THE MAN WHO
STOOD UP
TO BE SEATED

A CONTROVERSIAL
APPOINTMENT
TO THE
UNITED STATES
SENATE

Foreword by Kurt Schmoke
General Counsel, Howard University

THE MAN WHO STOOD UP TO BE SEATED

A CONTROVERSIAL APPOINTMENT TO THE UNITED STATES SENATE

The Memoirs of Roland W. Burris

Hunter Heart Publishing
Colorado Springs, Colorado

The Man Who Stood Up to be Seated:
The Memoirs of Roland W. Burris
Copyright © 2014 by Roland W. Burris
First Edition: December 2014

To order products in bulk, or for any other correspondence:

Hunter Heart Publishing
4164 Austin Bluffs Parkway, Suite 214
Colorado Springs, Colorado 80918
www.hunterheartpublishing.com
Tel. (253) 906-2160 – Fax: (719) 528-6359
E-mail: publisher@hunterheartpublishing.com
Or reach us on the internet: www.hunterheartpublishing.com

"Offering God's Heart to a Dying World"

This book and all other Hunter Heart Publishing™, Eagles Wings Press™ and Hunter Heart Kids™ books are available at Christian bookstores and distributors worldwide.

Editorial Staff: Ulysses Chambers, Gord Dormer, Deborah Hunter, Brenda Mates & Terri Liggins
Book cover design: Phil Coles Independent Design
Layout & logos: Exousia Marketing Group www.exousiamg.com

ISBN: 978-1-937741-75-4
Printed in the United States of America

Disclaimer

As I, Roland W. Burris, searched through the annals of my life in preparation for the numerous oral interviews I conducted that led to the writing of this book, I must admit there are many things from my past that I no longer clearly recall. Perhaps I have suppressed them due to their very negative nature. For the most part, though, I do remember enough challenging things juxtaposed to good things to share them accurately on these pages.

Some people, when reading about themselves in this book, may question me about the validity of the information shared. Please note that everything written is true to the best of my recollection. The truth as I know it has not been compromised nor has it been told with any effort to harm anyone intentionally or to discredit anyone's reputation.

This book is dedicated to:

My Parents, *Earl and Emma Burris, Sr.;*

My Brother, *Earl "Nick" Burris Jr.;*

My Nephew, *Joseph Giboney;*

And to the voters, donors, volunteers, workers, and all who helped to make my dream a reality through their votes and support, their sage advice, their campaign and election assistance, and their commitment to maintaining the highest standard of performance ;

- Office of the Illinois Director of General Services,
- Office of the Illinois Comptroller,
- Office of the Illinois Attorney General, and
- Office of the U.S. Senator from Illinois;

And to the members of the financial world and community organizations that helped me to gain much of the invaluable perspective, knowledge and experience I would need to sustain my journey as a dedicated public servant of:

- Office of the Comptroller of the Currency, Department of the Treasury,
- Continental Illinois National Bank and Trust Company (now Bank of America), and
- Operation PUSH., (now Rainbow PUSH)

In Appreciation

Throughout my life and career, I have found that few accomplishments are ever made without the combined effort of many dedicated and committed individuals. The completion and publication of this manuscript, *The Man Who Stood Up to Be Seated*, is certainly an accomplishment which falls into that category. As a measure of my gratitude to those who have facilitated my work on this project, I am very happy to acknowledge them and to express my deepest gratitude for their encouragement, support, technical assistance, and expertise at many stages throughout the conception, writing, editing, and finalization of this manuscript.

First, I would like to acknowledge the tremendous assistance and support provided by Mr. Donald A. Ritchie, Historian for the United States Senate, who has been widely recognized for his distinction in the field of oral history, particularly with his well-known editing of the transcripts of the hearings of Senator Eugene McCarthy. In addition, he has authored a number of highly regarded books, including *Press Gallery: Congress and the Washington Correspondents* that won the coveted Leopold Prize. I am especially appreciative to Mr. Ritchie for the exceptional expertise with which he guided and fine-tuned the series of oral interviews that took place in Washington D.C. between September 20, 2010 and October 15, 2010. They formed the foundation for this manuscript.

I also wish to thank Ms. Terri Liggins, who took on the professional responsibility of making the expert editorial adjustments in person, tone, and voice to transform the oral history of those interviews into a comprehensive, living memoir. She clearly articulated and illuminated the various phases of my life and career, including the goals and values that have been central to my development. Ms. Liggins also provided invaluable professional advice on the layout and design of the book and on important aspects of implementing an effective marketing strategy.

I express, as well, my gratitude to Mr. Ulysses Chambers who drew upon his considerable expertise as a former professor of English and his ten year tenure as my speech writer, to strengthen the authenticity of my voice in the

i

editing of this manuscript. He worked closely with me and performed hours of extensive research. This allowed us to elucidate unclear points, collaborate the facts and fill in gaps, to further authenticate and enhance the memoir. In addition, Mr. Chambers provided vital assistance with such technical matters as indexing and photo selection, scanning, captioning and layout.

Since I cover considerable detail about key individuals in my Senate Office in this book, I will not duplicate those comments here. However, my book does not highlight the extent to which some individuals played key roles in my professional life prior to my coming to the U.S. Senate. Therefore, I wish to recognize Tom Dodegee and Jimmy Voss, my top administrators; Al Manning, my communications director; Fred LeBed, my longtime assistant, advance man, political strategist, and friend; and finally, Wanda Gates (20 years in my Chicago office) and Gloria Schiesler (16 years in my Springfield office), the two ladies who made sure that all aspects of my professional life were in impeccable order.

In addition to the contributions made by these key individuals, I am also thankful for the dedication, professionalism, and expertise of all the un-named employees, volunteers, and others who contributed to my success in government or in the private sector. I pray they know how instrumental they were to me.

I feel a special obligation to extend my eternal gratitude to those who were with me in earlier phases of my journey who have passed on and are now no longer with us, like Ron Greer, Ron Smith, Bobby Joe Mason, Tony Harley, and others whose names may have escaped my memory, but whose dedication and service are permanently etched on my heart.

I also thank those friends and family members who helped to refresh my memory, provided me with new photographs and other pieces of valuable information, or otherwise assisted me in putting together the family history and other elements of my life story.

I have reserved my final acknowledgements for those people who mean the world to me: my family. I offer my special thanks and appreciation for the love and support I received from my son, Roland II; from his wife, Marty;

and from my grandsons Roland Theodore and Ian Alexander. They are the epitome of the future generations for whom this book is intended.

I am very grateful for the encouragement and inspiration I received from my daughter, Rolanda, who has always insisted that I preserve my story for future generations and who reversed our parent/child roles by displaying the "tough love" required to do so. She refused to listen to any more of my oral recollections until I had written them down properly, in the form of a manuscript. She followed up that challenge by buying me a tape recorder! For this relentless nudge, as well as Rolanda's unconditional willingness to roll up her sleeves and pitch in to help with any task in the preparation of this manuscript for publication, I will always be truly grateful.

It is most difficult to find adequate words to express my love and appreciation for my wife, Berlean, for her unstinting support and encouragement at all stages of bringing this memoir to fruition. She made time for me even while engaged in the major effort of writing, editing, and publishing her own manuscript: *Just Stand: God's Faithfulness Never Fails*. I am especially grateful for Berlean's willingness and ability to balance support provided to me along with the many demands placed upon her by family, community, and her own professional career as an educator and administrator. I hereby publicly acknowledge my successes are due, in part, to her love and dedication towards me for three-plus decades of my career as a public servant, and beyond.

Roland W. Burris
Chicago, Illinois 2014

Foreword

I was very pleased to be asked to write this foreword to Senator Roland Burris' memoir, *The Man Who Stood Up To Be Seated*. As a former elected official and former Dean of the Howard University School of Law, where Senator Burris earned his degree, I was intrigued by the prospect of introducing the senator's memoirs, since his elevation to the U.S. Senate drew such a great deal of national media attention and raised a number of unique legal questions. I am proud of the role I played as a senior member of the senator's legal team which helped him to address the issues surrounding his ultimately successful bid to become a United States Senator from the State of Illinois.

Even to the casual observer, the title of the book, *The Man Who Stood Up To Be Seated,* is obviously a metaphor for an *"everyman"* who at any period in history has refused to back down when he believes himself to be in the right. In a similar sense, the act of "being seated" which, conceptually, is quite different from "taking a seat" implies that while he is ready to fight for his principles, the senator is also a strong believer in following the rule of law and the protocol prescribed by the orderly and legal act of "being seated" in the Senate of the United States. Together, the image of the man who stands tall to protest intolerable conditions and the image of the man who fights for and wins the legal right to be seated evoke the strong sense of balance which has always been so characteristic of Roland Burris.

The images in the book's title are also very precise metaphors for the tremendous social, economic, and political progress that has been made by African-Americans in a country which once afforded them neither the right nor the privilege of "standing up" no matter how much they may have believed in or longed for equal justice. The denial of the rights of African-Americans took a variety of forms, ranging from institutional-ized racism to outright violence.

In addition to the obvious value of Senator Burris' book as an important historical record of his unique experience as a major African-American political figure, *The Man Who Stood Up To Be Seated* is also a refreshing reminder that real success is still achieved through such old-fashioned and straightforward means as a clear vision, a unifying mission, a strong sense of values, a belief in equality, and a commitment to hard work.

In 1978, Burris claimed the distinction of being the first African-American to be elected to statewide office in the State of Illinois when he won election as Illinois State Comptroller. After three terms as comptroller, he went on, in 1990, to become the first African-American attorney general in Illinois. In order to understand the significance of these achievements, it should be recalled that when Senator Burris was elected as Illinois Comptroller, there were only three black statewide elected officials in the entire United States. It was to this historical lack of African-American representation on both the state and national levels that Burris was referring when he noted in his *Farewell Address* to the U.S. Senate:

> *I am today the only Black-American Member of this Senate. Aside from myself, I can count the number of Blacks who have served in this body on the fingers of a single hand: Blanche K. Bruce, Hiram Revels, Edward Brooke, [and] the last two from Illinois: Carol Moseley-Braun, and our President, Barack Obama. Throughout 220 years of Senate history and 111 Congresses, only six Black-Americans have been able to serve. This is troubling in its own right. But when the 112th Congress is sworn in this coming January, there will not be a single Black-American taking the oath of office in this Chamber.*

Since Senator Burris made these observations, two African-American Senators, Tim Scott (R-SC) and Mo Cowan (D-MA), were appointed to fill vacant seats. Also an African-American, Corey Booker (D-NJ), was elected to the U.S. Senate. Despite these advances, however, in the main, Senator Burris' observations about the senate continue to be quite valid.

As the first elected African-American mayor of the city of Baltimore, Maryland where I had the privilege of serving for three terms, I can appreciate both the tremendous pride and the well-deserved sense of accomplishment that Mr. Burris takes in his achievements, which carry with them the awesome responsibility of maintaining the highest standards of transparency, professionalism, and personal integrity.

As former Dean of the law school Burris attended, I must note that even while he was a student at Howard Law School, Burris gave strong evidence of his leadership capacity by successfully taking on such roles as president of the senior law class and as a leader in such professional organizations as Sigma Delta Tau, a law school fraternity.

As a legal counsel to him in his quest for senate appointment, I can also attest the reason Senator Burris' detractors could find nothing in his actions, his record, or his character to preclude his admission to the U.S. Senate is there was nothing to find, other than a consistently exceptional record of outstanding public service.

As one who has been a friend to Senator Burris for many years, I can say Roland Burris was not *merely* eligible for the appointment to the senate, but *eminently* so.

To those who watched his development through the years, his early shift to the political arena and his eventual election to the office of attorney general was an inevitable part of his evolution. His appointment to the senate was then an appropriate addition to a distinguished and purposeful career.

The Man Who Stood Up To Be Seated opens with the *Prologue* in which we are able to "listen in" on the reflections of a man at the pinnacle of a remarkable political career who is literally polling family, friends, and political colleagues over whether or not to accept an appointment to the U.S. Senate. It is perhaps a mark of Burris' democratic nature that he seeks input and considers the opinions of others before making a decision, even though the appointment was one in which he had already publically expressed a strong interest. The overwhelming consensus among his family members and the hundreds of friends he approached was that the appointment was appropriate, well-earned, and richly deserved.

The enthusiastic support of his friends and family notwithstanding, it was probably not surprising that many in the political arena and in the media took quite a different view. What is surprising, however, were the extraordinary lengths to which they were willing to go to stop Burris' appointment, and the unsettling fact that they were willing to proceed at any cost, with little regard for truth or legality.

- First, they trampled over the concept of "innocent until proven guilty" by challenging the legality of *any* senate appointment by the beleaguered Governor Rod Blagojevich who, until his actual arrest and conviction, was still the legal governor of Illinois.
- Behind the scenes, they attempted to drum up support in the senate to reject any nomination that came out of the office of the governor of Illinois.
- Next, they appealed to Burris, himself, and attempted to use his unquestionable loyalty to his party to persuade him to reject the governor's appointment.
- Then, they refused to provide Burris with the certification of his appointment that the U.S. Senate required for seating.
- And when all of these efforts failed, without a shred of evidence, they helped to fan the flames of the media frenzy, which resulted in the senator being branded a liar who criminally conspired to "buy" a seat in the U.S. Senate.

Taken together, these efforts to prevent Burris from accepting the Senate appointment had one effect that his detractors probably never intended: that of fully provoking the Senate nominee to stand up and fight for what he believed to be right. In the end, of course, through the efforts of the Senator and his legal team, all contentions about the legality of the appointment and all accusations about the appropriateness of the Senator's actions were found to be without merit and totally discredited at all levels.

The Man Who Stood Up To Be Seated is the product of Senator Burris' deep reflections on important issues which affected both his personal and professional life, and, by extension, the lives of millions of others in his constituency. These issues included balancing the high honor of serving in the U.S. Senate with the regret of being only the sixth African-American in history to do so; and balancing the undeniably attractive prospect of service on the national level with the equally undeniable sting of the slurs to the sterling reputation he had labored for decades to build and maintain. Most importantly, however, the senator reflects on and draws hope from the invaluable lessons which young leaders might glean from learning about the struggles he faced and overcame, both after his appointment to the senate and throughout his long career.

Upon completing the figurative journey this book makes from the little town of Centralia, Illinois to the imposing chambers of the United States Senate in Washington D.C., one thing becomes quite obvious. In spite of the years that separate Senator Roland Burris from the young boy in Centralia who was moved to stand up in civil disobedience and break the unjust laws that prohibited him from swimming in the municipal pool, some things in our world have changed, while many others have remained the same.

As a result of the invaluable experience he has gained over his years of public service, Burris' vision has been sharpened and more finely honed, and his mission has become more and more inclusive as his knowledge and experience have accumulated and deepened. These changes are very encouraging, indeed.

Among the things that have remained the same are the degree to which Senator Burris has remained true to the strong ethical values instilled in him early in his childhood and the degree to which he still firmly believes in foundational principles like equal opportunity and hard work. *The Man Who Stood Up To Be Seated* is a powerful and encouraging testament to the stability and steadfastness of values and principles such as these.

Kurt Schmoke,
Vice President and General Counsel
Howard University, Washington, D.C.
2014

Table of Contents

Political Photographs

Senate Photographs

Epilogue

Appendix

Prologue

The Embattled Seat

alse allegations, indictments, perjury, and grand jury. Those were certainly not the words I expected to hear associated with the position I accepted on December 30, 2008, at the pinnacle of my thirty-plus-year career, a political career I can proudly say was characterized by integrity and resolve, and one which was free of sexual, financial, or other scandal. Although my entire career was one of public service, for the most part, I always maintained a low profile.

In fact, I would venture to say that prior to my appointment to the U. S. Senate in 2008, on a broad, national scale, most people had probably never even heard of me. They probably never knew that in 1969, a thirty-two-year-old Roland Burris became the first black bank officer at Continental Illinois National Bank in Chicago, Illinois and then, in 1972, became the bank's first black vice president. They never knew that in 1978, after serving for four years in the governor's cabinet, Roland Burris became the first black statewide elected official in the history of Illinois and went on to serve as comptroller for twelve years (elected three terms) and then as attorney general for four years. Sadly, after my senate appointment, most people would not come to learn those things or any of my other positive accomplishments, since the media seemed to care more about reporting a scandal centered on the appointment than about conveying the truth about the long and distinguished career of a straight-forward, history-making public servant.

Even the majority of the public, who for years viewed me politically or personally from *inside* the state of Illinois, had perhaps only gotten to do so on the more superficial level available through the sometimes limited, or often biased, filter of the media's lens. That is mainly because throughout my political career, I did not project a flamboyant and flashy-type of lifestyle. In other words, you would not find me calling press conferences every time I gave my opinion about the law or trying to generate publicity by hob-knobbing with big-named politicians. Instead, I operated unpretentiously under the radar, hopeful that people would recognize my steadfast commitment to those whom I served and would appreciate my use of the skills that qualified me for the positions to which I was elected.

So, there I was, thrilled at the prospect of becoming a United States senator, and joining a body that represents the most exclusive political fraternity in the world. I was thrilled that my fervent political ambitions had finally secured a spot for me in that highly exclusive office. There was no doubt I was thrilled that the national spotlight was suddenly focused on me, as I prepared to accept this prestigious assignment. However, much too soon and with far too much controversy, the thrill wore off.

Following my appointment by Illinois Governor Rod Blagojevich to the senate seat vacated by President-elect Barack Obama, the horrible media storm began. During a news conference several days later, Blago-jevich introduced me to the public as Illinois' newest junior senator. Immediately, a flurry of allegations began, centered around what some believed to be a fact: that Governor Blagojevich, who had been arrested three weeks earlier and charged with intent to "sell" the senate seat, no longer held any legal authority to appoint me, or anyone else, to that seat.

There I stood…right in the eye of that storm. After Blagojevich's arrest, it became clear the common assumption among leading Illinois politicians was even though he was still governor; he would not have the audacity to make an appointment to the senate. But he did make the appointment. There was also a common assumption among this group that no one would ever accept an assignment from such a tarnished figure as the governor had become. But I did accept the assignment.

Demands were hurled like darts from every direction, mostly telling me not to take the appointment because of the governor's scandal. One member of my own Democratic Party insisted I turn the governor down. Senior Illinois Senator, Dick Durbin, went as far as getting fifty-two signatures from Democratic senate colleagues stating they would not seat *anyone* appointed by Blagojevich. Even the Illinois Secretary of State, Jesse White, a black colleague of mine, refused to sign the required certification for my seating. I felt angry, frustrated and betrayed. Little or no attention was given to the fact that I was highly qualified for the senate seat and the fact I had done absolutely nothing wrong.

About a week prior to accepting the senate seat, I had discussed the situation with my lawyer; he felt I should accept the seat. Soon after that, I attended a Christmas Eve black tie affair that was attended by almost two thousand people. Throughout that entire evening, family members and friends from all over the state with whom I conferred were uniform in their agreement that should I be offered the appointment, I should accept, since I was certainly qualified for the position. However, in the aftermath, none of that mattered. The opportunity to achieve that coveted position—a position that most people who knew me, knew I'd had my eye on since Obama secured the Democratic presidential nomination—hung there in the balance. It dangled so tantalizingly close, yet so far away.

"Embattled," "beleaguered," "opportunist and worst of all... "liar." Those were certainly not the terms I had hoped to hear and see in the media juxtaposed with my name or my career. However, in numerous newspaper and magazine articles and in commentaries on T.V. sets across the nation, those words and more of the same lent the public a very incorrect first impression of me. I tried to fight back by explaining the facts, but the press didn't want to hear what I had to say. They were clearly more interested in taking my explanations and twisting them into something negative. Because of the incredible power of the press to twist the truth, my family, friends and lawyer begged me to stifle my urge to speak. I heeded their advice and kept quiet, until now, of course.

3

Needless to say, my newfound notoriety, compliments of that senate appointment, did not help me ring in a happy new year for 2009. Because of the tremendously negative implications of much of the media coverage of the situation, there were still many unanswered questions relating to my appointment to the U.S. Senate. Would I be indicted? Would I go before a grand jury? Never in a million years would I have imagined having to consider such options; however, they had suddenly become distinct possibilities.

The Sangamon County State's Attorney's office and the U.S. Senate Ethics Committee each began investigations into whether or not I perjured myself in my testimony regarding my appointment in the Blagojevich impeachment hearings which were convened by the Illinois House of Representatives. Those investigations consumed my every waking moment, for I knew their outcome would not only impact me, but my family and close friends as well. In the meantime, the magnitude of media-based attacks and parodies was already beginning to take a heavy toll on us.

I had come so far from my early childhood days in Centralia, Illinois. There in that small town, at the age of fifteen, I had set two career goals: to become a lawyer and to become a statewide elected official. In the midst of those investigations, as I reflected back on how I diligently achieved both those goals and many more, I asked myself, *"Was it all for naught?"* In that very moment in 2009, clarity emerged: the accolades I had received over the years had a larger purpose than I. Also in that moment, I knew sharing my story was the right thing to do, but I also understood I had to wait for the right time. Now, in 2014, that right time has finally come.

Introduction

Change Has Come to America

On November 4, 2008, the world watched history unfold. Some watched in despair; some in joy; but all in amazement. In his eighteen-minute, history-making acceptance speech, the nations newly-elected, 44th President, Barack Obama, cautioned the world that *"the challenges tomorrow will be the greatest of our lifetime."* Little did I know how accurately those words described the rough and acrimonious time that soon would overshadow my own successful thirty-year political career?

The challenges I would face during that tumultuous period *would* be among the greatest of my lifetime. It is a known fact that being the first of anything comes with a price. However, having been a trailblazer all my life, a destiny which I sincerely believe was one that was assigned to me, not one I personally chose, I can tell you the strides accomplished were well-worth the anguish.

In 1960, at age twenty-three, I arrived in Washington D.C., directly on the heels of a one year graduate stint at the University of Hamburg in Germany, which I began immediately after the completion of my undergraduate studies at Southern Illinois University. Thanks to an academic scholarship, I arrived in the nation's capital armed with two suitcases, an umbrella and a well-worn toilet kit, with my sights converged firmly on Howard University Law School. Never could I have imagined, though, how that one-way ride on the Baltimore & Ohio (B&O) railway train, with barely ten dollars in my pocket, would serve as a prelude for years of many accomplished dreams and for scores of unwarranted adversities.

Those early days in our nation's capital proved too "governmental" for me. In 1963, with law degree in hand, I told my newly-wed wife, *"Let's get back to Chicago so I can start my political career there."* I assured her that *"The only way I'd come back to Washington, D.C. would be as Vice-President of the United States or as a United States Senator!"* Why did I settle for a maximal goal of vice president and not president? One reason was that, like so many other Americans of my era, I honestly believed that in my lifetime, a black man could never become president of this country. I'm glad I was wrong.

I am pleased to say my time as a public servant was not a self-serving duty to me, regardless of the positions I held. It was an opportunity to break barriers and pave the way for other Black-Americans, especially for those among my constituency to hold political positions that for way too long had been reserved for my white constituents only. My political career began when Democrat Daniel Walker was elected governor of Illinois in 1972 and appointed me Director of the Illinois State Department of General Services. I served in that position until 1976, at which time I ran in, and lost, my first race for Illinois State Comptroller. Later, in 1978, after a second attempt, I became Illinois' first black comptroller. I was re-elected two times and served in that capacity for a total of twelve years until 1990. My election as Illinois Comptroller fulfilled the goal I had set for myself at age fifteen of becoming a statewide elected official.

In 1990, I was elected to the office of Illinois Attorney General, another first as a black man. After futile attempts of running for the U.S. Senate in 1984 and for governor in 1994, 1998, and 2002, I practiced law and ran a consulting firm in Chicago until December of 2008. At that time, I was appointed to fill the United States Senate seat left vacant by President-elect Barack Obama. Following a media frenzy of false allegations towards me and a widely publicized scrutiny of my credentials for the position, I proudly took the oath of office as a United States Senator on January 15, 2009, only the fourth black person ever to do so in our nation since the Reconstruction era, that fourteen-year period in U.S. history which commenced after the Emancipation Proclamation in 1863 and culminated in 1877.

Committees that I served on while in the senate included: Armed Services, Homeland Security and Governmental Affairs, Veterans Affairs, and several congressional delegations dealing with Military Affairs. I also received two Golden Gavel awards while there, each representing a hundred hours of service as presiding officer of the senate.

"From the chair," I stated to my fellow house members during my farewell speech on the senate floor, *"I have had the opportunity to listen to the words of my colleagues and reflect upon the great debate that unfolds each and every day—as it has always done throughout our Nation's history–in this the greatest deliberative body in the world. We come to this Chamber from every State in the Union–Democrats, Republicans, and Independents alike. Each of us carries the solemn responsibility of giving voice to the concerns of those we represent.*

Although we do not always agree, as the debate on this floor will often show, I am always struck by the passion that drives every Senator to stand in this singular place in the world and to speak their minds. It is this passion that will always define this Chamber for me."

The goal of becoming a U.S. senator I had set back in 1963 that prompted my return to Washington, D.C. in 2009 took longer to achieve than I ever imagined when I first left the capitol city as a fresh and eager law school graduate. Nevertheless, in a towering testament to the vibrancy of the American dream, it did occur. It is in this vein that these memoirs are produced.

I write this book with future generations in mind, generations that will hopefully never know the injustice of segregation I dealt with both as an individual and as a leader; generations that will hopefully never have to doubt whether a black male or a female of any race could be qualified as leader of our fine nation; generations whose dreams will hopefully be nurtured by the role models who chose to use moral legislative energy to improve our quality of life.

As I thought back over the years of my childhood, my education, and my early professional life in preparation for the numerous oral interviews in which I would be participating in partial preparation for the writing of this book, I knew there were a lot of things from my past that I no longer recalled. Perhaps I have suppressed them due to their very negative nature. For the most part, though, I do remember a great deal of the good stuff, as well as the more challenging stuff.

Some people, when reading about themselves on these pages, may even challenge me on the validity of the information shared. Please note that everything written is true to the best of *my* recollection. The truth, as I know it, has not been compromised nor has it been told with any intentional effort to harm anyone or discredit anyone's reputation. The stark reality of many events which took place during my political days will not allow me to paint a rosy picture of the life of a public servant, because it certainly wasn't always that. In fact, at times, it proved downright unbearable. With that said, if given the chance to do it all again, I would. Through the good times and bad times, when a way was needed, I, Roland W. Burris, either found a way or created a way. That's just who I am: a trailblazer.

PART ONE:

PERSONAL

MATTERS

Chapter One

My Foundation

I have lived almost my entire life as a public servant. My passion is to serve. I served as early as age eight, working alongside my brother as *Centralia Sentinel*'s first black newspaper route carriers. We put our hearts and souls into the task of delivering those local newspapers to the front porches of our customers with care and precision. We also knew there would be reprimanding by Dad if we didn't!

Over my next sixty-plus years, in every sector in which I served the people of Chicago, of Illinois and of these United States of America, my sincerity of heart remained a common denominator. I attribute that to my family, immediate and extended, who offered me unparalleled foundational truths and amazing unconditional love. Therefore, I would be remiss if I did not begin my memoirs with a proper introduction of them and an explanation of what their roles have been in my life.

As much as my heart has always been there for the public and perhaps too much in a Pollyannaish way at times, it's no secret that the public has not always been there for me. I naively believed that if you do a good job in office, people will *keep* you in office. That belief was proven false time and again. I believed if you accepted an appointment with the best interests of the people in mind, those same people would respect you for that. Instead, when I was appointed by then-Illinois Governor Rod Blagojevich to the senate seat left vacant by President-elect Barack Obama, daggers of persecution came at me, both directly and through every form of the media. What helped sustain me through all that turmoil was the strength provided by my family: both through the memories and lessons from those who have gone before me and through the love and support of those who are with me right now.

During the media frenzy following my Senate appointment, my integrity as an individual and as a public servant was undermined and my life of service was belittled. Many things reported about me were lies; many things I said were twisted. I even received death threats. My family's patience became challenged to say the least. Was it really worth all this? How long will this go on? How long could I endure so much maltreatment from people who didn't even know me?

Well, let me introduce you to the people who *do* or *did* really know me. They are the people who helped shape me into the person I am today. They are the people who have always cared enough to look at Roland W. Burris from the inside out—not through the lens of the media. Here are those loved ones…

My Dad

Earl Burris passionately desired to be a businessman. For him, that is what stood tallest among his many other ambitions. Being the industrious man that he was, I remember him always having some type of business of his own in addition to his job as laborer and car man for the Illinois Central Railroad.

Centralia, Illinois was a railroad town—home of the Illinois Central Railroad. My father was born and raised in Centralia. Therefore, it stood to reason that he, like almost every other man in town, would grow up to work for the railroad.

He put in over thirty years there, starting out by cleaning the clinkers, which entailed clearing away large ashes from the steam engines. Later he worked at the car shed helping to build freight cars. However, for Dad, that railroad job only represented his duty as the breadwinner of our household. His blood was in business. From raising and selling chickens and roosters, to selling all kinds of food, soda drinks and other merchandise, which eventually evolved into a bona fide business operated from a store; his determination, perseverance and personal pride brought business opportunities his way. Remember, we're talking about the 1940's, when it was hard enough to *get* jobs, let alone *create* them, so his business ventures were a huge accomplishment.

Every day, Dad would come home filthy from the rail yard environment in which he worked. He would head straight to the bath tub to take a bath and then dress up in his suit. Dad was a proud man. When he would put on his suit, white shirt, tie and hat, you knew he was about business! My father had a community service side to him as well, which is undoubtedly the source of my own passion for public service. He served as vice president of our local NAACP. As a, Republican, he tended to numerous political matters. For years, Dad was also active in the lodges as a 33rd degree mason. I remember watching him put on his apron and other Masonic regalia. You know, to a ten or twelve-year old kid, all that garb spelled importance! Even as a young kid, I placed a lot of value in everything my father did.

Dad never owned an automobile. In fact, I found out much later in life that he never even learned how to drive a car. Another thing he didn't own was guns. As the oldest of five kids, my father never forgot that his brother, Robert, was accidentally killed with a gun. Because of that, Dad would never let us have a gun. My friends would go hunting and come back talking about all the rabbits, squirrels and opossums they shot. I never experienced that. Truth be told, I probably couldn't hit the side of a red barn with a shotgun if given the chance. Dad was truly my hero in every sense of the word. I look forward to sharing my memories about him with you. Throughout my adult life—whether running for public office or running million dollar transactions for a bank—it has always been easy for me to discern impressions of the very fibers of my father's existence woven throughout my decision-making.

My Paternal Ancestors

My great grandfather, George Burris was born in Tiptonville, Tennessee. As the story goes, he became very successful in his own right, plowing the grounds for farmers using his old steel plow and his fine mules, which later became known as the best pair of plowing mules in all of southern Illinois. My grandfather, Blant Burris, told me his father could plow a field as fast as anybody from miles around, so farmers from all over would hire him.

Great grandfather George Burris married Josephine Tidwell. My research on Josephine Tidwell shows that she was born to William and Lola Tidwell in Tennessee, my great, great grandparents. Lola Tidwell was a Blackfoot Indian.[i] She and her husband, William, had four children, one of whom was Josephine, my great grandmother.

George and Josephine had fourteen children: seven boys and seven girls. Three or four of them, including my grandfather, Blant, were born in Tiptonville before the family moved to Pulaski, Illinois. My grandfather lived to be about eighty-six or eighty-seven years old, so I was privileged to have had many conversations with him about his family. He told me that his father, George, had three brothers. Two of them moved to Texas, while a third one moved farther west. The two who lived in Texas "passed for white,"[ii] a common practice employed by light-skinned black people during that time as a means of escaping racial discrimination.

In Pulaski, Illinois, Blant married Bertha Walters. In 1910, they moved to Centralia where Blant went to work for the Illinois Central Railroad, after being hired at a time when the railroad was hiring blacks as strikebreakers. Blant and Bertha had five children. My Dad, Earl, born in 1912 was the oldest of them. His younger brother, Robert Burris, died accidentally at a very young age. My father's three sisters, Gladys Burris Simons, Anna Mae Burris, and Alice Burris Birdo, were affectionately known to me as: "Aunt Gladys," "Aunt Anna Mae," and "Aunt Alice."

My Mom

My mother was born Emma Curry, in 1912, in Cataula, Georgia, just a couple of months before my father was born. Cataula is a small unincorporated town outside of Columbus, Georgia. She was the second oldest of eleven children born to Charlie Curry and Mary Green Curry. My mother, Emma, and six of the other children survived into adulthood, including my aunts Jimmy Curry Scott, Freda Curry Ricks, Minnie Curry Wilson, and Lola Curry Walker, and my uncles John Curry, and Elmer Curry. After my mother's father died, her mother remarried a gentleman by the name of John Elsey. As kids, my brother, sister and I spent a little more time at my Grandmother Elsey's house than at Grandmother Burris' home because Grandmother Elsey took care of us while my mother worked at the family store.

Mom was a woman of exceptional character; she was very well-suited to my Dad. She stayed active every waking moment of her day. When not running the household, tending to us kids, running the confec-

14

tionary or the Burris Grocery, you could find her managing civil affairs. She was an Eastern Star for many years. Like my father, she was very active in the community, whether attending PTA meetings or Republican political events.

Not only strong in character, Mom proved very strong in a physical sense as well. For instance, one day when I was about four years old, one of us kids was playing with matches and caused a small fire in one of the bedrooms of our house. My parents had just bought a new Maytag washing machine with the automatic hand wringer on it which was a very big deal to my mother, of course. Well, the washing machine was hooked up in the kitchen at the time the fire started.

Thanks to quick thinking and a serious boost of adrenaline, once my mother saw we were all safely out of the house, she picked up that washing machine and carried it out to the backyard! The fire engine soon arrived and dealt with the fire. Thank goodness it hadn't spread past the bedroom. Until she died at the age of fifty-three, Mom took care of her family the same way she took care of that washing machine that day. Her love, strength, her strong convictions, and her faith in God carried us through many trials and tribulations, ensuring our safety at all times.

My Maternal Ancestors

My grandmother, Mary Green Curry Elsey, was the second oldest of eight children born to a gentleman by the name of Major Green. Major Green married a lady named Mittie Biggest Green and they are my great-grandparents. I learned about my great-grandparents from a Pittsburg cousin of mine, Major Green IV, whom I only met a few years ago. According to this cousin, one of Major Green's granddaughters, who lived to be ninety-four years old, shared with him a good deal of information about her grandfather, our great-grandfather.

Major Green became a freed slave in Georgia, in 1865. He had always aspired to be a major in the military so he renamed himself "Major." Since he lived in Green County, Georgia, he took the name of his county. That's how he got the full name Major Green.

Major Green's daughter, Mary Green, married Charlie Curry and gave birth to eleven children. Four of them died in infancy—most during childbirth. Seven survived into adulthood. One of the eleven is still living at the time of this writing: Aunt Freda, who is eighty-three.

In 1917, when he heard that the Illinois Central Railroad[iii] was hiring black laborers, Charlie Curry left Columbus, Georgia, and traveled by himself to Centralia. Once hired, he sent for his family, which at that time consisted of my grandmother and their five children, including my mother who was about five-years old when the family moved.

Once in Centralia, my mother's parents had six additional kids before the death of my grandfather. My Grandmother Curry later remarried a gentleman by the name of John Elsey. To that union, no children were born.

My Brother

As big brothers come, Earl "Nick" Burris Jr. was among the best. He was the oldest of us three Burris children and, in his own unassuming way, a true leader. He certainly pointed me in the right direction, starting with allowing me to help with his newspaper route when I was just eight years old. We became *Centralia Sentinel's* first black newspaper deliverers. A couple of years later, Nick received a new route consisting of primarily white customers, and I ventured out on my own, taking over his old route.

Nick's new paper route served him well. He became so successful that he hired three young men to carry the papers for him. He and I would go around on Saturdays and collect the money for the papers delivered during the week. Unlike him, though, I still had to carry my own papers. I usually couldn't collect enough money from my customers to pay for the papers I had delivered that week.

Socially, my brother was very popular. Being a sharp dresser with a lot of class helped fuel his popularity. I gladly took care of his clothes for him knowing when he got tired of them; they would be handed down to me. In his junior and senior years of high school, his peers considered him a playboy, mainly because of the numerous girlfriends whom he courted, left and right.

Academically, Nick excelled in school. Good grades came easy to him. He attended Southern Illinois University in Carbondale, Illinois, earning a bachelor's degree. In 1963, at the same time I graduated from law school, my brother earned his master's degree. He and his wife, Shirley, had three beautiful children. So many goals set by my brother were thwarted by his illness and early death at the age of thirty. However, I can truly say his shoes are ones I still try to fill today.

My Sister

My Sister, Doris Burris Downey, was born two years before me. Growing up, there was always great sibling rivalry between the two of us. If you listened to her version of our childhood, she did more work than I did, whether helping me with my paper route or stocking shelves and servicing customers in our parents' grocery store. She even disputes that my swimming pool story happened exactly as I tell it. I'll share that story a little later because of its significance to my entrance into politics.

After she graduated from high school, Doris had her sights set on exploring life rather than experiencing college. She joined two of her high school girlfriends in Detroit where she worked for about a year before returning home to Centralia. She got married and eventually moved to St. Louis. Doris and her husband, Felix, had six children. Unfortunately, they lost their baby son, Joseph, in a drowning accident when he was sixteen-years old. Their other children, my nieces and nephews, are Felix Giboney III, Carol Nadine Giboney Young, Jill Giboney Williams, and Teresa and Keith Giboney.

I am grateful that through our sibling rivalry, my sister taught me from a very young age to stand my ground. No negative words about others are necessary when you let your own hard work speak for itself, just as Doris' hard work always spoke for her. Due to the respective illness, and eventual death, first of our mother and then of our father, Doris moved her family back to Centralia to help run the family business. Her willingness to do so and her valiant efforts to hold the businesses together speak volumes about her true spirit. I still love and appreciate her spirit today.

My Wife

Aside from her professional accomplishments, a lot of what I'll share with you about Berlean Miller Burris is written throughout my memoirs. I will tell you this much: I didn't know it at the time, but God sent me my very own personal angel that summer day in 1958 when I met Berlean who was then working at Provident Hospital in Chicago,

Illinois. In 2011, we celebrated our 50th wedding anniversary and, in hindsight, I know that no other lifelong partner would have so gracefully and masterfully fit the bill as my wife. I am truly grateful for her.

When I first met Berlean, she was a student nurse. When we married in 1961, she was finishing a three-year nursing program at Provident Hospital. After our two children were born, she desired to enhance her credibility in her field, so she obtained a bachelor's degree in nursing. In order to accomplish this feat within three years, in spite of being informed by her counselor that it couldn't be done in such a short period; she orchestrated her classes simultaneously through Loyola University of Chicago and two junior colleges.

With the determination Berlean had for excelling in her field, after she completed the bachelor's degree, it was only a matter of time before she was back in the books and in the classroom. Next, she attended the University of Illinois at Chicago where she received her master's degree in nursing. After that, Loyola University hired her as a member of its teaching staff, giving her the distinction of being the first African-American faculty member in the Loyola University College of Nursing. Berlean later accepted an offer as Assistant Professor at the College of Nursing at Chicago State University, during which time she felt it necessary to obtain a Ph.D. After completing her Ph.D. in Social Policy and Higher Education Administration at Northwestern University, she was promoted to Chairperson of the Chicago State University Department of Nursing and, after serving in that position for one year, she was again promoted to Dean of the Chicago State University College of Nursing, a position in which she served with distinction for eight years. My wife's many academic accomplishments didn't end with nursing, even after she received the ultimate accolade in that field: Dean Emeritus, for holding the dean position for a longer period of time than any other individual. Her continued thirst for learning, coupled with her love for God's Word, led her to complete a master of arts in Biblical Studies from Moody Bible Institute. Upon graduation, she was invited to join the graduate faculty of the Institute.

No doubt, I am very proud of Berlean for these obvious reasons and many reasons beyond these. It is beyond the comprehension of some people how she has managed to achieve all these personal goals while being a very involved mother and such an astute wife to a politician. I understand it though, because I have first-hand knowledge about her unwavering faith, as well as her conviction to follow *only* the path God has laid out for her. The proof is in the pudding, as they say.

My Daughter

On March1964, life as I knew it changed forever with the birth of our first child. Naturally, I felt the overwhelming pressure of financial responsibilities that any brand new father and household provider would feel under those circumstances. As a young bank examiner, forced to travel regularly across a wide region of the Midwest, that financial pressure would soon be matched with self-inflicted guilt over not being home often enough to experience our baby's many "firsts" and to help my wife with many of the parenting duties.

Berlean and I arrived at Augustine Hospital on Chicago's Near North Side to deliver what we thought would be a boy. Instead, Berlean ended up with the caesarian birth of a beautiful, healthy baby girl! I left the hospital to return to work before we had an opportunity to name our daughter. We hadn't picked out any girls names ahead of time, since we were under the impression that *she* was going to be a *he*. Under pressure to have a name for the birth certificate, my wife named our daughter, "Rolanda Sue Burris" before I returned to the hospital."Sue" is Berlean's sister's name.

In the years since my daughter's birth, the media had a field day with her name, saying *I* named her after me because I'm egotistical. How funny that their slander completely ignores the fact that I had no say-so in that decision at all. I had even asked my wife, *"Is that a name?"*

"It is now," she beamed. *"It's your daughter's name."*

Rolanda has grown up to become a beautiful, selfless person. Like her mother, she, too, holds a doctorate in higher education, which she obtained at Northern Illinois University. She also received a Masters of Arts degree in counseling from DePaul University and a Bachelor of Arts degree in communication from Bethune-Cookman University. As it goes with most father-daughter relationships, she captured my heart from her first breath and has had me wrapped around her finger ever since. There's nothing I wouldn't do to see Rolanda experience true happiness all the days of her life.

My Son

Three years later, in January, 1967, my son was born in the midst of the worst snowstorm in Chicago's recorded history. When we headed to the hospital on a Thursday evening for my wife's scheduled caesarian delivery on Friday morning, we had no idea what was in store for us over the next seventy-two hours.

Like thousands of other Chicagoans, our travel plans were quickly altered by the twenty-three inches of steady snowfall added to the foot of snow that was already on the ground. In our effort to reach the hospital, we were going nowhere fast, which I suppose was better than some people who were going nowhere at all. The travel time from our house on Chicago's Southside to the hospital on the Near North Side on a clear day would have been an easy thirty to forty-minute cruise up the expressway. We finally arrived at the hospital at 9:30pm, after a five-hour crawl!

Needless to say, as the snow continued, our hopes of seeing a doctor arrive in the morning to deliver our son waned. In fact, I couldn't even get home to relieve the babysitter we had hired to watch our daughter in our absence. Therefore, I spent the night in my wife's hospital room, while the babysitter spent the night at our house.

The next morning, I ventured home. It deeply concerned my wife that our daughter had been watched overnight by an older lady whom we barely knew, so snowstorm or not, I had to get home and see how things were. On my way to the south side, I passed stranded cars everywhere. A nearly paralyzed public transportation system got me only halfway to my house, due to unplowed streets that it would take city workers days to make navigable. I walked nearly twenty blocks—from 63rd Street and King Drive all the way to 78th Street and Eberhart Avenue—to complete my journey home.

It was quite an interesting couple of days weather-wise, especially given the fact that just four days earlier, we had hit a record high temperature of 65 degrees.[iv] That's Chicago weather for you. As most people know, Chicago's changeable weather is part of this city's notoriety; that, and its politics.

Well, a day later than scheduled (which wasn't bad considering the storm which was taking place around us), the doctor made it to the hospital just before I arrived. Within the hour, our handsome baby boy arrived as well! Today, Roland W. Burris II is an attorney following in the footsteps of his old man. He attended my alma mater, Howard University, where he received a bachelor's degree in Business and went on to Northwestern University for his law degree.

I remember right after he was born, Berlean stated his name, *"Roland W. Burris the Second."*

I said, *"Honey, you can't do that. He has to be junior."*

"No, I don't like junior," she said. *"I'm putting it on his birth certificate as 'the Second'."*

"Yes ma'am," was all I could muster up. I was barely in politics at the time, but already smart enough to know when to concede!

Currently, my son and his wife, Marty, have two beautiful little boys, Roland Theodore and Ian Alexander, age nine and six respectively, as of this writing in 2014. I love it that I am actively involved in my son's life, whether through joining forces with him in our consulting work with our law practice, or when my wife and I are performing our duty and privilege as grandparents of keeping our grandsons overnight.

Chapter Two
The Black Family
With Means

My Family

I am pleased with the person I have become and proud of all I have accomplished in my many years of life. It is because of these things that I am forever indebted to Earl Burris, Sr. and Emma Burris: the best parents this red-blooded black American boy could ever have asked for or had. Growing up in a small, southern Illinois, railroad town like Centralia from the late 1930's through the 1950's didn't offer the best in hopes and possibilities. We had to find them on our own. I deemed it necessary to conjure up big dreams in my early years to combat those big obstacles that stood in my way in that little town. Once I created the dreams, persistence and resolve kept them alive. That's where my parents came in.

Mom and Dad set excellent examples for their children; sharing similar work ethics that were second to none. In addition, they mastered disciplining. Oh, let me tell you! That was an era when kids could really be set on the right course with one good whipping. You know what I'm talking about: the real deal disciplining! In those days, parents would not *threaten* to straighten us out and then never follow through, as seems so often to be the case today. No, with my parents, as with so many other black parents of that time, threats did not enter into the equation, just action. Among my siblings and I, it was also a well-known fact that if our parents were not around when we misbehaved, grandparents, neighbors and other adults were granted the authority to spank us, chastise us or to do whatever else was needed. Therefore, my two siblings and I stayed very cognizant of the need to maintain our best behavior whether our parents were present or not.

My family was considered middle class, but some called us rich. No doubt, the fact that we lived on the edge of the black neighborhood, in an integrated neighborhood was probably one reason why some people in town thought we were a family of means. However, "rich" was not a term my father would ever have used to describe us. In strictly financial terms, none of us had any real wealth. My parents, like many others around us, struggled daily to make ends meet.

Staying very active in the community, they remained a center of influence in the schools through their involvement in PTA and in Centralia politics. My father was a Mason[v]; my mother an Eastern Star, a women's auxiliary of the Masons.[vi] At one time, my mother was also a Cub Scout Pack Leader, which kept my brother and me involved in the scouts, as well. In the scouts, I advanced all the way up the ranks to Assistant Scout Master.

I remember my mother as being very protective of her family, and that included her husband just as much as her three children. She was a proud woman who worked her fingers to the bone. Her father died when she was just a young girl, so she had always helped her mother and grandmother earn income by washing laundry and cleaning homes for their white neighbors. Mom was Baptist and attended New Bethel Baptist church, which was located right next door to one of the homes my parents rented before finally being able to afford to purchase a home of their own.

Dad was an astute businessman whose unstoppable ambition set the course for his multiple enterprises. Whether selling hens and chickens, miscellaneous goods from his confectionary, or groceries and other stocked items from Burris Grocery, his business acumen was impressive to say the least. I gleaned so much knowledge from watching him while my siblings and I helped to run the family businesses. He worked six days a week and, on the seventh day, attended Ricks Chapel AME Church down the street. Unlike my Baptist mother, he was Methodist.

24

Growing up, I had close relationships with both my brother, Earl "Nick" Burris Jr., who was born three years before me, and my sister, Doris, who was born two years before me. Being the baby of the family, though, meant my older siblings were, at times, expected to perform tasks on my behalf that they sometimes resented having to do. I remember when I was four and had an accident at the church door, while unsuccessfully trying to make it to the outhouse. After Mom made Nick and Doris clean up the floor, they took their revenge for having to clean up after me by taking me around to the side of the building and cutting off some of the long braids my mother always created when styling my hair. All in all, though, Nick was the best brother any boy could ever have. He was a very religious young man, who was likeable by all, and he was very smart. All those qualities made it easy for me to look up to him. The fact that his death at age thirty was commemorated with one of the largest attended funeral services that Centralia had ever experienced says a lot about the life he led and the high regard in which he was held by everyone who knew him.

As a child, the closeness my sister and I have felt for each other at times was expressed in the form of good old fashioned sibling rivalry. If you ask her about her memory of our childhood you will get a totally different story than you would get from me. For instance, she claims she helped me deliver my newspapers, a "fact" which I do not remember at all. In fact, according to her, she worked more than I did. Well, that may be true because when we were growing up, while Mom was busy running the store, Doris did become a great cook and housekeeper. Doris got married and started a family, instead of going to college. When my mother passed soon after my brother's death, without hesitation, Doris moved back to Centralia from St. Louis to help Dad run the store, readily splitting her time between Dad's household and her own until his death, which says a lot about the type of caring person she is.

Now only Doris and I remain from the family of our childhood and youth. With three-fifths of our nuclear family gone, I believe she and I have drawn even closer as a result of those losses. Suffice it to say, we've also passed the Lord's test of endurance in the midst of suffering that usually knocks many people off of their foundations.

Our Homes

Our small town of about twelve thousand people had approximately two thousand blacks. In spite of its segregation, Centralia was a good environment in which to live and grow. Of course, there always existed some disparity between the percentage of white professional people and black professional people in our town; but that was to be expected, especially in that era. One black doctor practiced there, but no black lawyers. The other black business people were folks like the barbers, the beauticians, the carpenters and families who owned stores. My family first owned a confectionary store and later grocery stores.

When I was born in 1937, my family lived in a rented house on Sattler Street in Centralia. That house had a porch that played a significant role in my bonding period with my father. When I was about three years old, I would get up every morning with my father as he dressed for work. Mom would fix him a bag lunch and would fix me a small lunch as well. I would sit on our porch steps at five-thirty or six o'clock in the morning waiting for the truck to come by and pick Dad up. He would bid me good-bye, climb into that truck crammed with all the other men from the area and head off to the rail yard.

Now, when Dad got in the truck, I got on my tricycle and rode on our block of Sattler Street: back and forth, back and forth. In my mind, I was going to work too. Once I got tired of riding my tricycle, I'd go back to our front porch, sit on the steps and eat my bag lunch. When finished, I would go back in the house, climb into bed and fall fast asleep. I will always cherish that early memory I have of bonding with and emulating my dad.

Soon, though, I had to start my day from a different front porch, as three kids sleeping in one bedroom proved to be a bit too crowded. We moved into our next rented house—advancing in that rented home to three bedrooms. Because of its location two blocks away on Sycamore Street, right next door to a Baptist church, we called that new house "the church house." In "the church house," Mom and Dad had a bedroom, my brother and I shared a bedroom, and my sister had her own room.

Our church house was right next to and owned by New Bethel Baptist Church where Mom was a member. Down the street was a Methodist church, Ricks Chapel AME Church, where Dad was a member. My siblings and I were forced to split our allegiance between the two churches.

I can remember Easter Sunday when I was four or five years old and I would go to say a little Easter recitation at New Bethel Baptist and then go down the block to Ricks Chapel AME and saying the same piece there. My favorite one was, *"He is risen, He is risen: the Son of Galilee."* Once the congregation realized I was done, everyone would clap real hard and loud. As a little kid already feeling good with his new Easter clothes on, I'm telling you, that applause felt like heaven to me! In August of 1942, as I turned five, our country was at war. After working hard and saving smart, my parents bought their first house: a big, white, two-story house with eight rooms: four downstairs, and four upstairs. Our big white house sat on Maple Street, on the edge of the all-black neighborhood, in an integrated neighborhood. Years later, that neighborhood, too, became entirely black populated.

When we moved in at the beginning of the month, the elderly white lady renting the upstairs still had thirty days left on her lease with the previous owner. The first thirty days, my family could only occupy the space downstairs. Mom and Dad had the downstairs bedroom. My brother and I slept in the dining room. My sister slept in the living room. With that house came a large kitchen and lots of closets. Since this house was so much larger than the church house, it seemed like a castle to us. Yes, a castle with no indoor plumbing. To celebrate our new home, my mother threw a dual birthday party for my sister, Doris, and me since our birthdays occurred on August 3rd and August 8th respectively. It was my fifth birthday and Doris' seventh. I remember kids galore running around for what seemed like hours in that huge front yard, as well as in the side lot that stretched clear to the alley. Everywhere we darted, our path seemed to be wonderfully obstructed with fully developed grape vines and fruit trees.

Our Businesses

Shortly after moving into the big white house, Dad officially opened his confectionary in a nearby rented building. He sold soda pop, candy and other goodies to the kids. His business did well because he was such an astute businessman. For example, if a product wasn't moving off the shelves, Dad created a packaged deal by taping the slow moving product to the more popular one and discounting the entire package. Perhaps some kids usually bought only a Payday candy bar for a nickel, and others usually bought only a pack of Juicy Fruit gum for a nickel. Well, to make kids buy both, Dad would band them together, offering the new two-some for nine cents.

I gained a lot of business knowledge by watching him, but after three or four years in the confectionary business, a fire broke out, badly damaging the building. Mr. O'Neal, who owned the building, repaired it but refused to lease it back to my Dad. Instead, he let one of his sons open his own confectionary. That put Dad out of business for awhile, until he entered into a partnership with, Mr. Owens, an elderly gentleman who had a lot of resources. Together, they started a grocery store called the Owens-Burris Grocery.

My parents had full responsibility for the operation of the Owens-Burris Grocery, with the help of my siblings and I, while Mr. Owens was responsible for buying all the stock and other products sold in the store. Customers of the store paid for their goods with cash or made their purchases on credit, agreeing to pay on their payday. Around where we lived, payday usually came either once a month with the arrival of public aid checks, or with the bi-weekly paydays of the Illinois Central Railroad.

About two or three years later, Mr. Owens and my parents got into some legal dispute. Mr. Owens sued my parents, but my parents won the suit. My father then counter-sued Mr. Owens and lost that suit. Needless to say, those estrangements ended their partnership, and that grocery store business closed.

Grandpa Blant Burris, my father's father, happened to own several vacant lots around town. He gave one of those lots to my father so that my father could build his own store on it. That's when Burris Grocery was born, built from the ground up. Let me tell you, opening that store was a total family affair! We all pitched in. Our foster brother, Richard Poore, built the new store with all of us helping him every step of the way, from hauling wheelbarrows and pouring concrete, to carefully stocking every shelf. Our collective fingers got worked to the bone throughout that entire summer.

Dad had set a goal to have Burris Grocery opened in time to sell back-to-school supplies. It was of major importance to him that the kids of our neighborhood could buy the supplies they needed before school started. And, we met that goal!

Once school started, my siblings and I found ourselves at that store every day after our classes ended. I was entering the fifth grade, Doris was entering the seventh grade, and Nick was entering the eighth grade. Not only did we stock the shelves, but now we also had to buy the food that went on those shelves. Sometimes our neighbor, Virgil Marshall, would drive us in his car to the wholesale company. Sometimes we purchased so much stuff that he needed to use his pickup truck to haul the products back to the store. Either way, Virgil refused to do any lifting. So my siblings and I did all the selecting and all the lifting.

We also had to go to the meat packing company owned by the Ray family, to buy various meats if they weren't delivered. If Virgil wasn't around to drive us, our bicycles had to suffice. The owner of Ray Packing Company had a son named Jerry who was my high school classmate. Jerry Ray still lives in Centralia, and we are still very good friends to this day. In fact, during a recent visit to the area, Jerry and I sat around chatting and laughing about the old Burris Grocery Store and Ray Packing Company days.

Our store became a community hub of sorts for political operations because of its location on the east end of town. All the white politicians would come to the east end and stop at Burris Grocery to talk about what was going on and who was lobbying for what. We didn't have any black politicians in our town to represent the interests of the black community, so we relied on the white politicians for that.

Dwight Friedrich was one such white politician. Mom and Dad swore by Dwight Friedrich and he listened to them about things going on in the black community. Friedrich served a long time as a state representative. He lost his seat for a while, but got re-elected years later and was in the legislature when I arrived in Springfield in January of 1973, as a cabinet member under Governor Dan Walker. Friedrich jokingly remarked that he couldn't understand how I had become a democrat.

Our Finances

In 1952, when I was a sophomore in high school, Mom became ill. She remained hospitalized for about two months and was away from the store for about three months. In her absence, the store suffered greatly—

29

especially administratively. That was the first time that she had ever gotten sick like that. In addition to the challenges that her illness presented at the store, my father's bank account was challenged by the hospital bill.

Mom's hospital bill for two months was $3,000. Dad's insurance company paid $1,500. Where the other $1,500 would come from, Dad had no idea. I remember Nick came to me one day and said, *"Dad needs $1,500."*

Without a second thought, between us, we pulled our money together: Nick came up with $900 from his savings and then I came up with $600 from my stash. When we handed Dad that $1,500, he was so moved by our gesture that he cried. He knew it had taken us years to earn that money through our paper route business. That didn't matter to us at that moment. We were just happy Mom was home and that we were able to help Dad pay the hospital bill.

Several years later, I came home from college for the weekend and became distraught when I examined the financial condition of the grocery store. A lot of our customers would run up their credit balances to thirty or forty dollars over a month's time. That was a lot of money back then! When they received their public aid or their paychecks, they would give us only fifteen or twenty dollars towards their bill and carry over a balance into the next month. I was shocked to find that those unpaid balances added up to thousands of dollars. All the while, my parents kept struggling along to keep the store afloat; paying the bills at the store, as well as at home as best they could.

Due to Mom's failing health and absence from the store, no one was collecting any of the past due money from the customers, and the customers certainly weren't voluntarily paying what they owed. By that time, my brother had graduated from college and lived in Springfield; my sister lived out of state. One weekend, while I visited from college, I stayed up half the night with an old adding machine tallying up all those back bills which I found in the boxes Mom had stuffed underneath the counter. I sensed the weight of all those bills resting squarely on my parents' shoulders as I calculated that enormous burden.

It was 1957 when I did that. Some of the receipts found were dated back to when we first opened the store some ten years earlier. Mom never wanted to see anyone go hungry. So her good grace of allowing customers to buy on credit allowed those receipts to total over $100,000! Can you imagine having $100,000 worth of debt on your books back in the 1950's? To say it presented a strain to my family's finances is an understatement.

All Dad could do was keep working at Illinois Central and let his paycheck cover expenses at the store and at home. All I could do was continue to get good grades in college so that I wouldn't lose the scholarship that covered my tuition. Even after tuition was paid, I still needed money from my parents for room and board. To facilitate that, my mother would send me twenty dollars a week. Ten dollars of that went towards my rent; five dollars towards my meal ticket that afforded me six dinner meals; the remaining five dollars covered everything else I needed.

Our Work Ethic

Yes, the life that I lived in Centralia was challenging; yet it was also exciting and rewarding. Perhaps *that* was why we were looked upon as the family with means or the "black society family." I believe it was my parents' strong work ethics that kept us looking unruffled, even while we were in the midst of financial struggles. Even though we did not have any real wealth, we always seemed to have some money in our pockets. Not only was Dad pretty strict about us always working, but also about *how* we did the work. My brother and I delivered newspapers. We did so with precision, or else we heard about it from Dad. We didn't mind his strictness too much, since it netted us a lot of money over the years.

My brother, Nick, was eleven years old and I was eight when we became *Centralia Sentinel's* first black newspaper deliverers. We truly put our hearts and souls into the task of meticulously placing those local newspapers onto the porches, and not in the yards, of our customers, regardless of the weather conditions. In fact, if it was a rainy or snowy day, we didn't just toss the paper onto the porch; no, we had to put the paper inside the screen door, so that our customers didn't have to brave the elements to get it. After a while, they came to expect that type of treatment and would report us to Dad when we did otherwise.

After several years, *Centralia Sentinel* gave Nick a new paper route in a predominantly white neighborhood. The *Sentinel* gave me his old route, where the customers were mostly black. Nick's paper route

31

became so successful that he hired three young boys to carry the papers for him. He and I would go around on Saturdays and collect the money for the papers delivered during the week. Unlike most of Nick's customers in the white neighborhood, some of my customers in the black neighborhood didn't always pay in a timely manner for the papers that were carefully delivered to them through the week.

Our newspaper responsibilities didn't stop at the end of the week, but carried over to the weekend as well. For instance, in addition to collecting our money on Saturdays, we also sold The *Pittsburgh Courier*,[vii] a weekly national black-owned newspaper, to people on the street. We would walk up and down the streets inviting people to buy those papers from us, most of them did. We then returned all the papers we didn't sell.

Sunday mornings, my brother and I would go get stacks of papers from Mack Downey's Grocery Store, the other black-owned store in Centralia. We would pay Mack twelve to thirteen cents for each paper; charge about fifteen cents to our customers and keep the two or so cents as profit. The papers delivered to that store and sold by us were: the *St. Louis Globe Democrat* and *St. Louis Post Dispatch*, as well as The *Chicago Tribune*, the *Chicago Daily News* and the *Chicago Herald-American*.

As you can imagine, that type of seven-day work schedule was great training for two young boys. Not only did we develop a good work ethic, but Dad taught us a thing or two about saving as well. For example, he introduced us to U.S. savings bonds. In order to purchase the bonds, we saved our pennies, nickels and dimes and bought stamps, which we turned in later in order to get the actual savings bond certificates.

I value memories of that little town; especially all those lessons my brother and I learned in business and finance. As I ventured into adulthood, I had many opportunities to put those lessons of persistence and resolve to the test.

Chapter Three
Two Goals and a Swimming Pool

My Early School Years.

I n spite of the fact that there were people who didn't pay my parents for the groceries they received and those who didn't pay me for the newspapers they read, our community consisted of some great people. These included the dedicated and committed school teachers of the eight elementary schools in town. The school I attended, Lincoln School, was the only all-black elementary school. There were seven other elementary schools that were all white, except for Fields Elementary School, which was located in an area of town called Southtown. Although Southtown had a white majority, some blacks lived there as well, so at Fields Elementary School, the town had integration by default, as the black kids and white kids were permitted to go to school together because Fields was the only school in the area and because the black kids had no way of getting all the way across town to Lincoln School.

Shortly after World War II, Centralia tried to integrate the schools. Two of the schools involved in the planned integration were Franklin, an all white school and Lincoln, the all black school. Probably one of the reasons school officials decided to integrate the schools is that some blacks lived right across the street from Franklin, the white school; and some whites lived only two or three blocks from Lincoln, the black school. The integration plan would have required both black and white students to attend the school closer to their homes.

Although this sounded like a sensible arrangement, it didn't work out. As it turned out, most of my black classmates who would have been affected didn't want to leave their friends at Lincoln, and I'm sure the same was the case with the white students at Franklin. There may have been some official reason why school integration did not work in Centralia during that era, but my recollection was that the blacks and whites just did not want to change mostly because kids liked being with their own friends. One of my classmates, who chose to keep coming to our school even though she lived across the street from Franklin, the white school, was Shirley Brown. Shirley later became my brother's wife.

Even though all of our primary schools had their own agendas and their own race of people, we all came together to attend the one high school in town. So, as all the students came up through the ranks of the eight mostly segregated schools, they became classmates at integrated Centralia Township High School.

During my high school years, all the teachers at Centralia High School were white. During all my grade school years at Lincoln, all the teachers had been black. To me, Lincoln Elementary School was a very impressive learning institution. I believe the teachers were very successful in equipping us for our next stages of learning.

The teachers at Lincoln Elementary School made such a vivid impression on me that to this day, I can remember the names of every one of them, while I only remember the names of most of my high school teachers and some of my college professors. At Lincoln my teachers were: Miss Mason in the first grade; Miss Bryant in the second grade; Miss Claybrook in the third and fourth grades; Miss Vonadore in the fifth grade; Miss Height in the sixth grade; Mr. Pope in the seventh grade, and in the eighth grade, Miss Tate for morning classes and Mr. William Walker, who was also our school principal, for afternoon classes. Miss Tate would get there early in the morning and in her meticulous script would fill the blackboard with great information. She would tell us, *"This is what you'll get when you attend high school."* She was absolutely correct. I entered Centralia High School well-prepared to compete with students from Irving School and the other grade schools around Centralia. I was in the fifth grade at Lincoln when Mr. Walker was hired as the principal of our school. He was a short, chubby fellow with a very heavy voice and a very energetic disposition. He had impressive credentials as a former Tuskegee Airman[viii] originally from Carbondale, Illinois, with a master's degree from Southern Illinois University.

I tell you, everyone admired Mr. Walker. He had the ear of the entire community. He and my dad were almost the same age and became good friends. Mr. Walker would drive Dad to all the school basketball games and other sporting events in which we participated, because Dad didn't drive.

Friends Galore

I was blessed with quite a few friends growing up. Among my closest ones were: Conrad Mays, the black doctor's son; Jackie and Lonnie O'Neal, whose father owned the building that burned when my father had his confectionary there; Lillian and Lillie Scott, whose parents were a barber and a beautician; and L.C. Weathersby, who became my friend in third grade. L.C. made straight A's. I really admired L.C. because he was super intelligent and would've easily been very successful in any professional career he pursued. Unfortunately, with fourteen children in his family, he had to leave Centralia High School and move to New York, where he lived with his sister and attended high school there. We comprised a middle-class kind of group. Some of us even lived a little distance from the all-black neighborhoods, as was the case when my family moved to Maple Street in an integrated neighborhood on the edge of the all-black neighborhood.

I certainly didn't let the segregation of schools and other places in our town keep me from having close friends across racial lines. A couple of them with whom I am still in touch today are Rod Snow, whose father was a successful doctor and Jerry Ray, whose father owned the meat packing company where we went to purchase meat for sale in our family grocery store.

Other close white friends throughout my school days were Fred Wham, son of a lawyer and Kenny Baur, whose family owned a dry cleaning business. Our schools had many sports, concerts and other programs with which we could identify. Even during my elementary years, my school, Lincoln, always looked forward to competing with Irving, the school with all the elite white students so we felt we had a lot to prove there.

Aside from all our schooling, working and competing, my friends and I enjoyed hanging out and getting into a little mischief here and there as young boys do. We were full of energy and pulled pranks and such, but nothing major. No doubt, compared to today's standards, the things we thought of as mischievous would now be considered trivial. For instance, I recall one night we drove around in the convertible provided by Carl Franklin, compliments of his dad. We headed to the outskirts of town where some of the white homes had the black lawn jockeys placed in their front yards.

Seeing those clay statutes which had been based on such discriminatory views of blacks infuriated us so much that we decided to steal them. We hopped out of the car at one particular yard and soon discovered a dog; correction, the dog discovered *us*! As it charged us, we made it back to the car in time, but the car stalled. Leonard Taylor, a big All-American football player who we called Moose, had to push the car until it started. What a hilarious, vivid memory I cherish of Moose scrambling over the trunk and into the backseat just in the nick of time!

Another of my friends, Conrad Mays who was the son of Centralia's only black doctor, provided the T.V. that we all hovered around every chance we got. In fact, the Mays were the first black family in Centralia to own a television set. We would go over there on Saturday nights and watch *Your Show of Shows,*[ix] which featured Imogene Coca and Sid Caesar. Boy, were we the envy of our other friends who didn't have access to a television set! The next day, the other kids would ask us for a play-by-play account of that show. That was around 1952. By 1953, my family was the second black family in town to own a T.V. Funny, even after we got our own set, I still went to Conrad's house to watch television with my friends.

Sports Galore

What Centralia High School lacked in diversified staffing, it made up for with its great athletic program. Our school's trophy case had so many trophies and championship pictures that, years later, when a new high school was built, the new display area wasn't large enough to house all the championship trophies and other memorabilia of victory which had been won by Centralia athletes over the years.

At Centralia High School, I played four years of football, four years of track, and was the basketball manager for two and a half years. Those were truly some unforgettable years! During my sophomore year, I didn't travel with the basketball team; I just stayed behind and laundered the team's uniforms. In my junior and senior years, I became manager and traveled with the team. Our team fared very well overall. We played thirty-one to thirty-two games per year and on average lost only two to five games each year.

My main sport was football, and I was good at it. My positions in my junior and senior years were quarterback and defensive safety. I made so many tackles and interceptions that I was written up for my defensive prowess and won honorable mention as an all-state back during my senior year. In my four years of playing football for Centralia, our team only lost two games—both to the East St. Louis High School Flyers.

At Centralia High School, if you played football or basketball, you had to run track. I wasn't that fast in track, but I did become a distance runner. I ran cross-country and the mile. Regardless of my lack of skill in the sport, Dad would always come out and watch my track meets. Since he didn't drive, someone had to bring him each time; yet, he never missed a single track meet. That was the kind of great support all my family members gave each other.

Dad loved to smoke cigars. I remember one track meet in particular in my senior year when he came out to see me run in a mile race. We lined up and the race started. We had to do four laps. Each time I came around the curve to finish a full lap; I passed my father's short, rather pudgy stature puffing away on his cigar. I can still see and hear him today encouraging me, while smoke rings swirled around his face, *"Pace yourself son, pace yourself!"*

As I sprinted around the second lap, I began falling behind my opponents. I approached Dad at that curve and he kept urging me on with his words, *"Pace yourself son, pace yourself!"* I got to the third lap realizing how much further behind I had lagged. At the fourth and final lap, all the other runners were done and I was still coming around that turn—just a-kicking. Dad continued his firm chant, *"Pace yourself son, pace yourself!"* He hung in there with me, even when I lost. My father was such a big inspiration to me.

Another sport I took part in was baseball—not as a player, but as a coach. I started coaching Little League Baseball teams when I was about fifteen or sixteen years old. My players were anywhere from eight to twelve years old. I must say, I had some very good teams. My coaching training actually started when I was thirteen or fourteen years old. I was the protégé of an older gentleman named Levy Leak. After he permitted me to work with him a couple of years during which I was able to glean from his knowledge and to pattern my coaching style after his, he gave up his coaching position and turned it over to me. He was a great coach and a gracious man who demonstrated his care for the kids he coached by using his own money to buy all the bats and balls for the team.

We practiced those kids hard and turned them into some very good Little League players. None of them ever went on to become profession-al baseball players or anything, but they were solid players nonetheless. We had seven or eight Little League teams around Centralia, and players from each team would all compete to be on one All-Star team. That Centralia All-Star team would then go on to play in championship games against teams from Salem, Mount Vernon, Carlyle and other surrounding communities. We generally won those championships.

I also coached my little cousin, Harry Duncan; or I should say *tried* to coach him. Harry was eight years old and would not stay in the batter's box when the ball was pitched. His uncle on his father's side was Melvin Duncan, a great baseball player with the Negro Baseball League[x]. Harry wanted to emulate his Uncle Melvin so badly; yet, he always stepped back to swing, as though he was afraid of the ball.

When I noticed it, I told him, *"Okay, Harry, we're going to solve this problem."*

I threw a couple of balls and each time he stepped back. I yelled, *"Harry, it's going to intensify. If you step back, I'm going to throw this ball right at your head!"*

Harry got so nervous and upset that his bat shook as his hand trem-bled. I went over to him, looked squarely down his face and pointed my finger at his chest with each word I spoke, *"If you want to be a baseball player, you've got to stand in that box."*

The next ball I threw hard close to him and he ducked. He started to cry, and he got back in the box. After several pitches, Harry stopped stepping back. When he got home, he told his dad that I threw a ball at his head and tried to hit him. I told his dad what I was attempting to work on with Harry. Fortunately, his dad sided with me. Eventually, Harry became one of the best Little League baseball players around town and even went on to play American Legion baseball for awhile. Today, though, he's a heck of a golfer, shooting in the high 70's and low 80's in a good round of golf.

Rewarding Honors

In September of 2010, my Centralia Township High School class held its 55th reunion. I was honored at that event for being named "Illinois African-American Man of the Year" by the National Council of African-American Men.[xi] Unfortunately, I couldn't make it to that reunion, due to my attendance at the Congressional Black Caucus[xii] meetings.

My friend, Rod Snow, accepted the award on my behalf. I was so flattered when he later told me all my classmates in attendance had something good to say about me and they felt fortunate to have known me over so many years.

I had also been honored by my classmates years earlier, at our 20th high school reunion, along with two other classmates, who achieved greatness in their fields. I was recognized for my appointment by Illinois Governor Dan Walker to his cabinet as Director of the Department of General Services. Another honoree, Bill Norwood, who attended Southern Illinois University (SIU) with me, became the first black pilot hired by United Airlines in 1965.[xiii] He later became the first black to attain the rank of captain at United. Bill also became SIU'S first African-American quarterback and was later recognized for his athletic ability by being inducted into the Saluki Hall of Fame.

Our other classmate, Bobby Joe Mason, was one of the greatest sports figures to ever come out of Centralia High School, having participated in basketball, football and track. He has a place in Centralia's Sports Hall of Fame as proof of that. He led his Bradley University team to two championships before going on to play for the world renowned traveling basketball team, the Harlem Globetrotters,[xiv] for fourteen years.

At the banquet, Rod Snow, stood and said in his talk, *"You know what, classmates? If it hadn't been for the black guys in our class, this class wouldn't have amounted to very much!"* There were more than a hundred classmates at the 20th reunion banquet and they all applauded his statement. When Rod accepted the award for me at our 55th reunion, he said, *"I'm going to repeat what I said at our 20th reunion. If it hadn't been for the blacks guys in this class, we wouldn't have amounted to very much!"*

Dirty Playing

In my junior year of high school as a quarterback, we played a football game against a high school from Salem, Illinois. We had just run an end around play, and I had done a pitch out to my halfback. Salem's defensive end hit me real hard, knocked me to the ground and then called me a "nigger." As I was getting up, he again sputtered, *"I'm gonna get you, nigger."*

Back in the huddle, one of my white teammates (either John Boswell or Bill Crain), who had also heard that Salem player, asked, "What did he call you, Roland?" *"You heard him,"* was all I said.

Well, that Salem guy looked to be about 6'6" and weighed over 200 pounds. I was 5'5" and weighed 140 pounds. Just as I was itching to go up against him again, the coach pulled me out of the game. I stood at the sideline crying, *"Coach, he called me a nigger!"* The coach urged, *"Just calm down, Roland. Calm down."* I did and soon returned to the game.

We beat Salem badly that night. We had several big players on our team as well. Two of them, John Boswell and Fred Wham—each about 6'5" and weighing anywhere from 220-250 pounds—came up to ensure me, *"Don't worry, Roland. We're going to take care of him."* Once Boswell and Wham dressed after the game, they headed out to the Salem bus with a vengeance.

When I found out they had left the locker room to confront that player, I ran out and stopped them. We were all pretty close as teammates and high school classmates. I appreciated their gesture, but didn't feel that the boy's ignorance in name-calling was worth my friends getting in trouble.

Let Them Swim

We experienced some of that same kind of small-minded mentality

40

around the Centralia community that built racial barriers upheld by injudicious rules. One such foolish rule still in existence in 1953 was that blacks could not swim in the Centralia public pool. Blacks tried to swim in that pool in 1951, but they had been denied entry. In 1952, the NAACP led an attempt to integrate the pool, but they, too, were denied. In 1953, Reverend Starks, the pastor of the church that Dad attended, became president of the NAACP. Dad was vice president of that NAACP chapter. Together, they decided to make another attempt at integrating the pool. Dad traveled to Chicago in search of a lawyer to come to Centralia to represent them, but could find no lawyer who would agree to take on the task.

The next day, after returning from Chicago, Dad traveled to East St. Louis, Illinois where he finally retained a black lawyer. He gave him a one hundred dollar retainer to be in Centralia on that Memorial Day to represent us should we get arrested. That one hundred dollar retainer was a huge amount in 1953. In fact, it represented more than a month's salary for my dad.

As the pool opened Memorial Day of 1953, Reverend Starks, my father, my brother, three friends of ours, who were the Lawson brothers and I stood there ready to swim in the pool. By coming to the town's public pool, we were demonstrating our right to swim there, as opposed to swimming in the muddy lakes and creeks which dotted the area. Until that time, those muddy watering holes were the only places blacks could go for their water recreation. To make matters worse, one of those creeks was where people watered their horses, cows, and pigs. It was named the "Pig Wobble."

When we arrived at the pool moments before the ticket window opened, white folks were already lined up along the fence just waiting for us to come, since word had gotten out that we would be there. Reverend Starks walked up to the ticket window with his money out and lo and behold, they sold him five tickets. We were very surprised to be able to get the tickets to the pool so easily. We proceeded into the locker room where we undressed and showered before heading to the pool. By the time we walked out there, the white folks were not only lined up along the fence, but they had also filled the bleachers, a gathering spot for parents, friends usually sat to watch the swimmers and a grandstand area for spectators when special competitions were held at the local pool.

41

I walked over very close to the high diving board and looked up to gauge how high it was. Just then, I decided to climb up the ladder and check out the board. Good board. At that point, with all eyes on me, I figured there was no turning back, so I proceeded to the edge and conjured up my most beautiful swan dive possible. I'm not sure how it looked to the spectators, but it felt good to me. After descending into the water, I opened my eyes and was shocked to note that the bottom of the pool was painted blue. As kids who grew up only seeing the pool from outside the fence, we always marveled at how pretty and inviting the water appeared. What a tremendous surprise it was for me to discover that the blue water that made the pool seem so inviting wasn't really blue at all!

Then the other guys in our little group jumped into the pool, and we swam and messed around for a little bit. During the entire time we were in the pool, we were apprehensive about what action might be taken since technically, we had "broken the law," but to our surprise, nothing happened. None of the white people said anything. None of them called us any names. However, none of them got into the pool, either. They just watched us. After a while, we got out of the pool, dressed and headed home. From that time on, the Centralia swimming pool was integrated.

When we got home, we started celebrating our victory. Reverend Starks and Dad went out to look for the lawyer who should have arrived in town by that time. Sometime later, Dad came in the house madder than I don't know what! I had never seen my father that angry. He looked at me and my brother and spewed, *That lawyer we hired didn't even bother to show up. If we had been arrested, there would have been nobody to represent us!* He carried on with his angry tirade and made this profound statement: *"If we, as a race of people are going to get anywhere in this society, we've got to have lawyers and elected officials who are responsible and responsive."*

My Two Goals

That statement hit me like a ton of bricks. I was only fifteen years old, but immediately began thinking about becoming a lawyer and a statewide elected official when I grew up. By the time I started my junior year of high school that September, my career goals were set. My attire that first day of school consisted of one of my brother's suits he had left behind when he went away to college and a white shirt and tie I got from Dad. If I was going to be a lawyer and a statewide elected official, I figured I needed to start looking the part. When I entered those school doors, some of my teachers didn't even recognize me dressed up. They soon learned that I was serious and got used to the fact that I meant business. That swimming pool experience motivated me to set those two goals: 1) to be a lawyer and 2) to be a statewide elected official. I fully understood that along with the privilege of operating in those two capacities came the power and authority to help the people who really needed help. I promised myself that once in those positions, I would not take advantage of people or purposely let them down like that lawyer let us down that day at the swimming pool.

Family
Photographs

Mrs. Josephine Ewing, great grandmother

Mrs. Mittie Biggest Green, great grandmother

Great Aunt Bertha Hinds

Great Aunt Ada Bell Scott

Great aunts: Mrs. Ada Bell Scott, Mrs. Bessie McGinnis, Mrs. Bertha Hinds at Burris Family Reunion

Uncle John Henry Curry

Uncle Elmer Curry

...ant Burris "Papa Burris," grandfather (far right), and his brothers, my great uncles: [from left] George Burris Jr., ...y Burris, Joe Burris, Russell Burris, and Sam Burris. Another brother, Robert Burris is not pictured

...urris family at Springfield Inauguration 1979: From left: niece, Kim Burris Holmes; nephew, Steve Burris; ...aughter, Rolanda Burris; niece, Jill Giboney Williams; Illinois Comptroller Roland W. Burris; niece, ...eresa Giboney; nephew, Felix Giboney III; sister, Doris Downey; nephew, Earl Burris III; wife, Berlean Burris; ...n, Roland W. Burris II

Mrs. Emma Burris, mother, and Mr. Earl Burris, Sr., father

unts: Mrs. Freda Ricks, Mrs. Lola Walker, and Mrs. Minnie Wilson

Brother: Earl "Nick" Burris Jr.

Roland Burris poses with son,
Roland Burris II, at his graduation
from Morgan Park Academy

Roland W. Burris II accep
congratulations at St. Ignatiu
College Prep Graduatio

Dr. Berlean Burris,
Hon. Roland W. Burris,
Roland W. Burris II, and
Rolanda Sue Burris
in the back yard of the
family home

Debutante Ball:
Hon. Roland W. Burris, daughter,
Rolanda, and wife, Dr. Berlean Burris

Rolanda Burris poses with he
parents and the roses sh
received at her Harvar
St. George High School graduatio

olanda S. Burris undergoes traditional "hooding" as part of her doctoral commencement ceremony at orthern Illinois University

Members of the Burris family look on at the Northern Illinois University graduation of Rolanda S. Burris. rom right, row two: father, Senator Roland W. Burris; mother, Dr. Berlean Burris; and brother, Roland Burris II; rom right, row one: uncle, Elder Cleotis Peacock; aunt, Susie Peacock, and aunt, Nellie Miller

The Roland W. Burris Family:
From left: Roland W. Burris II, Dr. Berlean Burris, Hon. Roland Burris, and Rolanda Burris

r: Berlean Burris' family celebrates her Ph.D. graduation, Northwestern University
rom left: brother-in-law, Cleo Peacock; sister, Susie Peacock; aunt, Mattie Townsend, sister, Nellie Miller;
ughter, Rolanda Burris; Hon. Roland W. Burris; Dr. Berlean Burris; son, Roland Burris II; sister,
amie Lewis; brother, Johnny Miller; sister-in-law, Hallie Miller; and brother, Henry Miller

Hon. Roland Burris and Dr. Berlean Burris pose after her Ph.D.
graduation at Northwestern University.

Hon. Roland W. Burris and Dr. Berlean Burris pose with son, Roland Burris II, after his graduation from Northwestern University Law School

Roland Burris II, Esquire, accepts congratulations from the Northwestern University Law School Dean at his graduation

Three Burris generations: Grandfather/father Roland W. Burris, son/father Roland II, and sons/grandsons Roland Theodore and Ian Alexander

Grandmother, Dr. Berlean Burris and grandsons, Ian Alexander and Roland Theodore Burris
Below:Son and Daughter-in-Law, Roland Burris II and Marty Burris, and grandsons, Roland and Ian

Chapter Four
Carbondale, Illinois

Wrapping Up in Centralia

A s I shared previously, I was a mischievous boy in my youth. Some would even have referred to me as a "bad little dude," because I would fight in a minute. I beat up a couple of guys in my day. One guy that I remember in particular was a boy named James Marshall. James had such a bad disposition that we all called him "Wildman." He thought nothing of beating up two or three boys in one day.

On the day that he and I fought, I was in the eighth grade, and Wildman was in the seventh grade. I can't even begin to tell you what caused the fight, but I know I fared okay. I have my bodybuilding and weightlifting to thank for that.

There were several popular professional wrestlers I followed in my younger days, namely Gorgeous George and the Mighty Atlas. I marveled at their muscles, so I gained an interest in lifting weights. In fact, all of us little black kids would go around talking about being Gorgeous George. I saw a picture in a magazine of him doing a body press, so that was what I did on that bully James "Wildman" Marshall. I had also witnessed Gorgeous George perform a back breaker, dropping his opponent across his knee. That, I definitely did *not* try on "Wildman." After all, I was a *bad* little dude, not a crazy one!

Some of those ill-conceived tendencies of mine spilled over into my first two years of high school, resulting in a couple of bad grades. I got a D in Latin and a D in Geometry. However, after that swimming pool situation—upon which my two life goals were established—I went back to school in the fall of my junior year with an entirely different attitude. I got serious. As a result, my grades improved substantially.

My friend Conrad graduated from high school after only three years, so by my senior year of high school, he was already gone and attending Northwestern University (NU) in Evanston, Illinois, a northern suburb of Chicago.

Since Conrad was at NU, my intention was to go there also—that is, until I found out how much it cost. I don't remember exactly, but in August of 1955, I believe tuition cost somewhere in the neighborhood of seven hundred or eight hundred dollars per semester, as opposed to thirty-five dollars per quarter at Southern Illinois University (SIU), in the southern Illinois town of Carbondale.

Northwestern's high tuition made my decision to go to SIU quite easy; that, coupled with the fact that I won a four-year full-tuition scholarship to attend SIU. My scholarship was for thirty-five dollars per quarter! Such a small amount for tuition sounds so funny compared to today's exorbitant tuition costs, but, for me, it truly made a huge difference. The only things left for me to come up with were my room and board.

Dish Washer Extraordinaire

To help lessen the college financial burden on my parents, I couldn't wait to get a summer job. In fact, just one day after I received my high school diploma on June 7, 1955, I headed to Chicago to start working. I spent almost the entire summer there, living with the family of my friend, Lonnie O'Neal. My godmother, Nellie Fields, was Lonnie's aunt. A group of us from Centralia lived at her home that summer.

The only job I managed to find that summer consisted of washing dishes at the lunch counter of a five & dime store, making ninety cents an hour. The store was located at 47th Street and South Park Avenue on the city's South Side. South Park Ave is now known as Dr. Martin Luther King Drive. That lunch counter served many customers every day, so thank goodness they had an automatic dishwashing machine. However, I found out all too soon—automatic machine or not—those dishes piled up faster than any one person could effectively manage to get them washed. And the funny thing was some of the regular dish washers did not know how to use the machine.

The head waitress there, a woman named Mozelle, was in charge of the other waitresses and a couple of chefs. Mozelle was so mean her looks would cut right through you, long before her words would. All the waitresses and cooks were afraid of her. I soon found out why, as she had the worst disposition of anyone I'd ever met. I figured if I could learn how to operate that machine, I could get on Mozelle's good side. My job was to ensure that the dishes were clean and to do so quickly. It took me a moment, but I finally got my rhythm. I learned how to collect the dishes, bring them back to the washer, and then operate the machine. I knocked those dishes out in no time, getting them to the stations for the waitresses to grab them. Every time a waitress looked for a plate or a glass, it was already there for them. When I first started, that wasn't the case, so all day long, I heard them holler and scream, *"Plates; more glasses; we have no cups for coffee!"*

After about three or four days of listening to that, I shocked them. First of all, because the other washers didn't know how to operate that machine properly, they did too many things manually. I forced myself to learn every detail of that machine and soon had those dishes steaming and zipping in and out of there, with no lipstick on the cups or glasses. I quickly inspected those dishes; grabbed any that needed a second run through, or special cleanup; and stacked the clean ones at the station.

Soon, the waitresses exclaimed, *"We just know this ain't true. We don't have to holler for our dishes?"*

Mozelle said nothing about my progress. I could tell she had no intention of complimenting me on my efficiency. Instead, she preferred walking around screaming at everyone. One day, after my third week on the job, I called in sick and in my absence; they had problems with the machine and with dishes not being ready.

When I returned to work, Mozelle muttered, *"Where have you been?"*

Mozelle was clearly upset my absence caused the stations not to be supplied properly. Within that one question of hers, I could tell this was her own harsh way of saying she appreciated my good work.

Around that same time, the chef had talked to the manager of the restaurant, and together they called me into the manager's office. I thought, *"Oh, my God, I'm going to get fired. What did I do wrong?"*

To my relief, both the manager and chef praised my work, saying,

"The waitresses are all pleased with your work. They tell me that they're getting dishes that are all clean, so we're going to give you a raise."

My boss gave me a ten cent per hour raise after just one month on the job. So my pay rate then became one dollar an hour. I was so proud! You talk about work! I worked doubly hard in hopes of getting another raise. My coworkers sometimes gave me a hard time about picking up dishes so fast. *"Just slow down,"* they would urge, *"you're showing us up."*

That was just my work ethic—the manner in which I had worked all my life. Luckily, my ethic included saving as well. I spent only a little of my earnings on my social life in Chicago, while keeping my focus on saving for college. My godmother kept me in line with saving for college, as well.

College Bound – Freshman Year 1955-56
Learning the Ropes

Early one morning in August of 1955, about three weeks before the fall quarter was set to start at Southern Illinois University (SIU) in Carbondale, Illinois, I sat on a train with four of my high school football buddies. About an hour after boarding in Centralia, the train rolled into the Carbondale station. We arrived at the campus and located the athletics department where we were to meet the new head coach and some of his new staff. Upon reaching the coach's office, we all sat there anxious to meet the coach and to hear his instructions. In addition to me, there was Bill Norwood, a quarterback like me; Leonard Taylor, an all-state lineman; Charlie Steptoe, also a lineman and cousin of mine whose grandfather and my grandfather were brothers; and Vernon Rush, a linebacker. All of us were academics. Rush was a mathematical whiz. Steptoe was a chemical whiz. Norwood excelled in reading, math and chemistry. My forte was math and talking. I could talk my way out of almost anything. After all, I *was* going to be a lawyer.

After receiving all the necessary information from the coach, it was close to the noon hour. Practice wouldn't start until the next day after our physical examinations, so that left us a lot of time to get acclimated to our surroundings. As we left our coach's office, we discussed getting some lunch before settling into the football players' dormitory.

The coach looked at us and said, *"You're going to get something to eat, huh?"* He then reached into his desk drawer and pulled out a sheet of paper and began to read off the names of the four restaurants where Negro players had to go to eat in Carbondale. All five of us gave puzzling glances at each other as if we shared the same thought: *"What is this? We only traveled sixty-five miles south from Centralia where we could eat anywhere!"*

"No, no, this is not going to work," either Taylor or Rush spoke up. *"Let's go back to Centralia!"*

The coach lifted his hands in an effort to stop our protest. *"No, no, no, calm down, we're going to feed you dinner and all the rest of your meals in the dormitory."*

For the time being, though, our lunch could only be purchased from one of the four places on his sheet of paper: New Era Dairy, Varsity Theater, the train station where we had arrived and a fourth place that I've since forgotten. I learned later that before our time, even the Varsity Theatre had been off limits to black students, until some SIU students had mounted a protest. Of course, we had no choice but to abide by the rules. We headed to town and ate without incident. Once back on campus, we got squared away in our dormitory. What a day that was.

Practice the next day—and every day after that—was intense to say the least. Unfortunately, it was too intense for Leonard, because after about one week of practice, he pulled out and went home. Rush followed suit the following week. That left Norwood, Steptoe and me to vie for positions on the team.

About three or four days before the first day of school, the coach came to me and said, *"Well, Burris, you're not going to make varsity, but we want you to come back when school starts and practice with the junior varsity. Make sure you come out for that, because I'm pretty sure you'll be able to run the junior varsity."* Well, that was discouraging and encouraging all at the same time.

Having made the cut, I headed home to Centralia for a few days before school. I was genuinely happy for Norwood and Steptoe, who made the varsity team. I returned to Carbondale several days later, ready to start classes. I was refreshed, recharged and mentally prepared to join the team as the junior varsity quarterback. We played nine games that year, winning maybe five and losing four games that season.

51

Integrating SIU

The university actually converted old World War II barracks used for servicemen into dormitories and a student center. I didn't get to experience barracks-living, however, because I stayed in the city with my brother at the home of a lady named Mrs. Edwards. It just so happened that right at that time, the university completed construction on the first major women's dormitory. It was named Woody Hall, and it was huge. Dr. Delyte Morris, who had been SIU President since 1947, was faced with a major racial question which emerged with the construction of that dorm: *"What are you going to do with the black female students?"* Well, Dr. Morris knew exactly what to do. He issued this edict: as the female students registered, they were to be assigned rooms without regard to race. There would be two girls to a room. The white parents registering their daughters were concerned with this arrangement. However, Dr. Morris stuck to his decision to assign the students as their names came up, regardless of their race.[xv] With that single, brave act, Dr. Morris integrated SIU housing. Some of the white students, as well as their parents, objected to that notion. President Morris stood by his statement and advised them to accept their roommate or leave the school. As I recall, a few parents did remove their students from the school.

I Can't Eat That!

As I mentioned, I lived with my brother. He was in his senior year at SIU, having lived all four years at Mrs. Edwards' home, which was only a short distance from campus. I stayed there only several months before I convinced Mom during Christmas break that I needed to stay on campus. I told her, *"I can't take it there at the house. Nick may have done this for four years, but I just can't."*

My main objection to living there was the food. I could not eat the food that was being prepared. The arrangement they had in place for years was that my brother would bring the food from my parents' grocery store and his classmate and roommate, Melvin Brown, would prepare it. Melvin's idea of a good meal was cooking some beans in one pot; corn in another. He would then heat up the spam and mix all three on the same plate placing the beans on top of the corn and the spam on top of it all. When I repeatedly asked Melvin not to mix my food that way, it fell on deaf ears. He basically mocked me, making light of my request. *"Oh, what's the difference? It's all going down the same way."* I knew that I needed to move.

Also, by that time, SIU allowed blacks to stay in some of the near-campus housing facilities, so that's where I went. My mom had agreed to give me an allowance of twenty dollars a week for room, board, and personal expenses. At that time, I could eat all my six meals at the University Drugstore (U.D.) The owner there was very supportive of me because I was an athlete. On Sunday, we were on our own for food.

Making the Grade

During my first year, I enrolled in the required ROTC program (Reserve Officers Training Corps). I was a government major, pre-law student and had a liberal arts curriculum. Grade-wise, I didn't do too well that first quarter, especially since I was playing football and trying to get used to my new surroundings. I made a "D" in my health sciences course and "C's" in all my other classes.

That caused my grade point average to fall just below the 3.0 minimal average my tuition scholarship required me to maintain. The dean threatened to put me on probation. That scared the living daylights out of me, because overall, I was a pretty good student who always tried my best in class.

No doubt, one of the culprits for my below-average grades was pledging a fraternity. Although I must admit, perhaps a bigger reason might have been all those pretty girls on campus. I realized all too soon I was not in Centralia anymore! I also met young men and women who came from across the country and from around the world, so it became tempting for me to pay more attention to my dynamic surroundings than to my studies. I knew I had some major convincing to do with Dean I. Clark Davis if I wanted to stay off probation.

While sitting in his office, I began my plea, *"Dean, whatever you do, please don't put me on probation. I promise you that in the next quarter I will do much better. As a matter of fact, I think I can make a 4.0 average."* (We were on the 5.0 grading system.) The dean said, *"You think you can do that? You're sitting here with a 2.9 right now, just one-tenth under the required 3."* I assured him I could do it and he accepted that. The next quarter I had five hours of chemistry, five hours of calculus, my first government course, ROTC and sports for a total of about eighteen credit hours. When all was said and done, I got an A in chemistry and an A in calculus and achieved a 4.5 average GPA the following quarter. And I maintained that average even while pledging for Alpha Phi Alpha fraternity during the second quarter!

I met with Dean Davis and showed him my grades. Needless to say, my complete turnaround helped to establish me as a person with some semblance of smarts, or at least showed I was serious about my education. The dean proudly said to me, *"I've never had a student make such a promise and keep it. I'm so glad that I did not put you on probation because it might have deflated you."*

Dean Davis turned out to be a very supportive figure in my college life and beyond. In fact, we became good friends. Over the years, Dean Davis often used me as an example when advising his future students. Anytime I visited SIU after graduation, I stopped by and visited him and we would often talk about the improvement I made during the second quarter of my freshman year.

After I proved to myself I could do well in college, the rest was history. I continued to do pretty well academically after that. Even though my academic record was good, I wasn't able to beat my brother's academic accomplishments, because he was so much smarter. Sports took up a lot of my time as well, but by the spring quarter, I had become totally adjusted to college.

That first year of college came and went very quickly. Before I knew it, it was time to head to Chicago once again for summer employment. It was the summer of 1956, and I no longer had to wash dishes. My godmother worked for a doctor who was a friend of a pharmacist at Provident Hospital in Chicago,[xvi] so they hired me for the summer. It turned out to be a fortunate "who-you-know" connection. Of course, the fact that I was a well-behaved and disciplined kid factored greatly into the equation as well.

So there I was, at a hospital, working in the pharmacy as a pharmacist's aide. I learned about different medicines, as my job was to drop off the prescribed medicine to the nurse's stations on the different patient floors. While making my runs to the various stations, I took note of a lot of pretty student nurses training at the hospital. Nonetheless, I stayed focused on earning some college money to take back to SIU.

College – Sophomore Year 1956-57
Proving Myself Again

I was supposed to go back to SIU in August for early football practice. However, because my job was going so well and I was making such good money, I decided to continue working a little longer. I finally got to Carbondale when school started in September. Upon returning for varsity practice, the coach pointed out to me, *"Burris, you didn't come back for early practice, so you have to go back to junior varsity."*

What an ego-deflator! That meant starting over and proving myself once again in order to play varsity. I played quarterback for the junior varsity. Another junior varsity player from Springfield, who *did* come back early, was a quarterback also and he was running the first team. So the coach decided to let us alternate as first team quarterbacks.

After our first or second game, we were preparing for the homecoming game. We had an open scrimmage which pitted the junior varsity first team against the varsity's first team. At SIU it was traditional that the best junior varsity players would be able to dress with the varsity for the homecoming game. I knew there could be no ifs, ands or buts: I really had to shine.

There I was at that scrimmage playing both quarterback and safety. On the defense, I tackled those 200-pound running backs at the line of scrimmage. I nailed them left and right; putting the hurt on those backs. The coach would yell, *"Don't crack up the varsity, Burris. What are you trying to do, hurt 'em?"* My reply came back, *"No, sir, just trying to make a play!"*

Mainly, I tried to move up to varsity. If hurting them was the way to show the coaches how good I was, then so be it.

The scrimmage ended. I don't remember specifically what the outcome was, but I do remember having sharp pains in my head later in the dressing room. It felt like somebody drove nails through my head. I didn't say anything; just got showered, dressed and went to U.D.'s to eat dinner. While sitting there eating, the pain got worse. I mentioned to the owner—who was very fond of athletes—that I wasn't feeling well. He had one of his workers to escort me back to the gym. It wasn't very far away, about two blocks maybe. Fortunately, the trainer was still there, and I told him about the sharp pains in my head.

End of the Line for Sports

The next thing I knew, I woke up in the emergency room in the hospital. They told me I had a brain concussion. That was the first time I had ever been in the hospital in my life. I spent three days there and, much to my chagrin, that ended my football career. There I was: depressed, 5'5," 150 pounds, left-handed, and black; I wanted so much to be a great football player. My goal was to make that varsity team.

The day after I went into the hospital, they posted the list in the morning indicating which junior varsity players would move up to varsity. I was in the hospital and the coach had not received word yet about what happened to me. At the top of that list to dress for the homecoming game was the name, Roland Burris. That gave me some consolation, but I didn't make it to the homecoming game at all because I was still recuperating.

After fully recovering from my concussion, I joined the wrestling team. We didn't have wrestling in my high school, so I didn't know the maneuvers and techniques. My experience was limited to the fighting I did as a kid and the wrestling I had done at home, but that was it. In spite of my lack of skills, a lot of good teammates and coaches taught me how to wrestle. In the end, I became a pretty decent wrestler.

I lifted weights all the time, so I didn't have an ounce of fat on me. I sported 40-inch shoulders, a 29-inch waist and my abs were rippled as well. We called our abs washboards back then. I stayed in training. I didn't smoke or drink alcohol. I didn't even drink coffee.

I did make the wrestling team, but didn't win many matches. Because they tried to get me in at 137 pounds, I often went up against some state champions. Despite all this, however, I held my own. I wrestled for the rest of my sophomore year and most of my junior year. After that, I called it quits for sports.

Carpenter Extraordinaire

In the summer of 1957, I got a break from having to train for sports for the first time in years. Also, that summer Provident Hospital didn't hire me back, so I didn't spend my time in Chicago. Instead, I stayed in Centralia and worked. My main job those two and a half months was as a carpenter's helper for Bill Norwood's father who had a carpentry business. I worked from 7:30am to 4:30pm, five days a week. Most of the time, I helped to rebuild the building that once housed my father's confectionary store, now called *Lonnie's Place*. Lonnie O'Neal's father, who owned the building, was the man who wouldn't lease the space back to my father after fire damaged the building when we were kids. My friend, Lonnie, had been an excellent chef at the Walgreen's lunch counter, and he had a great menu at his own place. We all loved Lonnie's hamburgers.

My other job during that summer was painting the outside of my grandmother's big, white two-story house. It wasn't just big, it was huge! Every day for almost a month, I would paint from 5:00pm 'til dark. Upon completion of that paint job, do you have any idea what Grandma paid me? Would you believe sixty-five dollars? As she handed me that sixty-five dollars Grandma said proudly, *"Son, you did a great job. Here's your pay."* I'm laughing about this now, but back then I wanted to cry! I just knew she was going to pay me a couple of hundred dollars so I could buy a car I'd had my eyes on. I felt my labor of love was certainly worth two-hundred dollars. It made me happy, though, to be able to help her out, so I quickly got over my disappointment.

College – Junior Year 1957-58 Frat House

I headed back to Carbondale to begin my junior year with a lot more excitement than I had experienced in previous years. Why? Well, I was vice president of my Alpha Phi Alpha[xvii] chapter at that time, and our fraternity had just successfully negotiated with the owner the rental of a large house which would be our frat house. When September of 1957 rolled around, there were fourteen or fifteen anxious Alpha members prepared to move into that house, which was about seven blocks from campus. Kappa Alpha Psi,[xviii] the other black fraternity on the SIU campus, was three years ahead of us in the housing arena. They had acquired their house back in 1954, compliments of the close relationship between one of the Kappa frat brothers, Carl Anderson, and Dean Davis. Since rivalry and competitive tension always existed between our two frats, we knew we had to get a house in order to remain competitive with the Kappas. The fact that their house was only one block from campus didn't bother us at all!

Halfway through my junior year, when our Alpha president, Jan Pe-

57

ters, graduated, I became president of my fraternity. That was a big deal to me, as I became the first junior in the history of our chapter to be president. With the presidency came not only the duties of the chapter, but also the duty of running the frat house. I had to collect the rent, pay the bills and make sure we had heat in the wintertime. In addition, there were other issues that needed to be monitored: brothers were cooking when they weren't supposed to be cooking and eating other brothers' food, so I had to referee things like that all the time.

Grease Sandwich, Anyone?

One student who pledged our fraternity really tore at my heartstrings. He was a freshman during my junior year. He came from a small town between Centralia and Carbondale called Du Quoin, Illinois. Floyd Smith was a smart young man. He got a part-time job near campus and tried to survive off the little money he earned. Having to put all his earnings towards tuition and rent at the frat house became such a huge strain on him. He just didn't have enough money to cover it all.

Floyd made it through September and then October. By the end of November, he kept looking each week for money to come from Du Quoin—money that never came. Floyd would come home in the evening from his classes and check the mail. If no mail had arrived for him, he'd fill up on water, drinking all that his belly could hold, and then go to bed. Floyd perhaps weighed about 140 pounds soaking wet. Although he was about six feet tall, he was mere skin and bones.

One day, we came home and Floyd had left us a note. In the note, Floyd informed us that he had dropped out of college. He just couldn't take the deprivation any more. Many years later, I met a young man from Du Quoin who worked for the SIU Alumni Association. He had gone to school with Floyd's kids. Floyd turned out to be a very successful handyman, painter and carpenter in Du Quoin. He died a few years ago, at about the age of sixty-five. Thoughts of Floyd's lack of money never left me; in fact, these thoughts have often haunted me. I will never forget how he tried to get a college education and how the lack of money, even to feed himself, had stood in his way and prevented him from doing so. Because of Floyd, I now sponsor an endowed scholarship at Southern Illinois University in Carbondale to help students in need. [xix] The scholarship offers funds for student emergencies, such as paying for transportation home, buying books or meeting other emergency needs. I will never forget how Floyd struggled because no helping hand existed to supply him with the money he needed to keep his education going.

Many of us experienced tough times at college. We couldn't get good meals on Sundays unless we had money, which we generally didn't. Therefore, Sunday became a miserable day in our frat house. I'm sure that kids today don't know about some of the things we went through, like having to eat grease sandwiches. I mean, we literally ate grease on bread to fill our stomachs and ward off hunger. We would first heat up some left over bacon or sausage grease. Next, we got some heel pieces of bread and would then dip the bread in the grease. That would have to suffice, since there was rarely extra money for food.

I recall a time when five of us sat around a table with one small can of tuna. Luckily, one of the brothers had a girlfriend who gave him a tube-shaped package of crackers to go along with the tuna. That Sunday, the five of us split up that tuna and crackers and enjoyed it as if it was a scrumptious three-course gourmet spread. We became skilled at stretching a meal like that and training our stomachs to believe we were full. We often rejoiced when Mondays rolled around so we could finally use our meal tickets. However, until Monday morning, we couldn't even get coffee and donuts. Most of us lived on coffee and donuts for breakfast. Since I wasn't playing sports anymore, I became one of those coffee drinkers.

Also, because I was no longer playing sports, I often drank this strange mixture of scotch and milk. An old friend of mine in Centralia introduced me to it. I got a little extra money one day, bought some scotch and tried fixing it myself. At first, it was some seriously nasty stuff! Then, it became just somewhat nasty. My frat brothers would talk about me like a dog whenever I had it. I drank it for a short while, but then finally realized that, sports or no sports, I just wasn't a drinker.

He Kept Us in Stitches!

In September of 1957, a week or so prior to the start of my junior year, some of my frat brothers and I had moved into our house early. One night, a group of us SIU students decided to hang out at the local Carbondale joint, where we knew we would run into some of the local

59

guys from Carbondale. We also knew that there was friction between the Carbondale boys and the college boys, and that it had been present for years. More than likely, it started because of the fact that the college boys tried to date the local girls in town. The Carbondale boys didn't like that one bit.

There we were hanging out when in walked this little guy, weighing between 120 and 130 pounds. Well, he started running his mouth about those Carbondale boys. The crowd got a little quiet and slowly divided: college boys to one side; Carbondale boys to the other. The guy stayed right in the middle, by himself, just a-talking about everything and everyone. I don't know if he was aware of the tension in the room or not, but he started cracking jokes. Fortunately, his jokes were so funny that the tension left the room and somehow there were none of the usual problems or altercations that night.

You may recognize the name of that little guy; because he went on to become a famous comedian and a well-known activist: Dick Gregory.[xx] Dick started at SIU with my brother and Carl Anderson, then dropped out and went into the service for four years. He came back during my junior year to finish up his last couple of years.[xxi]

We closed down the joint that night. As a fellow Alpha, he came on back to the frat house. We sat around from 12:30am until the sun came up. Dick had us in stitches that entire time, sharing his many stories. I ached from laughing so hard. No doubt he was born to be a comedian, but for the time being, he was just our funny frat brother and classmate. He was also a great sportsman, leaving his mark at SIU as a half-mile record holder. Dick was also very close to SIU president, Dr. Morris. He even had the privilege of spending nights with the Morris family as a guest in their home which was located on the campus of the university.

Just to give you an example of how he carried on, one time, we were sitting in the student union, and Dick got to talking about some of the girls sitting there. The boys would laugh, encouraging him to crack on them even more.

He looked at this one female student and said, *"Wow, honey, you sure are good lookin.' You've got some pretty blue eyes."*

"What do you mean blue eyes?" The girl inquired, knowing her eyes were dark brown.

Dick gladly clarified his statement, *"Well, one blew this way and the*

60

other blew that way!" Needless to say, the humiliated girl left crying. In 1958, during his senior year, Dick went around campus telling everyone that he received a telegram to appear on the Ted Mack Show in 1959. He approached me and some other frat brothers waving that telegram saying, *"I'm going to be leaving school."*

"Brother, let me see that," I said as I snatched the telegram out of his hand. I looked at it and blew his cover in front of everyone. *"Yeah, it says you're going to appear on the Ted Mack Show, but at the top it also says from Carbondale to Carbondale."* Everyone laughed, realizing he sent the telegram to himself.

Recently, I saw Dick at our 50th college reunion in Carbondale, where the university honored him. While at the microphone accepting his award, Dick started roasting me. I guess he was trying to pay me back for the telegram thing. One of the things he said was, *"You know, we were on the campus, and there was the senator walking around campus carrying a briefcase. Nobody carried a briefcase around this campus in the mid '50's. We said he's going to be some lawyer, carrying his briefcase. So, one day I asked, 'What do you have in that briefcase, Roland? You got your lunch in there?' He said, 'No, Dick, I don't have lunch in the briefcase.' 'What do you have in there then?' I grabbed it and opened it. 'Damn, he's got books in there! This guy IS studying!' Well, this boy is just too studious for me."*

Focused on Books and Beauty

Winding down my junior year, I really began to focus on graduating. With my athletic career coming to a halt, it was now all about the books. I took my first two German classes that year and another German class the following year to fulfill my foreign language requirement.

Even though I had a girlfriend there at SIU at that time, she knew how seriously I took my schoolwork. Therefore, if she wanted to be with me, she had to stay in the library where I was, rather than out on the lawn courting.

The summer of 1958 found me back at Provident Hospital for three more months of experience in the pharmacy. Again, I routed medicine to the patient floors. That time around. I noticed the many attractive female student nurses a little more than I had previously; one of them I noticed in particular. The pharmacist I worked for was dating a student nurse. I told him, *"You know, I'd like to meet some of those student nurses."*

So the pharmacist asked his girlfriend who was a senior in the Provident three-year nursing program, about any prospects. She knew of one: a very nice freshman girl who was assigned to her as a "little sister." The pharmacist and his girlfriend then arranged for us to meet.

At the appointed time, I went over to the nurse's dormitory and informed the lady at the lobby desk that I was calling on student nurse, Miss Berlean Miller. She paged her and momentarily, Miss Miller came down to the lobby and spotted me. Of course, I had spotted her before at a distance on the hospital floor, but boy, she looked even better when I saw her up close. We politely stammered through our hellos and then proceeded to the lounge to talk. I had the nerve to remain standing over her while she sat down. Standing confidently with my 40-inch shoulders squared; my 29-inch waistline; and my ripped washboard abs exposed through my thin T-shirt, I asked her, *"Now, why did you want to meet me?"* She darted a look towards me that instantly spelled trouble. *"What? I didn't want to meet you! You wanted to meet me!"* I responded, *"Oh?"* *"Is that how you feel about it?"* she questioned. I guess I don't have to tell you that Berlean immediately got up and left. She walked out on me! *"Whoa!"* I thought. The next day, I went back and sadly reported to the pharmacist, *"Well, that didn't work out too well."*

Berlean's "big sister" convinced her to give me another chance. The pharmacist encouraged me to go back over there to see her. Finally, we met again, wiped the slate clean and started over. The little talk we had at that second meeting led to us going to a movie. From there, we started dating and continued to do so throughout the remainder of the summer of 1958, and beyond.

Dating Berlean wasn't the only positive thing that happened for me that summer. I had finally saved enough money to purchase my first car. It was a used 1953 Pontiac that cost me about three hundred dollars. Finally, I had a set of wheels.

College – Senior Year 1958-59

In September of 1958, I started my senior year of college, and boy, what a full year that turned out to be! On top of maintaining the day-to-day frat house operations, I competed for a scholarship that would allow me to go to Germany as an exchange student after graduation; organized the planning of our fraternity's 25th anniversary; led an investigation into the discrimination that routinely took place there in Carbondale, Illinois; and remained an active member of the Young Republican Club. Yes, I tackled a lot of different things.

Of course, I still needed to study for my classes to keep up my GPA. I was a government major, with an emphasis in both history and psychology. I graduated with two minors and a major. The only way I was able to achieve all that in four years was to carry a full load, which consisted of fifteen to eighteen hours each quarter for all four years.

I certainly had a lot going on. In fact, I had so much going on that I wasn't able to make it up to Chicago for the Christmas holidays to see my new girlfriend, Berlean. Therefore, in an attempt to let her know I cared, I enlisted the help of a buddy of mine from college, John Holmes, who was visiting his brother in Chicago. John agreed to go meet Berlean and take her out to a nice dinner paid for by me. He also delivered a message to her that I missed her and an explanation of why I couldn't get up there for the holidays.

Berlean appreciated that gesture and understood my busy schedule. Throughout the remainder of the school year, she and I wrote letters back and forth as often as we could. In light of my very active schedule, it was a wonder I even got an occasional letter off to her, but she was important to me, so I managed to do so.

Connections

Overall, my experiences at Southern Illinois University were very rewarding. The icing on the cake was the fact that I connected with so many good and interesting people during my four years there. In the years since, in their various walks of life, some of them have made notable contributions to society. I am humbled to call them friends. In addition to Dick Gregory, another such friend is Carl Anderson, who was a senior when I met him. He and my brother, Nick, were classmates. He was so popular that he had become a BMOC (big man on campus), who was admired by all his peers. Carl finished his undergraduate studies in 1956 and stayed for two more years to complete his master's degree. At SIU, Carl became a housing residence fellow and later Director of Off-Campus Housing. As I mentioned earlier, Carl was instrumental in helping the members of his fraternity, Kappa Alpha Psi, to get their frat house. Later, as Director of Student Affairs at Howard University, he became my guardian angel while I attended law school there, helping me get a fellowship as an assistant dormitory director.

Another person I'm privileged to call my friend is Tom Burrell.[xxii] Tom and I met the first summer I spent in Chicago in 1955. His family lived across the street from my godmother, Nellie Fields. We were the same age, so we hung out together every summer. He attended Roosevelt University in Chicago. Sometimes Tom and I would sit on the porch chatting about what we wanted to be when we finished college. I told Tom I wanted to be a lawyer and a statewide elected official in Illinois. Tom said he wanted to be an advertiser and own a company. I didn't even know what an advertiser was back then, but I could tell by Tom's passion and conviction that whatever it might entail, he would achieve it.

Tom Burrell created Burrell Communications, the largest black advertising company in the country.[xxiii] Clients of Burrell Communications include companies, such as McDonalds, Coca-Cola, 3M, Toyota, and Walt Disney, just to name a few. Years after college, Tom joined me in an organization I created called Young Executives in Politics.[xxiv] I established this organization as a means of helping community leaders become role models for young black professionals in corporate America. My desire was for young folk to learn about the world of business, while also gaining exposure to the political process.

Another classmate I'm honored to know is Donald McHenry who was in graduate school when I met him in two of my senior year classes: political science and international law. While he was still working on his master's degree, the university hired him as an instructor in the speech department, which gave him the distinction of being SIU's first black instructor. Don later became Ambassador to the UN,[xxv] replacing Andrew Young,[xxvi] who was fired by President Carter for talking to the PLO. Don also worked at the State Department and was on President Kennedy's writing staff.

Lawyer at Large

Knowing people like those guys who were focused on their goals and purpose in life, helped me to stay on track as well. When I tell people today how focused I was in college, I'm not sure they really comprehend exactly what I mean, but I was. After I arrived at SIU, I got my pre-law

64

degree, and I kept my mind firmly focused on going to law school and becoming a lawyer. That's mainly it. Now, of course, I had my share of fun times and did some crazy and interesting things like most college kids do, but my main focus never wavered from my desire to study law. In fact, one of my more interesting occurrences at SIU allowed me to put my lawyer skills to work even before attending law school. It happened during homecoming weekend during my senior year when the sister of a friend of mine had come down from Chicago for the SIU homecoming festivities. The female students back then had curfews. Normally, girls had to be in by 11:30pm on weekends, but on homecoming weekend, the curfew was extended to midnight.

My friend's sister had gone out that night and missed curfew by about forty-five minutes, so the dormitory council agreed to bring disciplinary action against my friend because of her sister's violation. My friend came to me complaining about the injustice of the school making her pay for her sister's violation of the curfew. I asked her if she would like for me to represent her as her lawyer. She said "Yes," and I obliged.

I lost at the dormitory hearing level, but there was a student council appeal process. I appealed to the first level of the student council which agreed to sustain the dormitory council's opinion. Defeated again. Finally, there was an ultimate appeal to an overall council. I argued a mean case. I did my research and found out that on the evening in question; the car my friend's sister was riding in had broken down due to mechanical problems. The visiting young lady had no way of knowing where she was, was not familiar with Carbondale, and certainly did not know the direction or the distance to campus. I verified the fact that there had been car trouble, which had caused the delay, and I won that appeal. The punishment that was about to be applied to the student was lifted. Word traveled swiftly all around campus that Burris had won the curfew case. Everyone was calling me the campus lawyer. To me, however, this was just another step towards fulfilling my goals to be a lawyer and an elected state official.

Integrating Carbondale

Throughout my entire period of matriculation at SIU, from 1955 through1959, there was always racial segregation. This was also about the time the Civil Rights Movement was gearing up. In 1958, as president of our Alpha chapter, I was at the forefront of the planning for our fraternity's 25th anniversary celebration, which was to take place in 1959. As I began making plans to bring in guests from across the country, I hit a snag because in Carbondale, Illinois, blacks couldn't sleep in the hotels or eat in certain restaurants.

"Well, that's not right," I thought. Things weren't like that back home in Centralia, just sixty miles or so to the north. When I talked to people about this dilemma, I got a lot of shrugged shoulders.

"Well, Roland, that's just how it is," was what I heard far too many times.

So, as the fraternity president, I tried to get our other black Greek organizations together to try to do something about this situation, but nothing happened. I tried to get letters out a year in advance to start promoting our 25th anniversary at our Carbondale campus. When my junior year ended, there still had been no great progress.

When my senior year started in September of 1958, the pressure was really on me to get the event planned by April of 1959. I knew I had to talk to SIU President, Dr. Morris. I requested a meeting with Dr. Morris and soon sat in his office, along with some young ladies I rallied onboard for the cause: about four or five freshman and sophomore girls.

I voiced my concern, *"The Alphas are trying to hold our 25th anniversary here and there's no place for our guests to stay, because blacks are not allowed in the hotels."*

Dr. Morris countered with little resolve, *"I have no evidence of that. You'll have to collect evidence, and show the discrimination."* As a pre-law student, I knew a thing or two about strategy-building. My small troupe and I went back and tried to organize the other fraternities, but it ended up being just me and my Alpha brothers who were willing to go to work collecting the evidence that Dr. Morris had asked for.

"Look," I said, *"We gotta have proof. Dr. Morris says he has no evidence of this discrimination."*

I outlined an agenda, which entailed gathering evidence that one particular hotel wouldn't allow blacks to register as guests, and evidence that certain restaurants refused to serve blacks. We had no idea how to pull off such a scheme without the necessary finances and other resources. Well, my fraternity ended up putting up the money for the hotel room and the restaurants, so the money portion was resolved. Our only problem remained how to document the discriminatory actions of those service providers.

A classmate and very good friend of mine, a Jewish student named Lester Margolese, was also a government major and always talked about racial integration. Therefore, to me, he seemed the ideal person to assist us in this effort. I appealed to him in the name of equality, *"Les, I need your help. We've put together a strategy where you will witness some of us blacks being denied service in these public facilities. You have to do it. And you have to have other witnesses, too. It can't be just you, Les."*

He readily agreed, and we crafted our game plan. Les and about four or five of his Jewish friends would go into a restaurant, sit at the table and order beer or pop or something. Then four or five of us blacks would go in and attempt to be served. Of course, we were always refused service.

When we were refused service, we always made sure to insist on being served loudly enough to be heard by others in the establishment, including our planted witnesses. We documented that type of activity at different restaurants all over Carbondale. Also, at hotels across town, Les and his friends would go in, request a room and get it. We'd go in right behind them with the same request and would be told they didn't have any rooms available. Soon after we were denied, another friend of Les' would go in and rent a room without any problem.

Over a two month period, we documented the many instances of racial discrimination we encountered and presented all of our data in a report. That report included the names of every hotel and restaurant that denied us service and every clothing store that wouldn't let us try on hats and other articles of clothing. I enlisted the help of those freshmen and sophomore girls to type up all our findings.

We requested a meeting with the president in late February or early March. Unfortunately, no meeting occurred before our anniversary celebration in April, so no integration resolution occurred either. Our guests who traveled from East St. Louis, Illinois and from Chicago for our event had to stay in the homes of various local people. That didn't equate to defeat in our books. No, we continued our quest.

Later in April, we finally met with Dr. Morris and the general counsel of SIU, a gentleman by the name of John Rendleman. I started in,

67

"Dr. Morris, you said a few months back that you had no evidence of discrimination in the city of Carbondale. I would like to submit this document to you." A stunned Dr. Morris responded, *"What? Well, do you have a copy for the counsel?"* We did have a copy for the counsel. They took a few minutes and started reading and frankly could not believe what they read. Upon conclusion, Dr. Morris said, *"We'll get back to you. We have to meet with the Chamber of Commerce of Carbondale."*

In May, Dr. Morris called a large group of people together downtown in one of the office buildings. Four or five of us students were invited to the meeting. The meeting commenced with introductions and pleasantries, and then the president of the chamber spoke. *"Dr. Morris has some business that he'd like to discuss with the chamber."* Dr. Morris opened by reiterating what a wonderful relationship the university community had with Carbondale. He continued noting how we must employ unity because we have all types of students from all over the world. Our students must be treated equally. As he spoke, I could see all those white men—there was not a single white female or a single black person of either gender—in the audience just nodding their heads in agreement and "Uh-huh-ing" his comments. All of them fully understood the importance of the university to their own livelihoods and to the overall prosperity of the Carbondale community.

Finally, Dr. Morris' talk reached its pinnacle as he stated, *"We have here evidence that our black students are not treated equally in the Carbondale community."* Suddenly, the "uh-huhs" stopped and the utter silence fell across the room. Dr. Morris then read aloud the list of downtown businesses, and provided the documentation of discrimination with each one. I noticed the blood draining from the faces of those guys, as they listened and stared straight ahead. As Dr. Morris took his seat, the chamber president stood up and spoke, *"Dr. Morris, we appreciate what you've reported to us. The chamber will take that under advisement, and we'll get back to you."*

Well, that meeting took place in the middle of May. We graduated around June 9th or 10th of 1959 without a peep from the Carbondale chamber. In the Fall of that year, while studying in Europe, I received a letter from Willie Brown, one of the students who helped with those integration efforts. He informed me that the university opened up that

Fall quarter with the whole city of Carbondale integrated, except for one place, the "Rat Hole," which was a dive tavern that wasn't about to admit blacks, which was just fine by us.

That's how I took the leadership in integrating the city of Carbondale without an ounce of conflict, controversy or any demonstrations. It was accomplished with strategies and reports and most importantly, enlisting Dr. Delyte Morris to carry that banner for us. I had taken note of how he had integrated that SIU dormitory in 1955, saying that the school would not tolerate discrimination on the campus. From that, I knew he possessed the necessary passion to fight segregation in the city of Carbondale, Illinois.[xxvii]

Chapter Five

To Hamburg and Back

Qualified

During my junior and senior years at Southern Illinois University, I studied German as a foreign language. In 1958, early in my senior year, Professor Hardwick, who was German and head of the German Department, informed me there was an exchange student program with the University of Hamburg in Hamburg, Germany. The way it worked was students would compete for two scholarships through taking part in written and oral competitions conducted in German. The two winners would study at the University of Hamburg for one school year, while two students from Germany would study at SIU for that same period of time.

The prospect of studying in Germany for a year intrigued me, and I decided to enter the competition. I started digging into the German language as best I could. It seemed to be a difficult foreign language to comprehend. I knew I had to pull out my big guns in order to pull this off, because it was expected there would be about two-hundred applicants for those two slots.

In the end, I was selected along with a student named Edward Swick, who now lives in Chicago. Ed is of Polish heritage. While in college, he spoke Polish, Russian and German. His language fluency resulted from having studied German in high school and being raised by a family who spoke Polish in the home. After graduating from college, he taught German in a Chicago high school. Ed won the scholarship to attend the University of Hamburg and also qualified for a Fulbright scholarship. I have always felt that more than likely, I could not have won a Fulbright scholarship, simply because of my skin color.[xxviii] Remember, we're talking the 1950's.

With the Fulbright scholarship, special arrangements were made for the student to stay with a selected host family and to receive traveling funds. Although I also lived in a family's home when I first arrived in Germany, that temporary arrangement which had been made possible by the university was only intended to bridge the gap until classes started, at which time, I moved into a private dormitory near campus.

In June of 1959, I graduated from SIU with many plans of my future swarming in my head. I was due to leave for Germany in August. Before heading overseas, though, I spent part of the summer in Chicago, since Provident Hospital hired me back at the pharmacy. Fortunately, that meant I was able to continuing dating Berlean. However, in August, we experienced an abrupt interruption in our relationship, when I had to bid her farewell. It was a bittersweet time. As anxious as I was to get to Germany, I had no idea what awaited me on that ten-day trek across the ocean or during the year abroad, which lay ahead.

Getting There Was Half the Fun

On a Thursday night in mid August 1959, I caught a train in Chicago and rode all night to New York City, where a friend of mine, John Flamer, agreed to pick me up at the train station and accommodate me until time to board my ship on Sunday afternoon. I arrived in New York City late Friday afternoon.

I've been fortunate to be able to stay in touch with some great friends from SIU over the years. John Flamer is one such friend. By coincidence, he and I even celebrated our 50th wedding anniversaries about the same time. John had been a great track star at SIU and was a genuine Olympic hopeful at that. During the summer of 1959, John had decided to spend his break at home with his family in Yonkers, New York, which is why he agreed to accommodate me and help me get to my ship. So, late Friday afternoon I arrived at Grand Central Station and began looking for John. There was only one problem: John was looking for me at Penn Station! There I sat for about four hours with my two suitcases, my umbrella and my toilet kit, growing more uncertain by the minute as to whether he would show up at all. I had called John's house, but there was no answer.

It finally dawned on John, who had been looking for me at Penn Station; to try New York's other train station. Suddenly, in the fourth hour of my long wait, I heard a huge commotion in the main corridor of Grand Central Station, which seemed to be getting louder by the second. When I looked up to determine the source of this commotion, I spotted John with about twelve to fifteen of his buddies (three carloads of them) pressing their way towards me.

John exclaimed, *"There he is!"* To which his entourage responded with cheers, as they called out my name and ran towards me. What a great and unexpected greeting! They made me feel so special that I almost forgave John for the long and grueling wait.

I had eaten very little along my journey, so our first order of business was to stop at a fast food restaurant. Next, we went to a party that lasted until the wee hours of Saturday morning. Later on Saturday, we went to the beach. By evening, we were a group of twenty folks drinking beer and cheap wine. I didn't drink much; however, some in our group got pretty high.

Our marathon party continued well into that night, concluding around midnight on Saturday. We ended up in John's living room sleeping everywhere—on the floor, and on couches and chairs. His mother just about had a heart attack when she awoke Sunday morning to passed-out bodies all over the place.

My ship for Germany was scheduled to board at 2:00pm Sunday afternoon and to depart at 4:00pm. John was the only one who managed to wake up at my urging and drive me to the harbor. We had a two-hour trip ahead of us from Yonkers to the New York port, and John's old beat-up station wagon was our only means to get there. I made it on time to board the German ship, the *MS Berlin* which sailed out of New York City harbor. What a class act weekend send-off that turned out to be!

Our ship reached Germany ten days later, but due to perilous events along the way, to me it seemed like the trip was twice that long. First of all, just minutes away from the dock, with the Statue of Liberty still in full view, I succumbed to the consequences of nonstop partying and realized that I was as sick as a dog! I was reduced to leaning over the ship's railing and being violently sick.

As though that wasn't enough torture for my head and stomach, a severe storm soon impeded our journey. I remained in bed seasick from an unending rocky motion that, at times, seemed unbearable. That lasted for three days! Finally, I did recuperate and the crew helped me out of my cabin so that I could get some air, move around a little, and get some food into my system.

During that entire ten-day voyage, I saw only two other black people: a serviceman and his wife. Mainly, I stayed to myself. During the first five or six days no one said anything to me. Around the sixth day of the voyage, when the sun came out, I decided to relax a bit on the deck. As I lay there with a navy cap pulled slightly over my face to help shield my eyes from the sun, I sensed people slowing down or stopping momentarily, as they strolled in front of me. I began peering out from under my hat and sure enough, they kept staring at me as they walked past my chaise lounge. It soon became quite annoying to me.

Finally, one German guy got up enough nerve and sat down next to me. He spoke very plain English, offered pleasantries and an apology up front to what he was about to ask me. He wanted to know if I could get a suntan. My rather curt response came, *"What do you think?"*

Just as I shifted on my lounge chair, he could see the tanned difference on the part of my legs exposed to the sun, as opposed to the upper portion of my legs that was previously protected by my swim trunks. He turned beet red by his ignorance, apologized some more and then went about his way. That was only the beginning of the different kinds of reactions and questions posed by the people of the country where I was about to begin a year of study!

I realized I had to just get used to it. The Germans aboard the ship were extremely curious, which also made them pretty bold in their approach. For instance, even though we were assigned to tables in the ship's dining hall, some people even maneuvered their seating so that they could dine next to me and ask me lots of questions.

Ah, Land!

We docked at the harbor in Bremerhaven around August 20, 1959.

My school term at the university did not begin until the first of October, but my professor wanted me to get there early so that I could get adjusted to my new environment. So there I stood checking out posted signs to find the right train that would take me from Bremerhaven to Bremen where I would board yet another train to Hamburg. My train tickets were all arranged; I just had to find the appropriate train to Bremen.

The German trains contained first, second and third class sections. I rode first class. I engaged in a couple of conversations here and there, especially from Bremen to Hamburg, which was the longest part of the ride. The Germans' small talk was mostly about their considerable curiosity, both about me being black and me being American. They always asked if I were a soldier. I advised them I was not a soldier, but instead an American student. In hindsight, I can see how that first part of my journey, with all of its inquiries, helped set the tone for what the remainder of my year would entail.

Approaching my stop, I remembered my professor had instructed me not to get off at the main train station, but instead to get off at the Dammtor station. Once at Dammtor, I started unloading my belongings. I hopped off the train with one suitcase and my umbrella and set them down on the platform. As I turned back to get my other suitcase, the train had already begun a slow crawl out of the station! In America, trains wait; apparently not so in Germany!

The train stops of the German trains were similar in duration to stops of the "L" trains of Chicago, because neither stops for very long. However, I thought a passenger train like that would at least give a person time to unload. Not so. By the time I jumped back on the train and then off again with my other suitcase and toilet kit, I was halfway down the station's long platform. I walked back to where my other items were and nobody was around. Everyone dispersed that quickly. So there I stood, not knowing which way to go. I thought I was on the ground level already, but soon realized otherwise.

Finally, a worker who spoke no English came by. I tried to use my SIU German on him and got nowhere. He continued to look as puzzled as I did. Eventually, I came up with the word for taxi. *"Taxi? Ah ha! Taxi!"* The worker's face lit up as he was happy to finally comprehend. We went down the stairs and I finally felt relieved to see the main station. There were ticket counters, different stairs leading up to the various trains and lots of people everywhere. A wave of anxiety struck once again, as I realized I needed to get myself and those suitcases into the right taxi and to my right destination.

I hopped in a cab and again relied on my limited vernacular to instruct the driver to take me to a hotel near the University of Hamburg. After a frustrating dialogue, where nothing was getting accomplished, I just shortened the sentence to "hotel" to help him understand me.

"Ah, hotel!" said the driver and off we went on a fifteen to twenty minute ride. He drove me to the most expensive hotel in Hamburg, positioned right on the Alster, which is a big lake in the heart of Hamburg. I proceeded to the front desk where fortunately, they spoke English. I checked into the hotel with my two suitcases, umbrella and toilet kit and didn't budge from that room until the next day. One would have imagined as mentally and physically drained as I was by that time, that sleep would have been the easiest thing to do. On the contrary, I didn't sleep a wink that night.

There I was, this twenty two-year-old small town, American kid in Hamburg, Germany, thousands of miles away from everything I had ever known in my entire life. There I was, not sure if anyone would be able to understand me; not sure of where the university was or what it would be like; perhaps not totally sure if the trip had been the right thing for me after all. Do you think I was able to sleep under that kind of pressure? I was almost overwhelmed by my anxiety. I knew I had to improve my language skills very quickly.

The next morning, the hotel personnel helped me get a cab to the University of Hamburg and calculated how much the ride would cost. I had changed some money into marks in order to pay the driver. At that time, for one dollar, you would get 4.5 or so German marks. I monitored closely my modest stash of money.

Finally, I arrived at the university, found where to go for registration and presented the woman at the desk a letter showing that I was an exchange student from Southern Illinois University. She skimmed the letter's contents, spoke a few words to her coworkers and soon the very excited staff hovered around me in an overwhelming display of hospitality. In German, they exclaimed, *"He's here! He's here!"*

Dr. Hartwig had sent word that I would be coming in August—even though school would not be in session for almost another two months—

so they were prepared for me. They didn't know exactly what day I would arrive, but they had all this stuff planned out. They had even found a family for me to stay with temporarily.

Over the next several hours, I got all the university information squared away. I registered for classes and met a few key people. Thank God, they all spoke English, albeit broken English. It didn't matter that their English was rather shaky; at least we could all communicate. They soon found out that my German wasn't all that hot either. Throughout the course of the day, I began to learn my way around campus and other points of interest in the area around the university. Much to my chagrin, I learned that the Dammtor train station where I first arrived was right across the street from where the university property starts! That's why Dr. Hartwig had me get off at that station. Had I just looked across the street, I would've seen it. No wonder the taxi driver was so confused when I tried to direct him to a destination near the university. I was already there!

"*Mama, There's a Schwärzer!*"

After my first full day in Germany, I traveled back to the hotel and finally enjoyed a good night's sleep. The next morning, I reported to the home to which I had been assigned. The family who lived there consisted of a widow, two sons slightly younger than I and a daughter about my age. When I arrived at their home, I was surprised to learn that five or six other foreign students stayed there as well. It was a huge house capable of comfortably accommodating us all. It was equipped with a family's quarters at one end; students' quarters at the other end; and a long hallway connecting the two.

After settling into my bedroom, I joined the others in the students' area where we hung out and got to know one another. I met students from Afghanistan, Italy and Egypt. Some of them spoke broken English better than I spoke German. We began chatting about the 1956 Sinai War [xxix](also known as the Suez War) between Egypt and Israel and all the problems the Afghans were having.

In the meantime, the widow's children had telephoned some of their cousins, who soon joined us, very interested in learning everything about us. About three or four cousins around the same age—all of them young ladies—became particularly intrigued with me after finding out I was a

77

student and not a soldier. They kept asking me questions. I responded with my two or three good German words. Again, that's when I knew I really had to dig in and start getting my German speaking skills tightened up.

I remember how we had to put a quarter, which is a mark, into the television set to keep it going. That's one of the ways the widow earned her living. She also collected rent from us, several weeks' worth from me. Paying her to stay there was worth every dime, as the experience at her home really indoctrinated me into the whole German culture.

We enjoyed learning about one another's cultures during my stay there. One of the things that intrigued me about the Afghans was how they shaved each other's beards using fine thread. They wrapped the thread around one thumb and forefinger pulling it taut with their other thumb and forefinger. Then they twisted it to form an "X," which was the part of the thread that slowly rubbed against their skin yanking the hairs out from the root, as they moved the thread back and forth. I watched in amazement as I would have never imagined something like that could be so effective.

I began to socialize with more ease, yet I found myself still talking too much in English. In order to brush up on my German, I constantly tried to get the sons to talk to me only in German, but they wanted to talk to me only in English in order to brush up on their English skills! It got to be quite a scene when one of them would switch from English to German to try to express himself, while I would switch from German to English to try to express myself. Some of the conversations got to be very interesting with our hodgepodge of dialogues.

Even before arriving in Germany, I set two goals: to study hard and to maintain a calm temperament. In other words, I knew there would be curiosity about my race, so I wanted people to be able to discuss anything with me without consternation or aggravation on my part. Overall, I believe I handled the race issue very well; even accepting some insults from people who might not have recognized them as such.

One such experience with race that challenged me a bit occurred after being in Hamburg a few days. I went back to the train station to pick up my trunk that had been shipped over directly from the ship, because I wasn't able to put it on the train. While standing in line with a ticket to claim my trunk, a lady stood in line a few paces behind me with a young boy who must have been about ten or eleven years old. All of a sudden, I heard the boy exclaim, *"Mama, there's a schwärzer, a schwärzer!"* I happened to be familiar with the word "schwärzer" and its negative connotation equivalent to the "n" word here in America. I slowly and deliberately turned around to face the user of that word. Just as I did, the boy left his mother, dashed over to me and rubbed my hand several times. Astonished by his new discovery, he whispered loudly, *"It doesn't rub off!"*

My blood began to boil, but I immediately remembered my goal and remained calm. Now, my German was not that good; neither was that mother's English very good, as she stammered through an apology. I looked her square in the eye and said in English, *"Please teach your son that there are other kinds of people in this world."*

Of course, the folks standing around us saw the entire incident. You could see some of them shaking their heads in disbelief over the ignorance of that child. I knew I said the right thing to the lady. I couldn't get angry at the young kid, because he didn't know any better; his actions were based on the attitudes taught in his home. I must say, though, that incident was perhaps the most "in-my-face" and disturbing racial issue I experienced during the entire time I was in Germany.

Soon, the end of August rolled around. Since the university was only three or four blocks from the private home where I was living, I had already been going back and forth to the campus getting adjusted there. I purchased all my German books right away to study ahead of time, knowing as I did that all my lectures, labs and classes would be in German. Between those books and my conversations with the boys, I soon became more adjusted to the language.

In September, three weeks prior to the October 1st commencement of classes, along with some of the other foreign students, I moved into my Catholic dormitory. The building, which was called the Franciscus College, was operated by a priest and five nuns. We arrived before the German students were scheduled to move in, which allowed us time to bond among ourselves. I was especially excited to see four other American students move in.

Ed Swick, my fellow alumnus from SIU, had arrived too, but he lived in a dormitory off campus in the suburbs. As a Fulbright scholar, he initially lived with a family whose home had been designated as a boarding house for Fulbright students. His host family's household consisted of Dr. Schaffer, a dentist, his wife, and their three children. Their son, a twelve-year-old at the time I met him, grew up to become a renowned medical specialist. The father died about two or three years ago, but as of this writing, Mrs. Schaffer is still alive.

According to Ed, one evening during dinner, he and the Schaffer's engaged in an insightful discussion about the race problems brewing in America, which, at that time, was coming into the Civil Rights Movement era. Somehow, that discussion led to a contentious statement Dr. Schaffer made implying that America would never send a Negro to Germany as an exchange student, but only students like Ed.

Evidently, Ed took that statement to heart and felt he needed to prove Dr. Schaffer wrong. A day or so later, he phoned me saying that the Schaffer's would like to invite me to dinner. He had told them I was an American exchange student from his same school, so they were delighted and anxious to meet me.

It was a beautiful September Sunday when I boarded the S-Bahn, the German equivalent of the Chicago "L" train, out to Rahlstedt, a suburb of Hamburg. School hadn't started yet, nor had my roommates arrived, so the timing of this dinner was perfect, as I had free time on my hands. I found the Schaffer's beautiful home with no problem and proceeded to their front door with flowers and a bottle of wine in hand, as I had been informed was proper German custom when invited to dinner.

I rang the doorbell, and this young kid opened the door, looked at me and then without a word slammed the door right in my face! Whoa! I looked at my card and checked the address written on it. I looked at the name Schaffer on their mailbox. I rang the doorbell again. That time, Dr. Schaffer came to the door inquiring in German, *"May I help you? What can I do for you? What do you want?"* I quickly asked, *"Are you Herr Schaffer?" "Yes, I'm Herr Schaffer,"* he very curtly responded.

Ed stood in the background silently laughing his head off. I had no idea what the hell was going on; apparently, neither did Dr. Schaffer. Quite puzzled, I asked, *"Is Herr Swick here?"* Suddenly, Dr. Schaffer put two and two together and the blood just drained from his face. He apologetically concurred, *"Yes, yes, yes. Come on in, come on in."*

While stepping aside to usher me in, Dr. Schaffer noticed Ed behind him laughing. Realizing the trick his houseguest had played on him, the two of them began laughing hysterically together. I still didn't get it. By that time, the Schaffer kids joined us in the foyer and just stared at everyone. Mrs. Schaffer joined us as well and her eyes got big as saucers when looking at me, at her husband and then Ed. It was quite a scene—one I remember vividly to this day. Soon everything settled down and Ed filled us all in on his prank. He said he wanted Dr. Schaffer to see for himself how untrue his statement was that America would not send a Negro to Germany as an exchange student. After recovering from all the excitement, we had the greatest time at dinner and beyond.

Years later, Dr. Schaffer's son came to America for a medical conference and set aside time to see Ed in Chicago. I was invited to join them, but was unable to because I was out of town on business. I hated that I missed him, but thoroughly enjoyed the pictures he brought of us "back in the day."

There we were, Ed, Dr. Schaffer and me, sitting in the Schaffer's backyard in lawn chairs wearing our suits and ties! The Schaffer's had heard it was customary for Americans to sit outside on their lawn chairs, so Dr. and Mrs. Schaffer made sure we did that after dinner. That was so funny to me. That is by far one of my most pleasant memories of the time I spent in Hamburg, Germany.

School, People and Campus Life – German Style

Finally school started, and I got registered for all my classes. In the dormitory each foreign student was partnered with a German roommate. I had two German roommates during my year there; both were great. My first roommate was Volkmar Von Clause, whose father was a mayor (a Bürgermeister) from a town in southern Germany near Munich. My second German roommate was an exciting young man who lived in Osnabrück, a city maybe seventy or eighty miles west of Hamburg. His name was Dieter Weber. By the time Dieter became my roommate in December, I had finally begun to master German. Although I wasn't quite thinking in German yet, I could mentally translate English to German and then speak it.

At my dormitory, there were thirty different countries represented—from a tiny little island off the mainland China called Formosa; to great big countries like Algeria, Ethiopia and Peru; and to others like Spain, Russia and Hungary. The four other American students in my dorm were from Northwestern University, the University of Kansas, the University of Arkansas and the University of Pennsylvania. A few Americans and a few other foreign students lived in Ed's dormitory out in the suburbs. After being in school for about two weeks, we had to select our student council. I had met almost everybody there in those first two weeks, yet there were a few whom I hadn't had the opportunity to introduce myself or otherwise get to know. Nevertheless, I told one of my American dorm mates, *"I want to run for president of the dormitory."* He said, *"Nobody knows you."* I insisted, *"They pretty much know me. Put my name in the nomination."*

He did, and I got elected head of our dormitory. That meant I had to call the meetings and plan all of the events. It also meant working closely with the father and with the head mother, who was in charge of the sisters, to ensure the place ran properly. The most interesting thing about that dorm was it housed a bar in its basement. I'm talking about a real bar, with real alcohol, and with students rotating as bartenders. We could buy anything we wanted to drink from beer to hard liquor! And it was a Catholic dormitory at that! Every night we would wrap up our studies around nine or ten o'clock and go check out the bar before going to bed.

Our dormitory also hosted cultural nights at designated times throughout the Fall and Spring: Ethiopian night, Colombian night, etc. Every country had its turn. Of course, I made sure we put on a spectacular American night, where for the first time in Hamburg, Germany we feasted on good old American style hamburgers and hot dogs! We had contacted the American Consulate to get the meat and buns, and they came through with flying colors. I tell you, that was one of the best nights of all the cultural nights! Outside, we grilled those hamburgers and hot dogs. We dressed them up with mustard and ketchup with corn on the cob on the side. Those students kept saying, *"We come to America! We come to America!"*

I relished those happy cultural events, because often, the atmosphere in our dorm could become overly intense. Perhaps it was idealistic nationalism which caused a mini United Nations to evolve within our dormitory. Because of ideology or other reasons, groups sometimes had sharp disagreements with one another. We often had to keep the two Hungarian students away from the two Russian students. Seems they wanted to reenact the Russian-Hungarian war, when Russia put down the Hungarian Rebellion in 1958.[xxx] Little Joe of Formosa, who was all of 4'5"tall and weighing about 105 pounds, threatened to take back the mainland of China. Then we had the Algerian students always in conflict with the French students. Many of the students argued with the Americans, putting the five of us on the spot quite often. They tended to target me more than the others since, as dorm president, I was seen as the leader.

Two Ethiopians used to come at me especially hard, attacking me about the Lend-Lease program. Let me tell you, they talked about America like a dog. One analogy they used was the American promise to help with their farming, which they later discovered only to be true if they leased American tractors. In other words, we would lend them the equipment to get the job done, while demanding they pay us back for the "borrowed" equipment. So, in addition to trying to study my lessons at the university, I spent hours at the American Cultural Center digging up books, learning all there was to know about the Lend-Lease program and other issues. I needed to make sure I could properly defend my country during our heated conversations.

That led me to take the most patriotic stance I've ever taken in my life. I made sure those Ethiopians learned all about the boycotts and the Civil Rights Movement, which was heating up in our country at that time. I also shared the story of the integral role I had played in the integration of Carbondale. As we welcomed 1960, I continued sharing stories with my fellow students about America's plights, whether the topic was the Supreme Court *Brown v. Topeka* decision,[xxxi] the sit-ins, or the Freedom Riders.[xxxii] I was determined they were going to learn about these things that were taking place. The race topic was hot even in Germany.

Simultaneously, I was immersing myself in the American international structure and the German language. By the second week in December, progress inevitably occurred. I'll never forget it. While down in the bar, a few of us got into this big argument about something. Suddenly, in my best German enunciation, I yelled out, *"Der umgangssprachlich!"* That means "That's great" in German.

I didn't translate it mentally. I thought it in German; hence, I said it in German. From that moment on, I no longer thought in English and then translated—no, I was thinking in German. From that point, my German vocabulary expanded rather rapidly and easily and by Christmastime, I was about 85% fluent in German. Over time, I perhaps achieved 90% or 95% fluency, but never 100%. I began to understand some of the differences between German and English. For instance, the words "bear" and "bare" in English, you pronounce them the same even though you spell them differently, and they have different meanings. Well, in German, it's not like that. When using German terms like DES, DAS, and DIE, there was no way of getting around having to know when to use each term. That's why I still had some difficulty with words in the textbook when studying international law. I had to go to my dictionary often. On top of that, I still had to tackle those legal terms.

I recall another interesting experience in that dormitory bar involving a traditional drink that the Germans call bock beer. I was told bock refers to the bottom of the beer vat. Its brewing process included removing ice from the partially frozen barrels of beer resulting in a substance with higher alcohol content than regular beer. Today, the many versions of bock are mainly popular during certain times of the year that are generally associated with holidays or festivals.

As I mentioned before, I had never been drunk in my life. Well, one night in February, as several of us hung out in the bar discussing American beer and German beer, some German students bet that no American could drink two bottles of bock beer. As a matter of fact, they were willing to bet that I, being a non-drinker, couldn't even drink one bottle of the stuff. So, you guessed it—being the bold and crazy guy that I was, I put my three or four marks on the table and declared, *"By golly, I can drink a bottle of bock beer."*

I snatched that bottle off the table, turned it up to my mouth, put my head back and went glug, glug, glug. I got about halfway through it and the room started spinning! I don't remember anything after that. I do remember being sick for a week and losing my marks in the process. That had to be one of my sickest moments in Germany; in fact, it was even worse than how I felt when I was both hung over and sea sick on my journey over on the *MS Berlin*!

Perhaps one of the saddest memories I have of that year was the lonely Christmas Eve I spent in the dorm. All the German students had gone home for Christmas. Like me, a few other foreign students had not gone home for the holidays, but they had all decided to go out. My American buddies, Eric and Russ, were Catholic, so they all went to mass that evening. I was Baptist. I stayed in my room.

I remember savoring a bottle of wine and some cheese and crackers. There I sat on December 24, 1959 fidgeting with the radio, since we didn't have television, trying to get the American Army station, *Voice of America.*[xxxiii] It was our only English station. I soon found it and there began my marathon of favorite Christmas carols. Their familiar melodies made me even more lonely and homesick for my family. Finally, in my melancholy state, I drifted off to sleep. On Christmas day, I slept almost the entire day.

The day after Christmas, as previously planned, I went to visit my roommate, Dieter, at his home in Osnabrück. His family had a lot of out of town family members visiting them, which was the reason they had no room for me to stay with them for the entire Christmas break. That was ok. I was most grateful for the little bit of time I did spend with them, as it was indeed a very welcome alternative to the loneliness of my room.

All Roads Lead to Cultural Learning and Adventure

Studying, going to classes, speaking German all the time and learning about American affairs so that I can explain them when asked or defend them when challenged, drained me of a considerable amount of time and energy. How I eventually found time for yet another activity there at the University of Hamburg is beyond me; yet, somehow I managed to have some very interesting experiences with the American Consulate.

One day, I attended one of the many cultural presentations to the German people hosted by the American Consulate. It reminded me of a town hall meeting. When I was given an opportunity to speak, I began talking about a certain issue. Apparently, the Consulate General took notice of me. I'm sure he thought, *"We've got this black American here studying international law. He speaks German; and he's from Chicago. How can we best use him?"*

Soon, the Consulate General was specifically inviting me to participate in many other consular events. In fact, I became part of a speaking tour. One of the topics addressed on the tour was the race problem in

America, a problem about which I was able to speak with considerable authority, due to my first-hand experiences in Centralia, Carbondale and Chicago. Even though I'm from Centralia, Illinois, in order to keep things as simple as possible, I told everybody in Hamburg I was from Chicago. *"Oh, Chicago! Al Capone!"* was the response I heard quite often. During the same time period as our Civil Rights Movement was occurring back home in America, England was dealing with its own major race riots in Nottingham, which was home to large numbers of British Guineans who had migrated from Guiana and become English citizens. Our lecture tours stayed mainly in the northern parts of Germany, rarely venturing down south. The more tours I did, the more knowledgeable I became regarding American history, politics and what the Civil Rights Movement was all about.

I can remember, during one of my talks, some Germans insisted they would not be discriminatory towards blacks. They claimed, *"We are not that way towards black people."* I countered, *"Let me tell you something. You see what is happening in Nottingham and Notting Hill[xxxiv] and Nottingham,[xxxv] England? Those are race riots because of skin color, economic conditions and differences in attitudes. When people who talk to me find out I'm American and not African, I suddenly get nicer treatment."* I continued, *"If ten percent of your population were black, you would have a race problem that would be manifested in a similar manner to what we have in America."*

It never even dawned on them they lived in a homogenously populated environment. The Germans didn't get it because there weren't enough blacks in their culture to create a "problem" for them. Guess who they *were* having issues against? The Turks! The Turks were their minority. The Germans weren't even conscious of the fact they were discriminating in the ghettos against the low paid Turkish workers and gardeners. They didn't realize they were treating the Turks terribly.

I advised them as well about why most Germans treated me differently than they treated the Africans. I said, *"I'm getting excellent treatment because, one, I speak your language. Number two, when you find out that I'm a black American, I can't keep up with all the invitations I get to have dinner with your families."*

As my lectures continued across Germany, the Consulate General kept complimenting me, so I must've been getting my points across and helping to enlighten my audience. There is no doubt that this experience was also an enlightening one for me. Those lectures and being president of my dorm helped me to develop and hone leadership skills I could never have gained in a classroom. I was both pleased and amazed that in such foreign territory, a place where no one knew me from Adam and where almost no one else looked like me, I presented myself in such a way that they judged me based only on the characteristics of my personality I presented to them and not on my skin color. They had voted me president of the dorm, and they respected my presentations during those tours. I was thankful for that.

It wasn't all hard work, as I was also able to have lots of fun and received quite a bit of cultural exposure that year, as well. I met a lot of Americans who had also come over to Hamburg to study at the university. During school breaks, I went on trips with other students to other European countries. We visited such places as the Netherlands, Brussels and Paris. During one break, four of us American students got an Opel and headed south to Greece, sleeping wherever we could. We toured southern Europe, the Alps, Switzerland, and Austria and even ventured down into Italy, where we visited Florence, Venice and Rome. As we got over to the eastern side of Italy, we stopped at places along the Aegean Sea. Our money started running out before we ever made it to Greece, so we had to head back to Hamburg. As a matter of fact, we weren't even able to stop in Munich. Our wine and cheese supply got low, and we cautiously began conserving every mark to buy gas. Thank goodness, we did make it back to Hamburg without getting stranded. Talk about interesting and fun!

Another road venture involved a young Turkish girl from Ed's dormitory, whose father owned about a third of Turkey. She and I became friends and had a lot of good times together. In the spring of 1960, her sister came from Turkey to visit her. The two sisters, along with an American female exchange student from the University of Pennsylvania with a nice Volkswagen, wanted to visit Copenhagen. They felt it would be good for a male to accompany them. I volunteered to drive them up there, if they took care of all my expenses. Unlike my other European excursion, this time money was no problem, as her sister came equipped with a lot of it. We managed very well all the way to Copenhagen in that Volkswagen. I drove most of the way for them and we spent four or five days in Denmark.

Just as my classmates and I took trips to other countries and campuses, exchange students from other parts of Europe included Hamburg and our campus on their itineraries from time to time. I remember two very adventurous females from the University of North Dakota, who made their way to Hamburg while traveling across Europe. They ended up staying at our dorm for two or three months, working in the kitchen and dining hall to pay for their room and board. Janice and Arlene were their names. They became close to all of us American students at Franciscus College dorm. In fact, I recall acting like their big brother at times, protecting them in unfamiliar territory. By May of 1960, they were on their way, and I didn't hear anymore from them.

Fast forward forty-nine years to Christmastime of 2009. During a late night session in the Senate Chamber, my seatmate, then-United States Senator Bryon Dorgan, and I engaged in casual conversation. I mentioned how I met two young ladies from his state of North Dakota named Janice and Arlene. I told him they traveled through Europe in 1960, when I studied at the University of Hamburg. Dorgan seemed very curious about the Janice person; verifying the year I referred to and asking if I knew her last name. Dorgan excused himself from our conversation and left the floor. About five or so minutes later, he returned from making a phone call and handed me a piece of paper with Janice's full name on it, as well as her contact information. I had forgotten what her last name was, but recognized it right away. He also handed me the name and number of his friend, whom he had just called, who, as it turned out, is Janice's close friend.

I was totally astonished! The next day, I called the senator's friend and left him with my contact information to pass on to Janice. Lo and behold, Janice called me. It was truly delightful to reminisce about our Hamburg days and catch up on each other's lives almost a half century later; all compliments of a casual conversation with an unrelated third party. Now, that's what I call serendipity at its best!

Spies 'R Us

In June, two months before I was scheduled to head back to the states, I signed up for a ten day student trip to Berlin on a student bus. A few days prior to leaving, I received a call to report to the American

Consulate. I was told to ask for a particular gentleman. That's all the orders said. I obediently went to the Consulate, stopped at the desk in the lobby, and asked for that person. The gentleman seated behind the desk told me, *"Go down this hall. Turn right. Go to the room at the end of the hall and knock on the door twice."* I followed his instructions and knocked twice on the door at the end of the hall. A voice replied, *"Come in."*

When I entered the room, I noticed that there was a desk with a gentleman sitting behind it. On the desk was a manila folder. The gentleman gestured for me to sit in the empty chair across from him. After a cordial greeting, he wasted no time getting straight to the point. He opened that manila folder which, based on what he revealed he knew about me, apparently contained my entire dossier, which he began to discuss with me. *"How in the world did they know all these things about me?"* I wondered. The man's voice interrupted my deep thought. *"Mr. Burris, I understand your German is very good. You are taking a student trip to Berlin. What we would like for you to do is to help us get a little information from the German people in East Berlin."* *"What do you mean?"* I questioned, totally perplexed about the whole situation.

The man continued as though he didn't even hear me, *"You can catch the S-Bahn to go over into East Berlin."*

He proceeded to give me a ton of instructions. He wanted me to go into different restaurants and eat. I was to make sure I got a table close to a family that consisted of a husband, wife and maybe children. After the meal, I would try to pay with East marks, not West marks. One West mark was worth four-plus East marks. The restaurant personnel would insist I pay with West marks, unless I had a green card. So when I couldn't produce that card, I was to create some type of a ruckus trying to pay my bill. That's when I would reach out to the nearby family saying something like, *"Is this how you treat visitors in your country?"* I mean, those consulate people had that whole enactment down to a "T." The man finished up his instructions by saying, *"They probably won't talk to you at first, but see if you can get them to go with you on the S-Bahn back to West Berlin and then sit down and interview them. Ask them questions like how do they get their sugar and bread? How do they get their fruit? How do they get their clothing? Are they able to purchase automobiles? If so, how much do they pay? Collect various bits of information from those families."*

After being in Berlin for a couple of days, I got up enough nerve to conduct the consulate's "fact-finding" mission. I broke away from my student group and caught the S-Bahn into East Berlin. That was back before the Berlin Wall went up.[xxxvi] Despite the absence of a wall, there were certainly definite differences between the West sector, which was under allied control and the East sector, which was under communist control. I went into a restaurant, did as the man instructed, and it worked exactly as planned. I was shocked!

In my four or five trips to the East sector—one for lunch and several for dinner—I met about four or five different families. They did go back with me and I would say something like, *"Let's discuss this or that."* I spoke their language, so they were comfortable with me and would unsuspectingly allow me to collect all kinds of information from them. It was great! I merged back with my tour group each time after I finished with my mission. After the ten days, our group boarded the bus and headed back to Hamburg. The next day, I went to the American Consulate and turned in my little write-up to that same gentleman. That was the last I ever heard of it. Just as mysteriously as the opportunity came my way, it mysteriously went away.

One day in October of 1960, while at my desk at Howard University School of Law, I glanced at the *Washington Post* and my eye caught a pretty shocking title: *"Student spy arrested in Germany."* I opened the newspaper and read the entire article. A student was arrested for gathering information in East Berlin. He received a suspended sentence of six months in jail.

Imagine my horror when realizing a kid got arrested for doing the same thing I had done only a few months earlier. How naive I was not to have realized I had been an informant for the CIA! My heart skipped quite a few beats while reading that article and having the reality of it all settle in. I suddenly recalled a conversation I had with Ed back in June, upon returning from my ten day student trip to Berlin. I told him about one of the fact-finding missions I conducted while in Berlin. I remembered that he became very curious and how he had pressed me more than usual for details about that mission, obviously wanting to know more.

Apparently, during one of the periods when we were able to travel through Europe, while I was taking a student trip to Italy, Ed had gone on a student trip to Russia. He never talked about his Russian trip until we had the conversation about my fact-finding missions. That's when he shared with me the story of his own so-called spying adventure. Imagine that! The same guy at the consulate had him do the same thing on his thirty-day trip to Moscow that I had been told to do on my ten-day trip to Berlin! At that time, it still never dawned on me the "information-gathering" I was doing could be CIA-related.

Ed recounted one time when reaching the Russian border; all the students were ordered off the bus and told to line up alongside the bus. Those guards questioned all the students in English; however, when they got to Ed, they started speaking Russian to him, as though they knew he understood the language. Soon, all the students, including Ed, were ordered back on the bus, and they continued on to their next destination, St. Petersburg. While staying in St Petersburg, Ed said when he came back to his hotel room; he noticed items in his room were sometimes moved from the places he had left them. He knew then someone was on to him, but he couldn't figure out who and how. Either way, he figured his room had been searched and might have been bugged.

Next, Ed traveled on to Moscow, where his group would spend most of their time. After checking into his hotel room in Moscow, remembering what happened in St. Petersburg, he decided to put little pieces of paper in the door to prove to himself his room was being searched when he was away. He would also arrange furniture or other items a certain way, such as a lamp or the clothes in his closet, determining to check the position of those things upon his return to see if anything had been disturbed. Sure enough, when he returned to his room, he could tell someone had been there. That made him very uneasy and cautious.

After a few days in Moscow, he had met this Russian student, and they became friends. One evening, they were scheduled to go to the Opera together. Ed waited in the designated place and the student never showed up. The following day, in a conversation with another student on the trip, Ed found out that this same Russian student with whom he had become friends had been suddenly and mysteriously arrested by the Russian authorities, apparently while Ed waited for him to show up for the Opera!

Poor Ed didn't know whom to trust! Was his new Russian friend a set-up? How did this other student even know his new Russian friend was arrested? To this day, Ed will not talk about some of the experiences of that Russian trip. I understand. One thing's for sure, looking back on those experiences that Ed and I shared, I am truly thankful we weren't the ones being written about in that *Washington Post* article!

Heading Home

July 31, 1960 signified the end of my studies at the University of Hamburg. As I planned my trip home, the thought of once again enduring that ten-day journey by sea, with the likelihood of getting sea sick, became too much to bear. I convinced my parents to purchase a plane ticket for me, so I could fly back home instead. The cheapest one-way student fare they found from Europe to New York City was four-hundred dollars. That was a lot of money back then! God bless them; they came through, and I was scheduled on a flight in early August out of Frankfurt International Airport, which is known in Germany as Flughafen Frankfurt am Main.

A day or so before leaving, several of my friends who were still on campus, including my young lady friend from Turkey, gave me a farewell/early birthday celebration (my birthday being August 3rd). I don't remember details of our activities; however, I do remember that none of us made it to bed for those couple of days. Needless to say, I was exhausted by the time my friends bid me goodbye at the train station in Hamburg. I boarded my train for the 300+ mile trip to Frankfurt, while my trunk was shipped directly to Centralia.

Unfortunately, as with my ship ride *to* Europe, my plane ride home *from* Europe had a few snags as well. First, the plane had some mechanical difficulties preventing us from departing that evening. After spending the night in the airport, where I made an unsuccessful attempt to sleep on the hard chairs, I was happy and relieved when we were informed all aircraft repairs were completed, and we were cleared to take off the next morning. That was when problem number two occurred.

Without any prior knowledge of the difference between airline and railroad travel, I had shown up at the airport toting my two suitcases, along with my umbrella and toilet kit. As I approached the gate that morning to board the plane, the agent informed me I had too many bags. What? I couldn't believe it! I had no one there to take my excess belongings and ship them home for me, so all my luggage had to get on that

92

plane. Thanks to my quick thinking, I approached an American student whom I noticed was scheduled on our flight and explained my dilemma. He had been carrying only a briefcase, and without hesitation, agreed to carry on one of my suitcases.

In 1960, the total travel time from Frankfurt to New York was about twenty hours. That little Boeing four turboprop engine jetliner accommodated about one hundred passengers and, I believe, a crew of five. We first flew from Frankfurt to Iceland and actually had enough time to get off the plane for awhile. I was excited to be able to say, officially, that I had been to Iceland. To prove it to the folks back home, I purchased a few souvenirs and even a little decal sticker from the airport. After leaving Iceland, we stopped on the island of Newfoundland, Canada (the province now known as Newfoundland and Labrador) before finally landing in New York where my mother, my brother's son, Earl III, and my sister's daughter, Carol Nadine all awaited my arrival. Because Dad was an employee of the Illinois Central Railroad, they all rode on free passes. We felt it would be great for the oldest two grandchildren to experience a trip like that, so they traveled from Centralia up to Chicago and then on another train from Chicago to New York.

My friend from SIU, Les Margolese, was living in New York with his parents at that time. He and I had made arrangements for him to pick up my family members from Penn Station and then bring all of them to meet me at the airport. Our plans were well-executed. They picked me up mid-morning, right on schedule. We headed to Les' home, where we visited with his parents and got a bite to eat. Of course, we couldn't let the kids go to New York City for their first time and not take them sightseeing in Manhattan, so we did that for a short while before heading right to the railway station to catch the train bound for Chicago. What a whirlwind of a brief stay that was! On top of all that, I had not yet slept beyond a few moments here and there —and certainly not at all in a bed—for almost four days.

Twenty-four hours later, in the late afternoon August heat, we reached Chicago's downtown train station. My birthday had come and gone while I had been enroute home. We were picked up at that station, taken to Chicago's South Side for a brief visit at my godmother's house (where I had lived each summer during my college years) before being dropped off at the Illinois Central station at 63rd Street to catch our train to Centralia.

A surprise awaited me at my godmother's house. There, in a vase, were a dozen beautiful red roses. I could not imagine who sent them, until I noticed the "Happy Birthday" card from my young lady friend in Hamburg. My godmother and family members really teased me about that, saying I had gotten myself a girlfriend, and I was going to marry a Turkish girl.

Anyway, our all-night ride from Chicago to Centralia presented another sleepless night for me, which made it close to five nights without sleep. I still hadn't been to bed for a full night's rest and the seats of that train didn't offer any relief for one reason or another. There I was, fighting jetlag and operating on adrenalin only for energy. We arrived home in Centralia in the wee hours of the morning. I climbed into my bed and stayed there most of the day.

When I finally woke up from that much needed rest, I realized there was one thing I did not factor into my meticulously rigid travel arrangements from Hamburg to Centralia. I'm sure it was because I was so tired I wasn't thinking straight. During my short period in Chicago, I neglected to call a certain young lady of whom I had grown very fond: Berlean Miller.

Berlean and I had written each other rather extensively while I was in Germany, except for one period of time when she moved, and I lost track of her. I had to write my godmother for help in locating her. At that time, she had graduated from nursing school and was working at the University of Chicago Hospital. While in school, she had lived with her sister about twelve blocks away from my godmother's house.

I have vivid memories of that distance between their homes, as one very cold winter day while I was visiting Chicago during Christmas break in my senior year at SIU; I walked those twelve blocks without a hat. I have no idea why I didn't have a hat on but as a result, my ears became frostbitten. To this day, they still burn whenever the weather is cold, and whenever I forget to put on warm headgear which adequately covers my ears before I go outside.

I suppose to a young man in love, frostbitten ears must have been a small price to pay. As Berlean and I continued to correspond through letters, I pretty much settled on the fact that she was the one for me. In fact, I think I may have even mentioned that to her in a letter or two.

Nevertheless, what a horrible mistake I made in not calling her while passing through Chicago. I carefully began rehearsing my explanation, as I prepared to call her from Centralia. *"Where are you?"* That was one of the first things out of her mouth. *"Centralia,"* I slowly responded. *"You mean you were in Chicago and you didn't call me? You came all the way back home and you're just now calling me?"*

She fired away question after question; leaving no room for me to answer any of them. As the saying goes, she was fit to be tied! I eventually smoothed things over by promising to make it back there that following week to visit her. I got a train pass from Dad, rode back up to Chicago and kept my promise to Berlean.

Education
Photographs

Roland W. Burris (first row, third from left) and his first grade classmates Lincoln Elementary School

Roland W. Burris (first row, center) and his Lincoln Elementary School eighth grade classmates

Roland Burris smiles for his second grade school picture at Centralia's Lincoln Elementary School

Mr. William Walker, Principal at Centralia's Lincoln Elementary School from 1948 to 1975

Roland Burris at Lincoln Elementary School

Roland Burris in his Freshman year at Centralia High School

Roland Burris in his Sophomore year at Centralia High School

Roland Burris in his Junior year at Centralia High School

Roland Burris in his Senior year at Centralia High School

Roland Burris in his football gear (#12) during his Senior year at Centralia High School

Centralia Freshmen Football "B" Team. Burris is second from left in top row

Centralia Sophomore Football "B" Team. Burris is second from left in second row

Centralia High School Track Team. Burris, a sophomore, is far right on fourth row

Centralia Varsity Football "A" Team in Roland Burris' Junior year. Burris is third from right, first row

Roland Burris (far right, third row) Centralia High School junior and members of the Track Team

Senior Roland Burris (second from right, fourth row) and Centralia High School Varsity Football "A" Team

Southern Illinois University chapter of Alpha Phi Alpha Fraternity. Burris, president of the fraternity, is fifth from the left on row one

Southern Illinois University Inter-Fraternity Council. Burris is at far right in row three

Southern Illinois University Young Republicans. Burris is at far right in row two

Southern Illinois University football players including Roland W. Burris (#12, far right) and four of his friends from Centralia High School: Bill Norwood (#11), Leonard "Moose" Taylor (#31), Charles Steptoe (behind Taylor, number obscured), and Vernon Rush (#10)

Roland Burris in his Southern Illinois University Senior Class Photograph

...nator Burris poses with members of the Beta Eta Chapter of Alpha Phi Alpha fraternity at his alma mater, ...uthern Illinois University after the donation of the Senator's papers to the university

...ceremony marking donation of Senator Burris' political papers to the university's library (from left) Key Note ...eaker and former SIU trustee William "Bill" Norwood; David Carlson, Director of Library Affairs, ...orris Library; former SIU Vice Chancellor Harvey Welch; Senator Burris; Chris Shelton, president of the ...ta Eta Chapter of Alpha Phi Alpha fraternity; SIU Chancellor Rita Cheng; and SIU President Glenn Poshard.

Exchange student, Roland Burris, far left, with fellow students at University of Hamburg-

Howard University Law School Senior Class Officers. Burris, class president, is third from left

Howard Law School Senior Class, Roland Burris (far right in first row)

land Burris (far left) and members of Howard University Law School Moot Court

land Burris (seated far right) and members of the Howard University chapter of Sigma Delta Tau,
e only black legal fraternity in the country

Roland Burris (seated at far right) and members of Howard University's Sigma Delta Tau Fraternity

Roland W. Burris , Senior Class Photograph, Howard University Law School

Roland W. Burris poses in his graduation gown prior to his June 7, 1963 graduation from Howard University Law School

Burris: Law School Commencement speaker
From left: Law School Professor and former classmate, Jerome Schuman; Hon. Roland W. Burris, Distinguished Howard University Law School graduate and Commencement Speaker; and Law School Dean Earl Lane

Chapter Six
Howard University School of Law

All the Preliminaries

Soon after settling into my classes at the University of Hamburg, I had started mapping out the next phase of my life, when my year in Germany would be completed. That phase, still almost a year away, required that I make a major decision fairly soon, so that I could properly prepare. Should I go back to SIU and get a master's degree in international law (I had already checked and knew that I could get in that program)? Or should I go directly to law school? Decisions, decisions. In the end, taking into account that one of my two main goals in life was to become a lawyer, I figured I should go to law school right away, rather than delaying it.

I began checking out a number of law schools, and eventually narrowed my selection down to three of them: the University of Michigan Law School, the University of Illinois College of Law, and the Howard University School of Law. Before sending applications to those schools, I had to take the LSAT, the law school admission test. I found out that the closest testing site would be in Heidelberg, one hundred miles away from Hamburg. The LSAT was scheduled for February of 1960, so I had several months to prepare for that grueling exam.

I studied for that exam with extreme attentiveness. I skimped and scraped from various resources to come up with the test fee and travel costs. Finally, the time came to make the southeast trek to Heidelberg. I don't remember the exact results on my LSAT, but I do recall that my score was fairly decent. Good score or not, Michigan turned me down. However, I was accepted by the law schools of the University of Illinois and Howard University.

Next, I had to think about the finances required for me to attend law school, since I realized finances could somewhat dictate my final decision. Since it was closer to home, I really wanted to go to University of Illinois College of Law. When I inquired about scholarships, however, the University of Illinois admissions office indicated that there were no scholarships available for first-year students. That news hit me like a ton of bricks. It was a blow to my pride that I had worked so hard and gotten admitted into law school only to find that I did not have the means to follow through with matriculation. That was a hard pill to swallow. Shortly thereafter, I received a letter from Howard University School of Law. In part, it read, *"Based upon your academic standing, you will be considered for a scholarship… fill out these papers and send in this application fee."* I immediately wrote Mom asking for fifty dollars, which was the required application fee. Soon, the fee was paid, securing my next phase of life, even as I settled into my current phase in Germany.

Once my year at the University of Hamburg *was* completed and under my belt, there wasn't a whole lot of time for me to transition from Germany to Washington, D.C., mentally or physically. From the moment I stepped off that twenty-hour flight back to the states, it was do this, go there, to finalize things for law school. Throughout all that hustle and bustle, I barely found time to be excited. That seemed okay, since my father was excited enough for both of us. Dad was a very proud and hard-working man. He expected the best of people, especially his own children. When we worked hard and achieved what we set out to do, he had no qualms about letting us and others know how proud he was of us and how happy we made him feel.

For instance, just before I traveled to Germany, in August of 1959, I was honored by my Alpha Phi Alpha fraternity as *Midwestern Brother of the Year* for having received a scholarship to study abroad. Dad was already taking me out to a restaurant because of my going to Germany, but that fraternity award gave us a second reason for our feast. Dad told everyone around us that evening about the two reasons for our celebration.

You can imagine Dad's elation when finding out his son would be attending law school and Howard University School of Law at that! Now, *that* was a big deal to him.

HBCU's

Years before applying to Howard University, I had heard about the school and its legacy as one of the historically black colleges and universities in the U.S. I must admit, though, all I thought I knew about Howard University prior to attending was just the tip of the iceberg. After all, how could I even begin to imagine the huge impact such a physically small, but historically large campus, nestled in our nation's capital would have on me? No, I couldn't have predicted I was about to tread upon life-changing grounds, and not by simply calling it home for the next three years of my life.

In spite of its distinction as a leading black university, Howard University, from its conception in 1867, has been a nonsectarian institution. In more recent years, it has become distinguished as one of a number of colleges known as HBCU's (Historically Black Colleges & Universities)[xxxvii], a distinction it shares with the other one hundred and five schools of its kind dispersed throughout our country. Howard is open to both sexes and to all races of people. Even though some people may think these higher learning institutions were established as a place where *only* blacks could learn; in actuality, they were created, because blacks were not allowed to attain a college level education *elsewhere*.

For instance, Howard University's founder, Civil War hero General Oliver Otis Howard, was a white, Christian man concerned about the educational opportunities for freed black men of the 1800's who, prior to the Civil War, had been forbidden to enter any room or building in which a school might be convening or where school lessons were being taught. In 1866, Howard joined forces with men from various socially concerned groups in Washington, D.C. and discussed plans for a theological seminary to train colored ministers. As a result of those talks, Howard University was founded and then incorporated by Congress in 1867 with a founding mission of promoting social justice, educational access, and opportunities for Black and underserved populations .[xxxviii] Over the years, this mission has expanded significantly.

D.C. Bound

I was home in Centralia getting ready for law school when the trunk I shipped from Germany finally arrived. It contained all my sweaters and heavy items, some of which needed to be re-packed and taken with me to Washington, D.C. Packing and traveling had started to become second nature to me, and I was getting really good at traveling light. So, for my move to Howard University School of Law I only carried, you guessed it, two suitcases, an umbrella and a toilet kit.

Departure day finally rolled around, and my brother and his wife drove me to the B&O train station in Salem, Illinois, which was about ten miles away. I expected Nick to pick me up in my prized 1953 Pontiac I bought in 1958 while in college for the princely sum of three hundred dollars. I had asked him to keep it for me when I left for Germany. To this day, I cannot remember his explanation when I asked him how and why he had gotten rid of my car and bought himself a new one.

Once at the train station, I proceeded to the counter and presented my voucher to the ticket agent. I would be traveling to Washington D.C. on a train voucher called a "foreign pass," since I wasn't riding the Illinois Central train. After my parents had scraped up four hundred dollars to purchase my flight home from Germany, that foreign pass, plus a little traveling cash, I had used up most of their remaining dollars.

You can imagine how horrified I felt when that agent said my voucher was no good! Shock ran through me and I could sense my mouth hanging open as I tried to comprehend what I had just heard. When the agent just stared at me, never changing his story; never saying, *"Oops, I made a mistake and your ticket is good after all,"* numbness in my body replaced shock and my knees almost gave out under me.

I had planned so meticulously for that day, or so I thought. I had my luggage, proof of my admissions; my scholarship paperwork, some money in my pocket to help me to get settled in Washington, and what I thought was a valid train pass. Apparently, that particular voucher was not acceptable, so in order for me to get on that train, at that moment, my brother and I put our money together and purchased a one-way ticket to D.C. When all was said and done, I slid into my seat on the train with great relief and ten dollars left to my name.

I had never been to Washington, D.C. before in my life. So, even though I had traveled all the way to Germany and back, I still felt an overwhelming sense of anticipation about seeing our nation's capital. I spent almost the entire daylight hours of my twenty-two hour ride enthralled by nature's magnificent landscapes, as the train swooshed through the heart of America: Indiana, Ohio, West Virginia and Virginia. I marveled at the designs in the cornfields and the small country houses holding their own, although completely encircled by those massive corn and wheat fields.

I closely guarded the ten dollars left in my wallet. Midway through the trip, I got so hungry that I had to break down and spend some of it on food. I bought a ham sandwich and a Coca-Cola. While eating in the dining car of the train, I met a young lady. We struck up a casual conversation, mainly about our originating points, as well as our destinations. Her family lived in D.C. She had been off somewhere attending undergraduate school, but was heading back east to enroll in the nursing program at Hampton University.

When she found out I was Howard-bound, she informed me that her brother was the admissions director there. Our conversation culminated with her giving me her name and telephone number on a piece of paper. I cannot remember her first name, but her last name was Eaton. Whatever original intention I may have had for obtaining Ms. Eaton's phone number, my later use of it turned out to be far from what I expected.

When the train pulled into D.C.'s station, I had $8.25 remaining to my name. I got off the train and found a cab. I instructed the driver to take me to Howard University, and we arrived there within minutes. I paid the fare, unloaded my gear from the trunk and then followed the signs pointing to admissions, in search of the campus housing office. The admissions clerk told me to go up to the third floor and look for a long counter. Once there, I asked the lady if the housing director was in, and sure enough, a gentleman named Mr. Bush came to the counter.

I started right in, *"Well, hello Mr. Bush. I'm Roland Burris and I've been admitted to law school. I will be looking for some off-campus housing. Can you help me?"*

He looked at me like I had three eyes and said, *"No. We don't have housing for you. Did you apply for housing? Are you a law student?"*

"Yes, I am a law student and no, I didn't apply for housing yet." I apprehensively answered, suddenly afraid of what next would come out of that man's mouth. After all, how did he know there wasn't housing available for me without checking a list of some sort?

"Well, no, we don't provide any housing resources."

"Oh," I thought with a blank stare on my face. *"That's how he knew!"*

"Well, is Mr. Anderson available?" I had intended to look up Carl Anderson, a Kappa and my former schoolmate from SIU, as soon as I arrived. I had heard he was Director of Student Activities at Howard.

"No, Mr. Anderson is on vacation. He won't be back for a week."

I felt an immediate knot forming in the pit of my stomach. I looked around and—thanks to my quick thinking—asked, *"Is there an Alpha house available?"* One thing I learned early on after pledging is that you can meet a fraternity brother for the first time halfway across the world and there will be an instant connection, as though you've known each other for years. Brotherhood for life: it's a comforting feeling, especially when you're in a pinch like I was that day. Imagine my huge relief at Mr. Bush's next reply. *"Yeah, there's an Alpha house."* Mr. Bush started writing the address on a piece of paper as he spoke those words. Anxious to get rid of me and all my questions, I'm sure. He handed the address to me with a "good luck, kid" kind of smile and I thanked him.

I once again loaded my two suitcases, umbrella, and toilet kit into my arms and headed outside to hail yet another cab. This time, the taxi ride was not as brief as my taxi ride from the train station to the campus; instead, at the end of the taxi ride, I found myself all the way on the Northwest side of D.C. I don't remember exactly where, but I do remember the taxi fare ate up almost half of my remaining money; leaving me with a little less than five dollars to my name.

With no idea of where to stay, no off-campus housing offered and Carl not in town for a week, the fact that Howard had an Alpha frat house thrilled me to no end. Correction: there was an end to that thrill. It occurred immediately upon arrival to the frat house, which I immediately discovered to be closed for remodeling.

Staring at a big empty brick house in the late afternoon heat, I began to pray, *"Oh Lord, what do I do now? I'm here with nowhere to go and I know no one. Tell me what to do, God."* Just then, it dawned on me that I had that young lady's name and phone number on a piece of paper. I had previously tucked it in my pants pocket and frantically went fishing for it. Whew! It was still there. I made it to a pay telephone, called her and fortunately she answered. I stammered briefly, *"Uh, hi. This is Roland Burris. We met on the train."* *"Okay,"* she said, at first sounding slightly uneasy. Then I could tell she suddenly made the connection and her voice took on a more relaxed tone. I explained my plight to Ms. Eaton. She offered her assistance with total sincerity, *"Oh, Mr. Burris, I tell you what you do. Get a cab and come over to our house. There is a lady around the corner who keeps students. I'll call her for you."*

Thank you, God. I hailed a cab and soon arrived at the Eaton home somewhere not far from where I was—still Northwest. I paid the driver; after which, I had a mere two dollars and some change left over. I met the other Eaton family members: the young lady's mother, her sister and her brother-in-law.

They had called the lady who rented to students and left her a message. Next, they fed me. I had been too afraid to buy anything to eat since arriving in town, due to my lack of funds, so I certainly didn't turn down their offer of food. Finally, the lady around the corner called back and said she did have a room available for rent. I immediately called my mother and asked her to wire some money to me for the room rental. I went around the corner to face my last hope for a place to live. She was a nice and rather frail old lady who quoted me a room rate of thirty-five dollars a month. To that I replied, *"Okay, my mother is wiring me some money. When I get notice of the Western Union telegram, I'll come back and pay you the rent."*

I got word that my telegram had come in. The Eaton sister and brother-in-law drove me back to Union Station that evening, where I signed for the telegram and received the funds. Mom had sent me all of twenty-five dollars. I walked out of Western Union all smiles. I didn't let anyone know how much—or should I say, how little—money I had gotten. They drove me back to the old lady's house and dropped me off there.

I went inside and reported my situation. *"Mom didn't send me as much as I thought she was going to, so I'm kind of short. She did send me twenty-five dollars. I'll need something for my pocket, so I'll give you fifteen dollars and I'll need to take ten dollars to tide me over until I can*

105

get a job." She looked at me and said, *"Son, you look like an honest young man, I'll accept that."*

What a relief her kindness brought to my situation. What a relief her rented bed brought to my body that night. As I lay there, I reflected on my entire venture to D.C. starting with the bad train voucher in Salem. I had already crossed quite a few hurdles to get to that point, but I knew I had more awaiting me. Drifting off to sleep, I prepared my mind for the first of those new hurdles I would face starting that very next day: finding a job.

Start at the Bottom; Work Your Way Up

I had purposely arrived at Howard seven or eight days earlier than the beginning of classes so that I could find a job. I had the scholarship, yet I had to pay for books and my living arrangements, so I needed a job. Early that next morning, without even taking time to stop for breakfast, I headed back to the same administration building, to the same floor, except this time, I was looking for the Student Employment Office. There, I met a lady named Mrs. Cooms.

"You're here just in time," she announced. *"It's a good thing you got in early this morning, because over at Cook Hall there's only one position left. They need somebody over there right away." "Yes, ma'am, I can start now!"*

I could hardly get my words out fast enough to accept that position. In fact, I accepted it before even knowing what the job entailed! Anyway, I figured, how bad could it be?

Mrs. Cooms then told me the job paid one dollar per hour. She gave me a piece of paper and told me to report to a certain person over at Cook Hall. When I arrived at Cook Hall, the gentleman who would be my supervisor echoed exactly what Mrs. Cooms had said—that I had gotten the last position available. He handed me some gloves, a bucket, a scrub brush and led me to the room where I would be spending the next eight hours of my first full day at the university cleaning bathrooms. His parting words were, *"Young man, go to it."*

I stood there for a moment; observed my surroundings, took a deep breath, and got to it. I had never been too shy or too proud to do what I had to do and I felt certain this time would prove no different. I began cleaning the urinals, commodes, sinks and walls of each bathroom on each floor of the section of the building assigned to me.

By the end of the day, I had made eight or nine dollars. I still had the ten dollars from my mother, so I had enough money to eat that day. During morning break, I had bought a donut and a cup of coffee; for lunch, I had bought a sandwich. On my way home, I stopped for a hamburger or something like that for dinner. I had no clue how I was going to continue to make it on such a small amount of money.

The next morning, I headed back over to Cook Hall where I was assigned to another section of bathrooms. While I was cleaning, a tall young fellow walked in with his bucket and mop and started mopping. As we made small talk, I found out he was a senior in the undergrad school. He asked what year I was and I answered, *"Law school." "Law school! You're in law school?"* He chuckled slightly as he continued, *"I'm doing this crazy job because I need a little money."* I stated with dignified conviction, *"Well, I'm trying to get money for law school."* Not wanting to drop the subject, he queried, *"Why are you doing this grungy type of job, cleaning latrines, if you're going to law school, man?"* I stopped scrubbing, looked at that guy and said, *"Well, I'll tell you, sometimes you've gotta start at the bottom and work your way up to the top. I was the last one hired here, and this was the last job standing; so I took it."*

He shrugged his shoulders, somewhat accepting what I said. We went on with our business, cleaning all the bathrooms in that section of the building that day.

During my lunch break, I decided to go to the administration building to check on my scholarship. I suppose I needed assurance that I was still actually getting the scholarship, especially since no more money was coming from home.

The clerk at the counter pulled out my records and said, *"Well, yes, Mr. Burris, you've been admitted to the law school and yes, there's a scholarship that's going to pay your tuition."*

For the first time since arriving on Howard's campus, I breathed a real sigh of relief. I was definitely in and it was definitely paid for. The clerk started handing me all kinds of forms to sign and other papers from my file I needed to read. She then read something noted in my file and said to me, *"By the way, you sent in a deposit and since you received a scholarship that deposit is refundable."*

"It is? I asked pleasantly astounded. *"How much is that deposit?" "Fifty dollars,"* she responded. *"Do you want that in cash?"*

I'm sure that clerk did not understand why I started laughing and could hardly stop. Needless to say, that bit of good news made it easier to report back to my scrubbing duties. In fact, I was whistling on my way back to the latrines. That's when I ran into Mrs. Cooms, the job placement lady, in the hallway.

"What are you doing over here? You ought to be over there working!" Her reproach caught me totally off guard. It was as if she had channeled into an elementary school teacher, and I was the ten-year old lazy kid in the back of the classroom. I respectfully charged back, *"Ma'am, I'm on my lunch hour." "Well, you make sure you hurry back over there!"* she said completely ignoring my explanation and making sure she had the last word before proceeding down the hallway.

Talk about a high-deflator! As soon as I got back to my work location, though, I whistled through the rest of the day cleaning toilets. I felt even happier when I got home that evening and was able to hand my landlady the twenty dollars I owed her. She looked me straight in the eye as she smiled and spoke, *"Son, I knew you were an honest young man."*

At the end of the week, I received a small paycheck. By then, it was about time for classes to begin. My friend, Carl Anderson, had returned to work and learned I had been trying to reach him. By the third day of law school, Carl and I finally spoke on the phone. He delivered some excellent news to me, which was even more unexpected and exciting than the news about my refund.

"You know, Roland, there are fellowships available," Carl informed me.

"Fellowships? What do you mean, Carl?" I asked.

He began to spell it out to me, *"Well, as a graduate student, you could get a fellowship in exchange for agreeing to serve as an Assistant Dormitory Director. Under this arrangement, the university would take care of your room, plus they would pay you a monthly stipend of one hundred dollars."*

"They would?" I couldn't believe my ears.

As Carl talked, my mind raced. So many financial dilemmas would be resolved if that whole scenario actually occurred. We completed that phone conversation with Carl promising to look into that fellowship on my behalf.

Sure enough, as a man of his word, Carl called a couple of days later with the news, *"Roland, you're clear. You've got your fellowship. Come over here to fill out some papers and..."*

Three days later, I moved from the old lady's house four blocks away to my new dormitory, Carver Hall. Carver was a senior dorm for undergrads. My room was huge because I had to counsel students there. I realized counseling others while carrying a full load of classes could pose a strain on my studying, but I decided to worry about that bridge when I came to it.

A few days after moving in, I was working the front desk of the dormitory. In walked this young man and he looked at me saying, *"You look awfully familiar."* I agreed, *"You look familiar to me, too."* Then it dawned on him. *"Oh, yeah, yeah, you were at Cook Hall cleaning the latrines."* He continued, *"What are you doing over here at Carver?"* I said, *"Well, young man, remember what I told you about starting at the bottom and working to the top? Well, I'm now the Assistant Dormitory Director here at Carver."* He laughed as he nodded his head. *"I believe, Sir. I believe."*

Neophytes

My first year of law school was brutal, especially since I had to split my time between fulfilling my academic responsibilities and dealing with the many different concerns of the Carver Hall undergraduate residents who were in my charge. There were fifty-nine first year law students, including three women and two white male students. Retrospectively, I note only one of the three women graduated with the class. Of the two women who didn't stay, one transferred to a different law school, and the other one withdrew due to illness, although everyone really believed that the real reason she dropped out of school altogether was because of pregnancy.

One of my Howard classmates, Julius Johnson, from St. Louis had attended undergrad with me at SIU, where he was already a junior when I entered as a freshman. While I was completing my year of study in Germany, Julius was serving the final year of a three-year stint in the military. We both arrived at law school at the same time and re-acquainted ourselves as law school classmates.

I was characterized as a rather outspoken law student, which none-theless caused some interesting situations for me as a student. You see, I came from an environment at SIU where students were encouraged to speak up; and that they did. At Howard University School of Law, though, I learned that such free expression as I was accustomed to at SIU was far from the norm. I detected a serious competitive nature among Howard students, which was only accentuated by the horror stories that many of the upperclassmen told to scare the heck out of the neophytes. On our own, we first year students soon found out that some of the professors actually did live up to some of those horror stories.

One incident that occurred during the last few months of my first year in law school involved a student named Mr. Hopkins. At the time of my arrival at Howard, he was beginning his third year. Hopkins was a veteran in his mid-forties who had never failed a course in law school, that is, until that year. That's when he received two F's on two final exam papers and was dismissed from law school just before graduation. The rule called for the immediate dismissal of any student who received two F grades over the three year period of law school. I never knew the details of Hopkins' situation, but we all knew that he sued the school and lost. Mr. Hopkins never did get his degree from Howard. The Hopkins story was both scary and traumatic to us first-year law students. Knowing that it was possible to make it all the way up to your senior year and then be dismissed made all of us forget about slacking off in our studies. In the year following the Hopkins case, we would go around citing *"Hopkins '61,"* as a reminder to any of our classmates who appeared to be slacking off in their class work.

I started off with four or five classes that the professors made so tough that you really never knew what you were doing or how you were coming along doing it. To survive academically, I regularly spent many long hours in the library. This was easily one of the most academically intense periods of my young life! I read so much during those first six weeks that there were times when I actually thought I would go blind! In fact, my once 20/20 vision soon required the assistance of eyeglasses, which I had never previously needed.

In trying to get a full grasp of all the new challenges and demands which were part and parcel of the Howard law school environment, I queried this person and that person. I took pointers from upperclassmen who had learned the hard way, that is, whenever I was fortunate enough to find one who was willing to help me *avoid* the hard way myself. All my efforts and strategies evidently worked, because my three years at Howard Law School turned out to be a very positive learning experience for me overall.

My extracurricular experiences were positive as well. Although I was never on the *Howard Law Journal*,[xxxix] our school's legal publication, I had classmates who were at the first level of it. One of them was Earl White, who was the number one student in our class; another was Jerome Shuman, who became a law professor at Howard. Both of them are now deceased. The other classmate who worked on the *Howard Law Journal* was Tony Miles, who is currently with the Securities Commission for the District of Columbia.

As far as the *Law Journal* is concerned, from time to time in my first two years, I did participate as a volunteer gopher in mimeographing some of the briefs prepared for the cases to be filed for the U.S. Supreme Court by the civil rights lawyers. Ah, the wonders of the mimeograph machine! Long before the days of fast-performing laser-jet printers, we had to crank those huge machines to get our copies; not to mention dealing with the messy carbons and even the completed copies that came off the drum with the ink still wet.

Notable people

My three years at Howard occurred during the height of the Civil Rights Movement. That movement took over ten years of boycotts, sit-ins, marches and other displays of organized protest against segregation before the necessary legislature to abolish racial discrimination toward blacks within our nation was finally passed. The Howard University School of Law played an integral role in the movement, both through the participation and contribution of the students who passed through Howard's doors and through the legal knowledge, expertise, and connections of the professors and other staff and faculty members who graced the university's classrooms and administrative offices.

In addition, Civil Rights leaders, such as Thurgood Marshall,[xl] Constance Baker Motley,[xli] Jack Greenberg[xlii], and Oliver Hill,[xliii] all members of the NAACP Legal Defense and Educational Fund, Inc.,[xliv] a nonprofit law firm founded by Thurgood Marshall, were often seen on our campus. They came there to practice their trial runs, which were organized by Spotswood Robinson III, Dean of the Howard University Law School.[xlv]

Marshall, along with his team, won his most famous case, *Brown v. the Board of Education*, in 1954, at the start of the Civil Rights Movement. In 1933, he had graduated from Howard University Law School at the top of his class. I remember that soon after I arrived at Howard, Marshall was appointed by President Kennedy to the United States Court of Appeals. Then, in 1967, he was appointed by President Lyndon B. Johnson as our nation's first African-American Supreme Court Justice.

As Marshall's co-counsel, Motley became the first African-American female elected to the New York State Senate in 1964 and then in 1966, she was appointed by President Johnson as the first African-American female federal judge in the United States. Greenberg, as the only white counsel member of the Legal Defense Fund, succeeded Marshall as Director-Counsel in 1961. Among his many other law accolades, was an honorary degree conferred by Howard University in 2004.

Robinson, a Howard faculty member from 1939 until 1948, when he joined Marshall with the Legal Defense Fund, came back to Howard as Dean of the law school in 1960, succeeding Dr. James Nabrit, who left that role to become President of Howard University. When he had graduated from Howard University School of Law back in 1939, Robinson achieved the highest scholastic average in the history of the law school until my classmate, Earl White, broke that record by maintaining the highest grade-point average achieved by any Howard law student over a three-year period. In 1966, Robinson was appointed to the United States Court of Appeals for the District of Columbia Circuit by President Johnson, becoming the first African-American to hold that post. Previously, he had broken the racial barrier on the local level when he became the first African-American to become Chief Judge of the District of Columbia Circuit Court.

Of course, this list of notables would not be complete without naming Charles Hamilton Houston[xlvi] and his social engineering[xlvii] crowd. Houston, a prominent African-American attorney, played a role in almost every Civil Rights case put before the Supreme Court between 1930 and the 1954 *Brown v. Board of Education* decision. His active role against discrimination on the legal front earned him the title, "The Man Who Killed Jim Crow."[xlviii] The Charles Houston Bar Association and the Charles Hamilton Houston Institute for Race and Justice at Harvard Law School are just a few of the organizations named after him. As Dean of Howard University School of Law during the 1930's, he mentored many students who would go on to become some of the leading African-American law professors of the day. He also created a process called social engineering, which he used in his training of many black lawyers in strategies that would challenge the legalized segregated system. During his tenure, Howard University School of Law trained about one-fourth of the nation's black law students, including many of the most influential civil rights lawyers in the nation. Houston is best known for having trained Thurgood Marshall.

Many names are associated with the Charles Hamilton Houston's social engineering concept. Some of them are professors who actually taught me, such as James A. Washington Jr., (who became dean of the law school in 1969),[xlix] Herbert O. Reid, Sr.[l] and Dorsey Edward Lane,[li] just to name a few. I can't begin to express how awe-inspiring it was to me to be trained by professors who had received their training from a man like Charles Houston.

Notable Experiences

As I mentioned, some of the professors proved more than worthy of the horror stories that the upperclassmen shared about them. As I recall, one particular class in legal contracts, which was taught by Professor Newton Pacht,[lii] met two times per week. Professor Pacht sat at a long desk on a platform at the front of the room. The students sat at long tables across the room, with approximately ten or twelve students to each table. The rows were in bleacher fashion so that everyone had an unobstructed view of the professor.

On the first day of class, I sat in the second or third row. Professor Newton Pacht rushed into the room, slammed his book real hard on his desk, ran to the window quickly hoisting it open with a loud bang, then ran back over and stood in front of all fifty-nine of us and just stared at us for a few minutes.

He scared the living daylights out of everyone! You should've seen us looking like little sheep heading to slaughter. Finally, he asked a question, *"How many of you already had Business Law courses?"* A few students put up their hands. Some of these students began to smile and seemed to relax a little, confident that having taken business law had gotten them on Pacht's good side. They soon found out the contrary.

Professor Pacht leaned towards those individuals' and scoffed, *"Don't you all bring any of that business law garbage into my contracts class!"*

His first impression tactics worked. It was designed to get our attention and make us never forget certain things like the fact that applying business law concepts to a contracts class will mess you up! Fifty some years later, I remember that event as though it happened yesterday.

Another "lasting impression" professor was one of the few female law professors at Howard when I was in law school, a black woman named Mrs. Straker. Mrs. Straker taught *Legal Writing and Research.* She taught directly from a book with the same title. I had already taken that same course and had used that same book as an undergraduate, so I pretty much knew most of the material. Well, during one of our sessions, she gave us some information that I knew was incorrect. The more I listened to her, the more I knew it was wrong, so I figured I had to say something. I raised my hand and when she acknowledged me I said, *"Mrs. Straker, what you're putting on the board is not correct."* Boy, at that second, you could hear a pin drop. My classmates were probably thinking, *"Who is this fool?"* I continued to explain why she was wrong and told her to check it for herself. She did, and discovered I was right.

You can believe that from that point on, she started checking everything before giving it to us. Thank goodness she wasn't indignant about being corrected by me. I did get an A in the class.

In addition to memorable professors, I had some memorable classes as well—some good, some bad, some downright brutal. There was one that comes to my mind and it didn't even occur in law school, but *before* I got to law school. It was an international law class I took at the University of Hamburg entitled, *Conflicts of Law.* Fortunately, it was a pass/fail course. I passed the class, but the legal terminology involved and the way the things were in Europe made it one of the hardest courses I've ever tackled.

For instance, in Europe, we could travel to another country and speak that country's language with the same ease we travel from state to state here. The only difference is that here in the U.S. we would speak the same language regardless of which state we are in. In Europe, however, I spoke German when I was in Germany, but I could go a short distance to Holland where I would speak Dutch; or go a bit further to Denmark and speak Danish; or to France and speak French, etc. (That was all before the European Union.)

So, we had cases we had to study that dealt with multiple jurisdictions. One famous case was with a German citizen who married a French citizen in Switzerland. They were living in Spain and wanted to get a divorce (or something to that effect). We had to determine who had jurisdiction. Bottom line, it boiled down to the fact that the site of residency was the determining factor in terms of jurisdiction and how the law should be applied. We had to factor in currency rate differences when regarding monetary issues and take other litigation issues into account as well. Even though it was very difficult trying to master all the complex requirements of European law, that class ranked high among my most interesting courses in law.

Yes, that first year of law school was scary; it was brutal; it was fun, but most of all, it was life-changing. If I had it to do over, I wouldn't change a thing.

Just in Case

My freshman year Torts class taught by Dean Robinson was memorable as well—mainly for its brutal nature. That class lasted the entire year with not a single exam given until June. I still remember that the class met for one hour each Tuesday and Thursday.

In that class, we used the case method, which is otherwise known as "briefing a case." That meant we had to read the issues surrounding the wrongful act for which damages were being sought; then, we had to dissect the judicial opinion given the case and analyze it with legal reasoning. Finally, we would brief it, or summarize it, and present that summary to the class. The first month or so of the class was all procedural stuff; learning the steps involved in briefing a case, etc. It was around late October or early November when Dean Robinson started giving us assignments to brief.

The following week, Dean Robinson came into the classroom and immediately started calling on people to present their cases. The first several people he called on weren't ready. He then called on me and I gave my case.

Dean Robinson said, *"Okay, Burris, give the next case."* I gave him the next case.

He said, *"Burris, give the next case."* I gave the third case (by that time, my analyses were getting pretty weak).

He said, *"Okay, Burris, give the next case."* I gave the fourth case.

He said, *"Burris, give the fifth case."* I didn't have a fifth case!

I had only briefed four cases. Then he called on my classmate, Smitty, who didn't have any cases prepared. Another classmate had the fifth case. After the presentation of that fifth case, class was over. Dean Robinson then said, *"When you come in here, you must be prepared."*

So I told myself I had to have at least five or six cases before going back to class that next session. When the following Thursday rolled around, who do you think Dean Robinson called on first? *"Burris, give the first case."*

Not only did I do the first case, but the second case, third case, fourth, fifth and sixth cases as well! He asked me for a seventh, but I only had six, so he called on somebody else. No one else had the seventh case briefed.

The dean looked at me and asked, *"Burris, have you heard of the All-American Game?"* I said, *"No, Dean, what's that?"* *"It's baseball,"* he answered. *"Three strikes and you're out."*

For that following Tuesday, I must have briefed ten or twelve cases. At the next class, right on cue was Dean Robinson's request, *"Burris..."* I did eight or nine cases that day; ten or twelve cases the next class. That pattern went on until our Thanksgiving break. The only student briefing cases in that classroom was me! I thought surely that wouldn't be the way things transpired *after* the Thanksgiving break; however, I prepared ten or twelve cases anyway. I settled into my desk that Tuesday that school resumed. Dean Robinson walked in and, *"Burris..."*

I kid you not, I briefed all the cases each class up until the Christmas break. I could not wait to hit the road out of town for a break from that class and law school in general. I hitched a ride with a guy in my class who lived in Chicago.

The Engagement

Driving through those mountains of West Virginia was no easy feat in the years before interstate highways were built. On top of that, my classmate's car had three flat tires at various points along the way. We experienced our first flat early into the trip and used the spare tire in the trunk. We then got stuck somewhere in West Virginia, due to another flat.

Managing to the best of our ability as two broke law students, we pooled our money and purchased a used, retread tire. We suffered our third flat tire in Toledo, Ohio, and were totally out of money. I called Berlean, who wired me thirty or forty dollars to buy another used tire. What would normally be a twelve-hour drive from Washington, D.C. to Chicago, took us around twenty-six hours to complete!

Even though I could count on Berlean to help me out in any fix, she had a vested interest in seeing to it that I reached Chicago safely that winter break. Several months earlier after returning from Germany and before heading off to Howard, I made an important promise to her. We were sitting on her sister's porch back in August talking, when I envisioned her in a way I had never done before. Many times, I would pose the question in my mind, *"Who will be the right woman to be my spouse?"*

After meeting Berlean, I had dated other women, here and there, both in the states and in Germany, but each time that question would cross my mind, the only name that came in response to my question was, *"Berlean."*

So, perched on that porch on that warm summer day, I looked into her eyes and said, *"Now, I'm going to law school, but when I graduate I'm going to marry you."*

I know it wasn't the most romantic proposal, but Berlean appreciated it just fine. She was happy so that's all that mattered. My family was happy, too, when they found out. I called my father and told him I was going to get engaged during Christmas break and would need money to buy a ring. He obliged.

My parents arranged an engagement party to take place in Centralia during Christmas break. I told Berlean we would officially get engaged then. First, she had to help me past those flat tires that threatened to keep me from getting back home to her. Finally, we met in Chicago and drove

117

to Centralia where we celebrated our engagement.

A Marathon Exam

When my second semester began in January, grades were posted. Even though I hadn't taken any tests yet in Torts class, I also had four other courses to pass. I did okay with all my grades. Sadly, however, about seven of my classmates had failed that first semester of law school. We began our second semester with only fifty-two students. Also, as the semester got underway, it seemed like the young ladies came out of the woodwork. They came at me from this way and that way. Being engaged, I tried to be as honest and forthright as I possibly could be; however, there was one particular young lady who just refused to be turned away by my honesty. The situation created by the persistence of that young lady grew to be such a problem that Berlean and I temporarily broke off our engagement. In the end, however, Berlean and I worked everything out. I convinced Berlean that we shouldn't wait until I finished school to get married, but instead should get married at Christmastime, during my second year of law school.

As if my love life wasn't a big enough problem to handle, I still had that Torts class. We had the same book and everything. Dean Robinson started the class off in the same manner as well, *"Burris give the first case."*

I briefed at least ten cases. That went on for the entire month of January! I guess my classmates settled on the fact that I would be the only one called on to recite in class, because they stopped briefing their cases.

One day in February, Dean Robinson came in, looked around and called on Smitty. He didn't call on me.

When it turned out that Smitty had not prepared a case, he called on a couple of my other classmates. Again, no one had any cases briefed, so he came back to me, and I did a few cases. In the following class, he started with someone else, and they presented three or four good cases, but he eventually got back to me. Finally in February, he stopped calling on me altogether, except on a few occasions. In June of 1961, we had our Torts final exam.

Dean Robinson walked into the room at 8:45am for the 9:00am exam start time. He began talking about how when he was in law school, he had a professor who gave a final that lasted all day long. He went on and on about his experience. We listened, but I don't think any of us sitting there really took into account what he said, as our minds flooded with built-up anxiety over the prospect of our own final exam. Dean Robinson finally stopped reminiscing and scooped up an armful of blank bluebooks. *"Okay, I'm going to pass out the blue books. Make sure you write so that it can be read, because if I can't read it, I can't grade it."* Next, he passed out the questions. There were only four questions on the entire exam. Not bad, right? Wrong! Each question had a long list of sub-topics under it, each of which had to be addressed separately. I am not exaggerating when I tell you that those sub-topics went from about A to W on the first question; from double A to double N on the second question and so forth.

It suddenly sunk in why Dean Robinson told us about his own final exam taking all day to complete! We started writing about 9:15am. Dean Robinson herded us to lunch at 1:30pm. I don't think anyone had even gotten through the first question before lunchtime. Digesting my food proved no easy task, as we all ate solemnly before being ushered back to the classroom at 2:00pm. Smitty was the first one to leave the exam room at 4:30pm. I left at 9:30pm. The last person left shortly after midnight. I had never seen so many blue books stacked on everyone's desks in my life! I tried to answer every question in that twelve-hour period, which required about ten blue books to accomplish.

One of the questions had to do with a train wreck where a spark ignited the oil which leaked from the train and started a fire, eventually spreading to the nearby woodshed. We had to apply tort theory in determining the approximate cause and other legal distinctions that had to be made in the case. Definitely, this was the most grueling class and exam I ever experienced! As I recall, of one hundred possible points, I got a score of eighty-two or eighty-four. I received a B in that class, which was one of the highest grades given.

A classmate named Earl White, who was the number one guy in our graduating class, earned a grade somewhere in the low nineties on that final exam and as a class grade. Not only did Smitty drop out of law school that year, but we lost about twelve more classmates as well. As freshmen, we started with fifty-nine students. After first semester and second semester eliminations, we started our sophomore year the following Fall with approximately forty of our original classmates.

The Smart Order Picker

Prior to starting my second year of law school in September of 1961, I worked in Chicago during the summer. I had a tremendously difficult time finding a short-term job before finally landing one at a wholesale bookstore. It seemed that no one wanted to hire short-term workers, especially not a law student. They knew it would mean that the company's training time and money would be wasted since a student-employee would be likely to leave as soon as his classes resumed. In order for them to hire me, I actually had to stretch the truth a bit to make them think I was considering not returning to school.

My main duty at the wholesale company was to pack the boxes with books being shipped to retail stores. One of my co-workers was an older German immigrant, with whom I would converse in German. I told no one that I had spent a year of study in Germany—that would have been another point against the likelihood of my getting the job. The German guy was shocked that I could speak his language, but apparently enjoyed our conversations just the same.

In my department, we were called order-pickers. Almost all of the order pickers were black. Most of the order-pickers couldn't read the book titles, a fact which caused them to be very slow in filling the orders. I, on the other hand, pulled the books and filled the orders within minutes. The people in the front office were puzzled and felt threatened by my unusual proficiency, because they couldn't figure me out. *"Who is this guy?"* My boss called me into the office one day and began telling me things like, *"You've got a future career here."* As pleased as I was that he was happy with my work, I hoped that my future would be based more on my successful completion of my degree than on moving up in his company, however, all I could do at the time was to go along with him, because I needed that job. I also needed to get back to law school, which I did at the end of the summer.

Wedding Bells a-Ringin'

Starting my second year at Howard, I still held the position of assistant dormitory director, but I was assigned to Cook Hall instead of Carver Hall. Soon, though, being assigned to any dorm would pose a problem, as I would be married after Christmas break and not be allowed to live in the dorms. With the help of a classmate of mine, Earl McCaskell, I solved my dilemma, at least partially. Earl worked in the administration building with Dean Kerry, the Dean of Men in the Howard undergraduate school. Since Earl was single, he and I swapped positions, so that he could live at Cook Hall as an assistant dormitory director. I then took his position as graduate assistant to Dean Kerry. With that swap, even though I had to find a place off campus to live, I could still keep my one hundred dollars monthly stipend.

I went home during that Christmas break of 1961 and got married. Because she was already working, Berlean bought our rings. Our wedding took place on December 23rd in a small ceremony performed by Reverend A. P. Jackson in his study at the Liberty Baptist Church at 49th Street and South Park Ave (currently Dr. Martin Luther King Blvd) on Chicago's South Side. Berlean had started visiting that church when she was a student nurse, because it was close to Provident Hospital. We were both Baptists, which helped a great deal in our relationship.

The weather turned ugly in Chicago that day, dumping about twelve inches of fresh snow on the ground. That caused my parents and a few friends of mine as well, to have to cancel their trip up from Centralia to attend our wedding. The only friend of mine who made it was my best man, Lonnie O'Neal. Two of Berlean's sisters, Nellie Miller and Susan Miller Peacock, and her sister's husband, Cleo Peacock were there as well. I was disappointed that my parents couldn't make it; nonetheless, it was a great day. Lonnie and I looked real dapper in our tuxedoes and Berlean looked beautiful in her wedding gown. After exchanging vows, we drove to her sister's home, where we all enjoyed cake and ice cream and posed for pictures. As I look back now from this present vantage point in time, it is really difficult to imagine that all of this that took place only fifty years ago.

After spending the night in Chicago, we headed to Centralia the next day to spend Christmas with my family. We traveled in Berlean's new car—a very attractive 1960 white Thunderbird. She worked as a nurse at the University of Chicago Hospital, and that car was a product of her astuteness with her finances.

We had a joyous first Christmas as husband and wife. Mom fixed a huge, delicious Christmas dinner. Lots of family and friends came over to meet my new wife. After spending a few more days in Centralia, we drove back to Chicago where we stayed until just before New Year's Eve. In the comfort of our brand new car, we drove back to D.C. for the second semester of my second year in law school. Thank God, there was no worry of car trouble or flat tires on that road trip.

I Don't Cook, But I Will Do Laundry

It was New Year's Day, 1962, when we arrived back in D.C. with no place yet to live. A hotel room for the next ten days had to suffice. Within that time, we found an upstairs, one-bedroom, one-bath apartment at 1500 Monroe Street, NW. The landlady had furnished it as well, making it even more ideal for us, since we owned no furniture whatsoever.

I really buckled down that entire second year, as the complexity of courses magnified. However, as mindful as I stayed regarding my studies, I was that much more mindful of our money situation. I knew that the one hundred dollar monthly stipend I received working as a graduate assistant would not be enough to pay for things such as the electric bill, telephone bill and groceries. Therefore, Berlean needed to find employment. Since Berlean had completed her training and certification and had some experience in nursing, we knew it wouldn't take long for her to find a job.

As soon as we got settled into our apartment, Berlean began calling around setting up interviews. One friendly lady she spoke with at Doctor's Hospital told her they had openings for nurses and invited her in for an interview. I drove Berlean there and waited for her in the lobby. While watching the people come and go, I didn't see one single black person anywhere. A janitor came by to clean out the ashtrays and even *he* was white! Right then I said to myself, *"Hmm, something's wrong here; this doesn't look right."* Shortly after that, my wife approached me looking rather sad. She lamented, *"Honey, all of a sudden they don't have any jobs."* I tried to sound surprised, but I had already deduced as much by watching the people in the lobby, *"You're kidding!"* She replied, *"No, the lady said she would take my application and call me if there was an opening."*

I empathized with my wife, *"Well, you know Honey, it's not you. They just ain't hiring blacks. If they won't hire a black janitor, then they sure as heck won't hire any black nurses in this hospital."*

Berlean filled out an application at Freedmen's Hospital on my campus (currently named Howard University Hospital).[liii] Within a few days, she had interviewed, was hired, completed her orientation and began working fulltime as a nurse.

While living in the hotel, we ate out at restaurants a lot. When we finally moved into the apartment, we grocery shopped and ate things like lunchmeat and snack items purchased here and there, but that time we bought *real* food. I could hardly wait for the nice, big meal I was about to experience. That little "dream bubble" all too soon burst, when my beautiful new wife said, *"Well, honey, you've got to fix us some dinner."*

I halfway thought she was kidding, so I shot back, *"Fix dinner? Me? Oh no, no, you've got to fix dinner."*

She said, *"I don't know how to cook."*

"What?" I said, noticing that she wasn't kidding. *"Well, I don't know how to cook either."*

Can you believe that? In all our talking about love, the future and such, we never thought to talk about cooking! We laughed and joked about it for a little while, but then it got kind of serious. The first few times we worked together in the kitchen, we ended up with dishes like fried bologna or boiled pork and beans and hot dogs, but we both realized this just wasn't going to cut it. I needed some real food, and I delicately mentioned that fact to Berlean one day. So she said, *"Well, you've got to get some cookbooks and learn how to cook."* I said, *"I'm studying."* She said, *"Well, I'm working."*

I told Berlean I had never before cooked a dinner meal in my life. I was always busy and my mother and sister always cooked, so it was never required of me. Besides, in most households in those days, including mine, the men just didn't cook. I wouldn't know the first thing about *planning* a meal, either. After that conversation, the atmosphere in our apartment became pretty contentious and continued that way for about a week.

As soon as our telephone was installed, Berlean called my mother to confirm what I said about never having cooked a dinner meal. My mother never told Berlean specifically that I couldn't cook, but she certainly got a little upset over our arguing about the topic. In fact, Mom made my new bride feel so bad that Berlean knew not to bring up that subject ever again. I can still hear her authoritative voice saying, *"Now, you two young kids, you're a wonderful couple, just get along!"*

Nevertheless, being the dutiful wife that Berlean is, she got a cookbook and started reading and preparing good meals. One Sunday just recently, after enjoying a great home-cooked family dinner, I complimented her. I said, *"I don't know how you do it, Honey. After almost fifty years, I still haven't cooked a single dinner."*

Along with cooking, my wife fixed up our apartment pretty nicely with accessories. We went to Sears for drapes. Berlean has excellent taste: classic in style, but not overly expensive in price. Her sense of taste has always been perfect, even to this day. I was appreciative of the way she wanted our place to be "home," so I felt the least I could do was to help carry the load. And that I did, both figuratively and literally.

I bought the groceries and carried them up to our apartment. I also carried the laundry to and from the Laundromat. One day, three or four young kids, who lived across the street, were hanging around outside our building as I headed to the Laundromat, which was a block away on Fourteenth Street. As I approached those kids, one said, *"Oh, there goes Mr. Henpeck. Hello Mr. Henpeck."* I instantly snapped, *"Who are you talking to?"*

They turned to each other and started laughing. Apparently, they had heard their parents talking about me doing chores stereotyped as "women's work." As you know, in those days a man generally did not do household chores, lest he risked being called henpecked. I didn't let their jeering bother me and chalked it up to the fact that their parents had very sexist views of the duties of husband and wife. My wife, however, tells a totally different story and says that I *did* let that comment affect me and thereafter refused to do the laundry any more until we lived in Chicago and had a washer and dryer in our home.

Berlean and I had a great system going. She worked at the hospital from 11:00pm until 7:00am. After I dropped her off at work in the evening, I came back home and held a late night law study group at our kitchen table with guys like Schuman, Davis, McCaskell and a couple of others until 1:00am or 2:00am. After a brief night's sleep, I would pick Berlean up at 7:00am, and she would drop me off at school before driving herself home. I would get home from school in the evening, and we would spend a little time together before she went to work. We operated very successfully like that for the next year and a half.

I wrapped up my second year in law school with a multitude of great experiences. Some of those experiences were quite controversial, especially those issues surrounding the Civil Rights Movement. Things were really heating up; kids were protesting almost all the time about almost everything. One of the protests during my second year evolved when students found out that some students received scholarships under an unfair scholarship distribution system. The students called for a strike on the law school, and they went after Dean Robinson. I remember how we had the faculty of the law school sitting in the jury box. The dean was trying to preside over the meeting to actually determine what was fair and was not.

Not only were scholarships scrutinized, but who was eligible or not eligible for financial assistance was questioned as well. Students even began ranting about the conditions in the law school. In the end, I do not recall that anyone was punished for these protests, but those were truly some turbulent times!

Hanging Out at the White House

In the summer of 1962, with President John F. Kennedy in office, opportunities opened up for summer interns at various federal government agencies, including the White House. Lo and behold, I was selected as a White House intern. From June through September, I worked in the executive office building for the Office of Emergency Planning. The internship program was headed up by Attorney General Robert Kennedy. There were seven of us summer interns under his direction. He met with us as a group at least every other week to check on our progress.

I reported directly to John E. Cosgrove, Director of the Office of Emergency Planning. He was a fair-minded individual and over the course of the summer, became very supportive of me. Some of his department's responsibilities resembled that of FEMA in regards to floods and fires; however, during the time I worked there, the major concern was preparing for a nuclear attack on the nation with an emphasis on Washington, D.C. Those preparations took place just prior to the Cuban Missile Crisis,[liv] an event that took place in October of 1962 with the confrontation between the Soviet Union and Cuba on the one hand and the United States on the other.

I did a lot of the leg work for a group called the Executive Reserve.[lv] The Executive Reserves were the people poised to replace government officials if those officials were killed during an attack. They dealt with issues like how to keep the government going; planning access routes; securing locations to be used, etc. Because their work was so highly classified, I had top-secret security clearance. I also couldn't talk about any of my work with anyone outside of the job. I recall being in a meeting as a staff person in the executive office building where there must have been fifty or so top executive reserves who were being briefed by Director Cosgrove. A tremendous amount of planning took place. Towards the end of the meeting, Director Cosgrove introduced me as a summer intern and asked if I had any comments. Well, I had been listening intently to one particular topic they covered about the evacuation of D.C., the evacuation routes and the monitors who would cover those routes. That discussion had struck a chord with me, so it was amazing I was given an opportunity to comment on it.

I accepted his offer by stating, *"Mr. Cosgrove, I don't want to be presumptuous, but I've been listening to this and my assessment is that if there is a nuclear attack and you've got these evacuation routes for our top government officials, it's not going to work."*

At that point, total silence fell over the room. After all, they had done so much intense, meticulous planning and then a summer intern comes along and pokes holes in their plan? One would've expected me to be given a kind nod and asked to be seated. Instead, Director Cosgrove urged me on.

"What do you mean, Roland?"

I explained, *"Well, number one, I don't think the monitors are going to be at their stations. They're going to be trying to save themselves. They're not going to be trying to clear a way for these people to get out of Washington."*

"You don't think so?"

"I don't know, but I can see them doing more self-preservation than otherwise."

I may not have the exact words of our dialogue as it was, but that is a fairly accurate assessment. The fact that Director Cosgrove then looked out on those men and asked them what they thought about my comment spoke volumes about his character. The majority of those men nodded their heads in agreement that I may have been on to something. One person even said that the entire program might need to be rethought. It has always been my nature to speak up. Director Cosgrove appreciated it.

Even so, after I spoke in that meeting, in some part of my mind, I tried to convince myself that by daring to speak my opinion, I had done something wrong, that I had put my foot in my mouth or had simply talked too much. Director Cosgrove's response assured me that I had not. Also during my summer internship, Ted Kennedy was preparing to run for the United States Senate from the state of Massachusetts; a seat that he did win that November.

Definitely one of the greatest highlights for me that summer was sitting in a meeting where all three Kennedy brothers were present: the President, Bobby, and Teddy. As a young man with sights on becoming an elected official, I was indelibly moved by that experience.

The Final Go-Round

By my senior year, our original count of fifty-nine freshmen classmates dwindled down to about twenty-five individuals. Some had dropped out or transferred to other schools, others had failed. I ran for class president and was elected. My study group friends, Jerome Schuman, Ray Davis and Earl McCaskill served as my campaign team and proved to be a pretty good team at that.

That last semester of that final year was a busy one. On top of our classes and finals, we conducted job searches and attended to preparations for the graduation ceremony. I also found that the burden of job searching is usually lightened when you have built a great network of people. Just as I had formed many special bonds at Southern Illinois University, I had also formed many lasting bonds at Howard.

For years to come, many of those people played important roles in my life, far beyond what I could ever have envisioned at the time I met them at Howard. Although there are far too many names for me to mention here, I will be identifying and recognizing quite a few of them throughout the remainder of these pages, as I share some of the events which took place during my many years in politics.

When I look back at my successes, I see that usually they were a by-product of the excellent network of people with whom I was very closely associated, including five years of Howard classmates: two classes ahead of me and two classes behind me. For example, Bernard Ash was already a third-year law student when I was just in my first year. He became a terrific mentor to me. His leadership and friendship got me through a lot of difficult days in my first year at Howard. Today, Bernard and I are still in regular contact with each other.

During my second year of law school, I met another life-long friend, a young man from Atlanta, Georgia, named Ben Brown, who was in his first year. About fifteen or so years after law school, Ben and I created an organization that we named the National Alliance of Black Leaders. Ben was not only influential in helping to secure my appointment as an at-large member of the Democratic National Committee in 1980, but also encouraged me to run for one of the organization's vice-chair positions in 1981.

D.C. vs. Chicago

In my last semester, I applied for and received a job offer from the National Labor Relations Board in D.C., with a starting salary of approximately $5,400 a year. I did not accept this offer. Instead, there was an opening for a federal estate tax examiner with the Internal Revenue Service in Chicago that caught my attention, so I applied for that. My wife and I felt there was too much "government" for our taste in D.C., so we planned to head back home right after graduation.

I graduated on June 7, 1963. Dad traveled to D.C. to attend my graduation ceremony. My mother had just visited me in my last semester with my brother's daughter, Kim Burris Holmes, and my sister's son, Felix Giboney III, giving them a unique educational trip during their spring break, so she couldn't afford to come back so soon. As proud as my father was of me for graduating; however, he also berated me for not taking that labor relations job. He figured somebody being offered a position making $5,400 a year should be thankful and take it no matter what.

At the most, Dad probably made only $2,000 or $3,000 a year, and those earnings represented all the money in the world to him. He couldn't understand why I didn't think the same way. The way he saw it, the labor relations job was a definite means for supporting my family, and he felt strongly that I should have respected that. *"No, Dad, I don't*

128

want that job because I want to go back to Chicago," is all I kept saying to him.

In my heart, I knew I wanted to get my political career going. I also knew that Chicago was the ideal place for me to launch that career. It would just be a matter of time, that part was the only uncertainty. So, the day after my graduation from Howard Law School, Berlean and I packed up our belongings. Within a few more days, we had left that furnished apartment in D.C. behind us and made the twelve to fourteen-hour trek back to Chicago, where we belonged. It felt so surreal to be able to finally say I had graduated from Howard University School of Law! It was also a little sad, though, considering that of our original fifty-nine classmates who started out with me in law school, only twenty-two had stood there—donned in cap and gown amidst the strains of Pomp and Circumstance[lvi]—at our graduation. Actually, a total of twenty-five of us received our diplomas that day; the three additional graduates were holdovers from previous classes. Over the many years since that day, death has taken its toll on our alumni. Today, as of this writing, there are perhaps only eight or nine of us still alive.

Chapter Seven
Corporate Rise and Community Ties

Settling In

I n June of 1963, my wife, Berlean, and I were very excited about moving back home to Chicago. As the sun drove away the winter chill, warming everything in sight, diehard Chicagoans, along with the marigolds and daffodils that garnished their neatly edged lawns, emerged unscathed from the horrid winter. Earlier in the year while still in D.C., we kept hearing how cold it was back in Chicago and how the temperature had reached record lows. Even that didn't deter us from wanting to be in Chicago; neither did the city's tumultuous times brought about by war across the seas and the unjust treatment of black people right in our own backyard. On a lighter side, the music of that era, which ranged from the Beatles to Little Stevie Wonder on his harmonica helped to keep our minds momentarily off the ubiquitous events of those wars, political unrest, job and housing discrimination, Civil Rights protests and KKK assassinations.

Housing discrimination ran rampant in Chicago in those days, so we had our work cut out for us. When we arrived in Chicago, we stayed with Berlean's sister and brother-in-law for a short time before beginning our search to find our own place. We felt very welcome in their home, which was nestled in a "safe" neighborhood, meaning that it was

100% black populated. However, as we began our search for a furnished apartment, both in the classified ads and posted in windows, we encountered a reoccurring message: *"Whites only. Negroes Need Not Apply."*

Facing that type of treatment was especially difficult after experiencing firsthand the positive effects of a passionate Civil Rights Movement that had been taking place in D.C. Coming home to such restrictions made me think that the strong voices of civil rights hadn't yet reached the ears of black Chicagoans, that is, not until later in the 60's when a noticeable shift in Chicago's demographics took place. The large movement of black Chicagoans from a black area of the city to a previously white area was called "black migration," or the "black spread." [lvii] An influx of black families left the confines of their urban housing projects in exchange for ownership in the outlying Chicago neighborhoods previously dominated by whites. The more this movement occurred, the more frightened some white homeowners became. Rumors of blacks seizing new residential territory were perpetuated by white realtors, with the predictable result of spreading fear among white homeowners like wildfire. *"The blacks are coming! The blacks are coming!"*

With that foreboding cry, many white homeowners panicked. Some sold quickly to the black families and fled further out to the suburbs, and by doing so, created a term called "white flight." Other white homeowners relentlessly stood their ground and defended their space with whatever it took: violence, intimidation, or legal tactics.

Burning crosses appeared in the front yards of some new black families, as a clear message to the newcomers that they were anything but welcomed by their new neighbors. New property-selling restrictions were quickly adopted and put into effect in an attempt to combat the convergence of blacks and to slow down the "panic peddling," a term given to the practice of white homeowners hurriedly selling their homes in trepidation. [lviii]

Due to the "black spread" and the mass exodus of whites, every three or four years a new dividing line would emerge between the growing black community and those formerly all white Southside neighborhoods. Way back in the day, if one were to begin at Chicago's midpoint and head south, 63rd Street would have served as the invisible line beyond which blacks did not live. Then, slowly but surely, that line became 66th Street, 69th Street and then 71st Street. In the early '50s, when I stayed in

Chicago during my college summer breaks, I resided at 71st Street and St. Lawrence Avenue. Black homeowners were just crossing the prohibited 71st Street border to reside in the 72nd Street block. By the time my wife and I moved back from D.C., that dividing line had reached 79th Street.

So much hatred fueled the actions of white people in those neighborhoods. When realizing they couldn't keep black families out of their space, they made life a living hell for many of those black families who moved into formerly all-white communities. In fact, the home that Berlean and I currently reside in was previously owned by legendary gospel singer Mahalia Jackson. She bought it in 1958 from a white doctor. In a book that Ms. Jackson wrote, she tells how her windows were shot out when she moved into the home. Sadly, the atmosphere had not changed much between the time Mahalia Jackson brought her home and the time when Berlean and I were searching for housing in 1963.[lix]

Thankfully, Berlean and I settled into our own first home fairly quickly and without incident. We moved into a furnished apartment in Hyde Park; a few blocks from the University of Chicago Hospital where Berlean began working as a psychiatric nurse. While I focused on job hunting and studying for the bar exam, her paycheck temporarily covered our household necessities.

Before leaving D.C., I had applied for a federal estate tax examiner position at the IRS for the Chicago area. Soon after we arrived in Chicago, I went to the downtown office of the IRS with my completed papers, but when I got there, I was informed that due to new internal budget restrictions, the IRS had been forced to decrease the number of job vacancies from five to three. That left me, their fourth candidate, unemployed.

Shortly after settling into our apartment, Berlean sensed the need to take a pregnancy test. Her woman's intuition proved to be correct, and we began preparing for our first child. Soon thereafter, it appeared as though our guardian angels began preparing the extra space we would soon need, using a simple phone call to get the ball rolling. I was home one day studying for the bar when the telephone rang. When I answered the telephone, it was a real estate lady who, obviously, had dialed the wrong number. As I tried to inform the caller that she had the wrong number, my wife asked, *"Well, who is it?"* I cupped the receiver with my hand to respond, *"It's a wrong number. She's calling for someone about a house to sell."*

"She wants to sell a house? Tell her we need a house," whispered Berlean.

At my wife's request, I began querying the realtor, letting her know we were interested in purchasing a house. She happily promised to help us and called a couple of days later with what she described as the perfect home for us. I was quite hesitant to look at any houses considering the fact that I was jobless; however, the realization that we really did need more space for the baby drove me to proceed.

We met with the realtor, who turned out to be a very pleasant older white lady from Turnquist Realty. She drove us to a quaint two-bedroom bungalow at 7826 Eberhart Street on the South Side of Chicago. The home was nice, and my wife simply loved it. One big problem, however, was the fact that it cost $15,000; we barely had five hundred dollars. Within a few days, though, we managed to scrape up about $1,500, still a far cry from the $3,000 required down payment. That's when we headed to the Chicago City National Bank at 63rd and Halsted Streets to apply for a homeowner's loan. As Berlean and I sat in front of the loan officer, he pulled out a long, blank form and began filling in our names and address.

Then he asked, *"Who's your employer?"*

"I don't have one right now," I responded, *"but my wife has a job."*

"Well, we don't count the wife's income."

"What do you mean you don't count her income? She can make the mortgage payment."

He shook his head and reiterated, *"No, YOU'VE got to have a job."* I looked him square in the eyes, as I spoke with all sincerity, *"Look, I'm a law school graduate. That should tell you a lot about my potential."* That officer smirked as he answered in the most demeaning manner, *"Sir, we don't make loans based on potential."*

I wanted to reach across that desk and punch him! My wife and I still laugh about that today, although it was anything but funny back then. Back then, it was downright discouraging, knowing I had so much potential on the inside, but I could not yet monetize that potential.

Discouraging or not, I had to persevere; we had a house to buy. Putting that incident behind us, we went to the Hyde Park Savings and Loan

Association which the realtor had recommended to us. She even accompanied us when we completed our application. When we arrived at the Hyde Park Savings and Loan Association, our realtor introduced us to the loan officer, a black lady vice president by the name of Mrs. Wilma Sutton, and briefly shared our dilemma with her. With that, the loan officer began the paperwork. Even though things progressed a lot smoother there at the Hyde Park S & L, we still didn't qualify for a loan. That is, not until that sweet realtor put up $1,000 of her own commission as collateral! We could not believe she did that. We expressed our gratitude over and over to her, as we signed the contract on that two-bedroom bungalow in November of 1963.

The following month, we moved into our new place. It was a fairly easy move, since all we had were books and clothes. Soon thereafter, Berlean made sure we had furniture. Of course, not just *any* furniture would do for my wife. No, it had to be the best quality for the best price. In fact, if you come into our living room today (in 2014), you will see the same sofa and a couple of barrel chairs that we purchased back in 1963! Their longevity attests to the extremely high quality of the items that Berlean selected for our home. I've always admired my wife for being savvy with finance that way.

<u>100 Years in the Making</u>

One of the other jobs I had applied for while in D.C. was with the Office of the Comptroller of the Currency (OCC), which is part of the U.S. Treasury Department. The OCC was established in 1863 to regulate and supervise all national banks and their federal branches. The OCC ensures that these entities remain in compliance with the laws concerning their customers' deposits and assets.[ix]

I had actually almost forgotten that I had applied for that job until one day in the second week of July while I studied at home for the bar, the telephone rang. The person on the other end of the line said, *"We're calling from Washington, D.C., from the Comptroller of the Currency. You applied for a job. Would you be . . .?"*

"Yes!" I didn't even let the man finish his sentence.

He started his sentence over, *"Would you be interested in becoming a bank examiner for the trust department of the Office of the Comptroller of the Currency?"*

134

"Yes, yes, I would!" I could barely believe my ears as I accepted the job offer.

The conversation lasted for about ten minutes more, as I gathered all the details pertaining to the paperwork to be filled out. Several days later, my packet of information arrived in the mail. I completed the appropriate forms and took them downtown to the comptroller's office in the Federal Reserve Building on LaSalle Street in Chicago. Finally, I was hired! I started working on my birthday, August 3rd, when I went in for training at the Chicago office. I later discovered that I was the first black examiner hired in OCC's one-hundred-year history.[lxi]

I spent the first two weeks training and meeting the other examiners. Finally, they presented me with my briefcase, credentials, and some paraphernalia used by the examiners. At that time, I also received my first bank assignment: the Livestock National Bank on 43rd and Halsted Streets. It was customary when we examined a bank, not to inform the bank personnel that we were coming. That was certainly the case my first day on the job at Livestock National. I was supposed to report to the bank when they opened at 8:30am, but I got there about fifteen minutes early. The bank's huge glass door was locked, so I knocked on it since I could see some people bustling around inside. A guard came to the door and said, *"We're not open."*

I quickly responded with, *"I know,"* as I pressed my bank examiner's credentials against the glass. The guard squinted to read the small print on the paper. *"Hold on,"* he said sauntering off to an office in the back of the bank. The security guard returned to the door with the vice president in tow. Once again, I held up my credentials for them to see. They both read them and then looked at each other as if simultaneously thinking, *"Maybe we ought to let this guy in."* The door was unlocked. The vice president ushered me into the bank's small lobby and pointed to a chair. *"Young man, you sit right here until the other examiners come."*

Now, at that time, I was not so naïve that I missed what was going on. After all, that *was* the South Side of Chicago; that *was* near the stockyards; that *was* ultra conservative territory back in 1963. Most particularly, the personnel at the bank had never ever known a bank examiner to be black; therefore, to them I must've been a trainee or someone in an "observing only" position. However, because it was my first day on my first job, I really didn't know if I was being treated unjustly or if it was just procedural not to be allowed access to the files until the other examiners arrived. I sat there waiting powerlessly until the other examiners came, at which time we all were ushered into the office to begin our work.

Later, I happened to mention that incident to the head examiner, Mr. Lighter, when sharing how my first day went. Lighter was a forty-year veteran of the OCC force. I didn't tell him how I was treated with the thought, and certainly with the intention, that he would *do* anything about it. I guess I figured that after being around that many years, he'd seen it all and learned to turn his head to a lot of things. On the contrary, Mr. Lighter did not ignore the incident. After turning beet red from embarrassment while listening to me recount the incident, he immediately contacted the vice president of the Livestock Bank, whom he soundly chewed out for what he considered disrespect to my position.

Examining

I enjoyed my job as a bank examiner. I was thrilled about earning $6,000 per year. I wasn't thrilled, though, about the traveling part of the job. I examined banks all over the Midwest, going to cities like Peoria, Indianapolis, and Detroit. Typically, I would be gone all week, come home on a Friday night, and then leave again on Sunday afternoon. Having only one full day at home each week hardly constituted the proper conditions for studying for the bar, especially when that 24-hr time period had to be shared with a wife, a new home and a baby on the way. Even though I sensed that I hadn't properly studied for the bar exam, either while on the road or while at home, I sat for the exam anyway in August of 1963.

I wasn't really surprised when I didn't pass the bar. Deflated, yes; but surprised, no. I remember thinking that at least I was still a bank examiner. You don't have to pass the bar to have an examiner's job; and what a job it was. In one short year, I acquired many interesting stories! There was one bank I examined in Detroit that held a famous family account. The first time I verified the assets and trust funds of this family, I came across a thin envelope. I opened it and discovered fourteen government bonds worth one million dollars each, with a twenty-thousand dollar coupon attached to each bond. Those coupons are negotiable currency just like dollar bills. We had to verify that all fourteen were there and that all the coupons were still attached.

Over time, large dollar amounts passing through my fingers became routine, but seeing fourteen million dollars at one time like that really caught me off guard. My eyes got wide as I thought, *"Hmmm, some people really got it!"* Right after that, I began reading about banking and the stock market to learn all that I could about finance. I figured I needed to know as much as possible anyway about managing large funds, since I was planning on going into politics. In undergraduate school, I took a course in accounting for non-accounting majors. In law school, I took a course in legal accounting. Those two courses constituted the sum total of the financial exposure I had prior to the invaluable "hands-on" education I received through my examiner job; however, I had a growing desire to learn even more about banking and finance.

As an examiner, I traveled 75% of the time. After our daughter, Rolanda, was born in March of 1964, it became inevitable I leave my examiner's job and find employment, which would allow me to work a more normal schedule. Leaving Berlean alone at home from Sunday through Friday to care for our baby, manage her own work schedule, and deal with babysitting issues, just wasn't fair. Therefore, I left my examiner job after a year, but as I said, not before acquiring a lot of interesting experiences.

I remember a little incident which occurred on the road, while I was returning from examining the NBD Bank in Detroit with a fellow examiner and friend of mine, Ed Schneckenbeck, a lawyer who joined OCC shortly after me, which meant we were the two newest examiners on the force. The normal drive time between Detroit and Chicago was just under five hours. Ed and I rode together in my wife's 1960 Thunderbird, which had some serious get up and go, registering up to 140 mph on the speedometer.

At the end of a long, tiring week in Detroit, we were on I-94 heading home Friday evening when I put out the challenge, *"Ed, we're going to get to Chicago in four hours."* Ed egged me on, *"Let's do it, Roland!"*

So we barreled down the toll road out of Michigan onto the Indiana toll road! I got my toll ticket, but I think I only slowed down to about 40 mph while snatching it! As soon as I got that ticket, I goosed it up a little bit and we zoomed up to about 80 mph in a couple of seconds flat! Just then, came that dreaded siren sound: *"Whoop, whoop, whoop..."*

We were pulled over by the Indiana state trooper! He got out of his car and swaggered on up to ours, gearing up for his rehearsed routine. *"Gentlemen, do y'all know how fast you were going?"* I said, *"Wel-l-l, not really."* He said, *"You only slowed down to pick up your ticket."* I thought maybe he would let us off with a lecture if I could get on his soft side. I said, *"Well, officer, you see it's Friday evening and we're trying to get home to our families. We've been working in Detroit..."*

Ed and I poured out this song and dance, and the trooper coldly said, *"That's not a good reason for speeding, sir. You gentlemen are going to have to confront the Justice of the Peace. I want y'all to follow me. You're going to park your car in the oasis over here. I'm going to write you out a ticket, and I'm going to take you to the Justice of the Peace over here in Portage, Indiana. We're going to see what he has to say about it."* I said, *"Look, we're federal bank examiners, we've never been in trouble before..."*

In the end, Ed and I succeeded in softening him up a little bit, because he reduced the speed on my ticket from where he clocked me at 80 or 85mph down to 70 or 75mph. We still, however, had to go before the Justice of the Peace (JP). In that little town of Portage, that JP's office was in the back of somebody's house! As we went around to the side entrance, it looked like the door to a garage.

The trooper knocked on the door in a rhythm that sounded like some kind of code. We all went in and this old gray-haired guy with a beard sat at his desk chewing tobacco. He starts off, *"Ah understand you two boys was speedin'..."*

"Well, sir, we were just trying to get home to Chicago after a long week of work in Detroit," Ed explained. *"Whadda you boys do?"* The JP inquired, boring a hole through us with his resolute stare. *"We're federal bank examiners,"* I answered as confidently as possible. *"Federal bank examiners? What's that?"* Ed looked at me—his face pinkish with fear—to see if I wanted to educate the man. I returned the glance, shaking uncontrollably with as much fear as Ed felt. We both realized that we were totally out of our element and were not exactly sure about how to proceed.

I instinctively decided to avoid the explanation and instead repeated, *"We were trying to get home. We had a rough week and we just wanted to get home to our families."*

"Well, when you're speedin' that fast you know you'll kill somebody and won't get home at all." He continued with a short lecture that ended with him naming our punishment. He reared back in his chair and said, *"Now, we're gonna have to fine you boys."*

"How much is the fine?"

"It's gonna be $102."

Our mouths dropped. We couldn't believe our ears. One hundred dollars in 1964 was a lot of money! *"We ain't got that kind of money on us,"* I appealed, *"but what we can do, we can give you a check to hold and bring the money back later."*

"No, if you can't pay the fine right now, you gotta go to jail."

I gasped, *"What? I've never been to jail in my life, sir! No, let's talk this over. We're certainly not criminals. We are federal employees. We're trying to do the people's work."*

By that time, I was pretty much begging! *"Lemme tell you somethin' boy, I locked up two preachers last night."*

Ed and I looked helplessly at each other. Even with our legal training, we didn't know what that man was capable of doing within his jurisdiction, and we weren't about to find out. We knew we had to keep pleading our case to get the heck out of there.

Finally, I said, "Look, sir, we're really not bad people. One of us can leave our license here," I continued to cop a plea with him, *"We will fill out an envelope and leave a license with you. When we get back home, on Saturday morning you'll have a special delivery of our fine coming back to you. Then you mail the license back. Can you buy that? Can you be that gracious?"* He spoke slowly and reluctantly, *"Y'all look like a couple of good honest boys. I think we can agree to that."*

By that time, sweat was running down my face! Ed's shirt was soaking wet. We sweated through that ordeal and got the heck out of there! As the trooper drove us back to our car, he marveled, *"Y'all are some pretty lucky fellows. That SOB has never done that for nobody."* I questioned, *"Well, why do you think he did?"* He said, *"Hmm, I don't know exactly, but y'all touched him when talking about helping the people."* He added, *"Plus, you're a black and a white person and you get along together."*

As I drove the speed limit the rest of the way to Chicago, I silently reflected on how Ed and I always supported each other. That day, it really benefited us in a big way since we believe that's what impressed that old JP the most. Nine hours after leaving Detroit, we arrived home. Now, that was a record-setting drive time!

Another time, I recall working at a bank when one of the trust account files came up missing. It was a modest million-dollar estate, but the file couldn't be found anywhere. We had been there all week. We had to go through the files and verify the assets against the cards they had on record. Those bank employees were all up in arms, nervous was an understatement!

The vice president in charge of the Trust department sweated bullets during our entire visit. He was convinced, and tried to convince us, that somebody must have stolen that file from him. We prepared to write him up. From there, we were required to bring in FBI agents. That kind of fraud warranted the whole nine yards.

We called old man Lighter, the head examiner, on the scene first before calling the FBI. He started querying the bank officers, *"Where did you have this file? In this file cabinet?"*

"Yes sir, that's the one," the vice president said, obviously fearing for his job. Lighter then asked, *"Anybody ever move that file cabinet?"*

"No, we haven't moved it."

It was a huge file cabinet so most likely it had been in that same place since they moved into the building. I'll never forget how I sat there listening to old man Lighter talk to the bank personnel in a very deliberate, wise manner. He sounded neither accusatory nor frazzled. Instead, he worked to put them at ease so that they could think logically through the whole process. Lighter suggested, *"Well, in my day, sometimes things got lost. Sometimes people put things on top of the cabinet and they would fall over the side."*

They got some janitors to move the file cabinet and lo and behold the million dollar estate's file had fallen behind the file cabinet! That put a halt to the fraud investigation, as well as to the high probability of some lost jobs. Those bank employees were greatly relieved, to say the least!

I must say, that over the years there have been several situations to which I've tried to apply the "old Lighter" style of wisdom. That is something that is taught in law school as well: applying your experiences from other situations to the experience you're currently dealing with when trying to solve a problem. In law school we were taught to be very thorough in thinking things through, because there are no two legal matters that are exactly the same.

During that year of traveling as an examiner, there was always some concern on the part of the older examiners about where I would stay. In some of the towns we visited, blacks weren't allowed to stay in the hotels. In spite of these local policies, however, I never had a problem when I showed up at a hotel in one of these towns.

Now, of course, there was hesitancy, but because I traveled with a white male, they always gave us a room. In other places, even though my staying in the hotel may not have been an issue, it was the fact that I was a black bank examiner that raised the eyebrows. In those places when I checked into the hotel and when it became known that I was a bank examiner, like Paul Revere riding through town warning of the eminent arrival of the British army, some of the hotel people morphed into veritable town criers. Instead of *"The British are coming!"* their cry was *"Hey, there's a black guy staying here, and he's a bank examiner. The examiners are coming!"*

No matter how many challenges I faced as a bank examiner, the rewarding lessons I learned and the positive experiences I gained outweighed all the negatives. Still, I felt content in giving it all up, as it was certainly time to move on. I began interviewing at banks and was soon hired. After serving out my two-week notice as an examiner, my first day as a banker was August 3, 1964, exactly one year to the day after I had started working for the Office of the Comptroller of the Currency.

I left OCC with a great reputation and in good standing. My partners threw me a farewell party after I conducted my last exam at the Marquette National Bank of the Upper Peninsula of Michigan. Ed and I then drove from Marquette, Michigan, down through Wisconsin and into Chicago for our final ride together.

Banking

Having the trust experience from examining banks presented a solid enough background for me to go into banking. While examining those banks' activities, we had to review trust agreements and verify assets. A lot of accounting knowledge was required in order to verify the assets. We had to make sure that the trust was being administered according to

141

the agreement and that the investments were being handled according to law. We had to examine personal trusts, testamentary trusts and various other types of trust documents. The accounts had to match exactly what was on the bank records. I applied to two top banks in Chicago: Continental Illinois National Bank and Trust Company (now Bank of America) and First National Bank of Chicago (now JP Morgan Chase). While at OCC, I had examined Continental for seven or eight weeks and First National for four or five weeks, which is why they became my first choices. First National called me in for an interview. When I expressed my interest in working in their trust department, they responded with, *"Well, we have to give you some tests first."* I thought to myself, *"Okay, any accounting type test should be okay, given the things I learned as an examiner."*

Little did I know it would not be that type of test at all! They sent me out to a psychological testing firm and had me figuratively trying to put a round peg in a square hole. I answered many crazy questions and passed without a problem.

Next, I interviewed with a human resources person, who looked at me and he said, *"Well, let me ask you, Mr. Burris, why aren't you clean shaved?"* I heard him clearly, but responded with, *"What?"* He repeated himself, *"Why aren't you clean shaved?"* Highly insulted, I knew what he was getting at but continued the charades anyway. *"What are you talking about, the moustache?"*

"Well," he chose his words carefully, *"We don't have any moustaches at the bank."*

"You don't?" I answered sarcastically, as I leaned closer to his desk, *"Well, how many black men do you have at the bank? In fact, how many black men do you know?"*

That man jumped back in his chair a bit and started stammering. *"Uh, what do you mean?"* I firmly stated, *"It's a cultural thing, sir. You look at three out of four black men and we have moustaches. It's a cultural thing. We have moustaches, but we ARE clean shaven."*

That didn't go over too well with him! Needless to say, the interview went downhill from there and I never heard back from them. Next, I interviewed with Continental. The human resources guy at Continental was a young man named Bob Ganchief. Bob and I later became personal friends. During my interview with him I asked if they did psychological testing. Bob answered, *"No, not that I know of."*

"Do you all require black men to be clean shaven?" I wanted to get it all out in the open right away.

"What are you talking about?" Bob looked totally confused by my off-the-wall question. I briefly explained to him my First National Bank experience (without mentioning their name) and he said he never heard of such a requirement. After one more interview with Continental, the bank made me an offer which I accepted. As I mentioned, my first day at the bank was Monday, August 3, 1964, which was a nice way for me to spend my birthday.

As a young man with my first in-office, nine-to-five job, walking into that bank building everyday gave me a great sense of pride. The bank's splendid 1920's classical architectural design, which boasted six massive Roman ionic columns on the outside of the entranceway and magnificent marble floors on the inside, instantly humbled each visitor and employee alike. As if mirroring its impressive architectural stature, Continental's operations as a unit bank with no branches in Illinois firmly held its own in the banking industry, until its eventual demise some years later. Over the next couple of decades, dating from the time I was hired, Continental grew to become the sixth-largest bank in the U.S. in assets and deposits. Continental also led the nation in commercial and industrial lending and had approximately $40 billion in assets by 1984.[lxii]

Once my paperwork was squared away, I went through initial training. Banks during that time seemed to hire a lot of post graduate students for entry level positions. Those employees worked by day and attended law school or pursued their MBA degrees by night. Their training program was generally geared for employees with the potential to become future bank officers. The major problem I encountered with Continental was that they *really* didn't know what to do with me. Even though I went through the same training designed for future officers, it was decided that since I had experience as a bank examiner, I would be placed in the bank's trust division.

I had been at the bank for three months; yet, they continued to send me from division to division to take part in different training programs. After the first month, I noticed that all the other trainees had been assigned to their permanent positions. Some went to estate administration; others went to personal trusts; still others went to investments and to other parts of the bank. On the other hand, I went nowhere! For a while, they kept me down in the training section. At one point, they sent me over to the commercial side of the bank to work for a short while. During that time, I was still trying to pass the bar. By this time, I had made two futile attempts to do so. Certainly, I could not entertain the notion that I could not pass the bar; so, instead I blamed my lack of success at passing the bar on the grueling traveling schedule I had been forced to maintain as a bank examiner. I guess I was afraid that unless I could identify some logical reason for not passing the bar, I would begin to second-guess the possibility of ever becoming a lawyer.

Once I started working at the bank, however, my daily routine proved more conducive to spending productive and uninterrupted hours in intensive study of Illinois law. I was even able to get a couple of those bar exam review courses under my belt. Finally, time for the bar rolled around and, although I shuddered at the prospect, I went in to attempt the exam for the third time. The only thing worse than *taking* the exam, was waiting on the exam results.

Finally in October, I was permanently assigned to the Trust Tax Division of the Trust Department, where the floors were tiled and the desks were a kind of industrial metal. That department prepared the income tax returns for trusts and estates and also completed federal estate tax and Illinois inheritance tax returns. In addition to myself, there were two other black gentlemen in that department. One was Cecil Butler, who was a lawyer, and the other was an accountant named Oscar Williams. As of this writing (2014), Cecil is still alive. Oscar is now deceased. Both of them had been hired earlier that year. In 1962, Continental Bank's first black employees were two light-complexioned female tellers who could pass for white. Both of them worked on the commercial side of the bank.

I also met another black guy on the commercial side of the bank, in the loan division where lending documents were processed. His name was Ron Greer. Ron was a graduate of the University of Illinois with a bachelor's degree in accounting. Ron had also acquired a master's degree, making him very well-qualified for most of the entry-level administrative positions at Continental. Yet, there he sat in the back room; not even making the loans, but simply pushing through the paperwork that processed the loans.

I realized very quickly there existed so many limits that were next to impossible to penetrate. One day, from my metal desk with the tile floor under my feet, I decided I had it with limits. I spoke aloud, *"Why would they assign me to the Trust Tax Division and not to the Estate Administration program to work with the officers, as they did for my fellow white trainees? Why did those trainees get the mahogany desks on carpeted floors, while I got the metal desk on a tiled floor?"*

Cecil, Oscar, Ron and I knew the answer without uttering a word: *"Race."* After all, it was 1964.

You Can Bank on Racism

It had taken Continental three months even to assign me to the Trust Tax Division. My first job there was stapling together computer-printed income tax returns. After a couple of weeks of that mundane work, I became concerned and complained to my boss, Bob Mullen. *"Look,"* I told him, *"I'm a lawyer. Why would I then be assigned to the Trust Tax Division stapling returns when the other white lawyers and law students were assigned to the Estates Administration Division?"*

Naturally, Mullen, who was a second vice president, couldn't give me a logical answer, because there wasn't one. In the chain of command, Mullen reported to William Funk, Vice President of Estate Administration. So, Mullen referred me and my questions to Mr. Funk. When he also proved unable to provide me with a response, Mr. Funk directed me to the Vice President of Human Resources.

I posed the same question: *"Why wouldn't I be assigned to the training program to learn to administer the estates like the others who were hired with me?"* I forget that man's name now, but I will never forget what he said as he looked me straight in the eyes, *"Now look, Roland, I didn't create racism in this society and I, as an individual, cannot change it. If you're going to make it in this bank, you're going to have to be ten times better than your white counterparts."*

Having been raised in a strict manner by my parents, and with the steadfast work ethics they bestowed upon me and my siblings, that HR man told me nothing that I hadn't already heard spoken by my father hundreds of times. Somehow, though, hearing this said right to my face by the very person I'm supposed to be ten times better than, caused my

145

sensitivity to rise. Add to that the other factors to the equation: it was the 60's; I was only twenty-seven-years-old with my whole career ahead of me; and there was a wife and baby at home depending on me. It seemed to me that the stakes against me were suddenly stacked a mile high. That reality awakened my cynicism and momentarily shattered all my youthful illusions of achieving great things. Those words rang in my head for the rest of that workday, *"If you're going to make it, you've got to be ten times better than your white counterparts."*

I went home that evening disturbed and discouraged. As I shared the turn of events with my wife, I started crying. My wife started crying because I was crying. Our baby started crying just because that's what babies do. There we stood as a snapshot of racism's sting, captured from the extremely harsh and unsympathetic collage of pre-civil rights America. After dinner, I continued to lament over what to do. Do I quit? Do I start a picket line at the bank? Do I get a brick and throw it through the window? Lord, what do I do? I prayed until I fell asleep. That night, like many other times, His succinct answer settled in my spirit. My answer from God emphasized what that vice president already told me, *"Roland, you MUST work hard to present yourself ten times better than your white counterparts."*

I arose the next morning with a smile on my face that stay planted there as I headed to work. Instead of picketing or throwing bricks, I arrived at the bank with a new attitude. Knowing that my personality would always challenge a system whenever I perceived it to be broken, I realized that I couldn't "right" that system until I had diligently worked in it and contributed to its success. Therefore, not only did I prepare the tax returns regularly assigned to me, but also the returns of departed co-workers that were also assigned to me. Soon, I progressed through the ranks from doing 941 and 1040 returns, to doing the federal estate taxes and Illinois inheritance tax returns. I also networked with lots of influential people inside the bank and within the community. I brought in a lot of new customers to Continental Bank.

I performed all the tax work on the Abe Saperstein estate. At the time, he was the deceased owner of the Harlem Globetrotters.[lxiii] I also had a major tax filing on the estate of one of the largest ranches in the United States. The owner was an eighty-eight-year-old lady who lived in a high-rise in downtown Chicago. She had inherited a ranch in Texas that was thousands of acres in size. Due to the prevailing racism of the times, I was not allowed to go down to Texas in person to look at the ranch's assets, including the land, the cattle and the other range animals, even though I had to depreciate them for tax purposes. I very skillfully handled all my accounts that I had been assigned. After three years, there was a vacancy in the bank's tax consultant position. It was a management level position to which was assigned responsibility for the bank's more complicated tax issues. The person who held that position was also responsible for teaching new employees how to prepare tax returns. Although I was next in line for that position, I wasn't confident that things would go in that direction.

Therefore, I approached Mr. Funk, Vice President of Estate Administration, to remind him of how qualified I was for the vacant position. I'll never know if what I said made a difference, but I was promoted. I'd like to believe that the promotion came strictly as a result of my strong work ethic and diligence.

In my new position, a trust officer named Jack Glazer sat behind me. Jack was an older white gentleman who recognized that he had reached his peak within the banking structure and wasn't going any higher. He was content with that; yet always encouraged *me* to go higher. He repeatedly said, *"Roland, if you want to make it in banking, you've got to get out of the trust side of the bank. You've got to get to the commercial side."*

"How the hell am I going to get to the commercial side of the bank? I asked myself. *I'm busting my butt now, teaching these tax classes, handling all the difficult tax issues and all the problems that come with it!"*

Continental Bank was growing by leaps and bounds during that time and so were my job responsibilities. With approximately four-thousand employees came a lot of turnovers, a lot of hiring and consequently a lot of tax training conducted by me. I couldn't complain, though, as I remembered my earlier challenges at the bank just trying to be recognized and promoted. Throughout my career, I had achieved both recognition and promotion.

In October of 1964, Berlean called me at work one day. We didn't have individual phones at our desks, so I had to go to the desk of Mr. Peterson, my supervisor, to retrieve her call. Berlean greeted me with,

"Honey, you got a thick envelope."
"I got what?"
"You got a thick envelope."
"Well, open it."
She did and within seconds exclaimed, *"You passed the bar!"* I let out a resounding *"YES!"* I pulled the receiver from my face for a moment and exclaimed to Mr. Peterson, *"I passed the bar! I passed the bar!"*

It felt great to have passed that exam, as I felt it would help establish myself more securely at the bank. I arrived home from work that evening and Berlean and I celebrated. I then prepared to head down to Springfield to acquire my license.

Cracks and Potholes

Early 1965, after settling at the bank as a tax consultant, I approached my wife regarding my becoming more active in the community so that I could pursue my political ambitions. *"Honey, I'm pretty content at the bank, but you know what I've got to do, right?"* She hesitated, probably afraid to learn the answer, but asked anyway, *"What's that?"* *"I've got to get involved in the community. Now that I'm a lawyer, my second goal is to be a statewide elected official in Illinois."* A nonchalant, *"Um-hmmm,"* was all she could muster.

To begin my journey into the community arena, I started joining organizations. I joined so many of them that sometimes it seemed like I spent as much time at meetings as I did at work. One of the first meetings I attended was held by the Jaycees.[lxiv] My co-worker, Oscar, had invited me to one of the meetings, and I soon joined. That group consisted of young men who performed a host of community projects.

The Jaycee work was intense. I ended up becoming vice president, then president of the South End Jaycees, a faltering chapter which I helped to bring back to life. It intrigued me that the Jaycees had chapters all over the state. What I didn't know was that most of the Jaycees in other parts of the state were Republicans, a fact which ended up working in my favor in later years.

Next, I joined one of the major mental health organizations in Illinois.[lxv] Since I lived in the Chatham neighborhood, I also joined the Chatham-Avalon Community Council. In those days, those neighborhood councils really kept up the neighborhoods they represented by aggressively tackling issues like zoning, building and infrastructure deterioration, empty buildings and other community concerns. Finding that there were other lawyers on the Chatham council, I soon became close friends with the majority of them. One lawyer I got to know was a Jewish gentleman named Herb Fisher. Herb, who lived right in the heart of the majority-black community, had passionately served that community for many years. Another lawyer, Bill Cousins, went on to become an alderman and later an appellate court judge. Other council members whose names I can remember include Milton Lamb and Washington Burney. I was the newest kid on the block.

At one of the council meetings, there were questions about all the potholes in the streets, cracks in the sidewalks and deteriorating curbs throughout the community. Since I had recently been elected Conservation Chairman, I was assigned the task of preparing and presenting a report about the condition of the streets, sidewalks, and curbs in the Chatham and Avalon communities.

I don't believe they knew what they were in for by giving me that assignment, because I intensely surveyed our community from 76th Street on the north to 87th Street on the south, and between State Street on the west and Cottage Grove Avenue on the east. I marked every single pothole found in the streets; noted every cracked up sidewalk; and documented every section of broken or deteriorated curb.

After about a month or so, I presented the thick report at a council meeting and the members of the council looked at me like I was crazy.

"What in the world is this?" they inquired.

To one of the council members I said, *"Well, right in front of your house at 77th and Rhodes there's really a bad section of sidewalk."*

To another I pointed out, *"Near your house over on 87th and Langley there are several potholes."*

To a third council member I said, *"You've got a curb that's just deteriorating at 8229 Langley."*

I had all their addresses and told them what needed fixing on their blocks. They sat there with their mouths wide open as if to say, *"My God, what have we got here?"*

The president of the council decided that the city needed to take notice. He ordered, *"We need to get this report to city hall, because nobody has ever done anything like this before."*

After several phone calls to city hall and a brief wait, our council President Bill Cousins was granted an appointment with Mayor Richard J. Daley to present our report. I was invited to tag along as well. In fact, that report put me in good standing with the council members, who, from that point on, considered me a detail-oriented person who was unafraid of taking on any assignment.

It was 1965 and my first time meeting Chicago's first Daley mayor (his son and future mayor, Richard M. was just finishing college and serving in the Marine Reserves at this time). Daley was in his third of a total of six elected terms. I had heard all kinds of stories about him, which led me to imagine him as mean and gruff. In real life, he presented himself as anything but that.

Make no mistake, he *was* a straight-forward, no-nonsense kind of guy, but in a very professional way. The mayor readily welcomed the report presented by our council president and promised to see that appropriate action was taken. Within the course of several months, all of the work on those streets, curbs and sidewalks was repaired by the city. It felt good to see results follow the efforts of that community group.

The Machine

At the mayor's office, the council president introduced me to Daley as the Conservation Chairman, to which the mayor nodded my way. That was the extent of my interaction with the mayor, which was fine by me. It thrilled me just to be there, considering the political aspirations I had nurtured since my teenage years. In spite of growing up one hundred miles from the state capitol and three hundred miles from Chicago's political scene, from the time I was fifteen years of age and had set my goal of becoming a statewide elected official, I kept a pulse on Chicago's politics. In my senior year in college, I even wrote a term paper about "The Daley Machine," a political organization which was also known to some as "The Chicago Machine." The organization originated in the 1930's as "The Chicago Democratic Machine."[lxvi] My paper examined how the tight organizational structure of the machine dictated the political and economic landscapes of Cook County Illinois.

That term paper was inspired by my desire to bring about change in politics. The ill treatment of blacks served as one of the catalysts fueling my desire for change. That aspiration for correction deepened each time I witnessed trainloads of blacks migrating up from the southern states on that Illinois Central train, as I traveled numerous times back and forth between my home in Centralia and my college in Carbondale.

On those trains, those northern-bound blacks toted their worldly possessions in tattered suitcases and boxes held together by crude ropes. They also carried grease-stained sacks of food to eat along their journey, since they were not permitted to eat in the dining cars. On the north-bound trains coming up from the south there were segregated, "Colored Only" cars where blacks were forced to sit. Black people traveling on the Illinois Central knew that they were restricted to the seats in the "Colored Only" cars from Cairo (pronounced Kay-ro), a racially-riddled little city at the southernmost tip of Illinois.

On the other hand, when coming out of Chicago and traveling *to* the south, blacks could sit anywhere they wanted. You'd better believe, though, once they pulled into Cairo, Illinois, black travelers knew they had to get back to the "Colored Only" car for the duration of their trip south.

During that time, there were two premier passenger trains operated by the Illinois Central Railroad. One, *The City of New Orleans*, ran from New Orleans to Chicago. The other one, *The Panama Limited*, was a train on which blacks were not permitted to ride on at all, until the Civil Rights Movement and the subsequent passage of federal civil rights legislation. Blacks traveling those tracks from the south looking for opportunities in the north found them under the patronage of 'The Daley Machine' in Chicago.

There, a particular job would be given to a person, and that person's entire family became tied to that job in terms of benefits. That person would be governed by precinct captains or ward bosses. If that person didn't produce, or didn't do exactly what that boss ordered him to do, that individual would be fired, a circumstance which, consequently, affected the welfare of the entire family. This is how many people would get trapped by those bosses into certain jobs for a long time. The bottom line was that you got your job based on who you knew, and you kept your job based on what you did and on how well you followed orders.

For those under the economic control of "The Machine," following orders was particularly important when it came to voting. During elections for city officials, those affiliated with "The Machine" were expected to vote a certain way in order to keep their jobs. They also used their influence to ensure that their families and everyone else they knew voted that way as well. It was a well-known fact that if a person didn't bring in his "quota" during elections, it was very likely that he would lose his job.

In terms of elections, "The Machine" was a powerful force, one to be reckoned with! The ballots showed that "The Machine" was very instrumental in John F Kennedy's 1960 election, when he won Illinois by only 9,000 votes, but captured 450,000 votes in Cook County alone.[lxvii] The more I watched "The Machine" in action, the more I wondered, *"What about those NOT within that organizational web?"* Say there was a precinct of six hundred people with only about two-hundred and fifty of them controlled by "The Machine." *"Where were the other three hundred and fifty people?"* I asked myself, *"Why weren't they participating?"* I figured my job in the political arena in Chicago would be to activate that other three hundred and fifty headcount. I knew I wasn't going to change the minds of those two hundred and fifty folk whose livelihood depended on their jobs and whose jobs dictated their votes. As I studied and analyzed all that, my goals were to become more active and visible in the community, which I had begun to do in 1965, and to begin battling "The Machine."

To initiate that twin strategy, I became a gofer for Congressman Bill Dawson's top guy, Lawrence Woods. Congressman Dawson[lxviii] was the second black congressman to come out of Chicago; Oscar DePriest[lxix] was the first. Dawson helped Richard J. Daley[lxx] become mayor of Chicago for his first term in 1955. In my role as gofer, I would chauffer Woods around, and hang out and listen to what was being discussed at Dawson's headquarters in the Second Ward. Congressman Dawson had a close friend, Leslie M. Bland, who was a successful realtor (and whose ninety-year-old widow still lives a block from my current home at the writing of this book). Les had a big office on 79th Street right around the corner from where I lived. As a new lawyer, I joined forces with Les, and we worked together in representing various local home buyers in their closings. I was moonlighting as a real estate lawyer while still working at Continental Bank and pursuing my political ambitions.

As the 1966 even-year elections approached, one of the new realities on the horizon was the creation of a new Illinois state senate district, called the 29th senatorial district. At that same time, both the 1967 aldermanic and mayoral elections loomed large in Chicago politics. That's when I joined an organization called Committee on Illinois Government.[lxxi] This group included people like corporate executive and future governor, Dan Walker; Vic de Grazia, from Walker's campaign; Illinois State Representative Adlai Stevenson;[lxxii] and other young rebels. We were all independent democrats anxious to battle that all-too powerful democratic machine. At about the same time, Gus Savage, editor and publisher of *Citizen Newspapers*, a chain of independent weekly newspapers in Chicago,[lxxiii] teamed up with Bill Cousins who had advanced to Chairman of the Chatham-Avalon Council along with Bill, headed up a committee called the 29th District Voter Education Conference.[lxxiv]

Our goal was to find candidates for that senate seat. In the Primary Elections of 1966, two democratic candidates for Congress in the Second District, Abner (Ab) Mikva and Barratt O'Hara locked horns. We brought in Charles Chew, Jr. as an independent six-year alderman from the 17th ward to run for that new 29th district senate seat. Charlie was pitted against Russell DeBow, who was the candidate of "The Machine." On election night, Mikva lost to Barratt, but Charlie Chew beat Russ. Winning the primary nomination was tantamount to winning the office, because there would be little or no republican opposition in November.

We had campaigned nearly non-stop, day and night for Charlie: tracking reports, delivering literature, making phone calls and canvassing door to door. Fortunately, back in the day, when we went knocking on hundreds of doors, people opened them and listened to what we had to say. Unfortunately, back in the day, while we were out there in the neighborhoods, we often were forced to go toe-to-toe with precinct captains of "The Machine." Nevertheless, with Bill Cousins as Charlie's campaign manager and a committed crew of hard workers, we landed that big win, which gave us both credibility and a leg to stand on. Soon after that win, while the effervescence yet remained in our celebratory champagne, we heard that Chew had gone downtown to meet with Mayor Daley. Charlie Chew sold out to The Daley Machine right after the primary election! Rumors had it that he got a heap of money with the deal. One only had to look at the Rolls Royce and several Cadillac's he soon drove to know his price tag must have been high. That was Chicago

153

politics for you.

Later, I challenged Chew's ethics with an article in the *Citizen Newspapers* that I wrote about him. He never responded. Chew went on to become a popular, hard-working state senator. He was also chairman of the Senate Transportation Committee. He was never defeated in the senate and served that position for twenty years, until his death in 1986.[lxxv]

Aldermanic wars

We rode the wave of the 29th District Voter Education Conference's victories right into the aldermanic and mayoral elections that followed in February 1967. People figured no one would challenge Daley, but that's exactly what we did in those aldermanic spots. Most notably, there were three South Side wards that had a vestige of independence during that time. They were the 6th, 8th and 21st wards. The results of the aldermanic races in those wards were as follows:

- 6th Ward – Independent Samuel "Sammy", a big funeral home operator in Chicago, worked with a young guy, Phil Smith, as his campaign manager to beat incumbent, Bob Miller, also a Chicago funeral director.

- 21st Ward – Gus Savage, Chicago newspaper publisher, battled James Montgomery, an attorney, in the primary. Both ran and split the vote, allowing The Machine's candidate, Wilson Frost, to win with 50% of the vote.

- 8th Ward – Independent Bill Cousins, managed by me, did not get 50% of the vote, which necessitated a run-off election with challenger, Leslie Bland. That run-off election was held in April of 1967, and Cousins won.

I gained a great deal of political experience during Bill Dawson's 1966 campaign because of my working closely with Dawson's top guy, Lawrence Wood, and because of my work on Chew's campaign. That hard-earned experience made me an easy choice to become Bill Cousins' campaign manager, even though I lived in the 6th ward, and he was running in the 8th ward.

I didn't think Les would run against Bill, but Les' close friend, Congressman Dawson, encouraged him to do so and financed him heavily as well. That caused me to have to end my moonlighting real estate work with Les. That race was tough. I didn't want to part ways with Les, either, but I had no choice.

So I felt the strain of that campaign both physically and mentally. After working at the bank all day, I would get home, eat dinner, kiss my wife, hug my daughter and head back out to the campaign office until two or three o'clock in the morning. I had never run a campaign before, so I had to learn the ropes and manage volunteers all at the same time. Talk about not sleeping for many nights!

As if all that weren't enough, Berlean was expecting again, this time with our son, and we were experiencing the biggest snowstorm in Chicago history! Continental Bank and all other businesses in the city were closed down. Twenty-four hours later, on the 28th of January, the streets were somewhat cleared. The doctor finally arrived at the hospital just before I made it there. Berlean and I welcomed our beautiful son into the world. All too soon, though, after my fatherly duties were performed, political duty called. I kissed my wife and new son good-bye and headed back to Bill Cousins' aldermanic campaign.

Celebrity
Photographs

Chicago Bulls and NBA superstar, Michael Jordan and Hon. Roland W. Burris

Burris and Chicago Bulls center, Bill Cartwright

Burris shares a light moment with native Chicagoan and NBA star, Isiah Thomas and NFL star, Ahmad Rashad

Burris and Chicago Bulls guard, John Paxton

Chicago columnist Irv Kupcinet, Roland W. Burris, and Chicago Mayor Eugene Sawyer

Former SIU classmate, Don McHenry, U. S. Ambassador to the United Nations and Hon. Roland W. Burris

John Johnson, owner of Johnson Publishing, Dr. Berlean Burris, and Hon. Roland W. Burris

Chicago Bear and Pro Football Hall of Famer, Richard Dent, greets Roland W. Burris

Illinois Comptroller Burris meets with Israeli Prime Minister and future President, Shimon Peres

...adio and television host, Larry King, and Roland Burris

Illinois Attorney General Roland W. Burris delivers the "knock-out" punch to World Heavyweight Boxing Champion Mohammed Ali

Burris with Chicago Bears running back, Walter Payton, and quarterback, Vince Evans

Professor John Hope Franklin, historian; Etta Moten Barnett, noted contralto; and Roland W. Burris

Illinois Comptroller Roland W. Burris with Tadeusz Mazowiecki, Prime Minister of Poland

Burris with Tommy "The Hit Man" Hearns, the first professional boxer to win titles in four divisions

Burris with Eubie Blake, composer, lyricist, and pianist of ragtime, jazz, and popular

prah Winfrey accepts award from Roland W. Burris, founder of Young Executives in Politics

urris with Liza Minnelli, Actress, singer, dancer, and choreographer

Burris greets Sammy Davis Jr., actor, dancer, and singer

Roland W. Burris and Dr. Berlean Burris meet with Nelson Mandela, South African anti-apartheid revolutionary and politician who served as President of the Union of South Africa

Chapter Eight

From Banking to Politics

Organizing

In 1967, as the snow melted and springtime broke through, the long awaited run-off election resulted in a Bill Cousins win. Cousins' victory did not come without a true fight to the end. Remember, he and Les Bland were involved in a run-off race against one another in the 8th Ward, right? Well, it turned out that Les' primary residence was *not* in the 8th Ward, but in the 21st Ward. He had a nice big home, too, on the corner of 85th Street and Indiana Avenue. We obtained copies of his utility bills and anything else that we could get our hands on that associated his name with that address, demonstrating that Les was ineligible to run for the 8th Ward office. Les was very upset with me about the part I played in this, but it helped to secure the win for Bill Cousins.

I remember one of my law professors, Professor Daniel, telling us that once we were out of school, we would be social engineers. He said that in order to facilitate constructive social change we might discover a need to create new organizations. I guess I took his advice to heart, as I created several groups in addition to joining them. I formed one of them soon after Cousins and Samuel "Sammy" Rayner became aldermen. Once in office, Cousins and Rayner had quickly joined forces with a Jewish gentleman from the 5th Ward, named Leon Despres. It was said of Despres that he "represented the black community, even though he wasn't black and represented the poor community, even though he wasn't poor."[lxxvi] He died only recently at the age of one hundred and one, a couple of years following the death of his wife of seventy-five years. His tenacity and passion for civil rights had pitted him against Mayor Daley in city hall since 1959.[lxxvii]

After the election of Cousins and Rayner in 1967, we were happy to send our two new warriors to assist Despres in the ongoing battle with city hall. It soon became apparent that the newly minted alliance formed by Despres, Raynor, and Cousins, needed an even tighter and stronger coalition to take on Daley successfully. That is when I formed the group called the Independent Political Organization (IPO).[lxxviii] My main goal in creating this organization was to set up an operation that was comparable to the Regular Democratic Party and which could counteract the party's tendency to tie up a whole family with political patronage and then turn their heads on unfair labor and housing laws.

Our first IPO conference at the University of Chicago proved a success. Of the fifty wards in Chicago, perhaps twenty of them were represented at that initial conference. That was very good, considering the fact that Chicago only had five or six black aldermen. Some of the individuals in attendance would later go on to become elected officials at many different levels of government. We had representatives like Anna Langford from the 16th ward and Gus Savage from the 21th ward, who later became a congressman. Even though Gus had lost his race in the 21st ward, he continued his independent work. We also had people from the West Side, like Luster Jackson and Fred Peavy. Peavy eventually became a Republican.

Also in attendance was a very distinguished socialist, Timuel "Tim" Black, who became a guru within our independent movement. He was of the same district as Despres, the Hyde Park area, and was instrumental in electing another independent state senator from there, Richard Newhouse. As of the writing of this book, Tim Black, Professor Emeritus of the City Colleges of Chicago is alive and well at age 95. A celebrated historian, he has authored a number of important books, with some of them being researched and written even when he was in his 90's.[lxxix]

Our group members became members of another group, one which I did not create, called the Committee on Illinois Government (CIG).[lxxx] Among the members of that group were Dan Walker, a gentleman who later became governor of Illinois, and another gentleman, Vic de Grazia, who worked as his campaign manager. We also had a woman named Dawn Clark Netsch, who became state comptroller and who, years later, beat me in a primary gubernatorial election. There was a very resourceful activist, Lucy Montgomery, whose husband was a wealthy attorney. She helped fund such political efforts as Cousins' aldermanic win and Mikva's congressional loss. Our membership stretched all the way up the Lakefront to folks whom we called the "North Shore Liberals." Our members also included individuals like the heirs to the Britannica Encyclopedia estate, a big time developer named Philip Klutznick and his daughter, Betty Lu Klutznick Salzman. Klutznick, chief developer of the Village of Park Forest, a southern suburb of Chicago, later became U.S. Secretary of Commerce in President Carter's cabinet.[lxxxi]

All in all, many influential people came together for our cause, even though some of them later moved back toward the Regular Democratic Party. There wasn't much of a Republican Party in Chicago back then, so the political battles were primarily between the Independent Democrats and the Regular Democrats.

After organizing the IPO, I was elected its first chairman, barely beating out Phil Smith, who had been Rayner's campaign manager while I was Cousin's campaign manager. I was elected to this position by one vote, a fact which caused some of my friends and associates to refer to me, jokingly, as "old Landslide Burris."

It was after that win, though, that I really set my sights on running for public office. Since I had already managed Bill Cousins' successful 1967 campaign, I knew what to look for in a manager and found exactly what I was looking for with a young man named Ron Bean. I prepared to run for state representative in 1968. At the time, Illinois had a voting system called "cumulative voting."[lxxxii] We had three state representatives for every senatorial district.

Under cumulative voting, you could cast one vote for each of three candidates; three votes for one candidate; or one and a half votes each for two candidates. In essence, each person could cast three votes in their district. It may seem complicated, but that's how our state House of Representatives kept a good balance of republicans and democrats.

159

Depending on the district, there would be two democrats and a republican or two republicans and a democrat. At that time, there were one hundred seventy-seven House members and fifty-nine senators.

The current governor of Illinois (as of the writing of this book), Pat Quinn, paved his entrance to the political world with his successful movement in 1980, while still a law student, to repeal cumulative voting. Before then, however, my chances of being elected as a state representative were fairly good with that type of voting.

The only real problem facing me was the fact that I was still an employee of Continental Bank. How in the world could I run for office and stay at the bank? With a wife, two small children, a mortgage and all our other living expenses, staying at the bank was a necessity. I began to put some serious thought behind it all.

From Banking to Campaigning to Banking

I approached my boss, Bill Funk, to inform him about my seeking a state representative spot and to find out whether that would be a problem with Continental Bank. He said he would have to get back to me with an answer, which he did a few days later.

"Roland, you will be invited to a meeting with the president of the bank, the vice chairman of the board and a couple of other top officials," he reported.

To say I was anxiety-ridden was an understatement. In my four years at the bank, I had never seen the president of our bank, Tilden Cummings, let alone met him. So, without even a full day to prepare, Mr. Funk ushered me up to the carpeted second floor, past the top brass at their mahogany desks, past the secretarial gatekeepers and through the huge mahogany double doors into the grand splendor of the president's office. There I sat staring at President Cummings; Vice Chairman, Donald Graham; Executive Vice Presidents, John Perkins and Roger Anderson; Operations Officer, Joe Fitzer; and my Vice President, William Funk.

As eloquently as possible, I explained to that room full of big wigs my desire to pursue a political career, while maintaining my banking career. I knew I did not want to leave the bank, since being a state representative was only a part-time salaried job. I began selling my socks off as to why they should consider my two requests.

My appeals were: number one, I should be able to run for office while continuing to work for the bank; number two, once I won, I should still stay on as an employee of the bank. As I spoke, I suddenly figured out their hot button. I promised, *"If I'm in Springfield, you will have an inside helping hand to lobby for branch banking."* They perked up on that note and began asking me a few questions.

We didn't have branch banking in Illinois at that time, and our banks had not had much success with getting the legislature to make the changes in the law that would allow branch banking. One of the bank officers asked me a question regarding the possibility that I might change my mind and leave the bank after getting a taste of politics. I assured them otherwise. *"Well, you see, gentleman, I really don't want to leave Continental. In fact, someday, I would like to be president of this bank."*

Dead silence, as Cummings' face froze: red and expressionless. A few awkward seconds later, Mr. Perkins broke the ice in an optimistic manner. *"Roland, that's great. I wish we had more of our young individuals who came here with that attitude."*

That lightened the thick air in the room slightly; albeit, their frozen-faced smiles appeared to be hiding one communal thought: *"Who does this young black kid, who is nothing more than a tax consultant working in the tax division way in the back among the tile floors and the metal desks, think he is?"*

I just knew I'd gotten myself fired. Instead, Graham, rising from his seat as he spoke, gave me a glimmer of hope with the words, *"Well, Roland, we'll take this under advisement. We'll discuss those two matters one at a time and get back to you."*

About a week later, as promised, Mr. Funk called me and reported, *"Roland, the officers met and they have come to a conclusion. Yes, you can run. You can take some time off to campaign. We'll give you a leave of absence with pay so you can run. And about your ability to stay at the bank? We'll get back to you on that one later."*

I had crossed a major hurdle! I almost couldn't believe what I heard, talk about grateful! Then, wouldn't you know it? For the first time ever, the primary election was changed from its normal date in March to a new date in June. The strategy behind that 1968 change was to encourage a stronger voter turnout, since historically; we couldn't count on fair-weather, sunshine-only voters to come out in the somewhat brutal Chicago winters. The primary election had always been held at that earlier date because the Regular Democratic Party never had a problem getting its people to the polls in the cold and snow. So, there I was, having to campaign longer and wait longer for my fateful result.

A week after I received the officers' first response, Mr. Funk called me again and said, *"They met again, Roland, on your second request. They decided to give you an answer before the election instead of after. That answer was also a yes. When you win the state representative office you can stay at the bank. We'll settle on something as to where you can fit in during the days that you're in Springfield and how they're going to work out the compensation."* He continued, *"By the way, some of the officers want to contribute to your campaign."*

No one could imagine how that made this little black kid from Centralia, Illinois feel! Not only did I convince those titans of the banking industry to give me thirty days off with pay, but I also sold them on financially supporting my campaign! That gave me that extra boost of confidence, which helped me to campaign even harder. I had my wife out on the campaign trail as well; passing out literature along with my two little kids: my son in the stroller and my daughter walking on her own.

It seemed as though everyone and their brother ran in that democratic primary election! The two incumbents were Lewis Caldwell and Raymond Ewell. I was one of the three new candidates, along with Caleb Davis, who worked with us in the independent movement and Charlie Gaines. Gaines had previously run as a Republican and then as a Democrat, only to become the Republican State Representative a few years later. Of the four other candidates, I knew I could knock off one of the incumbents and, at worst, come in second. I took over the old headquarters where I had previously assisted Cousins in his win. It was the IPO office, too, so we were still paying rent there. My fund-raising efforts, with the help of my campaign manager, Ron Bean, brought in a little money. We held several bake sales and cookie sales, mostly hawking cookies for 15 or 20 cents each, here and there, but these efforts did not raise enough to afford such luxuries as yard signs, bumper stickers, posters and some of the other things that certainly would have been desirable and helpful in our campaign.

Finally, Election Day arrived in June of 1968. The votes were cast and tallied, and the outcome was revealed late that night. Of the five candidates, Ewell and Caldwell were re-elected. The incumbent Republican was reelected as well; so there was no change in the state representative. I came in last place, ouch! That slaughtering served me a painful helping of reality.

As it turned out, losing that election proved the best thing that could have happened to me. Of course, I couldn't see that at the time. At that moment, my ego emerged from the race bruised. Suddenly, I dreaded the impending jabbing from my colleagues at the bank. The biggest thing I worried about was facing the executives and others at the bank who had contributed to my campaign. I had raised a total of about $10,000 or $11,000, of which $5,000 or $6,000 had come from the bank.

But regardless of how I felt, it was time to face the music. Soon after the election, I picked myself up by the bootstraps and reported back at work. Everyone was kind to me, but I kept a rather low profile—still licking my wounds, I suppose.

Movin' On Up

Shortly after my return back to work in early July of 1968, I was summoned to Funk's office. *"Oh, God,"* I thought, *"this is it; I am going to be fired."* Once in his office, Funk began, *"Roland, we checked the results and saw that you didn't do too well out there campaigning. But guess what? We like that kind of action. We like that kind of involvement in the community, and you're pretty well known. We've come to the conclusion that you should not be in the trust tax division. You should be in the commercial lending division. So we've made arrangements to transfer you down to the lending section on second floor."*

Jack Glazer kept telling me I should get out of trust tax and get into commercial. However, crossing over between the trust department and the commercial department was an almost unheard of transition. Once a person started on a particular side of the bank that was typically the career path he stayed on while traveling up the ranks. So, as you can imagine, the likelihood of a black guy in the 60's crossing departments like that was slim. To this day, I believe my run and subsequent loss for state representative helped to get me out of that trust division.

Grasping the fact that I needed to be ten times better really paid off for me. During my first four years at Continental, my promotions advanced me from Accountant to Senior Accountant to Tax Consultant. When Cecil, the other black accountant, quit in my second year, they never replaced him. Instead, I ended up cranking out double the number of tax returns: his load and mine.

After the Chinese tax consultant quit, I was then promoted to his position. Even though the bank finally hired more people, I continued to be given a double load of assignments. The demands at work were overwhelming at times. I put in long grueling days at the bank, often getting home and having only enough time to get a couple of hours of sleep.

The advice to be ten times better also led me to become a true Continental Bank loyalist. I was always out there hustling my tail off on behalf of the bank. For instance, whenever I was around people, whether family, friends or strangers, and for business or for pleasure, I asked them, *"Do you have a checking or savings account? Why not open up a checking account and a savings account at Continental?"*

No matter where I was, I usually asked those questions, and they frequently resulted in the opening of an account. Every time someone whom I referred opened an account, my name would appear on a certain list. The number of new customer accounts I solicited steadily increased, usually with between $2,000 and $3,000 here and there in checking and/or savings accounts.

It was on my birthday, August 3, 1968, that I began training for commercial lending. I had to learn about the doctors and lawyers group, which was the exclusive client of the section in which I worked. One of the things I learned during that training was that loans were certainly being granted to those professionals.

The bank also had a small business lending section. It became a known fact that there existed a problem with loans *not* being extended by big banks to minority owned businesses around town. The small business lending section, called Group 4, was headed by Vice President, Fred Shewell, who was in his late fifties at that time. Shewell had advanced all the way up to that position from the mail room. He was a high school graduate, who had never attended college. Despite his lack of college training, he grasped banking, and lending in particular, and that's all it took for him to climb that corporate ladder.

Someone in Shewell's department became aware of all those new accounts being opened to my credit. Rather than keeping me assigned to the doctors and lawyers group, it was figured I would be best utilized in the small business group. I then attended several weeks of very intensive training for that group. I still remember those three C's of lending: character, credit, and collateral.

Soon thereafter, Shewell approached me and said, *"I've heard about you, but I haven't read any of the information in your personnel folder. If you're going to make it over in this small business group, you're going to have to prove yourself to me."*

I responded with much gratitude. I assured him I was up for the challenge and would hopefully not disappoint him. I immediately started assessing Continental's loan situation, after which, I went out into the community with a strong desire to make things fair where bank loans were concerned. I began meeting with small businesses and groups.

Dr. Martin Luther King, Jr. had been assassinated several months earlier in April. Marches and unrest in hundreds of cities across the nation led to rioting in some places. Chicago's West Side was one area that had fallen prey to a tremendous amount of burnings, lootings and killings. From those tragic events emerged groups throughout the black community organized by black business leaders who led a renewed effort to convince banks to finance minority loans to help newer businesses to grow, and to help those businesses, which had been destroyed by rioting and looting, to regroup.

Some of those groups would help the various business owners to write their business plans. Other groups would help package their loans. Because of the assistance provided by these groups, the loan applications which resulted from their efforts had a much greater chance of approval. Oscar Williams, an accountant I worked with at Continental, worked with these groups after leaving the bank and putting his accounting skills to use in packaging loans.

The 1968 U.S. presidential election was approaching: Nixon versus Humphrey. I was definitely not a Nixon supporter, but I was intrigued by the fact that one of his campaign talking points was promoting black capitalism.[lxxxiii] This sounded very much like what I was doing through Continental Bank: providing black businesses throughout the Chicago black communities the assistance they needed for growth and development. None of the other big downtown Chicago banks were involved in this early effort to finance minority businesses, only Continental. Because of Nixon's emphasis on support for black capitalism, though, some of the other large banks soon began to respond to the pressure to do so.

Nixon was elected. He appointed David Kennedy, Chairman of the Board of Continental Bank, as his Secretary of the Treasury.[lxxxiv] Vice Chairman, Donald Graham, moved up to fill the vacated chairman spot. Continental didn't have to fill the vice chairman position, as long as we had a chairman and president, which we did since Cummings remained president. Roger Anderson and John Perkins vied for that CEO position. Nixon also appointed Robert Mayo, one of our vice presidents from the commercial side of Continental, as his Budget Director.[lxxxv]

I found out later that it was Chairman Graham who, when he was vice chairman, had given orders to Funk for me to be moved out of trust tax and into commercial banking. Also, I was close to Mayo, since he helped me with my commercial training. So, as you can see, things just fell into place. I had direct access to the top of Continental, through Graham. In fact, I had a direct pipeline to the White House through Mayo, who had a direct pipeline to Treasury Secretary, Kennedy.

In April of 1969, I got a call to go see Senior Vice President, Sheldon Swope. I admit that this request gave me a bit of concern. Everyone joked that Swope had been with the bank for one hundred years. He wasn't known as the most pleasant guy around, but instead, a nononsense, old line banker. Most employees, like myself, had never even gotten a glimpse of the old guy. If the stories we heard were true, then that was just fine by us. Naturally, my co-workers wanted to know what I had done wrong to warrant a trip to the "principal's office."

I arrived at Swope's office, and greeted him with a smile. He nodded then gestured towards a chair near his desk. *"Have a seat young man. You know, we're about to make history here in this bank."*

"Oh really?" I asked, not sure what else to say. *"How so?"*

"Well, son, the board of directors is scheduled to meet this afternoon. If there's a quorum, your name has been submitted to be voted on by the board to become an officer of this bank."

Everything went blank in my head. I only remember saying, *"What?"*

He kindly repeated, *"We'll know at about two o'clock this afternoon whether or not you will become an officer of this bank. Of course, you can't say anything to anyone until after it is official."*

"Holy cow!" was all I could say to myself, over and over on the way back to my desk. It was only eleven o'clock in the morning. Can you imagine how slowly time passed by for me until the afternoon? Trying to contain my excitement for those three hours was pure torture! Needless to say, I could barely concentrate on my work the rest of the day.

My mind raced back to my earlier days at the bank when some of us black guys would be in the employees' cafeteria together, talking about race problems and other things happening at the bank. I remember that during one of these conversations that I used the term *"we"* in referring to bank policies, instead of the term *"they,"* which most employees used. My close buddy, Ron Greer, looked at me and said, *"What do you mean by 'we'? It's 'us' and 'them.' Man, they don't care anything about black folks in this bank. We've got to be on our P's and Q's because they want to run 'us' all out."*

The other guys agreed with Ron. I stood alone on that issue, as I replied, *"Well, Ron, you know, they're paying my salary. I made a commitment to work hard. In return, I'm giving them five years to make me an officer of the bank."*

Ron chuckled, *"They won't have a black officer in this bank for another fifty years."*

"Well, if I don't strive for it, then I'll never know if that will be true. So I can't be at odds with them and try to move up in the ranks, too." My word on that topic was final. I guess those who knew me felt that it would be pointless to argue with my level of determination on this issue.

Some of the guys actually started seeing my view on things in our many conversations, so it wasn't like we were ever at odds with each other on every issue. Even so, I would venture to say they were all shocked when later that day, just four months shy of my five-year goal, and contrary to all previous speculation concerning the likelihood of black executive advancement in the bank or in corporate America in general, they heard that Roland Burris had been appointed Continental Illinois National Bank's first black bank officer.

My new title as bank officer was assistant cashier. At two o'clock sharp the announcement list came out, and my name was at the top of the list. With the officer title came some nice perks: free lunches on the 23rd floor; my own key to the men's room; a special checking account; and best of all, my own special expense account. It was a really big deal!

Not only was I Continental Bank's first black officer, but I was the first one among Chicago's big banks in the LaSalle Street financial district. It took no time at all for the word about my promotion to get out on LaSalle Street. By four o'clock that evening, the First National Bank of Chicago, the second largest bank in the city, named their own first black officer. Their selectee, Hamilton Talbert, who is now deceased, was a friend of mine and a fellow trustee in our church. His title was also assistant cashier.

Making Things Happen

After my promotion, the small business and minority lending activity really accelerated. By April of 1969, Continental began making some of those loans and shipping them off to the Small Business Administration (SBA).[lxxxvi] Shewell grew concerned about the long length of time that the SBA took in completing its part of the loan process. Also, Shewell and I were apprehensive about whether or not enough credit-worthy standards were put in place to protect Continental from the threat of default.

To help put our minds at ease, we held a seminar for all those organizations helping the black businesses, and gave them instructions on how we operate and what we looked for in loan packaging. That effort did help to streamline the processing of paperwork coming to us. It also allowed us to send loans to the SBA that were apt to receive SBA approval.

Even with the extra measures we had in place to insure credit-worthiness, the paperwork was still bottlenecked at the SBA. One of the main complaints by applicants was that the SBA wouldn't reply until two or three months later. Shewell said to me one day, *"That's not right. I mean, if we're doing all this, and we do want to use the government guarantee from the SBA, they ought to provide us some timely processing."*

To get the matter straightened out, Shewell talked to Mayo, who talked to Kennedy, who talked to Nixon and the Small Business Administration people. The sentiments expressed loud and clear pointed to a much needed change in SBA rules. This strong sentiment eventually led to a major policy change in the rules and regulations of the SBA.

Around June of 1969, a new decision stated that the SBA had 72 hours to reject or approve a loan. If the bank that sent in the package was not notified within 72 hours, that loan would automatically be approved and 90% guaranteed. As one can imagine, in the interest of protecting our deposits, that ruling provided a major cushion for us.

After that ruling, we started processing so many applications that I soon felt I needed an assistant. Shewell decided we needed more than that and got approval to create an entire new subdivision that I would manage. That gave Shewell two divisions: his previous one, Group 4, and my new division, Group 4B, called Government Guaranteed and Minority Loan Division. My lending team of seven people consisted of bankers and clerks. I personally brought onboard my friend, Ron Greer, who in the past had always tried to convince me it was always "us" against "them."

As an officer, my lending authority, without another officer signing off on the loan, was up to $5 million. We financed and established many major companies. So many businesses were being helped that the SBA created the Small Minority Business Capital Corporation[lxxxvii] to enable implementation of extra types of funding.

That SBA group became a great source for organizations like Chicago United which was, a mentoring-type group made up of black and white corporate CEO's of mid to large-sized corporations throughout the Chicago metropolitan area who came together to strategize about the revitalization of the black community. A few of those black CEO's were: John Johnson[lxxxviii] of Johnson Publishing Company (*Ebony* and *Jet* magazines);[lxxxix] John Sengstacke[xc] of *The Chicago Defender*;[xci] Daryl Gresham of Parker House Sausage;[xcii] Cecil Troy of Grove Fresh Distributors,[xciii] Inc.; George Johnson[xciv] of Johnson Products; Edward Gardner of Soft Sheen Products;[xcv] and Dempsey Travis owner of Travis Realty Corporation and a former championship boxer.[xcvi] The members of this group made it a point to do business with the new companies that came into existence with the help of Continental loans through my division.

Always an Election Around the Corner

In 1969, while the loan contracts were flourishing through my Group 4B, my involvement with the Illinois Jaycees picked up momentum. I had already advanced through the ranks of the South End Jaycees, moving from member to vice president to president of that local chapter. From there, I became regional vice president in charge of about twenty chapters. I was also national director of Illinois' Northeastern region, which covered fifty chapters throughout Chicago, its suburbs, and surrounding cities like Joliet. I served on the national board of the Jaycee organization, as well, which met with our national president twice a year in Tulsa, Oklahoma. With my Jaycee plate already quite full, I was slated to become their Jaycee's unopposed nominee for Illinois state president.

I reluctantly approached my boss, Shewell, to inform him of my plans to travel to Decatur, Illinois for the Jaycee election. All the big corporate executives had young men in the Jaycee organization; however, I knew that the direction in which I was headed with the Jaycee organization wouldn't allow me to continue as head of my lending group at Continental. *We've got so much work here that you cannot do both,"* Shewell stated, confirming my fears. *"Given the workload you have with Group 4B, you would not be able to head up that lending group and the Jaycees; however, we can certainly find something else for you to do at the bank that requires less of your time. That way, if you run for the presidency of the Illinois Jaycees, we'll just put you on a leave of absence."*

That was the first time I had that tough of a decision to make between two very favorable positions. I headed to Decatur with the weight of the world upon my shoulders. If I left the lending division at Continental, I knew I wouldn't be able to get that position back. I also knew that in order for me to realize my dream of becoming national president of the Jaycees, I had to start with becoming Illinois president first. From there, I could run for one of the ten Jaycees national vice president slots. Four or five of those ten leaders would compete to become president of the U.S. Jaycees. I contemplated that entire trail as my entrance to achieving my life goal of statewide political office, which was the reason it became such a hard decision to make.

In the end, I turned down the Jaycee presidency opportunity and returned to Chicago distraught; yet, relieved. Deep down I knew I made the right decision to stay and run Group 4B and not to move to another department within the bank. Besides, I still made good contacts with all those statewide Jaycees while in Decatur, relationships that would serve as helpful influences in my future political career.

Election season rolled around again for Chicago: the 1971 mayoral and aldermanic races. At the urging of my friends, I thought briefly about running for alderman, but declined. In 1967, Sammy Rayner had beat Bob Miller, the incumbent 6th ward alderman. Rayner decided not to run again, allowing Eugene Sawyer to be elected 6th ward alderman. Just as losing the state representative race three years earlier had proven to be a blessing in disguise, I would later find out that not running for alderman was a wise move as well.

My lending duties kept me far too busy at the bank to give running for alderman any serious consideration. In fact, my Group 4B division was so profitable during that time that a 1969 issue of *Fortune Magazine*[xcvii] featured me as a young future leader or something like that for 1967. I wasn't even aware of the article, let alone the significance of it, until one of my colleagues informed me about it. In those days, it was quite an accomplishment to be featured in Fortune Magazine, so a lot of my white colleagues were jealous.

Money, Money, Money

As busy as we were granting loans, we certainly weren't just giving money away at Continental. We turned down a lot of people because we stuck to our guns about credit worthiness being a key factor in successful application for a loan. In fact, I sometimes became the brunt of derogatory comments, as I received a lot of flak from within the community. Statements like, *"Burris is just protecting the white man's money,"* and similar crazy statements were some of the things I had to listen to from those whose applications had been rejected, usually for very sound financial reasons.

As a result of the riots that took place following Dr. King's death, Continental Bank had been collaborating with Reverend Jesse Jackson[xcviii] on some of the issues occurring within the black community. Jesse and his group were really bringing pressure on the downtown corporate community to get involved in the effort to break down racial barriers that still existed in our city.

At one point, I explained to Jesse how important it was that he and I stay on the same page. Working together, with me on the inside and him on the outside, we had a great opportunity to positively impact the black community. He seemed to buy into that idea, or perhaps he just appeared so to appease me. After all, because he worked alongside the late Dr. King for years and was by his side until his death, Jesse was accustomed to dealing directly with the chairman of the board of Continental, instead of just a lowly officer like me. That was fine by me, as long as the goals of organic community growth and revitalization were accomplished.

And did we ever accomplish things! As I look back on those lending days, I can see a number of things of which I am very proud. I'm also thankful that I got to be a part of making some big dreams happen. One of my boldest moves as a banker was when I helped a preacher buy a hospital on the South Side of Chicago. There was a hospital called Evangelical Hospital that was owned by the Evangelical church which had decided to close and liquidate the hospital. A good friend of mine, Dr. Andy Thomas, began appealing to me as a banker about acquiring the Evangelical Hospital. He insisted, *"Our community has got to have a black-owned hospital."* Andy knew that the founder and pastor of Tabernacle Missionary Baptist Church, Reverend Louis Rawls, uncle to the legendary singer, Lou Rawls, was interested in purchasing the South Side hospital. Andy assured me, *"We can buy this hospital for little or nothing: about a million dollars."*

My hesitation was whether or not the hospital was worth that much, so I got a CPA firm involved. They performed an analysis of assets and every other check-and-balance task possible over a period of seven months to assure me of the soundness of the institution. I finally made the decision to go for it.

I remember Shewell looking at me very questionably, *"Is that your decision, Burris?"*

"Mr. Shewell, we've got to do this."

Collateralized by the assets of Tabernacle Missionary Baptist Church, I made a loan of one million dollars, which enabled Rev. Rawls to purchase and create Tabernacle Community Hospital and Health Center. Dr. Rawls, who over the years established other businesses including a funeral home, paid every penny of that loan back plus interest in just five years.

For a number of years, in its unique identity as a black-owned healthcare institution operated by an African-American church, Tabernacle Community Hospital and Health Center [xcix] continued to serve the health care needs of some of Chicago's most needy communities. Bottom line, Continental made money on that deal, and I had played a role in the establishment of what may have been the first black church-run hospital in America.

A few of my many other loan successes ran the gamut from a day care center to a bowling alley. One of our great success stories involved a housewife, named Mrs. Finch who earned a living by providing day care services for small children in the basement of her home. When Mrs. Finch decided that she wanted to expand her daycare business, she approached me about borrowing $500,000 to expand her facility to accommodate three hundred and fifty children. Although initially I questioned her ability to pull off a feat of this magnitude, after a lot of convincing on her part and a lot of detailed analysis on mine, I made the decision to make the loan. According to our assessment, it would take Mrs. Finch about one year to identify and enroll three hundred and fifty children whose parents were able to pay for day care. To our surprise, in only three months, she had identified and enrolled three hundred and fifty eligible children. Today, the center, Les Finch's Learning Tree Day Care Center, is still in operation, although it is now operated by Mrs. Finch's daughter. [c]

A white owner of Starlight Lanes at 87th Street and Cottage Grove Avenue on Chicago's South Side had suddenly decided on leaving the neighborhood and wanted to sell. As it happened, at the same time, Jacoby Dickens and radio personality, Daddy-O Daylie, ran a bowling league that was outgrowing the facility in which it was located. They were presented the perfect opportunity to acquire the eighteen-lane Starlight Lanes business. In 1969, I loaned them the $140,000 necessary to purchase it. Their successful acquisition of that bowling alley allowed them to become very successful businessmen.

Soon after the bowling alley acquisition, Jacoby Dickens began purchasing shares in a newly established bank called Seaway National Bank (now Seaway Bank and Trust Company) on Chicago's South Side. The bank relied on a group of black investors selling its stock to raise the necessary charter capital. Due to his loyal affiliation, Dickens became Seaway's Chairman of the Board and its main stockholder in 1982. Seaway Bank became the largest African-American-owned financial institution in the country in 1983.[ci] Continental's loan for Dicken's bowling alley had served as a stepping stone to his later banking success. Those are just some of my business experiences. I highlighted the success stories but believe me, there were failures as well. With each failure, my Government Guaranteed and Minority Loan Division continued to improve, as we gained more insight into the applicants and sharpened our lending skills.

All in all, my lending group remained profitable from the time our division started in 1968, until I left in 1973. We learned quickly to spot what we called the "hustling riff raff," people who came in with their get rich quick plans, expecting to borrow $100,000 to catapult themselves to their golden nest egg. Also, on one occasion, a borrower wanted me to participate in his kickbacks: *"If you loan me the $100,000, 10% of it is yours."* People like that were put out of the bank in a hurry. Most of this information I had never shared with anyone before. I guess I didn't find it appropriate to go around talking about what I loaned to people like Rev. Rawls and Mr. Dickens. Even many of those who are close to me may be learning about these efforts in the area of minority small business loans, for the first time.

Not only was it gratifying to have been able to play a role in encouraging business growth within the minority community, but it is also very gratifying to note that some of the more visible evidences of those successes are still among us today. In 2010, I attended an anniversary celebration of one of the companies I loaned money back in the early 1970's. A young man named Don Jackson materialized his dream of running his own company to produce and manage marketing and T.V. programming geared primarily towards the black community. He qualified for a $50,000 loan from Continental Bank to launch Central City Productions, Inc. (CCP).

Today CCP is the largest black production company in the country, with the production of over one thousand shows for broadcast television under its belt.[cii] Forty years from its inception, CCP flourishes with Don and his wife, Rosemary, still at the helm. I was humbled when asked to speak at their celebration, as the banker who loaned Don the money to start his company. The "Don Jackson's" of the world, and many others I helped, fueled my passion to do what I did while in the banking sector.

Chapter Nine
Family and Politics

A Great Ending to a Good Vacation

W hen my children were very young, I made a commitment to my wife that I would always take time out so that our family could go on vacations and spend quality time together. And we did. For the most part, those vacations would consist of driving tours. In the summer of 1972, however, when my daughter was eight years old and my son was five years old, my family planned our first major trip, which was to Disneyland in Anaheim, California. We loaded up our Thunderbird with all our gear and headed west on that ten-day journey.

Most of the way, we drove on the old Route 66, except for intervals when we made use of Interstate Highway I-40, stopping in cities like Oklahoma City, Gallup, New Mexico, and Las Vegas before reaching Anaheim and settling there for three days. The kids were so excited! To tell you the truth, those Holiday Inn swimming pools may have made a more positive impression on my daughter than Mickey Mouse! At each Holiday Inn, she took full advantage of the pool. As soon as we loaded the car and left one motel complex and headed down the road, she started asking how long it would be before we arrived at the next one.

After spending time with the family in Anaheim, we headed north to San Francisco. I had always heard about driving Highway 1 along the Pacific Ocean from Los Angeles to San Francisco, so the anticipation of that fueled my excitement. I must say, Highway 1 was just as incredibly scenic as I had heard. The awesome beauty of the scenery and the realization of the closeness of the ocean, on that narrow winding road, left me speechless. Thank goodness we drove on the inside northbound lane, as that made me feel a little safer. I marveled at the speed at which most of the southbound vehicles jetted around those curvy and steep drop offs with no guardrails.

After our brief stay in the Bay Area, we headed home to Chicago by the more northern route of Reno, Salt Lake City, Denver, and Lincoln, Nebraska. During our overnight stay in Salt Lake City, we had just returned to our hotel room after a long day of sightseeing when there was a knock on our door. I opened it and the hotel bellhop stood there holding the biggest and most beautiful basket of fruit I had ever seen.

"Sir, you've got the wrong room," I quickly informed him.

"No, no, no, it's your room number," he responded.

My wife approached the door and inquired, *"Well, whose name is on the tag?"*

The bellhop read the little envelope propped in the middle of the arrangement, *"To Roland Burris."*

"Well, that's me," I said. So I took the envelope, puzzled that anything would be sent to me on a vacation road trip. Who even knew where we were?

The card read, *"Congratulations to the Vice President of the Continental Bank."*

It took me a couple of seconds to collect my thoughts and then I shouted, *"Oh my God, I got promoted! I got promoted! I got promoted!"*

I started jumping up and down as I repeated myself! My wife started jumping up and down! Realizing the bellhop was still there, I reached into my pocket for his tip. Although I didn't have much money on me, I gladly gave him a twenty dollar bill. He started jumping up and down!

After gathering my composure, it suddenly dawned on me why Shewell had asked for a copy of my itinerary before I left for vacation. Waiting until I was on vacation to promote me and then surprising me with the announcement of it in such a unique manner was precisely the way Fred Shewell operated. I truly value the time I spent under his leadership.

Even though I did not see that promotion coming, I was not totally surprised when it happened. I had always worked hard in hopes of climbing the corporate ladder at Continental Bank. In fact, one time while having lunch with fellow officers in the bank officers' dining room, my work ethic became the topic of our conversation.

One officer said, *"You know, we used to sit around this table and talk about you, Burris. Now you're AT the table."*

"You were talking about me?" I don't know if I was more stunned by the fact that they even noticed me among that huge sea of metal desks in which I labored enough to talk about me, or that the guy was telling me that they had talked about me. *"What were you saying about me?"* I inquired with genuine curiosity.

"Well, we'd heard all these reports about how good you were. Oh yeah, I remember one guy said that you told him you were going to produce a document for him by Friday and instead, you produced it earlier; by Wednesday. He was very impressed."

Reputation: The Challenge to Protect It

That is how I've always operated. I give myself enough leeway on projects to make sure I complete them ahead of time. I learned from the conversation at that officers' table that people are going to talk about you one way or the other—either good or bad. You might as well let it be good. So, if a person wants a good reputation, one sure way to get it is to operate through honesty and a strong work ethic.

These days, I lecture to young people about gaining and maintaining a positive reputation. I am passionate about helping them to become more mindful of what people would say about them in their absence. It's important for young people to realize that while it may take a lifetime to build a positive reputation, that same reputation can be destroyed overnight with one bad decision on their part.

People used to take pride in saying their word was their bond, which simply meant if they made a promise, they kept it. I try to instill in young people the fact that if you keep your word, people will think highly of you. I also tell them even if you can't do something you promised to do then you should go to the person you made the promise to and tell them, *"I'm sorry, but I am not going to be able to do that."* I learned early in life how important it is to build a good reputation. Even without thinking about what the full effect of doing so would be, my modus operandi was that I would stay a step or two ahead of my bosses or whomever I dealt with in business. That was not always an easy thing to do, especially when one considers the heavy workload that I was assigned at Continental Bank.

I remember one particular situation where this big time bank officer, whose family owned Inland Steel, wanted me to do an audit on a customer file and I just didn't have time. He kept trying to get me to do it. Anxiety built up in me each time I had to tell him I was too busy or tied up. After two or three months of that, it finally occurred to me that I just had to say, *"No, I'm not going to do it."* I never did do that audit. A situation that had grown to be a challenge and had potentially negative consequences was effectively diffused by honest, clear communication.

Over the years, the challenges of juggling business, community affairs, racism, politics and family, at times, have seemed almost insurmountable. Life does not always allow us to control *how* challenges come at us, but we can control *what* we do about them. For me, having a firm sense of faith equipped me to overcome, rather than dwell on these challenges.

That same faith in God taught me to hold my family in high regard. Their foundational roles in my life greatly contributed to my success. So as I write about the tragedy of their deaths on the following pages, I know my words can't even begin to capture the depth of despair I felt as those tragedies unfolded in the midst of my career triumphs.

Gone Too Soon: First My Brother...

My brother, Nick, graduated from high school in 1952. He was such a smart student all throughout school that in everyone's mind, college was inevitable as his next step—everyone's mind, that is, except Nick's. He planned a different route. He headed to Chicago with his classmate, Cecil Coleman, where they planned to live with Cecil's uncle, Weldon Tide, and work for about a year.

My father didn't find out about his eldest son's change of college plans until *after* Nick had left for Chicago. Boy oh boy, was there some fussing going on. *"What do you mean he's not going to college?"* Dad yelled.

Mom tried to calm Dad down and rationalize Nick's actions simultaneously, *"He's going to work and try to make a little money. Give him about a year."*

"No, he's got to go to college! And he's going now!" Dad had always let it be known that his boys were going to college, especially

179

given the fact that Nick had always excelled academically.

I also had good grades, but, unlike Nick to whom academic excellence came easily, I had to study hard for mine. Nick made "A" grades without ever having to carry books home or studying. Although Nick had already left for Chicago, obviously without my knowledge, a good bit of serious negotiation took place between him and Dad.

The next thing I knew, that September, Dad boarded the train to Chicago. After he arrived at Mr. Tide's home; he and Nick packed up all Nick's belongings, and the two of them traveled back home that same evening. The next morning, Dad and Nick caught the train to Carbondale where Nick was enrolled at Southern Illinois University. That was how my brother's college experience started.

Back in those days, black males at SIU were not allowed to stay in campus housing. They had to stay with families throughout the Carbondale community. Therefore, Nick and three other roommates rented their rooms from a lady named Mrs. Edwards.

Every weekend for four years, Nick came home. He took food from our family's store back to school on Sunday for him and his three roommates to survive on for the week. The only problem was that the food he took was all starchy stuff: canned corn, peas, green peas and such. Their mainstay was spam and hotdogs. Since Nick provided the food, one of the other roommates cooked while the others alternated cleaning up the dishes. That system worked for them for four years.

Although that system worked for *them*, it turned out that it didn't work for me. When Nick was a senior, I began my freshman year at SIU. I lived with Nick and his roommates for the first semester, after which time I begged my mother to let me move to a dorm. Luckily for me, SIU had just integrated student housing, so the option of living on campus, which had not been open to my brother and his friends, was open to me. All I knew was that I could not continue to live in that house anymore where I was constantly forced to eat corn mixed with peas, topped off with baked beans and a slice of spam. Apparently, my mother agreed with my constant complaints, because eventually I was able to move into a private Christian dorm, which was conveniently located just next door to University Drugs (UD's) cafeteria where I often had my meals.

After graduating with honors, Nick, along with his wife, Shirley, spent a couple of years working in Springfield before returning to

Centralia, where he taught seventh grade at Lincoln School. As well-liked as he was as a student, Nick was even more popular and well-liked as a teacher, both by his students and the community. He loved teaching and wanted to expand his capabilities in that field, so he went back to SIU. He received his master's degree in the summer of 1963 around the same time I received my law degree.

By that time, Nick had been married for awhile and he and Shirley had three young children, Earl III, Steve, and Kim. Things were going great for Nick, as they usually did throughout his life. He and his family had just moved into a newly built home, and he bought a brand new car. Nick barely had time to make even one house payment and hadn't yet made any car payments when he began to have problems with his health. In the Fall of 1964, Nick was diagnosed with serious digestive problems, which explained his practice of popping an excessive number of Alka-Seltzer tablets to relieve what he thought was simple indigestion. Medical tests indicated that he needed surgery. He was admitted to the hospital exactly one week before Thanksgiving; the same day I returned home from Springfield where I had just been sworn in as a lawyer that morning.

Nick called my home that Thursday evening to voice some of his concerns about his impending surgery with Berlean and to ask her opinion from the perspective of a nurse who was highly trained in the provision of health care services. Berlean counseled him, comforted him and left him feeling a little more assured about his surgery. His surgeon happened to be a former high school classmate of mine by the name of Dr. Jerry Beguelin. We knew Jerry to be skilled at his craft, so that knowledge helped to put the family at ease. After all was said and done, it didn't matter how good Jerry was, because Nick was in pretty bad shape. During the surgery, they found that his digestive juices were not properly breaking down his food. They had to re-open a collapsed duct through which those juices were supposed to travel by inserting a tiny tube in the duct.

Unfortunately, however, even with this surgical alteration, they could only get the duct to open a fraction of its normal width.

That following Tuesday, Shirley reported that Nick started feeling a little funny. By late Wednesday, he took a turn for the worse. Early Thursday morning, on Thanksgiving Day, as Mom and Shirley sat by his hospital bed, he asked his wife to hand him his Bible. My brother was very religious. He served as secretary of his church, and in other capacities as well. He usually had his Bible somewhere nearby. He opened it up to the twenty-third chapter of the book of Psalms and read the full passage. After reading the Twenty-Third Psalm, my brother, closed the Bible, handed it back to Shirley, laid back in bed, and died at the age of thirty.

At around 5:30am, my phone rang; awakening me from a deep sleep. It was my mother in Centralia. *"Roland, your father is on the train. He's on his way to Chicago to see his dad, who is in Illinois Central Hospital."* I didn't even know my grandfather was in the hospital in Chicago. *"Really?"* was all I could muster, as I began to sit up to register the information. *"What happened to Granddad?"*

As though she didn't hear my question, Mom continued, *"He is on the train and you need to go meet him at the station. Take him to see his dad and then bring him back home."* Before I could answer her, she then dropped the bomb, *"Your brother is dead." "What?"* I asked so loudly that Berlean awoke and sat up in bed trying to find out what was going on.

Mom repeated somberly and almost robotically, *"Nick is dead."* One of the hardest things I've ever had to do in my life was to tell my dad that his oldest son had died. I rushed to get dressed, wondering the whole time what I would say. I got to the Illinois Central Station platform at 63rd Street and Dorchester Avenue before his train arrived. He was going to walk the several blocks from the train station to the Illinois Central Hospital, near 58th Street and Stony Island Boulevard.

Dad's train arrived. I struggled to maintain my composure while flagging him down among the other passengers arriving for their respective Thanksgiving celebrations. There would certainly be no traditional celebration for us I surmised. Finally, Dad saw me and looked happy to see me. *"Hey, son!"* he said cheerfully.

I greeted him, keeping my disposition as cheery as his. Mom had specifically instructed me not to tell Dad anything about Nick until after I'd taken him to see his father. Then, I was to let him know he had to get home to make arrangements for his deceased son.

Everyone seemed to have hustled off the train platform pretty quickly, motivated, no doubt, by their impatience to greet loved ones and to share a scrumptious turkey dinner. On the contrary, my dad and I seemed to walk at a snail's pace, as I conjured up small talk inquiring about his train ride. Suddenly Dad stopped, looked at me and said, *"Wait a minute, Roland, you didn't know I was coming in town. Why did you come and meet me?"*

Within those few seconds that I paused—searching for the right words—my pain showed and Dad knew. He looked me square in the face with a gaze of undesired discernment that haunts me to this very day. *"Is my son dead?"* I nodded and managed to utter, *"Yes."*

We silently continued our walk off the platform like troopers; allowing only a tear or two to fall, lest anyone around would learn of our pain. I felt the heaviness upon my dad, as I supported his arm down the platform stairs. Once in my car, I could no longer hold my composure. Neither could he. Dad and I sat there and cried like babies for what seemed like an endless period of time.

I eventually convinced Dad to continue with his intended visit with his father at Illinois Central Hospital. In fact, we went together and, somehow, got through that visit, although much of it occurred in a nightmarish fog. We did not tell Papa Burris about the death of his grandson.

Once back at my house, I packed and made necessary phone calls for the next couple of hours. There were certainly no Thanksgiving festivities going on that year for us, except of course for thoughts of gratitude for having had Earl "Nick" Burris, Jr. among us. Dad and I drove back to Centralia that evening to begin the daunting task of helping Nick's wife to finalize things at the hospital and to plan the service. My attention was divided between funeral arrangements in Centralia and orchestrating the train trip from Chicago that my wife and baby would be making the next day or so to join us in Centralia.

The funeral was held that Sunday afternoon at Nick's family's church. It was by far one of the biggest funerals the town had ever experienced, since Nick had been so young and so well-liked. Many of his friends from grade school and high school were there. His college classmates from undergrad and graduate school were there. His colleagues from work were there. His students and their family members were there. Family friends, neighbors, and people from every walk of life, were there.

My sister and her family made it in from St. Louis. Nick's in-laws and lots of our extended family members and loved ones from various towns attended as well.

November of 1964 was a trying time for the Burris household. We believe Nick's demise was due to a pancreatic attack caused by the backing up of pancreatic juices produced when his ducts possibly closed down again after the surgery. Dr. Jerry Beguelin wanted to do an autopsy but Shirley refused.

... Next My Mother...

The year 1964 culminated in the most difficult way for me. My family endured a tough first holiday season without Nick. During that same time, my job had me going in circles for no apparent reason. As mentioned earlier, after being hired at Continental Bank in August of 1964, I spent the first three months being bounced from division to division in various training programs. Finally, they had assigned me to a metal desk in the Trust Tax Division, while my fellow trainees went to the mahogany desks of the Estates Administration Department. After raising a question about the unfairness of it all, I had vowed always to be ten times better than my white counterparts.

In mid-February of 1965, just as things were beginning to look better all the way around, I received a call from my sister, Doris, saying that Mom was not doing too well and that she was in the hospital. I dropped all that I was doing—the "busyness" at the bank and all the community work with the Chatham-Avalon Community Council—to go see Mom in the Centralia Hospital. Before I returned to Chicago that next day, Mom was looking better and appeared to be recovering. Two days later, on February 22nd, I got a call from Doris saying, *"Mom is dead."*

My mother remained a strong and constant figure for me and my family throughout our entire lives. Then, in an instant, she died at the age of fifty-three and that constant, positive force of her presence was suddenly not there. I flashed back to the many years of watching how hard she always worked so that we could achieve our goals. When we were kids, my mother had helped her mother wash the clothes of white neighbors and clean their homes. She canned fruit for us to eat during the winter. She maintained an active role in community organizations, such as the school PTA, and was very involved with political matters.

As Burris Grocery's mainstay, Mom kept the store running while Dad went to his job at the Illinois Central Railroad and my siblings and I went to school. In 1957, when Mom was momentarily sick and had to be hospitalized, we all felt the pressure of running the store in her absence.

Even though medically my mother's death was attributed to liver failure, I believe she passed away because her heart had been broken by the loss of her oldest son. She had made a couple of statements in the past that one could interpret to mean she was somehow "ready" to take leave of this life. For instance, one day in the summer of 1963, when Nick had just received his master's degree and I had just received my law degree, we visited with Mom and Dad at home. My mother was overcome with joy at our accomplishments and stated, *"My two boys have achieved so much. If the Lord takes me home now, I'm satisfied."*

Another time that she made a pointed statement of that nature was at Nick's funeral. Our family was perched on the front row of the church, with Mom seated between me and Dad. All of us had a pretty hard time getting through the service, as we consoled each other. Therefore, Mom's emotional outburst that day while the preacher performed the eulogy didn't strike any of us as anything other than her way of express-ing the grief that all of us were feeling: *"Don't worry son, it won't be long before I join you!"* Those remarks made by my mother at Nick's funeral took on much more prophetic implications, as we revisited those utterances, just three months later, after her own death.

At first, when telling Mr. Peterson, my tax manager at the bank that my mother died and that I would need time off, I got the feeling that he wondered just how true my story was. It had only been three months since I requested time off from work to bury my brother. It was a very well-known fact that many of my young co-workers had grandmothers who died at least five times over the course of a year or so, requiring these workers to take time off from work to attend the funeral every single time the "mythical" grandmother passed away. Even back in those days when it was a fairly common occurrence, the idea of fabricating the death of even a distant relative was absolutely repugnant to me. In the workplace of today, I can't imagine that kind of scheme working, simply because the advanced technology and social media of today make personal matters so easy to verify. Of course, though, based on the fact that I had always been scrupulously honest with them in every respect, I knew that my bosses had no reason to doubt me. Along with their sincere condolences, they also sent my family flowers.

... and Then My Father

It was understandable that my father went into a deep depression when Mom died, especially since they had been married for so long and had developed such a close and interdependent relationship. Of course, they had had their share of disagreements over the years; however, my parents' marriage was a wonderful and strong one, which provided my siblings and me with a very positive pattern for our own married lives. And no matter how they may have disagreed from time to time, we rarely, if ever, heard them argue with each other.

In 1957, Dad went to the hospital due to a nagging cough. They detected a cancerous spot on his lung and wanted to do a treatment to remove the cancerous growth. He told his doctor, *"Let me go home and take care of my business matters and I'll come back."*

Dad did not end up returning to the hospital until 1971. When he got there, some fourteen years later, he could hardly walk and had quite a bit of trouble with his breathing. He was a stubborn, tough dude who put up a very good front for many years. For so many years, he continued to work and carry out other daily routines in agony, refusing to stop, determined to keep going for the sake of those who depended upon him.

That one day in September of 1971, must've been a rough one for him because he skipped work and instead hopped the train to the Illinois Central Hospital in Chicago. When they checked him out, they told him the cancer had metastasized throughout his entire body and that they couldn't do anything for him. He stayed in the hospital for two or three days before returning to Centralia with a prognosis of six to nine months to live. Dad lived fourteen more months and died in early November of 1972, right after the election. In the meantime, he was in and out of the hospital many times. I traveled down to Centralia on several of those occasions, as each time seemed to herald the end for him. Each time, though, despite the fact that the end seemed imminent, my Dad would somehow manage to pull through.

During this phase of Dad's illness, the Government Guaranteed and Minority Loan Division that I ran at Continental Bank from 1968 through 1973, experienced immense success, which kept my days both

186

long and full. Also, since 1971, I had been backing a gentleman by the name of Dan Walker, as he prepared for the 1972 Illinois gubernatorial race. Walker, a lawyer, Naval Academy graduate, naval officer and executive for the Montgomery Ward Corporation, was an Independent who faced Paul Simon in the Democratic primary contest. Simon was lieutenant governor, serving under Republican governor, Dick Ogilvie.

I called on my Jaycee network to assist us in raising funds, in spite of the fact that most of them were Republicans. I knew my involvement in that race presented me with a great opportunity for good political exposure, since I still had the goal of one day becoming a statewide elected official. In fact, I began supporting all the local candidates for state representative, for congress, and for state senator -- trying to hook things up throughout the entire state of Illinois.

Walker prevailed in that primary election over Simon, but only by an extremely thin margin. Therefore, we knew we would have to campaign hard at that point from March all the way into November to ensure there would finally be a Democratic governor in Springfield, and one who was *not* under the influence of the regular Democratic machine. During my very intense involvement in the general election campaign, my father's health took a turn for the worse. It was Election Day eve when my sister called me with some unsettling news, *"Dad is calling for you, Roland. You'd better come down here."*

"Well, Doris, tomorrow is Election Day. I'll go to the poll at six o'clock in the morning, cast my vote, and then I'll be heading to Centralia immediately." That was the best I could do to accommodate everything. That's just how important voting was to me; I could not do anything to change my father's condition, but I could make a difference with my vote.

The next morning, found me in front of the polling place sitting in my car, which I had already packed for the trip to Centralia the night before, well before the polls opened. As soon as the polls opened, I voted and then headed straight to the highway to Centralia. Five hours later, I sat at my father's hospital bedside where he recognized me and was so happy to see me. The hospital staff's only task at that point was to make him comfortable throughout his extreme pain, as they expected him to pass away at any minute, but he didn't. Dad was released from the hospital two days later, on a Thursday, and died the following

Sunday or Monday. He was only sixty-years-old when he died in 1972. It was obvious to all who knew him that his spirit had died seven years earlier after losing both his oldest son, Nick, and his loving partner, Emma Burris.

With the successive losses of our brother, our mother, and our father, only my sister, Doris, and I were left. Three-fifths of our strengthening foundation was gone, leaving us only with each other to lean on. I cannot communicate in words the grief I experienced over the loss of those who were so dear to me, but I always considered those losses to be a test from the Lord, and I knew it was a test I had to pass. I also knew it was part of a larger plan wherein I had to continue to push on to realize my ambitions and to achieve the many goals which lay ahead of me. Although I knew that the loss of those loved ones and the inspiration they provided would make these achievements difficult, I maintained the positive perspective that nothing was impossible.

Statewide, Here I Come

Dan Walker narrowly beat the incumbent governor, Dick Ogilvie,[ciii] in the General Election. Shortly thereafter, during Walker's transitional period, I received a call from Victor de Grazia, [civ] Walker's campaign manager. He was positioning the transition team and they wanted to put me in the governor's cabinet as head of General Services Administration (GSA) for the state government. Today, this department is called the Illinois Department of Central Management Services (CMS).

I talked to my boss, Shewell, about my future at the bank. Going into a four-year term with the governor's cabinet, I knew they couldn't give me that lengthy of a leave of absence. So I necessarily, but reluctantly, resigned. Shewell was very happy for me and my new appointment. He assured me that if I ever wanted to come back to the bank, he would be open to discussing possibilities. My friend, the other officer, Ron Greer, was then promoted to head Group 4B. Several resignation parties were thrown for me, as the chapter closed on my Continental Bank years.

After attending Dan Walker's inauguration in 1973, I began commuting weekly from Chicago to Springfield, a commute which I would make quite often over the next four years. As GSA director, I traveled non-stop supervising state items like all the vehicles, all the garages, all the telephone systems, all the leases and all the state-owned personal property. My office also did almost all the purchasing for state government. That made it very important for me to work with minority businesses such as Hispanic, black or women-owned companies, and open up opportunities for them to bid.

During my first year, I was in charge of the state's architecture office and construction projects. I chose Ken Groggs as the first black state architect in the history of Illinois government. Once again, my goal was to make sure we got the state apparatus geared up so that minority companies could fairly bid on state work. History had already proved this simply would not happen without our directed efforts.

Coming in behind my Republican predecessor in GSA meant correcting the fact that in all the contracts granted over a four-year period, we could identify only one that was given to a black company. This single contract was a $40,000 moving contract. I knew something had to be done to even out the playing field, so my office organized a minority business operation and set it up within our purchasing section. We worked closely with minority companies, teaching them how to bid for contracts and how their state government really works.

By the end of the first year, GSA was responsible for about $400,000 of revenue paid to minority companies across the state for contracts they had won. By the end of the next year, this figure had risen to a million dollars. By the conclusion of the third year, minority companies had won state contracts which totaled two million dollars. In my fourth and final year, minority business owners doing business with the state of Illinois were being paid approximately four million dollars.

One key area we targeted to help build the revenue stream for qualified minority businesses was in moving contracts. Movers were sought out, trained and hired to help move people who were on public aid. In doing that, we helped fulfill a great need on both ends.

The second targeted area was janitorial services. We discovered that janitorial contracts with downtown businesses and unions contained clauses that were totally illegal. In simple terms, it meant the only way a cleaning company could even bid on a contract to clean an office in downtown Chicago was if that cleaning company already had clients in that vicinity. So, if you never had a client in downtown Chicago, you could never get a client there!

We went after those contracts legally and wiped out those clauses with no resistance. We got on those unions which were involved in this practice and let them know they had been exposed. Finally, many other companies were allowed to bid. They joined the unions if they needed to and they bid low if they had to in order to introduce themselves to the downtown arena. That's how we made sure the wealth was shared.

In 1974, I was approached by the telecommunications staff about a need to do something called "teleconferencing" within the state government. According to their request *"We want to be able to sit in a meeting in Chicago and a meeting in Springfield and talk to each other and see each other on the screen without having to do all that traveling back and forth."* After they explained all the details, I said, *"Okay, let's go study this. Let me run this by the Governor."* I met with Governor Walker, who replied, *"Roland, if that's what you want to do and if it makes sense to you, do it."*

We started right away developing teleconferencing methods, but guess when we finally got the first teleconferencing session up and running? Not until 1992—eighteen years later! When I was back in Springfield as attorney general, they called me over to the Central Management Services office and let me sit in on the first teleconference meeting. Just think of all the different governors and directors we went through over that period of time.

Governor Walker also gave me the task of cutting waste in Illinois government, so I became the bad guy to a lot of folks. I collected automobiles. I cut out printing presses. I ended leases. I consolidated working spaces and much more. Most changes were not made radically, mind you, but perhaps in a rather unprecedented manner. Either way, the governor trusted me with those types of decisions. He was always very supportive because of his confidence in me.

Because of the amount of responsibility he turned over to me, I had to go around some of his staff people in order to get things done. Typically, a person had to report to the chief of staff or the deputy in charge of their agency to pass information on to the governor. The governor's reply would then be directed to you from his office along that same route. A staff member would tell me, *"The governor wants you to do this or that."*

I would always say, *"I need to hear that from the governor, himself."*

Then they tried to prevent or delay me from getting in to meet with the governor, so I'd have to call him personally on the phone. *"Governor, I need to talk with you."*

"Yeah Roland, what's up? Well, let me look into that," would be his response.

If I didn't hear back from the governor, it was because his answer traveled through his normal chain of command and someone on his staff intercepted those answers. Several people within that chain wanted to push their own agendas. Some orders I did receive, I later learned were given to me by some self-serving deputies, not the governor. They had their own little program going, so they could look good in the eyes of the governor.

Governor Walker also supported and respected local municipal officers. Even though Mayor Daley was among those local officers the governor respected, it was a known fact that he harbored a total dislike for the mayor. Actually, the feeling was mutual between them; they just coexisted as oil and water. Their relationship was so bad that if they stood beside each other in a receiving line, they wouldn't even greet each other. Daley had been known to say that he was the mayor of Illinois against the governor of Illinois.

Walker, who is ninety-one-years-old as of the writing of this book, is a very brilliant man. In my opinion, he had a good grasp of the issues facing the state of Illinois and good political sense. The combination of those two qualities made him a good governor. I believe what was unfortunate to us is there was a lot of decision-making and delegating done in his name, but without his knowledge or approval, that ultimately hurt him.

First Run

As we approached the 1976 elections, I knew my opportunity to run statewide had come, but for what office? Lieutenant Governor? Attorney General? Secretary of State? State Comptroller?

Our current lieutenant governor was Neil Hartigan. Oh, was there ever an oil and water relationship between him and Walker! At age thirty-four, Hartigan was the youngest lieutenant governor in the U.S. and was a Daley person. During his tenure as lieutenant governor under Walker, Hartigan was never really involved in any of the governance.

191

There was also the attorney general position, which was then held by Republican, William J. Scott, whose occupancy of that office was the longest on record. The secretary of state position was held by Democrat, Michael Howlett, Sr. There was also the state treasurer position held by Alan Dixon, a Democrat. As you can see, the constitutional officers had a very mixed political representation.

The position that appealed to me most, however, was that of state comptroller. The Office of the State Comptroller was newly created in the state's 1970 constitution. In 1972, the citizens of Illinois elected the first state comptroller, George Lindberg, who was a Republican. I figured that position would be a great one for me, since my banking background gave me both accounting and finance experience.

I put it out there that I was going to run for state comptroller. Victor de Grazia, the Governor's Chief of Staff, didn't take the announcement too well. I respected de Grazia as the brilliant and tough political guru that he was, even if he didn't want me on the ticket. He didn't think a black candidate could appeal to the voters in a statewide election.

Of course I disagreed and told him, *"Well, that's fine that you think that way; I'm going to run anyway."*

In the end, de Grazia and Walker did put me on their ticket along with a whole slate of candidates. Mayor Daley put together a slate for himself for that 1976 run. It was the Walker team against the Daley team. Unfortunately, all the primary victories went to the Daley team. Here is how the results stacked up:

- Secretary of State, Howlett, ran against incumbent Governor Walker. Howlett beat Walker in the Primary, but lost to James Thompson in the General Election.
- Lieutenant Governor, Neil Hartigan, won the nomination as lieutenant governor, but he and Howlett, his running mate, were defeated by the James Thompson-Dave O'Neal ticket in the General Election.
- Senate President, Cecil Partee, Illinois' first black in that position, was slated for attorney general. He won the Primary making him the first black statewide office nominee in the history of Illinois. In the General Election, however, he was defeated by incumbent William J. Scott, who maintained his position.
- Former Illinois State Superintendent of Education, Michael

192

Bakalis, ran against me for state comptroller and beat me in the Primary. Democrat Bakalis went on to beat George Lindberg who had previously held the state comptroller's position. The state comptroller's office was the only office that was won by the Democrats in the General Election.

- The state treasurer position was not up for re-election then, so the incumbent, Alan Dixon, remained in that position.

That lost election brought my time in Springfield to an end—at least for that season. In January of 1977, I was faced with the decision of where to go and what to do. I had an opportunity to go to a law firm, and I also considered going back to the bank.

Back Home

By that time, Continental Bank had changed its policy, with the result that if I decided to run for office again, I could no longer work at the bank. Also, the 1970 Illinois constitution redefined office terms. As a result of that redefinition, the people elected to statewide office in 1976 only served two year terms which ended in 1978 at which time they would all have to run again, thus moving Illinois off the four-year presidential election cycle. So I knew it was only going to be a year before I could run again. I had to make a decision about whether I should go back to Continental Bank or whether I should seek elective office in a future statewide election. History shows which one I chose.

Right at that time, I was approached by a couple of businessmen about joining a non-profit organization as a paid officer. George Johnson, Founder and CEO of Johnson Products, and Daryl Grisham, head of Parker House Sausage, were two very strong supporters of Rev. Jesse Jackson and his newly launched *Push for Excellence* program. Rev. Jackson was receiving grants and relying on prominent businessmen to raise money towards his efforts to get educational changes supported in Chicago.

I was flattered that Grisham and Johnson requested my assistance based on the work I'd done for black businesses while in the governor's cabinet and at the bank. However, because I had never been that close to Rev. Jackson, I really had no way of knowing what I might be getting myself into. I accepted their offer anyway and became the National Executive Director and Chief Operating Officer (COO) for *Operation*

193

PUSH, which later became *Rainbow PUSH Coalition.*

On January 17, 1977 at 12 noon, I left my GSA office in Springfield for the last time and flew back to Chicago. One hour later, I landed at Meigs Field Airport and headed straight to my new office ready to dig into the massive amount of work waiting for me there. I had brought my executive assistant, Wanda Gates, with me from my Chicago office to help me tackle the load at *Operation PUSH.* Fortunately for me, Wanda continued to assist me for years to come, running all the Chicago operations for my campaigns and remaining as my secretary throughout my entire political career. Perhaps you have heard or even been the one to note how Rev. Jackson was always showing up here, showing up there, and being always right in the media's camera lens anytime something happened within black communities across the country.

Once I was inside the *PUSH* organization, I discovered that Rev. Jackson was constantly pulled in many different directions by issues which arose all over the country. Because so much was required of him, a lot was required of me as well: organizing, raising money, overseeing money, dealing with the activist community, and more.

Those phones never stopped ringing at *PUSH*! Calls came in from every corner of America. All kinds of people requested Rev. Jackson. They wanted him to do this; they wanted him to get in that dispute; they wanted him to get involved with this person being shot; they wanted him to help settle that contract being violated; they wanted him to pull the plug on this company discriminating against blacks.

Rev. Jackson has always been a major national and international figure, yet in those earlier years, his group consisted of a few people working themselves to the bone with very little pay and with a lot of commitments on their individual and collective plates.

The people in that small inner circle definitely stood by him out of sheer dedication. Since Rev. Jackson stayed on the road so much of the time, my job, as National Executive Director, was to build a stronger and more cutting-edge infra-structure capable of handling the headquarters operations more effectively and efficiently.

In a short period of time, I put some of the following actions in place: a talking memorandum, preliminary memorandum and an action memorandum. Those were necessary steps to help workers and volunteers become more effective in turning initial preparation into completed action. As the COO, I had to make sure that we made payroll. That was always tough to do when relying on financial backing from fundraisers and regular contributors.

Rev. Jackson is a tough taskmaster. During the eleven months that I worked with him, there was a time or two where we went toe-to-toe in a little tussle. Since my tenure was backed by two of his top supporters, he couldn't cross me too strongly. All in all, though, Rev. Jackson and I were very professional with each other and kept our focus on the cause.

In late June of 1977, Bakalis, after being state comptroller for just six months, announced he was going to run for governor in 1978. My ears perked up right away to that news! Aha! There would be a vacancy for state comptroller. I immediately called my previous campaign manager, Fred, to get the ball rolling.

Part Two: Political Rings

Chapter Ten
Political Beginnings in the Land of Lincoln

Getting Slated

By 1977, some major changes had transpired in Chicago city politics. One such change was that Mayor Richard J. Daley, while serving his sixth term, died from a heart attack on December 20, 1976. As it turned out, the sudden and unexpected death of the mayor was the beginning of the deterioration of the strength of the vaunted Democratic Machine. Michael Bilandic was selected as acting mayor to finish out Daley's term.

In June of that year, I shared with my wife my desire to run again for state comptroller. At that news, Berlean responded with a statement that soon became the under girding for my campaign, a new revelation for reinforcement, if you will. She said, *"You already ran for Comptroller and lost. Why? Because you didn't have the party backing. If you're going to run this time, and I see that you want to, the only way you're going to win is if you get the party backing."*

"Honey, how can I do that?" I then reminded her, *"I'm with Dan Walker. I'm an Independent."*

"Well, there's no way you can win if you run again for State Comptroller unless you get the party support." She stood firmly on that conviction. I began thinking about just how right Berlean was in her

observation. It was easier said than done, though, since I had fought the Regular Democratic Party hard since 1965. That was a good twelve years of opposition that I somehow had to change on a dime. I needed a plan; a major one. I put together a strategy that began with a list of people I needed as allies, instead of enemies. But how was that ever going to happen? I didn't know, but with the Primary Election in March of 1978, slating needed to happen soon. At this time, I was still working at PUSH. Rev. Jackson became increasingly worried about all that was going on, since he knew he couldn't have somebody on his payroll running for office. I assured him I would step down once the slating process started. He was in agreement with me.

Several of the men on my list of those I needed to approach included: Illinois Senate President Cecil Partee; Gene Sawyer, Alderman and Committeeman for the 6th Ward; John Stroger, Committeeman for the 8th Ward; Wilson Frost, Alderman of the 21st Ward; and two aldermen from the West Side, Walter Shumpert and William Carothers. Since I lived in the 6th Ward, I decided to speak with Gene Sawyer before approaching the others on my list.

Gene was the nicest guy on the Illinois political scene. Although I had been fighting him on issues for many years, he had never gotten angry or lashed out at me. Actually, he never got angry with anyone. He would always say to me, *"Burris, you're on the wrong side. You ought to come join us."*

Finally, the time had come to test those words of his. I requested a meeting with him, and he readily agreed. I expected Gene to take advantage of our meeting as an opportunity for him to gloat with, *"I told you so."* Instead, it turned out quite the opposite. *"How' ya doin',"* Gene greeted me in his usual friendly manner, as I entered his office.

A couple of his brothers who were present greeted me warmly as well and prepared to sit in on the meeting. I returned the pleasantries and then got right down to business. *"I would like to join your organization. What do I have to do?"* Gene quickly replied, *"Nothing. You're in. You're in my organization."* That completely took the wind out of my sail. *"Well, how much does it cost?"* I just knew there had to be a catch.

"It doesn't cost anything," he assured me. *"You're in the 6th Ward Democratic Organization, Roland. Now, what do you want to run for?"*

"Well, thank you for accepting me, Alderman. I'd like to run again

for State Comptroller." "You would?"

"Yeah, I tried it once and lost the Primary, but now there's going to be a vacancy."

"I know all about that, so you know what? Let's do it! Let's have you run for state comptroller."

Shocked once more by the rapidity with which he gave me his approval, I thanked him again for his acceptance of me. Within a short time of putting my strategy into action, I had succeeded in getting one committeeman in the Regular Democratic organization on my side. Gene's support influenced Partee and Stroger to back my candidacy as well.

I knew the real problem would be with Wilson Frost; he certainly didn't disappoint me. As soon as we sat down together, He began firing away at me. *"You want to do what?"* he started in, *"You want to get the nomination for state comptroller?"* He chuckled incredulously. *"You want the support of the Regular Party?"*

Finally, Frost stared me square in the eye and gave it to me straight, from one black man to another. *"Look Roland, you've got three strikes against you: Number one, you're working for Jesse Jackson. Number two, you worked for Dan Walker. And number three, you're black."*

I appreciated his frankness as much as he appreciated my audacity. We continued to talk until finally, Frost came around and decided to support my candidacy for state comptroller. Together, he and I got the committeemen from the West Side to come onboard. That was August of 1977; my plan was beginning to meet with some successes.

Word got out very quickly that I was seeking the Regular Democratic Party's support in my run for state comptroller. It is commonly known when the Party slates a candidate, it is usually the candidate the committeemen put on the ticket. I wasn't quite there yet, because there were still some committeemen who were looking to do their own thing. I knew I still had to approach and win the support of some of these individuals.

One evening, there was a major fundraising reception for Alan Dixon. I made it a point to attend this event, so I could talk to more of the people on my list. While there, I spoke to a state representative, informing him about my desire to be on the ticket for comptroller.

"Well, that spot's gone," he immediately responded.

Dumbfounded, I replied, *"What do you mean?"*

"That's going to go to State Senator Dick Luft."

"Wow," I said, totally taken aback. *"Well, then what about State Treasurer?"*

The man confidently offered, *"That's gone too."*

"That's gone?"

"Yeah, that's going to go to a fellow named Jerry Cosentino."

By the time I left that fundraiser, my hopes and dreams were so deflated that I don't even remember going through the motions of driving home. It was about eight or nine o'clock in the evening when I found myself in my garage. I went in the house, ate dinner, and decided to devise an even more aggressive party-backing strategy.

I got out my legal pad, ready to brainstorm. Before I started writing, however, I pulled a book entitled *The Banker*, off my shelf. [cv] This book is about a big New York banker who, when faced with the task of preventing other bankers from taking over his bank, carefully planned a strategy designed to accomplish that goal. After carefully reading the last four or five chapters of that book, I felt I was ready to create my own plan. I wrote pages and pages of notes: what steps to take and when; who to talk to about what. I was working very hard to get slated!

The next day, having outlined my new course of action, I began making phone calls. The first person I called was George Dunne, Chairman of the Cook County Democratic Party. In a previous meeting I had with Dunne, he told me that everyone who presented themselves would have an opportunity to be slated; in other words, slating would be open.

In my phone conversation, I asked the Chairman, *"I thought you told me that everyone was going to have a chance, and that the slate was going to be open?"*

"What do you mean, Burris? It is open."

"Well, they tell me that Dick Luft is already the guy for State Comptroller."

"Who told you that?"

"A State Representative."

"And how do you think he knows this information?"

"I don't know, but what about Treasurer? He told me that was gone too."

"What? There's been no pre-slating; everyone will have a chance to be slated," the Chairman assured me.

I figured that information would touch a nerve with Chairman

Dunne, since he had previously said slating would be open. His statement was already public knowledge, so he couldn't go back on his word. Shortly thereafter, the reaffirmed word went out amongst the committeemen that there would be no pre-slating, but open slating only. At that point, the committeemen who were supporting me were in a position to demand that the Cook County Central Committee place a black candidate, such as myself, on the ticket.

The Cook County Central Committee, which consisted of fifty ward committeemen and thirty township committeemen, made the initial selections for slating. From there, the State Central Committee, this is made up of two representatives from each of the twenty congressional districts, made the final decision on the slating of statewide candidates. With the backing of The Cook County Central Committee and the vote of the State Central Committee, I would officially become the slated candidate for Illinois state comptroller.

Before the State Central Committee had made its final decision, I kept my promise to Rev. Jackson and resigned from *PUSH*. Truth be told, he was rather happy to see me go. No one had ever really challenged him the way I had. We had some good times together and some bad times together, but what mattered most was that we solved a lot of problems together.

It was November of 1977 when I became the slated candidate. Having been freed up from my *PUSH* responsibilities, I had nothing else to do but become laser-focused on turning my candidacy into an election win. Getting me on the democratic slate proved a major victory for the black ward committeemen. Even my wife could not believe what happened. *"How in the world...?"* She laughed. *"I didn't think you could pull it off!"* Nonetheless, she was proud of me; not just because of *how* I had implemented my plan, but mainly because I had even taken on the challenge. That whole series of events perhaps became a pivotal point in Berlean's belief in my political skills and abilities. She had always heard me speak of my goals, one of which was to become a statewide elected official. However, after that effort in 1977, she knew for certain that serving the citizens of Illinois was in my blood.

My Hat in the Ring

I wish I could say the battle was over at that point; but saying so would be lying. I mentioned that Dunne was Cook County Chairman, right? Well, in addition to *his* chairmanship, there were another one hundred and one county chairmen. In Illinois statewide politics, it was always the downstate counties versus Chicagoland's Cook County. Well, the majority of those one hundred and one party chairmen got together and said *"No,"* they were not going to accept Roland Burris on the ticket, regardless of the decision of the State Central Committee. So, there I was, in the midst of a Primary race for state comptroller against State Senator Dick Luft from downstate Illinois.

One evening, I attended a fundraiser on behalf of Mike Madigan, which was held in Chicago's western suburbs. At the event, there was music playing and lots of people having a great time. As I approached a circle of about ten white ward committeemen talking, I heard my name being mentioned in their private conversation. I decided to hang back behind one of the men in the circle to listen to what they were saying about me. I had to get very close to hear their comments over the loud music, so being short in stature paid off, as they never saw me.

Tom Donovan, Mayor Bilandic's chief of staff, was in the center of that group telling the committeemen how to deal with the prospect of having me on the ticket: *"You're going to carry Burris like you carry everybody else in your ward on that ticket!"* He was really laying it out to them, and there I was taking it all in. I couldn't believe Donovan did that, but I was certainly glad he did!

The next day, I told Gene Sawyer about my eavesdropping episode, and we shared a good laugh about it. We forged ahead with new confidence in my likelihood of winning the race for comptroller, knowing that we stood to gain a good base of the white vote with the support of the white ward committeemen.

Despite Donovan's stern suggestion and despite the State Central Committee's selection of me as the slated candidate, there were still plenty of the county chairmen who refused to acknowledge me as such. Those who supported me could not believe the audacity of those chairmen, revolting against the State Central Committee's decision and continuing to support Dick Luft!

After that, word traveled throughout Cook County that the black Committeemen who were carrying me on their ticket would cause a major split in the Illinois Democratic Party if I was not supported by those downstate county chairmen as well. In fact, the black committee-men, including Sawyer, Partee, Frost, Shumpert and Carothers, even held a press conference over the matter. In that press conference, they stated their unequivocal position emphatically: *"All downstate county chairmen are expected to carry Burris because he is the slated candidate by the State Central Committee. To do anything otherwise will cause a major split in the Illinois Democratic Party."* After that, a few white county chairmen did join forces with the black ones and, together, they made me their slated candidate, with race becoming a minor issue in the Primary election. I did go on to beat Dick Luft in the Primary. I got just as many votes in the majority white wards as the other slated candidates.

Finally in the Race

There I was, running again for state comptroller in 1978 as the Democratic nominee. My race was against a very tough, wealthy republican, John Castle, a member of Governor Jim Thompson's cabinet. His father had been a two-term attorney general of Illinois. He lived in Sandwich, a small, northern Illinois town. His family owned a bank, and John flew his own twin-engine Cessna plane. What all that meant was that I not only campaigned against John Castle, the man, but also against his money and name recognition.

I didn't have much money to do T.V. commercials, or any other major kind of advertising for that matter; instead, I relied on a network of contacts. One of the networks I counted on was the Jaycees network. Even though most of them were republicans, they knew me personally. They said, *"Party or no party, Burris is a good Jaycee,"* so, for the first time in their lives, some of those republican Jaycees supported and voted for a democrat.

Every major community in Illinois had a Jaycee chapter. Like me, many of the directors of those chapters had moved up the ranks, so I had been acquainted with them for quite a while. Generally, they were older, highly-respected individuals with a lot of status in their respective communities. According to Jaycee regulations, members were prohibited from continuing their membership beyond the age of thirty-five. No doubt, they were in excellent positions to collect on a lot of IOU's from family, friends and colleagues. They did an excellent job of "selling me" throughout their communities.

The positive effect the Jaycees had on my campaign brought great relief to my team, whose outreach was severely limited by low funds and limited resources. My modest campaign was led by Fred Lebed and Wanda Gates, both of whom I had worked with extensively since hiring them while I was in the governor's cabinet in 1973.

Wanda began as my secretary when I was head of the General Service Administration (GSA) office under Governor Walker. When I went to work for Rev. Jackson at PUSH, I took Wanda with me. So naturally, when I left *PUSH*, I wasn't going to leave her behind. She actually remained a very loyal and astute assistant to me throughout my entire sixteen-year political career.

Fred had come to work for me during the summer of 1973, as a nineteen-year-old intern. He ended up working full-time at GSA and managing my campaign in 1976 for comptroller. Despite my loss in that race to Mike Bakalis, Fred and I and the other members of our team worked our tails off and brought in 250,000 votes with very limited campaign resources. Running with Independent Dan Walker meant that there was no established and well-heeled organization in place which could provide funds to help me promote myself. In fact, our main resource was an old borrowed and beat up station wagon.

In those four months, during 1976, Fred and I literally wore that station wagon out, putting about 25,000 miles on it going from South Beloit on the northern border of Illinois, all the way to Cairo, Illinois on the state's southern border, and everywhere in between. Fred drove; and I navigated. Driving me everywhere was just one of many responsibilities Fred took on in those days. He also served as my scheduler and advance man.

He would schedule my appearance somewhere, drive us to that location, park the station wagon a block or so away, and go inside the venue incognito to check out the place for its suitability (hence, his "advance" title). If the place checked out okay, he would tell the people there that the candidate should be arriving soon. *"Let me go outside to check on where he is,"* is what Fred would tell them just before running back to me in our car parked around the corner. We would then pull up in front of that place as though that had been our intention all along. Those were some fun and trying times! In 1978, when I was going up against John Castle, naturally I wanted Fred back in the saddle as my campaign manager. Fred had left GSA when I did and was helping his father in the family's business. He happily came back on board to run that '78 campaign.

Wanda ran the campaign office, assisting Fred from inside. I selected my buddy, Ron Greer, who was still at Continental Bank, as chairman of my campaign. I also cashed in on the political expertise from people like Vic de Garzia and David Green.

Political strategist, Green, could work numbers like no one else I knew. He, working alongside de Garzia, was Dan Walker's guru and key fundraiser when Walker ran successfully for governor. On a side note, his son, Howard Green, is currently very active in the Jewish community with the American Israel Public Affairs Committee (AIPAC), which is one of the most powerful lobbying groups in our country.

I Won! Or Did I?

On that November 1978 election night, thank goodness I had David helping in the backroom when the votes came in. He and the others reported to me, *"Well, you won this election by 153,000 votes!"* Of course that was great news; however, it wasn't official news. Even though we were getting our numbers throughout the night directly from the county clerks of each of the one hundred and two counties, *our* figures were not being considered by the press.

The press never reported me as the winner that night. We knew in our gut and on paper that we had won the election, yet the media would not declare me the winner. Everyone running in that General Election had been officially declared a winner by the prognosticators in news rooms across the state that night, that is, everyone except me. Because none of the various reporters had declared a winner in the comptroller's race, my campaign office strongly suspected that someone was trying to steal the election! When I finally went to bed, the media was finally reporting that John Castle had beaten me by 4,500 votes.

That Wednesday morning, I got in touch with Cook County Board President, Dunne. I got in touch with Mayor Balandic. I called the Regular Democratic Party's lawyers. I informed the whole Party's structure that the press' figures are not matching our figures, even though our figures were confirmed by the counties. I told them that we would be calling for a full investigation of possible election fraud.

On Wednesday afternoon, I called a press conference. The members of the press came to the press conference with the expectation that I was going to concede, and were very surprised when I didn't. In that conference, I did not mince my words, but with much conviction, I stated, *"I'm calling for the U.S. Attorneys' offices in the northern district, central district, and the southern district of Illinois to impound the ballots, because they are trying to steal the election."* In the meantime, the Democratic Party lawyers were reaching out to the states' attorneys in the various counties.

First thing Thursday morning, I had my group investigate to see where exactly the press received *their* numbers. As it turned out, the Associated Press (AP) was the culprit. When I couldn't get through to the local AP office, I called the Associated Press in New York and demanded to talk to the president of the company. *"He's in Europe,"* the voice on the other end of the phone told me.

"Who is next in charge?" I explained my quest and was told to hold while my call was directed to the executive vice president.

"Hello Sir. I don't know anything about Illinois politics," came that man's response right off the bat, obviously fully informed of the nature of my call by the receptionist. I reiterated in a calm, but stern, manner, *"Well, just know that something is wrong with the count of the votes that your people are giving to the media."*

He soon realized I was not backing down from my claim, nor was I going to hang up the phone until he promised to take some sort of corrective action. He concluded our conversation stating, *"Well, let me call Illinois and find out what's going on."*

As he promised, that executive made a call to pass on the concerns we had about the accuracy of the AP reporting of the election results. An hour or so later, a very arrogant man from the Chicago AP called our campaign office and curtly asked, *"What is this all about you guys calling New York?"*

Fred immediately jumped all over that guy demanding results. *"We want you to go over your numbers! We want you to go over your numbers!"*

The AP man conceded. We pulled out our tally sheet and went through it alphabetically, county by county, comparing it to their sheet.

We were determined to find out why ours said we won by 153,000 votes and theirs showed we lost by 4,500 votes. There are one hundred and two counties. A, B, C, D...M. When we got to Madison County, the AP man read, *"Burris 39,000 votes, Castle, 179,000 votes."* *"Whoa, whoa, back up,"* Fred demanded.

The man read the line again, *"Burris 39,000 votes, Castle, 179,000 votes."*

"Castle got 179,000 votes? In Madison County? Impossible," fumed Fred. *"Hell, there ain't even 179,000 people in Madison County!"*

Our sheet had 19,000; theirs had 179,000. Someone tried to manipulate the election by placing a seven in between the one and the nine in their vote count! Someone actually thought that was going to just slip by us, obviously not realizing how familiar my staff and I were with the demographics of all the Illinois counties. Around three o'clock that Thursday afternoon, we corrected the so-called error and AP finally put the word out across the wires that Burris was elected to the Office of State Comptroller by 153,000 votes!

I held a press conference that Thursday evening, two days after Election Day, declaring my victory. Those two dreams I had set twenty-five years earlier as a justice-driven fifteen-year-old kid: to become a lawyer and to become a statewide elected official of Illinois had finally been fulfilled! Little did I know when I set those goals that I would become the first black statewide elected constitutional officer in the history of Illinois?

Inauguration Day

Inauguration Day on January 15, 1979 was not just a special personal moment that will exist forever in my mind and in the minds of my family and friends who were in attendance at the event, but it also became a swatch which will be embroidered forever into the historical tapestry of the State of Illinois. Since our state joined the union back in 1818, a black man had never been elected by the people to a statewide constitutional office. Even after all these years, I am still humbled to have been the first individual to be chosen for such a signal honor.

Not to be slighted from the list of significant occurrences, the weather made a statement as well. Funny how a temperature reading of fifteen degrees below zero (actual temperature, not counting the wind chill factor) can easily remain etched in one's mind years later. Funnier still was the fact that in all the excitement of that day, I left home without my overcoat, hat and gloves! I went the entire day on such a spiritual high that I didn't even need those winter outer garments. It was only after the entire day's festivities had ended that I even learned of the grueling low temperature, and even after the fact, I got cold just thinking about it!

That historic day was filled with activities from morning to night. First, my family and I were whisked from our home in a marked state trooper's car to Meigs Field Airport, downtown Chicago where, along with that state trooper, we hopped on a state plane to Springfield. We attended a church prayer service before the inaugural ceremony, and I hosted a private reception at my new office after the inaugural ceremony. Once nighttime fell, we danced and mingled until well into the wee hours of the morning at the inaugural ball. As you can imagine, we snapped numerous pictures throughout that entire day.

However, before falling into the throes of all the business and fanfare of the day, I did something that was most the memorable of all the activities. As soon as we landed in Springfield that morning, I had our driver take us immediately to Oak Ridge Cemetery. There, I visited Lincoln's Tomb; the final resting place for our nation's 16th president and his family, its huge separate acreage, at some distance from a sea of surrounding headstones. I ventured inside that marble-walled tomb and stood in front of the beautifully carved block of marble in the middle of the room, signifying the location where Lincoln lies buried ten feet below.

I spent a private moment reflecting and conversing internally with the one who said in his Gettysburg Address that our nation was *"conceived in Liberty, and dedicated to the proposition that all men are created equal. "*[cvi] I asked him what he thought about the great thing that was happening in his state of Illinois that day: that another barrier blocking the truth that all men are created equal had been broken. *"How about that, Mr. President? The people of Illinois have spoken."*

Before leaving that burial room, I glanced at an inscription on one of the walls that historians have pegged as the most famous epitaph in American biography. Those inscribed words, *"Now he belongs to the ages,"* were the words spoken by Edwin Stanton, Lincoln's Secretary of War moments after Lincoln was pronounced dead.[cvii]

As I sat on the stage later that morning, waiting to give my inaugural speech, I thought about that inscription in the tomb and how "the ages" have actually played out for "my people." Would our struggle ever *really* be over in the days that I'm on this earth? It's funny, but the mere fact I was even giving a speech that day was the result of a struggle.

Soon after winning my election, it had occurred to me that such a historical feat deserved a few moments of a public address. Since the inaugural rules stated that only the governor could give a speech during the inauguration, I sought permission from the inaugural committee to say a few words in celebration of such a historical moment. Their response was an unsympathetic *"No."* No other speeches besides Governor Thompson's would be allowed. In pure Burris style, I persisted for the sake of principle.

The inaugural committee, with Thompson at the helm, soon realized the issue was not going to go away. On top of that, once word got out about the whole ordeal, Jerry Cosentino, our newly elected state treasurer, added his demand. He told the committee, *"If Burris gets to speak, as the first African-American elected to a statewide office, then I should get to speak as the first Italian-American to be elected to a statewide office."*

Under so much pressure, the committee gave in and changed the rules. In order for me to be allowed to speak and for Cosentino to be allowed to speak, it was decided that ALL elected officials would be allowed to speak. The committee also imposed a five-minute limit on all speeches.

In my speech that day, I told the crowd about my visit to Lincoln's tomb. I shared with them about how, in the stillness of that marble tomb, I asked Lincoln what he thought about the significant change happening in his great state of Illinois that day which marked the first time in history a black statewide elected official would serve the people of Illinois. After several other sentiments, I closed by telling the crowd that I heard in my spirit the answer from Lincoln was that he was well pleased that the people of Illinois had spoken. Was it an oversight on my part, or a deliberate act, that my speech ran longer than that five-minute limit? The inaugural committee would never learn that answer from me!

211

Celebrations
Photographs

Banker Roland Burris (second from right) chairs meeting of members of Continental Bank's Group 4 B, the small business lending section which he headed

Roland W. Burris (center) with friends and colleagues at Continental Bank Alumni Reception

Banker Roland Burris confers with Fred Shewell, Continental Bank Vice President

Burris speaks at Ten Year Tribute for Outstanding Service as Illinois State Comptroller

Burris shares humor with Secretary of the Navy and former Governor of Mississippi, Ray Mabus

Burris (bottom left) greets friends as his party arrives at Goodwill Industries Man of the Year Award Ceremony

Burris accepts the congratulations of Patricia Roberts Harris, former Secretary and Human Services in the Carter Administration

The Black Book Award (1981) Congressman Walter Fauntnoy; unidentified person accepting the award on behalf of Atlanta Mayor, Maynard Jackson; Alabama Democratic Conference President, Joe Reed; Mayor Richard Hatcher of Gary, Indiana; Alderman Marian Humes of Chicago's 8th Ward; Illinois Comptroller Roland W. Burris; and Rep. Maxine Walters (D-CA)

Roland W. Burris greets Ruby Dee as Illinois Representative Benny Steward (1st Congressional District), and businessman Ted Jones look on

Comptroller Roland W. Burris is awarded the Presidential Citation by Dr. Benjamin Alexander, President of Chicago State University. Dr. William Sutton, University Provost, is in the forefront

Roland and Berlean Burris with Burris' former Centralia High School classmate, Bill Norwood and his wife, Molly, at Bill's retirement as the first black captain with United Airlines

Burris celebrates 50th birthday with family and friends at Chicago residence

Former Attorney General Neil Hartigan joins Attorney General Roland W. Burris; wife, Dr. Berlean Burris; niece, Kim Burris Holmes; daughter, Rolanda Burris; son, Roland Burris II; and nephews, Tony Burris and Steve Burris, in birthday celebration

Members of Comptroller Roland W. Burris' Springfield office celebrate his 50th birthday

Members of Comptroller Roland W. Burris' Springfield office celebrate his 50th birthday

Roland W. Burris at 50th Birthday celebration in Centralia, Illinois with Dorothy Brady, mother of former Presidential Press Secretary and gun control advocate, James Scott "Jim" Brady on left and Burris' great aunt, Bertha Hines, on right

Burris amuses son, Roland Burris II; sister, Doris Downey; wife, Dr. Berlean Burris; and daughter, Rolanda Burris at his 50th birthday celebration in Centralia

50th birthday celebration Son, Roland W. Burris II; daughter, Rolanda Burris; wife, Dr. Berlean Burris, Roland W.. Burris; and Burris' Centralia High School classmate, Betsy Kourdouvelis

The Burris's and their children, Rolanda and Roland II, celebrate the couple's 20th Wedding Anniversary at the Drake Hotel in Chicago

On 25th Wedding Anniversary, Roland and Berlean Burris renew their wedding vows at St. John Church Baptist in Chicago, with Dr. Reverend William A. Johnson, officiating and with son, Roland Burris II, daughter Rolanda Burris, and sister Nellie Miller in attendance

Roland W. Burris (left) and Dr. Berlean Burris (right) celebrate their 25th Wedding Anniversary with friends, Dr. and Mrs. Conrad May (center)

Roland and Berlean Burris prepare to cut their 25th Wedding Anniversary cake

Chapter Eleven
First Black Illinois
State Comptroller

First Term (1979–1983)
Working as a Statewide Elected Official

O vercoming lack of name recognition, lack of funds, and other obstacles as well, I had persevered through a hard-fought campaign to become Illinois' first black statewide elected official, as state comptroller. There were plenty of naysayers on hand to negate that my victory had anything to do with my own merit. Instead, they could only accept my election win as a fluke, implying that I had ridden into office on the coattails of newly elected secretary of state, Alan Dixon. My comptroller's number five spot appeared on the ballot immediately following the Secretary of State's number four spot. The fact that Dixon had won by such a huge margin over his opponent was their explanation as to how I had gotten so many votes overall. Also, in some of the black communities the word on the street was that a lot of people hadn't even known that I was black. They claimed, *"The name 'Burris' on the ballot didn't sound black."* That explanation was often used by political analysts to justify how I received so many white votes.

Despite the theories of these naysayers, I knew that I couldn't get sidetracked by all those crazy rationalizations about how I had gotten there. *I* knew that I had worked hard and played fair to get there, so that was all that mattered. It was 1979; my inauguration was over; and it was time to get down to business. Thompson, already serving a two-year governorship, had beaten Bakalis in a 1978 election to remain Illinois' republican governor. Dave O'Neal remained lieutenant governor. The other positions were as follows: Attorney General Bill Scott, Secretary of State Alan Dixon and State Treasurer Jerry Cosentino. We were three Republicans and three Democrats. On our license plates, we were described as: governor 1, lieutenant governor 2, attorney general 3, secretary of state 4, comptroller 5, and treasurer 6. I was number five.

In Illinois, the constitutional officers had to reside in the state's capital city, so the state paid for our homes in Springfield. The governor lived in the mansion, and the rest of us lived in leased or purchased homes. Since Illinois is such a big state, we were given access to a couple of modes of transportation: automobiles and airplanes. I also had five state troopers assigned to me because along with my elected position came a few death threats. In the midst of all the good people living amongst us, there are always those few crooked folks out there whose minds cannot accept major changes, especially when race and gender are involved.

In the executive department, we were free to set our own schedules, so I made it a point to get back to my family as often as possible. I spent two or three nights a week in Springfield or elsewhere if business took me to the other parts of the state. Anytime I had business north of Peoria, I spent the night in Chicago with my family. My executive assistant, Gloria Schiesler, was instrumental in making all my travel arrangements and for scheduling events for me anytime I was outside of Chicago. In fact, I remain forever grateful for the nurturing, mother-like administrative care Gloria extended to me for sixteen years.

My young son and daughter were growing up fast and were already in elementary school. Much of the burden was on Berlean to take care of their daily needs, which she did without complaining too much. She and I would joke about the fact that my name, as comptroller, was on her university paychecks, since I wrote all the checks for the state. I told her if she complained too much or got out of line, her paycheck might come up missing! We got through many tough times with humor like that.

For two people with such equally demanding careers, the notion of "tough times" was an understatement and humor was, and still is, a lifesaver for our marriage. At the same time that I was working at the bank and beginning my career in politics, Berlean was leading an extremely demanding pursuit of her own goals. She was already a registered nurse prior to our marriage. During our marriage, while tending to our children, she acquired a bachelor's degree in Nursing from Loyola University of Chicago; a master's degree in Public Health Nursing from the University of Illinois at Chicago; and a PhD in Social Policy and Higher Education Administration from Northwestern University.

During much of the time, she also held positions as Associate Professor, Chairperson, and Dean of the College of Nursing, and finally as Dean Emeritus of the College of Health Sciences, all at Chicago State University. Later, she also obtained a master's degree in Biblical Studies from Moody Bible Institute and was subsequently hired as a professor in Moody's Graduate School.

One would have to wonder where Berlean found a spare moment in the day for herself, but she did. Recently, she published a book about her life story entitled *Just Stand, God's Faithfulness Never Fails*. In the book, she talks about the unique experience of being the spouse of an elected official, the struggle to maintain the faith needed to remain supportive during trying times, and especially about how our faith helped all of us through my Senate experience.

I remember back in the early days of my political career, as I ran for state representative, Berlean had our little son in the stroller and our four-year old daughter by the hand, as she went up and down the streets passing out campaign literature. Through all her experiences, she came to know, as did I, the importance of that "first black statewide official" title being worn by me. In addition to that weighty honor, the Office of State Comptroller was still a fairly new position for Illinois. My work was truly cut out for me!

From Cash to Accrual

Just seven years earlier, in 1972, George Lindberg had become Illinois' first state comptroller. As the first person to hold this newly created position, a lot was required of him to get the office up and running in a manner that was also constitutionally sound. Lindberg had hoped for a second term to continue fulfilling that task, but had been defeated by Bakalis in the 1976 election. Bakalis soon set his sights on the governor's race and only served as comptroller for two years, clearly not enough time for him to complete most of the initiatives begun by Lindberg. The reason it was so important that operations of that position followed the new constitution was because of the fact that then, and probably now, most people don't understand the difference between the role of the comptroller and the role of the treasurer in state government. In essence, the comptroller writes the checks and directs the treasurer as to the fund into which the money should be deposited. The treasurer banks the money and invests the funds for the state. At the time I took office, there were approximately three hundred of those funds to manage, including the general fund, the roads fund, the common school fund, the lottery fund and many other special funds.

A lot of states in the U.S. don't have a comptroller. Illinois established this elected position in our new constitution in 1970 as a result of an auditor who, years earlier, had embezzled millions of dollars from the state. Orville Hodge, who served as Auditor of Public Accounts from 1953 to 1956, absconded with almost $3 million of taxpayers' money before getting caught and eventually serving prison time. To accomplish this crime, Hodge had set up a network of "ghost pay-rollers" and regularly printed checks to these non-existing people. He forged state warrants and committed a host of other misappropriations to which he pled guilty once the detection of his crime brought his spree to a screeching halt.[cviii] Obviously, Hodge's ability to misappropriate state funds so easily, clearly illustrated the need for a more transparent system of checks and balances.

Due to the nature of our warrant processing system, I remained concerned about somebody putting through fake information and stealing money from the state as Hodge had done. When I came into office, we had a paper system that required the manual keying in of all state vouchers. Our check-writing machine would not allow us to print any one check in excess of $9,999,999.99. Still, I was concerned that someone knowledgeable of our number and voucher system could send through false documents up to that amount; key in the proper codes; and voilá...fraud.

In fact, three men from the Department of Public Aid did just that.

They put through three separate vouchers for their dummy company for $14,000, $28,000 and $8,000. The only reason they got caught was because one of them tried to cash the $8,000 voucher at a currency exchange rather than at a bank. They were eventually each sentenced to five years in prison. We were able to recover all of the state's money.

One of my main objectives during that first term was improving the effectiveness of our accounting system by modernizing its operations. In order to achieve that goal, I took us from a cash accounting system, where transactions were not recorded until they were paid, to an accrual accounting system, where transactions were documented when initially received. That new system helped us to better determine our state's true financial obligations. It also made us a leader among states that improved their accounting systems and helped Illinois to become the first large state in the nation to process financial statements in accordance with cutting edge technology.

In order to be in compliance with GAAP, it required us to retrieve and reconstruct financial transactions dating all the way back to the 1940's, a daunting task, which we diligently managed; and thereby, earned still more national recognition. The entire process took a year and a half to complete. Finally, in 1984, with the cooperation of the State Auditor Robert Cronson, we produced our first financial report for Illinois, having met all the requirements for certification by the Government Financial Officers Association (GFOA) of the U.S. and Canada, in accordance with GAAP.

"It's Your Money"

Once in the comptroller's office, it didn't take me long to realize that there was more to my job than managing all those funds and modernizing our accounting systems. Another important aspect of my role, which sometimes seemed to be all-consuming, was battling the governor's budget director: Dr. Robert Mandeville.

Dr. Mandeville was a major financial guru for the state. Prior to my election as state comptroller, Mandeville had mastered the art of making Bakalis, the previous comptroller, to look really bad to the press, apparently all because Bakalis had previously challenged him on some state spending issues.

To undermine the previous comptroller, Mandeville had fed many unconfirmed and troubling reports to the press about Bakalis' operations. Whether these reports were factual or not, the press believed Mandeville because after all, he was Mandeville. As a result, the members of the press would not give Bakalis the time of day, and, in the process, diminished both the man and the office he held. Coming into an office with such a dubious reputation meant that I had to pull double duty in building up our credibility; otherwise, we would certainly have fallen prey to that same poor treatment from the press.

In forming my staff in 1979, I kept a lot of Bakalis' people and added my own personal team to the mix. I decided first to tackle the reputation issue by studying all there was to know about those three hundred funds, including all the trends and the nuances. I also looked at such issues as how the appropriations were handled and how the checks were written. Then, and only then, could I begin to come up with solutions as to how to better serve the public.

One such solution was a pamphlet I devised called *"It's Your Money."*[cix] I instructed my team to put out a financial statement each month. In that statement, we published what monies we took in, what we spent, and where we currently stood in the general fund. What we could see from those statements, and, more importantly, what the public could finally see was that the government was spending more than it was taking in. The press started eating that information up! As much as the members of the press couldn't believe our transparency, they loved our transparency. It made for great headlines. They couldn't wait for the statement to come out each month. What those statements were saying to the public was, *"Yeah, this is your money, but if you send it to Springfield, guess what? We're surely going to spend it."* I told the public, as well, on numerous occasions, that *"If you send it, politicians will spend it."*

My pamphlet and the wide interest it commanded led Thompson to realize that he needed to start releasing a periodical publication or statement of his own. Eventually, he did just that, and had his office produce a small publication which was designed to make the governor's office look good. Usually these publications also gave Thompson and me something to lock horns on. We challenged each other often, but outside of work, we remained fairly good friends; and were always very cordial to one another. I recall someone had observed me chatting and

218

laughing with Thompson one evening at a big dinner at the Palmer House Hotel in Chicago. That person later asked out of curiosity, *"You guys were fighting, weren't you?"*

"What are you talking about?" I asked, before realizing he was referring to the war of words we recently had in the press as Roland Burris, the comptroller, and Jim Thompson, the governor.

"Oh, that's government stuff," I replied.

When I first went to Springfield as head of GSA in the governor's cabinet, I learned that when legislators are on the floor talking about each other, or battling it out in front of the media, there's nothing personal about it between them, it's all political stuff; it's their passion for their work and for their beliefs. If you take it personally, that means you're too thin-skinned and definitely in the wrong business. I like Thompson as a person, while at the same time, I went toe-to-toe with him on political issues. For instance, I felt he didn't pay close enough attention to the income levels compared to the spending levels. In 1980, Thompson had made a big pledge to put $500 million per year in the education fund over the next five years. Right away, in his 1981 budget, things appeared quite differently. He only put $250 million in the education fund, only half of what he had pledged! The remaining $250 million was spent on a variety of new programs.

When Dan Walker was governor prior to Thompson, he managed the budget very well and did great things budget-wise for education in Illinois. Because of all the savings our state incurred under his leadership from 1973 to 1977, Walker was able to put into the common school fund, in addition to the base funding, over $660 million. Therefore, under Walker, the state's share of education rose to a high of 48% of the cost of all the elementary and secondary schools in Illinois.

In referring to the level of support the state will provide for education, the Illinois Constitution states that, *"The state of Illinois shall be primarily responsible..."* Even though the word "primarily" doesn't give an actual percentage, most people would interpret that word to mean 51% or more. So, under Governor Walker, we were just three percentage points under what was expected, which was not bad. Just as important was the fact that Walker had brought this about without any tax increase. In fact, his 1972 win over Governor Ogilvie was credited largely to the fact that Ogilvie *did* pass the state's first income tax law.

On the contrary, Thompson never kept his pledge to fund education fully. Using those pledged funds elsewhere, in my opinion, was what started the structural problem that Illinois still experiences today.

Next in Line

Financial mayhem surrounding that 1980 budget wasn't the only kind of disturbance going on during that time. Our state's capitol was experiencing a bit of an upheaval among the six constitutional officers, as well. In 1980, lieutenant governor David O'Neal left his post to run as the republican nominee to fill the U.S. Senate spot vacated by Adlai Stevenson III. Democratic Secretary of State, Alan Dixon, also ran in that race and beat O'Neal. O'Neal decided not to resume his lieutenant governor duties. Instead, he resigned and headed back to his downstate Illinois home.

According to our state constitution, the lieutenant governor position, when vacated, had to stay vacant until the next General Election, which in that case was 1982. As a result, Governor Thompson could not appoint anyone to fill O'Neal's spot.

The lieutenant governor assumes the powers and duties of governorship when the governor can no longer serve or is absent from his position. With that position open, the succession to the governorship, if ever needed, would have occurred in the following priority order: first, the attorney general; secondly, the secretary of state; thirdly, the comptroller; and lastly, the treasurer.

Our attorney general in 1980 was Bill Scott. Scott, however, was *not* eligible to take part in the succession to the governorship because he was in the process of being tried for tax evasion, a charge on which he was later convicted. When Scott had been convicted and forced to step down from the attorney general's office, Thompson had subsequently appointed Tyrone Fahner to take over as attorney general.

Our new secretary of state at that time was Thompson's former legislative staff member, Jim Edgar, who also had been appointed by Thompson to fill that position when it was vacated by Alan Dixon, who had just been elected to the U. S. Senate. Therefore, *neither* Fahner nor Edgar was eligible to succeed to the governorship since our constitution stated that only an elected official, not an appointed one, could do so.

As third in succession to the governorship during that period from

1980 through 1982, and as an elected constitutional official, I became Illinois' lieutenant governor in David O'Neal's absence. I would venture to say that most of the public did not know that if something had happened to Governor Thompson, I was next in line to succeed him.

It was fine by me that this was not public knowledge. I had enough going on with all my comptroller duties that I didn't need the unnecessary distraction that would have come from the press and from the public about a possibility that might not occur. I even felt a sense of relief when George Ryan became Illinois' lieutenant governor in the 1982 elections and took office in January of 1983.

Second Term (1983-1987)
A Second Go-'Round

I ran for a second term as Illinois state comptroller in 1982. By that time, my on-going financial battles with the governor gave me greater name recognition on the ballot. Four years earlier, the name Burris on a ballot was not associated with a black candidate or a white candidate, but was just an unfamiliar candidate. Once in office, though, I traveled throughout Illinois raising awareness about government spending and getting a lot of press coverage with my publicized financial reports. The press began listening and believing what my office reported about the state's overspending. We soon gained the respect we deserved. In late October of 1982, in the final days of my General Election campaign, I hosted a huge fundraiser dinner in Springfield. U.S. Senator Ted Kennedy was flying in as my guest speaker, so, needless to say, I remained quite occupied by all the preparations and last minute details. Berlean couldn't attend my dinner because of an important nursing conference she needed to attend in Minnesota. With our daughter away at college, our fifteen year old son, Roland II, was home alone.

Two hours before my fundraiser began; I received a phone call from my sister-in-law in Chicago. Roland had gotten ill, and she was at the hospital with him. I tried to reach Berlean, but she was in flight. I knew I couldn't cancel the dinner; after all, it was *my* fundraiser. I did, however, make arrangements to leave immediately afterwards, explaining matters to Senator Kennedy when he arrived. As soon as the dinner came to a close, I hopped on a state plane to Chicago, and my state police escort got me quickly to Mount Sinai Hospital on the West Side.

Berlean was paged in the Minneapolis airport upon her arrival and caught the very next flight back to Chicago. Funny, but she and I arrived at the hospital at the exact same time: around 10:30pm. The doctors had diagnosed Roland with acute appendicitis. He was released the next day and scheduled to return a week and a half later for an appendectomy.

A few days after that ordeal, I was re-elected to the office of Illinois State Comptroller by a plurality of 1.1 million votes! My November 1982 landslide win warranted a great celebration; however, so many other things were demanding my attention that there was no time to celebrate. For one, Roland's surgery was coming up the following week. Also, the entire city of Chicago was in high anticipation of a big announcement to be made by Congressman Harold Washington.

Governor Thompson had just stirred up the media with his own big announcement. The day after that General election, he had reported to the public that the state's October 1982 receipts had fallen far short of the amount of revenue that had been predicted. He called for a $2 billion tax increase, which at that time was the largest in the history of the state! I opposed that increase and put forth the position that although we would need a tax increase, only $900-$950 million would be necessary. Members of the legislature agreed with me late in their session. They passed a temporary tax increase for 18 months that proposed to bring in about $1 billion to solve our deficit crisis.

Harold Washington

Harold Washington[cx] had been an Illinois state representative and state senator since 1965 and was currently a congressman for the 1st Congressional District. In several key ways, however, it turned out that Harold was perfectly situated for what was about to happen: he was much loved by "the people" and much feared by the Democratic Machine. Months earlier, amidst speculation about his running for mayor of Chicago, he had told the press he would make an official announcement in November. So much pressure came at Harold from different directions during that very hectic time that even in the moments before his big announcement; he often was not sure what his statement would be.

On a Monday, about a week after my second-term win, our son was wheeled back into his hospital room around two o'clock in the afternoon after a successful operation. Berlean and I sat there waiting for him to awaken fully. At about three o'clock, Ron, my buddy and chief of staff, called to inform me that Harold Washington would be at my house at four o'clock. The topic to be discussed: Harold did not want to run for mayor.

I hung up the phone and anxiously turned to my wife with a look that pleaded for her understanding that I needed to leave the hospital. My look apparently wasn't working too well, because her initial reaction was anything but understanding. Nevertheless, being the trooper that she is, she soon relented with the words, *"Okay, go and have your meeting."*

Ron, Harold and I met at my house as planned and talked about the mayoral race. Harold shared his sentiments with me, *"I'm in Congress. I'm enjoying being in Congress, and I really don't want to leave the Congress. You should run for Mayor, Burris."*

I replied, *"No, not me. I just came off of a big victory as the only black elected statewide in Illinois. My sights are on a higher office statewide. Illinois can always get another black congressman; whereas, it would be harder to get another black statewide official. Besides, you can keep the black voters excited and voting."*

There we were, going back and forth debating what would be best for the public and what would be best for us personally. The press was coming down hard on Harold for things in his past, such as not filing taxes and having been arrested and serving jail time because of it. Because of these problems, some of the black committeemen were trying to stop Harold. Some of them had come to my house the day after the election and tried to get me to run for mayor, in the hope that a Burris candidacy might stop Harold from running. I had declined to do that. Some black businessmen in the community were upset and said, *"There's no way we can put up a guy like Harold."*

However, the activists in the community stuck by Harold. They wanted him in office; and a large portion of the black community wanted him in office. Even with those supporters favoring him and standing behind him, he just didn't want to go through all that rigmarole. Frankly, I couldn't blame Harold one bit. The media attacks are bad enough, but when total strangers who know nothing about you jump on the press' bandwagon slandering your reputation, it becomes more than one can handle. Because of that, I finally said, *"Okay, Harold, if you get out there in the race and it just so happens that it's too much and you don't want to handle it, just talk to the community, let them know that I would be more than happy to run if they would back me instead of you"*

"I gotta show up on Wednesday with this announcement, and you can show up with me." Harold said.

"No, it would be best if you showed up alone, Harold. But again, if it turns out that the situation becomes too bad, I will run with the support of the community."

That was the agreement Harold and I made. He left my home and two days later, on Wednesday, announced that he was running for mayor of Chicago. With that announcement, all hell broke loose in the media. They had a field day reporting and regurgitating all of Harold's personal background information. I'm sure Governor Thompson welcomed the diversion created by that frenzy, as it took some of the spotlight off him and his budget shortage and too-close-to-call election result against opponent, Adlai Stevenson. Thompson's win by a mere 5,000 votes out of 3 million votes cast did not finally became official until days before the inauguration. That's when the Supreme Court refused Stevenson's request for a recount.

Unlike Thompson in that General Election race, I easily beat Republican State Representative, Cal Skinner. In fact, I led the ticket in my number five spot beating Skinner by 1.1 million votes! Remember when my win in November 1978 was by only 153,000 votes? Winning by a million votes could definitely be attributed to years of exposing Thompson's spending of the people's money. In other words, my win served as a testament to the newfound credibility of the Office of the Illinois State Comptroller.

My 1982 win as Illinois state comptroller stood for a long time as the third highest plurality in the history of Illinois. Thompson held the number one plurality spot with his 1976 win over Mike Howlett at 1.6 million votes. Also in 1978, Alan Dixon beat the Republican secretary of state candidate by 1.3 million votes.[cxi]

Helping Harold

In Illinois politics, it's always been upstate versus downstate. During my time as comptroller, I really took a firm stance to promote a one-state mentality: the idea that Illinois could not exist without Chicago and

Chicago could not exist without Illinois. Because of my southern Illinois upbringing, and the time I spent living in Chicago, I found it both easy and necessary to stand before the people of southern Illinois and defend the people in Chicago, and vice versa.

My dual experience proved a major catalyst in bridging the gap between upstate and downstate. Even so, my accomplishment in 1978, as Illinois' first black statewide elected official, didn't cause much of a ripple in the black community. As huge of a milestone as it was in Illinois political history, people in the upstate, where Illinois' largest black population resides, didn't seem to embrace the significance of the election of an African-American to the comptroller's office since it was statewide politics, not Chicago politics.

On the other hand, Harold Washington's 1983 mayoral race electrified the Chicago black community. Harold's major accomplishment was not only becoming Chicago's first black mayor, but also the way that he energized black voters to go to the polls in record numbers. Had they *not* shown up in that fashion, there would never have been a Mayor Harold Washington.

Many people never knew just how narrowly Harold won that Primary Election. Even though there was a split between Richard M. Daley, the son of deceased Mayor Richard J. Daley, and his Southside Irish followers, and the incumbent Mayor Jane Byrne and her Northside Irish followers, every black vote was crucial in helping Harold squeak past those two in order to win. He beat Byrne by only 40,000 ballots with 36 % of the vote. Byrne herself got 34 % of the vote and Daley 30 %. Thus, more than half of the vote, 64 % did *not* go to Harold in that Primary Election.

At that time, the General Election in April was a partisan one, meaning the candidates' political designations were listed. The Republicans had put up state representative, Bernard Epton, who lost to Harold by only 25,000 votes out of 1.2 million votes cast. An astonishing 90% of the black voters came out and voted in that General Election! Harold received between 96-98% of the large black vote and only smithereens of the 85% white voters who came out in overwhelming support of Bernard Epton, causing the election to be that close.

Predictably, Harold's first term was riddled with conflict, making it extremely difficult for him to govern. The media certainly didn't help, using every opportunity to exploit Chicago's political turmoil. For instance, in 1985, an article about me entitled, *"The Man Who Should Be Mayor"* became a cover story of the city's monthly *Chicago Magazine*. I had conducted an interview with a writer not knowing that the story resulting from the interview would be used as a cover story. My picture even appeared on the cover of the magazine. As you can imagine, that did not sit too well with Mayor Washington, especially since we were friends. He had been coming down to Springfield enlisting my help in several areas, and then to have an article like that smack him square in the face.

Part of Harold's ongoing conflict resulted from him having only twenty-one aldermen on his side in the city council and an opposition group of twenty-nine aldermen led by Alderman Edward Vrdolyak. With such prevalent racial division and partisan conflict, Chicago was referred to as "Beirut on the Lake."A court's decision not to accept the city council's redistricting map, called for special elections to be held in four of the city's wards. As a result of those elections, Harold was able to gain four favorable aldermen, bringing the number of aldermen to 25-25, instead of 21-29. That gave him control of the city council with the ability to break any gridlock with his vote, allowing him to move forward with his agenda.

More Accounting Upgrades

During my second term, I continued to modernize our state-wide accounting system. A total overhaul was required to turn our system into an electronic one. The total project was estimated to cost $33 million, an amount we were told could be recouped in the first three years of the system's operations. I set precedence with that project with my requirement for the contractors to perform the work. For the first time in the history of Illinois, each of the five big-eight accounting firms working on the project had to partner with a minority or female-owned company.

The lead firm on that project was Price-Waterhouse. The minority firm with which Price-Waterhouse partnered was the accounting and management consulting firm, Washington, Pitman and McKeever, LLC,[cxii] led by Lester McKeever.[cxiii] This minority firm was founded by Mary T. Washington.[cxiv] In 1939, Ms. Washington earned the distinction of being the first black female CPA in the United States. Another one of the minority companies on that project was a CPA firm, Bronner Group, LLC,[cxv] headed up by a young woman named Gila J. Bronner,[cxvi] who continues today to provide consulting services to local, state and federal agencies throughout the country. Those teams were all well-qualified to implement the system we needed. All together, there were approximately sixty people working harmoniously together. The project started strong, and by the end of my second term everything remained on track, with about $15 million already spent: $7 million by the end of the project's first year and $8 million by the end of the second year. Unfortunately, later during my third term, the tide began to change for this new centralized accounting system.

Third Term (1987-1991) A New Party

In 1986, Adlai Stevenson, who lost in his 1982 gubernatorial race against incumbent Thompson by less than 1% of the vote, threw his hat in the ring for a second-go-'round with Thompson. With that news, Neil Hartigan, who was going to run for governor, backed out and instead ran for another term as attorney general. Hartigan's decision erased all my plans of running for attorney general. As the list of candidates came together for our primary race, I decided to run for a third term as comptroller.

Unbeknownst to us, Lyndon LaRouche, [cxvii]a political activist and head of the LaRouche Movement, [cxviii]had been preparing a place in our Democratic Primary as well. As we learned of this, he presented enough signatures on petitions to participate and soon filled a whole slate of candidates. On Primary Election night, as fate would have it, two of those LaRouches won: Mark Fairchild for lieutenant governor and Janice Hart for secretary of state. They defeated George Sangmeister and Aurelia Pucinski, respectively.

This turn of events caused a major dilemma for our Democratic ticket, mainly because Stevenson refused to run for governor with a LaRouche candidate as his lieutenant governor. Stevenson came up with a solution to that dilemma by creating a third party called the Solidarity Party. [cxix] The plan was to enter the Solidarity Party in the general election as a third party with Stevenson as its candidate for governor. Stevenson selected Michael Howlett, Jr. as his Solidarity Party lieutenant governor running mate. We moved forward to the general election as a divided party with no Democratic gubernatorial candidate.

In that 1986 General Election race, our Democratic ticket consisted of: Mark Fairchild for lieutenant governor, Neil Hartigan for attorney general, Janice Hart for secretary of state, Roland Burris for comptroller, and Jerry Consentino for treasurer.

The Republican ticket consisted of: Jim Thompson as incumbent governor, George Ryan as incumbent lieutenant governor, Bernard Carey for attorney general, Jim Edgar for secretary of state, Adeline Jay Geo-Karis for comptroller, and Mike Houston for treasurer.

The Solidarity ticket consisted of: Adlai Stevenson for governor, Michael Howlett, Jr. for lieutenant governor, John Ray Keith for attorney general, Jan Spirgel for secretary of state, A. Patricia Scott for comptroller, and William Skedd for treasurer.

That race brought forth no Solidarity winners and no LaRouche winners either. Of the six positions, three went to Democrats and three to Republicans. Thompson and Ryan maintained their governor and lieutenant governor positions. The remaining results were: Attorney General Hartigan, Secretary of State Edgar, Comptroller Burris and Treasurer Consentino.[cxx]

The Truth Comes Out

Just as had happened previously after the 1982 election, following the 1986 election, Thompson once again admitted to the state's income shortfall that my office had been reporting all along. Earlier that year in January, midway through our fiscal year, we had tracked the under-funded liability of our state's pension fund. That's when I warned the public about the governor's excessive spending, letting it be known that there were no ifs, ands, or buts about it: financially, Illinois was in dire straits. As they had done in the past, Thompson and Mandeville fired back at me regarding my pension fund reporting, falsely leading the public to believe that there was no financial problem.

Thompson could no longer deny the state's financial condition. In January of 1987, at one point during our inauguration ceremony, Thompson leaned over and whispered to me that we would have to go out and borrow some money to cover our current shortfall. Shortly after that, he publicly called for a $2.5 billion tax increase for his upcoming July '88 budget, the largest in Illinois history! Again, I opposed his tax increase because we had not corrected our spending ways after the '82 tax increase.

Later in 1987, as Thompson signed off on his '88 budget, he retaliated against me for opposing his increase. He not only vetoed the $9 million in my budget earmarked for the completion of the centralized accounting system, but he was careful to veto it in such a way that I could not override it. That action derailed the entire project!

With two years already invested into it; sixty people working on it, $7 million spent on it in 1985, and $8 million spent on it in 1986, that system became null and void with the stroke of his pen. Fifteen million dollars of tax payers' dollars literally went down the drain. In the years since, I don't believe that state officials ever got back to that particular project to bring about a centralized accounting system. That situation is an unfortunate example of bad politics entering into good government.

Chapter Twelve
First Black Illinois
Attorney General
(1991-1995)

Another First

n 1990, I began looking at my political clock. At the age of fifty-five and with twenty years in state government service, I was nearing eligibility for a full pension, which would be equal to 85% of my salary. With four years in the governor's cabinet and twelve years in the comptroller's office, I contemplated needing just four more years of service. At that point, I would be fifty-seven-years-old with twenty years of service. Suddenly, though, I couldn't view my situation as "counting the days until I could receive my retirement check." No, my time in office meant more than that to me. Besides, I had a lot more than just four years of service left in me. That's when I knew I had to run against Jim Edgar in 1990 for the Illinois governorship. Neil Hartigan was also running for governor, so he and I were ready to battle it out in the Primary. There was also a state senator by the name of Dawn Clark Netsch running for attorney general. In looking at the big picture, someone in the Democratic Party suggested that we not have "a conflict on the ticket," but rather that we take a different collective approach in order to better secure our party's win in the General Election.

That suggestion resulted in us backing a ticket of Hartigan for governor; James B. Burns for lieutenant governor; Roland Burris for attorney general; Cosentino for secretary of state; Netsch, taking my spot, for comptroller; and Pat Quinn--Illinois' governor as of this writing--for state treasurer. We all agreed and signed off on that ticket. The results were:

- Democratic candidates Hartigan and Burns lost against Republicans Edgar and his running mate, a state senator by the name of Bob Kustra.

- Democrat Cosentino also lost to Republican George Ryan, who had stepped down as lieutenant governor to Thompson, since Thompson didn't run for re-election.

- Democrats Dawn Clark Netsch and Pat Quinn won the comptroller and treasurer positions by defeating Republicans candidates Sue Suter and Greg Baise, respectively.

In the race for attorney general, I went up against a tough opponent, prosecutor of DuPage County, Jim Ryan and squeaked by with 51.48% of the votes compared to his 48.52%. Sandwiched on the ballet between Hartigan and Consentino, who both lost by small margins, I prevailed by almost 96,000 votes to become Illinois' first black attorney general and only the second black to have won election to the statewide office of attorney general in United States history.[cxxi] I remained in that office until 1995.

My main job as our state's chief legal officer was to represent the citizens of Illinois and the state government of Illinois. During my term, one of the ways I carried out those duties was through various support operations. I was the first Illinois attorney general to set up a women's advocacy division to deal with domestic and other violence against women. My office also sponsored a program for violence against children. I led the efforts to amend the state's constitution to include rights for victims of crimes. The Attorney General's office had statutory authority to set up a civil rights division, but none of the previous attorneys general had done so; therefore, I created the first civil rights division and one of our main legal actions was to attack racial profiling.

Services provided by my office covered a broad range of needs, from business and labor to protection and advocacy; these services reached citizens in every corner of Illinois. We handled criminal cases when a county state's attorney was understaffed or had a conflict. We handled environmental violations and anti-trust representation. For the first time in the attorney general's office history, I obtained the authority through the legislature to empanel a grand jury to prosecute statewide drug offenses.

I had about three hundred lawyers on my staff and another one hundred or so lawyers in various state agencies who reported to me. At any given moment of any given day, there was some legal action going on somewhere in the state keeping those lawyers busy. All the work of that office is done in the name of the attorney general. In other words, even though I deputized about four hundred assistant attorneys general and some special assistant attorneys general to handle cases statewide, at the end of the day, the only name on the litigation that went in the court on behalf of the people of Illinois was mine.

Just One Vote

A lot of those initiatives created within my office would perhaps not have occurred if Governor Edgar had his way. Edgar began his governorship at the same time that I came in as attorney general. The state was in such bad financial shape that his first order of business was to cut everyone's budget by 5% across the board. His proposed 5% cut in my budget required me to lay off one hundred and thirty people, about a third of my legal and support staff! At that time, some lawyers were making only $22,000 per year and had not had a raise in over four years. During the two terms that Hartigan had been attorney general, he had taken great care to act prudently with taxpayers' money, holding down his budget from increases for his staff in preparation for his possible run for Governor.

Had they been enacted, Edgar's budget cuts would have rendered my office virtually ineffective, which I believe, quite frankly, was his ulterior motive. Edgar figured that at some point I would try to run against him for governor, so he needed to ensure I wouldn't excel in my current office. I fought that budget cut by putting into place an operation to override his veto. Fortunately for me, unlike Governor Thompson who earlier had employed a sophisticated and irreversible veto for the central accounting system, which I had attempted to install as state comptroller, Governor Edgar had simply line-item vetoed the proposed

5% cut to my budget. This meant that all that was required to override his veto was a simple majority vote of the legislature.

It was also fortunate for me that we had a Democratic House and a Democratic Senate which was able to produce this simple majority which required sixty democratic votes in the House and thirty democratic votes in the senate. Although I realized it was going to take at lot of work on my part to stop my budget from being cut, I was determined to get it done.

First, I had to lobby the House of Representatives and get the sixty votes needed for the override of the governor's veto. I did that and got sixty-plus votes in the House. In the senate, President Phil Rock, the president of the senate, had a total of thirty-one Democrats; only one vote over the simple majority required overriding the governor's veto cutting 5% of my budget. Believe it or not, during the time that I needed to get the senate to vote on the override, one of the Democratic senators was admitted to the hospital in critical condition. So in actuality, there remained only thirty Democratic senators, exactly enough for the override to be successful.

In the midst of all the negotiation about the override, I learned that another democratic senator, Senator Ethel Alexander, from the Southside of Chicago, would not be in session, because she was under the weather and also had to transport her husband to his doctor appointments. That left us one vote short of the thirty state senate votes required for the override. The twenty-nine Democrats who supported me overriding the veto proceeded to help me get that one vote.

In light of Senator Alexander's absence from the senate floor, where that thirtieth vote would come from was the big question. There was no possibility at all of picking up a Republican vote to override a Republican governor's veto.

Since there was only one day before the vote, we immediately began calling Alexander at her home. All day and into the evening, we rang her phone off the hook. Finally, she answered. After listening to our request, she replied, *"Well, I'm sick; my husband's sick; and I can't come."* Out of pure desperation, I replied, *"We can send the state police to come pick you up, get you to the airport and fly you down on a state plane."*

"Well, I don't like to fly on those state planes."

"Okay, Ethel, we'll have them put the sirens on and drive you down

to Springfield."

Everyone understood that we had to get Ethel Alexander there for that deciding vote. That next morning, we called Alexander again to see whether she would be coming to Springfield. After we convinced her of the critical importance of her vote, she expressed her concern over that fact that she needed someone to take her husband to the doctor. I told her that we would make arrangements to get her husband to the doctor and that someone would be at her house to drive her to the Capitol. She still wasn't sold. That conversation took place around nine o'clock in the morning. Within the hour, we found out that they were going to call the vote at eleven thirty that morning—clearly not enough time for Senator Alexander to make the two and a half-hour trek to Springfield.

At eleven o'clock, I called her back and pleaded, *"Senator Alexander, this means everything in the world to the Attorney General's office; you've got to come."*

She finally agreed. Little did she know, we already had a state police waiting in front of her house along with someone to take her husband to his doctor's appointment? Soon, she was on the road to Springfield. In the meantime, I went over to the senate and asked Senator Rock if they could take a recess and hold off the vote because Alexander was in route. Rock obliged and recessed the senate at noon to reconvene at 1:30pm.

Just when things were starting to come together, they started falling apart. Two or three of the Democrats from down-state heard that Ethel Alexander was coming to the session to be the thirtieth vote. What did they do? They started to backpedal; suddenly changing their minds about their own votes. *"Well, Burris, we don't know about this vote now. You closed down the office in West Frankfort. I want the West Frankfort office reopened."*

Another senator took this stab at me, *"In that asphalt situation, you went against my son. We want you to let up on that asphalt case."*

They were coming at me in all sorts of ways, trying to box me in; trying to get something for themselves, especially regarding that asphalt situation which was a legal matter involving one senator's son who was being sued as a contractor for putting the wrong asphalt down and not following environmental protection regulations. I let them know right away that they weren't going to get me to cut corners on violations just for their benefit. I told them I'd go public with that information. Suddenly, they backed off and kept their votes in.

About two o'clock that afternoon, Senator Alexander arrived, still rather sick. A half hour later, President Rock called the vote to override the governor's veto. We got our thirty votes and managed to keep my staff intact! When the word got back to Edgar about the override, which he had thought to be dead because we had been one vote short in the senate, he was fit to be tied!

Up to that moment, I had not slept for forty-eight hours. I had been involved in a whirl wind of nonstop phone-calling, lobbying and strategizing, not to mention the extraordinary effort it required to convincing Senator Alexander to come to Springfield. It was the first of many hair-pulling experiences I was to experience as attorney general.

A "Wheely" Tough Situation

Another tough encounter was when my office received advance notice that there would be a major protest at the state office building in Chicago. This building is under the management of the department of Central Management Services (CMS), one of the state agencies. The individuals staging the complaint were wheelchair-bound paraplegics. They were protesting the unfair treatment of disabled individuals and wanted Governor Edgar to back them on their right to be able to ride public transportation. We anticipated having to go into court to get an injunction to keep them from demonstrating at the state office building. That next morning, the protestors in wheelchairs assembled in great numbers. Some positioned themselves in front of the building's entrances. Some made it inside the building. That state building, called the James R. Thompson Center in honor of former Governor Thompson, has an atrium lobby that ascends sixteen stories high. There I stood on the 12th floor, looking down over the balcony railing on a sea of wheelchairs, as more converged by the minute! Soon, the protesters had all the elevators and escalators blocked, effectively denying access to state workers and the general public. The situation quickly devolved from a simple protest to a public safety issue, which under a worst case scenario, might have had much more potentially serious consequences.

The ordeal started around mid-morning. We thought for sure that we would receive assistance from the court by noon, but our lawyers' attempt to obtain an injunction was denied by the court. That really allowed the protestors the opportunity to continue their protest by locking their wheelchairs together and taking over the entire ground floor.

Joining me while I stood there on the 12th floor, looking out over to the atrium, were two groups. On one side, were my lawyers representing CMS who were chiefly concerned about the safety of the public, and especially with the issue of building ingress and egress, particularly in the event of a fire or other emergency. On the other side of me, were my advocacy division lawyers, whose major concern was the disabled and their right to protest. As attorney general, pledged to protect the rights of both groups, I was caught in the middle.

I ordered my staff to contact the Chicago police. When we got the city's Deputy Superintendent of Traffic Control on the phone, his response was that it was a state police, and not a city police, problem. So, we got the director of the state police on the phone, who informed us that it was not a state police problem, but a CMS police problem. Those in charge of CMS police told us that CMS police could not arrest the protestors, because they wouldn't be able to accommodate all those wheelchairs in available lock up facilities. The inability of CMS police to deal with the situation, and the unwillingness of city and state police to do so allowed the protestors to remain in and around the state office building for hours and prompted them to assert that they wouldn't leave until they had heard directly from the governor.

Some of us, who knew our way around the building, used the back service elevators to gain access to the protestors. Through our advocacy action, we were able to impress upon them the fact that that they had made their point with their protest, but because of the danger they were causing to the public and to themselves, the protest should be ended. After learning that Governor Edgar wasn't even in town, they agreed to disperse. Around four o'clock that afternoon, in an orderly fashion, the hundreds of wheelchairs slowly vacated the building. As attorney general, I was the only lawyer who could be on different sides of the same situation like that without it being a conflict of interest. However, that circumstance did resolve itself peacefully.

Troubled Waters

Another very difficult situation I encountered as an attorney general was a seven-year-old case which was in process when I took office. It concerned three Illinois citizens who had been arrested by some Kentucky Department of Fish and Wildlife officers. The three men had been charged with fishing in the Ohio River without a Kentucky fishing license, while standing on the Illinois shore. The U. S. Supreme Court was already involved and had appointed a special master to hear the dispute between Kentucky and Illinois.

In 1792, when Kentucky entered the union, the state claimed its boundary as the northern shore of the Ohio River along the Ohio, Indiana and Illinois shores. Hundreds of years later, with that original boundary changed many times over due to the changing of the flow in the river, Ohio, Indiana, and Illinois raised disputes against Kentucky over that shoreline territory.

Ohio and Indiana had previously settled their disputes, by reaching an agreement with Kentucky which allowed each of these states the rights to the territory one hundred feet off of their own shorelines. My predecessor, Attorney General Neil Hartigan refused to settle so easily on behalf of Illinois. In fact, he practically bragged about having Illinois Congressman Dan Rostenkowski, his friend and one of the most powerful U.S. legislators, on his side to help in settling this long standing disagreement; that is, until he found out that Congress couldn't do anything about a dispute of this nature. The U.S. Constitution provides that when there is a dispute between two states, that dispute must be settled by the U.S. Supreme Court. A case such as this one could not be settled by Congress or by the President of the United States. Additionally, the only person who can represent a state before the U.S. Supreme Court is the attorney general of that state.

In fighting that case, we searched Kentucky's records all the way back to 1792. It was amazing to see how satellites, charts and graphs were used trying to figure out the true boundary that ran along those jagged, irregular lines on the maps! To complicate matters even further, during all those hearings, Illinois passed a gaming license law allowing Illinoisans to have gaming boats on the river. Therefore, a boat was going to be anchored at the small Illinois town of Metropolis, which sits right on the Ohio River.

When the Kentucky attorney general heard about that he warned, *"That's still Kentucky waters. You're not going to put a boat in Kentucky waters."* With lawyers from each of our offices battling it out, their attorney general then threatened, *"Any boat that is being put into the Ohio River would violate Kentucky law, and therefore we'll treat that as a violation, and we'll seize the boat."*

I shot back with my own threat, *"If you touch that boat which will be anchored on the Illinois shore, I would treat that as a belligerent act. Illinois has two ships in its Navy. We will float those ships down the Des Plaines River to the Illinois River to the Mississippi River and on to the Ohio River and protect that boat."*

Weeks later, Illinois had a boat in the water and Kentucky did not seize it, mainly because of a newly built hotel in Paducah, Kentucky along the river. Investors of that hotel encouraged gamers on that Illinois boat to stay in their hotel. That new economic interest caused the Kentucky attorney general to back off, making the whole Supreme Court case more contentious than ever.

Finally, in 1991, a settlement in *Illinois v. Kentucky* was agreed upon. The U.S. Supreme Court ruled in Illinois' favor, stipulating the boundary on the Illinois side the same as the Ohio's low water mark of one hundred feet off the shore and more. The new boundary went out as far as twelve hundred feet in a straight line along the river, granting land and water to Kentucky on the south and to Illinois on the north. The Kentucky attorney general and I agreed to this and proceeded to draw up the settlement.

When the negotiated settlement was ready, I proposed that we sign it first, on the Illinois side and then a second time on the Kentucky side of our common border. The Kentucky attorney general objected to this proposal. I then proposed we sign the document at the center of the bridge that joined our two states. Again, the Kentucky attorney general objected.

When it finally became clear to me that the Kentucky attorney general wanted the signing to occur on neutral ground, I agreed to those conditions. The Kentucky attorney general and I finally signed the settlement between Illinois and Kentucky in Washington D.C.; thereby, resolving and concluding that seven-year litigious conflict that had existed between the two states.[cxxii]

Educational Funds

Every day is a "major issue day" for an attorney general. One of my more memorable major issues occurred when some of our citizens sued the state over the disparity in funding for primary and secondary education. The people claimed that Illinois government should pay at least 51% of the cost of education; yet the state's actual educational funding had already gone down to just 33%. The people wanted a commitment from the state to increase funding for education.

To handle that claim, first I had to call together my team of lawyers. In that meeting, some lawyers said when the suit was filed we should go for a summary judgment on the matter. Others suggested we go for a motion to dismiss. Yet another group of them said we should not dismiss the claim, but file an answer and litigate it. It was up to me to make the final decision regarding what position we would take. I directed my staff to go with a motion to dismiss as some of us believed it to be a legislative matter and not a judicial matter; therefore, requiring it to be solved by the legislature.

After three or four days of options, we came up with our response to that petition and presented it to the circuit court of Cook County. Sure enough, after the judge heard our motion to dismiss, he agreed with us that it was a legislative matter. The appellate court and the Illinois Supreme Court agreed with that decision as well. Therefore, the citizens' case was dismissed. They could not hold the state accountable through filing a legal suit, but instead had to get legislation passed to change the funding process.

Three Sides to the Coin

The attorney general can be on all sides of an issue. One case I dealt with was a child abuse matter in Peoria, Illinois. Peoria County has its own state's attorney with a rather large staff; however, the Peoria State's Attorney's office was already involved in a major conflict and could not handle that particular situation. Therefore, the child abuse matter was turned over to my office, causing me to have to represent three sides in that particular case. First, through our advocacy division, I had the duty to protect the child who was thought to have been abused. Secondly, it was my duty to defend Department of Children and Family Services

(DCFS) staff against the allegations of wrong doings that had been brought against them. Thirdly, my office had to prosecute the individual who had been charged with abusing the child. I assigned a team of lawyers to each one of those issues. Whenever there's an abused child, DCFS generally investigates. In this situation, however, since charges were also being filed by the accused person against DCFS, I had a team of lawyers defending DCFS. Through all that, our child advocacy division had to ensure that the child's rights weren't violated. In the end, DCFS was exonerated and the abuser was convicted.

Save Jobs, Not Toxins

I recall a case that dealt with a manufacturing plant in Sterling, Illinois, a small northwestern town well known in the manufacturing and steel industries. The plant, which employed about fourteen hundred people at that time, had improperly stored, then dumped, toxic waste. Toxic waste is no small deal; such material is dangerous. Misuse of toxic waste and its improper removal can be a criminal violation.

The dilemma for me was that, if I rightfully sued that corporation, that company would likely close and I would put about fourteen hundred people out of work. To have done that in a small town like Sterling would have been economically devastating to that community. How could I live with myself knowing I had hurt all those families? It seemed only right that I would go for a compromise. That way, even though the corporation would certainly be indicted, it would also be saved, as would be the jobs of the citizens of Sterling.

Our lawyers indicted the officers of the corporation. The compromise was that the chairman and five officers plead guilty and received a sentence of three years in jail. They all served time. The company then got a whole new management team in there to address the toxic waste issue, and most importantly, the jobs were saved!

Winding Down

I entered the Illinois gubernatorial race in 1993, running in the Primary against Dawn Clark Netsch, the woman who had succeeded me as comptroller, and Cook County board president, Dick Phalen. That 1994 Democratic Primary race was the first one for the governorship since

1976 when Dan Walker lost to Mike Howlett. My toughest opponent was Netsch, with her backing of all the unions, as well as the party officials. I lost that race by less than 40,000 votes, and much to my surprise, Phalen received only 15% of the vote.

The loss to Netsch was a tough loss for me. It ushered in my "lame duck" period: the time from that Primary in March of 1994 until January of 1995 when I merely existed, until the end of my service as attorney general. During that time, as I contemplated my next political move, I realized that others were planning it for me. Talks of who would be running in the 1995 Chicago mayoral race began swirling and my name kept coming up. Every time it did, I rejected the idea. After all, my aim was to take another shot at the governorship in '98, not to become mayor of Chicago. I was soon reminded that the road to one's desired destination usually contains many side trails, which for me included working as a private attorney and managing partner with Jones, Ware and Grenard, the largest minority law firm in the country. Although I did eventually mount two additional campaigns for governor in 1998 and 2002 respectively, despite my intention to remain out of the Chicago mayoral race, all the support from my friends did cause me to become a candidate for mayor in the 1995 elections.

Chapter Thirteen

Serving on a National Level

...as an Organizer at Heart

P rofessor Daniel, my ethics class law professor from Howard University, planted the "organizing seed" in me. He said that if an organization did not exist in order to serve a particular purpose, then we, as social engineers, should create one. I joined a lot of organizations. I also created or advanced the existence of several of them. One group I created in 1967, the Independent Political Organization (IPO), was created in order to counteract many actions of the Regular Democratic Party, such as the party's tendency to tie up an entire family with political patronage.

Another organization, the Young Executives in Politics (YEP), was created to teach young black middle managers in large corporations how politics operated. Some of those managers even went on to become elected officials and to take active roles in political campaigns. I later created The Young Professionals[cxxiii] (YP), a group that replaced the YEP's as they aged, to capture that same demographic of older executives.

I was also involved in Jimmy Carter's 1976 campaign. In 1979, during his presidential term (1977-1981), I became Illinois' first black statewide elected official. Shortly before President Carter's term ended, along with State Representative Benjamin D. Brown, the first chairman of the Georgia Legislative Black Caucus, I formed a group called the

National Assembly of Black Elected Officials.[cxxiv] At that time, there were only five black statewide elected officials in America, and four of us participated in that organization. That national group not only anticipated the future election of additional black statewide elected officials across America, but also paved the way to my involvement with the Democratic National Committee.

...as an At Large Delegate Democratic National Committee Member (1980)

In 1980, President Carter played an instrumental role in my appointment as an "at large member" of the Democratic National Committee (DNC). In 1981, as Charles Manatt became chairman of the DNC, Carter's people, particularly Ben Brown, encouraged me to run for one of the DNC vice chair positions, the one earmarked for black members. I hesitated, not wanting to jump in the middle of the already heated battle for that position between Coleman Young, the mayor of Detroit, Michigan and Richard Hatcher, the mayor of Gary, Indiana. Finally, at the urging of some of Carter's people, who were very concerned about the direction of our party, I joined that battle.

As chairman, Manatt let it be known he would support the black candidate who received the most votes in the black caucus for the vice chair position of the DNC. Hatcher, Young and I competed for those votes which would be cast by the caucus' forty to forty-five members. After all our speeches were heard, we conducted the formal vote for the DNC vice chair position. The voting results were Hatcher nineteen, Young seventeen and Burris five.

With no one receiving the majority vote, a second election was scheduled for the next day. That night, prior to that second voting, Hatcher, to whom I was closer than I was to Young, requested a meeting with me to discuss our positions. Since he had nineteen and I had five votes, he encouraged me to deliver my five votes to him.

"Well, Dick, what about this," I conspired. *"If my people don't want to give up the five votes and no one still has the majority, would you then give your votes to me?"* After mulling that around for a few moments he replied, *"Well, that's fair. If there is a stalemate on the position, I would encourage my supporters to vote for you."*

We settled on that agreement; after which, I convinced my people that selecting Hatcher was in our best interest. I gave my five votes to Mayor Hatcher and he beat Mayor Young to become our black DNC vice chairman. I wish I could say our choice turned out to be a great one. In actuality, Hatcher's tenure was one characterized by confusion. He gave very little attention to DNC matters, and was often unreachable when problems and issues arose concerning actions at the DNC. Each time we assembled, the atmosphere grew more and more chaotic.

...as Candidate for the Illinois U.S. Senate (1984)

Sometime in 1982, with my own growing interest in running for the U.S. Senate, I approached Illinois Congressman Paul Simon and questioned him about any future plans he had for running for the senate. I knew that if there was anyone who could easily be elected to that position, it was Simon. His reply was that he was really happy in the House where he had been for the past ten years and had no plans to run for the senate. That response sent my antenna up, knowing that the strongest opponent would be out of the way.

In late May of 1983, after Harold Washington had been sworn in as mayor of Chicago, my desire to become a candidate for the senate really increased. I called Paul again and said, *"Paul, I'm putting together my campaign. Next month, I'm going to announce my candidacy for the senate."*

Paul replied, *"Roland, go right ahead. I'm not interested in it. As a matter of fact, at the right time, I could even support you."*

By the middle of June, I had confidently prepared my announcement, still keeping Simon's words of endorsement on reserve for the right time, when I got a phone call from him.

"Roland, there are people out here talking to me in Washington about the senate race. They want to do a poll to see how I would fare in that race."

Stunned for a moment, I responded, *"Oh, are you going to change your mind now and run?"*

"Well, I don't think I am," Simon started, *"but I've got to see how this poll comes out."*

"Well, Paul, I'm announcing my candidacy in a couple of days."

Sure enough, about two weeks later, as I began raising money, forming my committee and getting all the other activities involved in campaigning underway, Paul called me back, saying, *"Roland, that poll looked pretty good, and they are going to back me with a million dollars to start; so I think I'm going to be a candidate."*

"Paul, I appreciate that, but I already announced my candidacy, so we're just going to see which of us can win this thing." We spoke briefly and before hanging up I added, *"We will challenge each other in the Primary, but when it's over we need to support the winner in order to take the seat away from Percy."* Simon agreed, and we ended our conversation on that promise of alliance.

The man referred to by Simon was Republican Senator Charles Percy, who was also head of the Senate Foreign Relations Committee. A lot of my Republican friends had been telling me that Senator Percy was not really paying attention to the issues which most concerned the voters of Illinois. Because of that, many of those friends were not planning to vote for him. I actually liked Percy and regarded him as a good guy. My friend and fellow church trustee, Hamilton Talbert, was Percy's best friend. However, after speaking with my Jaycee group, I came to my own political assessment of Percy and easily agreed with Simon that either he or I needed to take Percy's seat away.

There were four candidates in that senate race. Besides Paul Simon and me, there was Phil Rock, Chairman of the Democratic Party and president of our state senate; and a lawyer by the name of Alex Seith, who had challenged and almost beaten Percy in his last election. Naturally, the Democratic Party backed Phil Rock during that November 1983 slating period, as we all prepared to go to battle in the March 1984 Primary Election.

The entire time I fought through that race, my heart told me I couldn't beat fellow Democrat Paul Simon. So if the press had reported that opinion or if anyone had voiced that feeling to me personally, they wouldn't have been telling me anything new. Still, however, I did have a personal obligation to give it my all during that race. Because of that, I pretty much ran up and down, and crisscrossed, the entire the state of Illinois in my campaign efforts. The election had soon come down to a two-man race between Paul Simon and Roland Burris. At the end of the

Primary, Simon won by a little over 100,000 votes. I had no idea I could come even that close to beating him.

As promised, I immediately got behind Simon and threw all my support his way. I gave a fund-raiser for him at my Chicago home a couple of months before General Election Day. Paul Simon did go on to beat Percy and become Illinois' U.S. senator for the next twelve years. Paul and I maintained a respectful friendship until his death. Whenever the opportunity warranted, he made a point to tell people about our senate commitment and how I had kept my commitment to work with him to help him get elected to the office of United States Senate. I considered him to be a true gentleman.

...as Candidate for Vice Chairman of the Democratic National Committee(1985-1989)

In 1984, as Texas Congressman George Thomas "Mickey" Leland[cxxv] and I were being honored in Montreal, Canada by the National Medical Association, we began talking about the DNC. Mickey, who was chairman of the Black Caucus at the time, voiced his concerns about how Vice Chairman, Hatcher, was operating. He, along with many of the rest of the caucus members, disliked the fact that no one could get in touch with Hatcher during a crisis. We certainly couldn't get any information from him during times when the DNC was not meeting.

Since I had run before, Mickey urged me to run for vice chair in order to "take out Hatcher." I agreed and began my preparations for the February 1985 election. My team of people made calls all over the country announcing my upcoming run. Also, in that election, contenders for the position of chairman of the DNC to succeed Charles Manatt, were Paul Kirk and Nancy Pelosi. Since I was closer to Kirk, I let it be known to Pelosi that I was in Kirk's corner. For various reasons, their race grew very contentious, as did mine and Hatcher's.

Some black caucus members tried to convince Kirk to follow the example of his predecessor, Charles Manatt, and support whomever the majority of the caucus members recommended to take the Black Caucus' vice chair spot. As was his right, Kirk disagreed and insisted the issue be taken to the floor so it would be up to the whole DNC to select the vice chair candidate. The question then remained was whether or not the Black Caucus would still take a vote within the caucus. Mickey had said they would not, which I thought was a good move. My team had canvassed all the state DNC members, so we knew how many votes we had. What we didn't know was whether or not we could win in the caucus. Win or lose, it looked like it would be really close.

The afternoon before the meeting, Mickey, Deputy Chairman Ron Brown and I met privately for a brief while. Mickey again promised Brown and I there would be no vote in the Black Caucus, yet just thirty minutes after making that promise, he went into the Black Caucus meeting where the first item on the agenda was a vote to see what their position was on Hatcher and Burris! Ron and I looked at each in total disbelief. *"What is going on?"* Apparently, Mickey along with some of the members of the caucus had decided there would be a vote. I huddled with my people for a few last seconds of strategizing. I told them I didn't think I could beat Hatcher in the caucus, but that if I got more than 40% of the vote I would not allow the caucus vote to be the final say-so. After all, if Kirk was going to stick by his word and take the issue to the floor, then the outcome of the Black Caucus vote was not the final word as far as I was concerned. Sure enough, the Black Caucus took its vote, and Hatcher beat me by three or four votes. That next day, voting from the floor was scheduled to take place for chairman and vice chairman.

Paul Kirk was being challenged by Pelosi, and I was being challenged by Hatcher, so there were more than a few litigious attitudes all around and plenty of bitterness as well. My team of people and I were up all night calling people and taking the many calls that people were making to us. Jesse Jackson and Mayor Marion Berry were just a few of the folk calling and attacking me for going against the decision of the Black Caucus. Some of the members of the Congressional Black Caucus called as well. Seems like everyone wanted to know, *"What are you doing Burris?"*

It was decided my people would take all the phone calls; I would no longer talk to anybody. I was kept isolated from all the distracting opinions. That morning, as the sun rose, none of us had been able to sleep. We had been caucusing, counting votes and politicking all night long. I did take a call that morning from one of my strongest backers, a young state representative from Gary, Indiana, Hatcher's city. Her name was Earline Rogers. *"I know you're catching the heat,"* Earline began, *"but I'm committed to your candidacy. I don't care what you do, don't you back down."*

"Thanks Earline," I answered appreciatively, *"but the heat is getting to me, and it's coming from all directions."*

Finally, around noon, it was voting time. In the vote for the DNC Chairman which took place first, Paul Kirk won over Nancy Pelosi. He then officially opened up the process for the vice chair candidates to speak. Just before I headed to the podium to speak as the DNC Vice Chairman Candidate, Black Caucus Chairman Mickey was finishing his nomination of Hatcher for vice chair. As Mickey left the podium and headed off the stage, I passed him on my way up to the stage. When he saw me, his expression alone revealed it all as his glaring eyes literally dared me to take another step. Through gritted teeth he warned, *"Don't you go up there and speak. Don't do it. I'm telling you, don't do this, Roland."* I looked at him and said, *"Congressman, you've got a problem."*

At those spoken words, Mickey looked like he was going to have a heart attack. He was so angry! Had he thought that I had just been blowing smoke that whole time? I looked at my aide who was standing next to me, shook my head and went on up to the podium to present my platform for the vice chair candidacy. After that brief confrontation with Mickey, I had fresh new tension, which helped to fuel the delivery of my speech. Hatcher spoke next.

More tension arose as the vote went down. I knew that many of the issues I raised in my speech had resonated with a lot of people; I hoped my words had resonated with enough of them to warrant my receiving more than the one hundred and fifty votes needed. On stage, I talked about how we had to move forward. I appealed to the party to cut out all the bickering and fighting because when we're beating up on each other at the DNC meetings, it left us with no energy to beat up on republicans. We counted one hundred ninety-three votes. The real turning point occurred when Ernest "Dutch" Morial brought the four Louisiana delegates over to my camp because he said he liked what he had heard. As those last votes were tallied, we had one hundred ninety-seven votes, and I won the Democratic National Committee Vice Chairman spot.

Soon after I was elected, Hatcher called a press conference during which he and Mickey called me all kinds of names. I didn't find out about it until later, but apparently I was labeled an Uncle Tom, a house n----r and a traitor. I traveled back to Chicago where I held a press conference the following day. The media was all over that issue, asking me what I thought about what had been said. What can one say about that type of bitterness? The attacks came at me from all directions, too. Some of the activists in the black community were upset that I had taken Hatcher out. Jesse Jackson was upset. Even though I had worked with him, he was closer to Hatcher than to me. Both Maxine Waters and Willie Brown of California were upset. Dr. C. Delores Tucker,[cxxvi] who had succeeded Mickey to become the new chairman of the Black Caucus, wasn't fond of me either, since she and Hatcher were allies. I was pretty much *persona non grata* among many of the black democratic leaders.

I ignored it all. I put together my small staff which consisted of a secretary and a staff director, Gordon Gant, and went to work right away on my agenda of uniting our party. I convinced Paul Kirk to let my duties include statewide elected democrats, an option which would give me the ability to travel around the country helping to elect statewide officials (i.e. governors, comptrollers, etc.). For example, I had to beat up on some democrats to get them to see that we needed blacks elected in Mississippi and in Alabama. When I talked to the then-state party chairman of Alabama about electing blacks, I remember how he just about laughed his head off at my request. *"We can't even get white democrats elected down here in Alabama!"*

Gordon and I traveled to many states, raising money for the Democratic Party. In 1985 we helped to bring about the election of the Virginia Democratic statewide ticket, as the voters of Virginia made history by electing, in addition to a white male, also the first female and the first African-American to statewide office: Gerald Baliles as governor; Mary Sue Terry as attorney general; and Douglas Wilder as lieutenant governor. We laid the groundwork in the party for coalitions to work with the Gay and Lesbian Caucus, the Hispanic Caucus, and other factions, and helped many of these groups to elect their local candidates during the 1986 election. Within just twelve months, people began to see the results of what Gordon and I were doing to bring about a more unified party. As we geared up for the 1988 presidential election and the DNC meeting, we got things very organized. We had an agenda. People had been notified of our agenda and other matters up front. The problem with lack of information within the caucus was a thing of the past. Those who benefited from these improvements would never give Gordon and me the credit we had earned and deserved for it, but we knew the truth.

In 1987, while working on the committee to help get Michael Dukakis elected for president in 1988, we went in search of his running mate. We had a promising meeting with John Glenn of Ohio. We also traveled to Dallas, Texas where we ended up in a high-rise clubroom full of big time democrat millionaires with belt buckles bigger than my head and hats bigger than my whole body. One of those guys spoke up, *"By golly, y'all put Lloyd Bentsen on this ticket and not only will we carry Texas, we'll carry every thang in this here country."*

So Lloyd Bentsen ended up being Dukakis' running mate. As it turned out, though, not only did Dukakis not carry Texas, but he lost the 1988 presidency to George H. W. Bush. Bentsen, after losing the vice presidency, was re-elected senator from Texas.

Even after three years, while leading up to that 1988 convention, there was still a lot of bad blood in the Black Caucus over my defeat of Hatcher. Soon, this bad blood began to manifest itself. On top of that, in February of 1989, the DNC was preparing to elect its officers for the1989 DNC's officer's election. In July of 1988, Jesse Jackson and several other powerful democrats cut a seat out for the then-mayor of New Orleans, Sidney Barthelemy to become vice chair. In essence, they negotiated me out of the picture, which was okay with me because my sights were already set on running for governor of Illinois in 1990.

I was in my third term as comptroller, and I did not know whether or not attorney general Hartigan was going to run for governor, but I decided to run. Incidentally, Ron Brown ran for the chairmanship of the Democratic National Committee that year and, with hardly any opposition, became the first black to be elected chair of the Democratic National Committee. Although I would have enjoyed serving under Ron, the timing was right for me to move on. As I turned my attention to my candidacy for the Illinois governorship, I held no hard feelings against my Black Caucus contenders.

Chapter Fourteen

An Illinois Candidate
Again and Again

... for Governor of Illinois in 1994

I had just announced my candidacy for governor in 1993, when I found out that Dawn Clark Netsch, the woman who had succeeded me as comptroller, had decided she was going to run for governor as well. Her decision to run meant that a Democratic Primary race for governor would occur in 1994 when there had not been one for an Illinois governor since 1976 when Dan Walker had lost to Mike Howlett. Even though there were three of us in that '94 Primary, my toughest opponent was Netsch, since she had the backing of most of the unions as well as the party officials. I lost that race to Netsch by about 40,000 votes. I knew that beating an incumbent like Edgar in the General Election would be next to impossible because of *his* popularity; however, I had never considered the possibility that Netsch's own popularity would ruin the opportunity for me even to get to run against Edgar.

Part of my loss can be attributed to money, and more specifically, to the lack of it. Raising money had been my biggest challenge in all my campaigns, as it was the hardest thing for me to do. About $1 million was all I could come up with for that '94 gubernatorial Primary race and even that came only as a result of constant fund-raising and using up the small political stash I had accumulated as comptroller. Netsch, on the other hand, had no problem raising money. Not only was she a great fundraiser on her own, but she also had a wealthy husband funding her campaign as well. To raise money for his wife's gubernatorial campaign, apparently, Walter Netsch, who was an architect at Skidmore, Owen and Merrill, sold a single painting of theirs for about $2.5 million and used some of the proceeds to fund his wife's '94 campaign. With all that money, Netsch bought a commercial that I believe was the clincher for her win. The commercial featured Netsch, an elderly gray-haired lady, making a combination pool shot while saying she was a "straight shooter" in solving the educational problems facing Illinois by funding the schools. The woman in the ad went on to state that the funding would come from raising income tax from 3% to 4%. According to Netsch, this would amount to a total tax increase of only 1%.

I was in a St. Louis, Missouri hotel room getting dressed for a fundraiser when I viewed that commercial on T.V. It caught my attention right away for a couple of reasons. First of all, Netsch's commercial caught my attention because of the time slot when it was aired, which was four thirty in the afternoon! I thought, *"Oh my God, where did she get the money for that primetime slot, and how can she afford to run it in St. Louis for people who aren't even voting in the Illinois election?"*

Secondly, Netsch's commercial caught my attention because the statement she made about her tax increase being only a 1% tax increase was entirely false! In terms of percentages, when you go from 3% to 4%, the actual rate of the tax increase involved is a whopping 33%, not the single percent that Netsch claimed! I tried to challenge Netsch on the error of her calculation, but I simply did not have the funds to create a commercial of my own to correct the total misconception that was being disseminated by Netsch's ad.

Later that year in July, Governor Edgar underwent bypass surgery to correct three or four blocked arteries. A few weeks before Edgar's surgery, Lt. Governor, Kustra, had turned in his resignation with no effective date. However, upon learning about Edgar's severe condition, Kustra immediately withdrew his resignation. With no lieutenant governor in office, had Edgar's surgery taken an unfortunate turn, once again, as had been the case between 1980-82 when I was state comptroller, as attorney general, I would have been next in line to succeed the governor. November of 1994 rolled around and a fully-mended Edgar went on to beat Netsch in that General Election. He did so by a large margin, receiving almost 70% of the vote. At that point, Netsch's percentage of the vote was the lowest total of any gubernatorial candidate in Illinois history.

... for Mayor of Chicago in 1995

Harold Washington suffered a fatal heart attack in November of 1987 while in office; in fact, the attack literally occurred in his City Hall office. When he died, Washington was just six months into his second term as Chicago mayor. Vice Mayor, David Orr, became acting mayor for a couple of weeks until my friend and Mayor Pro Tem, Eugene Sawyer, was voted in and went on to serve as mayor for a portion of the remainder of Harold Washington's term, because a lawsuit required that a special election be held in 1989 to elect someone to complete the remaining portion of Washington's second term. In that 1989 mayoral run, Cook County State's Attorney, Richard M. Daley, son of former Mayor Richard J. Daley, became Chicago's new mayor.

When I ran against Daley in the 1995 mayoral race, Daley had defeated four other Primary candidates: Incumbent Eugene Sawyer and Timothy Evans in '89; Congressman Danny Davis and Judge Eugene Pincham in '91. As it also turned out, in '95, Daley would also defeat two additional opponents: activist Joseph Gardner and yours truly.[cxxvii]

In all honesty, I must say that I really had never wanted to run against Daley. Actually, I just wasn't interested in running for mayor of Chicago, period. My interest and focus had always been on the statewide rather than the city level. However, right after I lost the 1994 Illinois gubernatorial race, some business people in the Chicago community approached me and encouraged me to do so. Soon after I was approached by these business people, another contender suddenly appeared on the scene, also vying for the mayor's seat. Black Southside activist and commissioner of the Metropolitan Water Reclamation District, Joseph Gardner, indicated that he was going to run for mayor. When I heard that news, I said that I definitely would not be running.

To persuade me to run, the people who supported me came to my home, negotiated with me, promised my family that we'd have their support, and ultimately convinced me that I would get their full backing. One activist even told me, *"We need you to run. We want to get Joe Gardner out."*

"Look," I countered, *"I've been looking to run for governor again in '98. I'm thinking I can really become governor, and I don't want to get into the mayor's race."*

The activist remarked, *"Well, if you want to run for governor in '98 you'd better think about running for Mayor in '95."*

I wasn't totally sold on the mayor-to-governor transition, but it sort of got me thinking. Mainly, though, with so many people requesting me to get in the mayoral race, I began feeling a huge obligation to answer the call of the community. I finally gave in to that call, but only with conditions. I made it perfectly clear to my supporters that I would run only if Joe dropped out. My campaign people started circulating petitions for me. Gardner and his people started circulating his petitions. We decided on a date when Gardner was supposed to drop out, which was sometime in early December. Well, early December came and went, and Gardner was nowhere to be found. He didn't re-appear until a week or so after the drop period had passed. So he missed it and stayed in the primaries.

Once again, I stated, *"I can't run against Joe."*

A spokesperson from my supporters came to me all fired up and, as a result of his enthusiasm, got me fired up too, *"We still got a shot at this, Roland! What we are going to do is run you as an Independent."*

"Wait a minute now! No, no, no." I tried to put the brakes on that guy's enthusiasm real quick.

"Oh yeah, we're going to get the petitions..."

"It's going to take a lot of petitions." I interrupted.

He continued, *"You're going to need 50,000 signatures."*

"You ain't going to get no 50,000 signatures." I insisted.

He queried, *"Well, if we could get 50,000 signatures, would you run?"*

"No, because the opposition will challenge all the petitions and will not allow me to get on the ballet."

He gave one last challenge, *"Well, how about if we get 70,000-80,000? How about if we get 100,000 signatures?"*

I challenged him by saying, *"When you all get 100,000 signatures, come back and talk to me."*

In order to run as an Independent for the April General Election, candidates had to file petitions in January. Lo and behold, my supporters went out and obtained about 95,000 signatures before the January deadline!

"Okay, I'll run as an independent to honor that request of all those individuals who are asking for an alternative," I conceded to the wishes of my supporters and announced my candidacy on March 3rd of 1995. The general election was April 4th, which gave me only thirty days to pull a campaign together, and to do so with scarcely any money. As an Independent candidate, my supporters raised about $200,000-$250,000, which meant that we could not afford any T.V. commercials. I lost. In that General Election Daley received 63% of the vote. I received 36% of the vote, which was the highest percentage of any candidate against Mayor Daley. The Republican candidate, Raymond "Spanky the Clown" Wardingly, who helped children and could always be seen in parades and games, received the other 1% of the vote.

A Break from Candidacy (1995)

The big question for me at that time was what do I do next? I really needed to figure out what my next career move was going to be. Prior to running for mayor, I had interviewed and agreed to a very lucrative position with a major law firm in Chicago: Mayer, Brown. The persons I interviewed with were the head of that law firm, my good friend Ty Fahner and Mayor Daley's brother, Bill Daley. As I began that 1995 mayoral race, Ty called me sounding very shocked, *"Roland, what are you doing?"*

I immediately put him at ease, *"Ty, don't worry, I'm not coming to work at the firm. There's no way I could put you through that kind of consternation. The community kept coming to me so I'm going to run. I'll just figure out what to do about another job later if I lose."*

By June 1995, I started working for the minority law firm, Jones, Ware and Grenard. Mark Jones was a black former judge; Mitchell Ware was a very prominent black lawyer; Frank Grenard, was a prominent white lawyer. They owned the largest minority firm in the country. I joined them as a managing partner because although they were extremely skilled in practicing law, they lacked an individual with the expertise at the partner level to direct the administration of the law firm.

... for Governor of Illinois in 1998

While still at the law firm of Jones, Ware and Grenard, the political bug hit me hard again in 1997. I knew I didn't have any campaign seed money to start a gubernatorial campaign; therefore, I borrowed the $100,000 from personal life savings that would have been my kids' inheritance in order to provide the seed funds. With those funds available for the campaign, I got my office space, and hired a small staff; my campaign for Illinois governor was off and running.

John Schmidt, a lawyer from the law firm Mayer, Brown and also a good friend of mine, put his hat in the ring, as did Congressman Glenn Poshard and Jim Burns. The four of us battled it out in the Primary race. I lost, coming in behind Poshard by about 30,000 votes. Poshard went on to lose to George Ryan in the General Election. I stayed at Jones, Ware & Grenard and never did recoup my $100,000. My daughter jokingly accused me of spending her inheritance.

... for Governor of Illinois in 2002

By 2002, Jones, Ware and Grenard had dissolved, and I was now at a much smaller firm working as of counsel. I began telling myself that I had one more shot at the governorship. I had to have another time at bat so that I could either have three strikes or hit a homerun. I knew that until one of those things occurred, I wouldn't be satisfied. The only difference with that third opportunity to swing at the ball was that this time I really had no money to advance. I did, however, have enough resources to secure a headquarters and put together a small group of people to rally behind me.

I had recently met a young businessman who, when I told him of my plans to run, showed a considerable interest in investing in my campaign. I was scheduled to announce my candidacy on September 20, 2001, so we met at the man's office the morning of September 11, 2001 to begin strategizing. Soon after arriving to his office that morning, my gubernatorial plans took an immediate back seat in terms of importance when the news of not one, but two tragic plane crashes in New York was announced to us. As we sat glued to the T.V. sets in the office of that businessman's broadcasting company, we witnessed a world-changing event, as planes crashed in different cities, into the Pentagon and as the

World Trade towers crumbled to the ground. About an hour later, after trying to analyze the reason for these tragic events and trying to process in our minds the magnitude of this tragedy for New York City and for our entire country, we decided to get back to work. Talks about my campaign resumed. I had previously worked out my budget and shared the figures that indicated I could run my whole campaign on $2 million. With all the information presented to him, that businessman mulled it over for a few minutes and then said, *"Okay, I'll give you half of the $2 million."*

I questioned in disbelief, *"You'll do what?"*

He repeated, *"I'll contribute half of it."*

Even though I asked him for the money, it caught me off guard when he so readily agreed to invest $1 million in me on the spot. *"How do you plan to do it?"* I inquired.

"Well, how do you think I should do it?"

"I don't know. Giving a million dollars to a candidate is a lot of money. And I don't know whether or not I really want you to put that much money into the campaign."

"Look, I want nothing in return. You're a friend, and you should be Governor. I just wanna help out."

We brainstormed some more, then I came up with a plan with which we both were comfortable. I asked him to start off with a smaller amount as seed money. He wrote me a $200,000 check that day to launch my campaign and promised the other $800,000 before I filed my campaign disclosure report in December of 2001.

"Okay," I said graciously, *"I'm taking this initial money, but I think we should make the remaining $800,000 a loan."*

"Why? What do you mean a loan?" he asked.

"Well, if you loan it to me, when I win, I can pay you back your money."

He finally agreed to that, and I made it official by having a promissory note drawn up between him and the Burris gubernatorial committee. I assured him the loan was between him and the committee, not between the two of us. Again, he agreed to everything; that launched my whole '02 campaign.

In that Democratic Primary race, there were three candidates: a congressman named Rod Blagojevich, Paul Vallas, the former Chicago

School District CEO, and yours truly, Roland Burris. I thought to myself, *"Now I should be able to beat these two guys, Blagojevich and Vallas. Who can even pronounce Blagojevich's name?"*

Blagojevich's father-in-law was a big time alderman and committeeman in Chicago by the name of Richard (Dick) Mell. He was wealthy, but more importantly, he was a big party influencer with contacts all over the city and downstate. Even to this day, everyone knows Dick Mell takes no stuff from nobody; he is tough. He's also a good friend of mine. Friend or no friend, I believed that I could beat his son-in-law, so I announced my campaign for Illinois governor. Upon hearing that announcement, Eddie Read, a close friend of mine who owned a mobile home, volunteered to drive me throughout the entire state to announce my candidacy. With Eddie driving tirelessly all the way, we visited six key cities, and three other smaller cities, on our six-day tour.

One thing I had not counted on along the campaign trail was the inroads that Paul Vallas would make in the black community. He was a Chicago native and the CEO of the Chicago public schools working under Mayor Richard M. Daley. Daley had dismissed Vallas and Gerry Chico, the Chairman of the Chicago Board of Education. As a result, Vallas remained in limbo, so to speak, until deciding to run for governor. I knew I couldn't count only on black support in my race; I had to count on downstate support as well.

My friend and former nominee of the Democratic Party in '98, Glenn Poshard, said he was going to stay out of it; yet, he ended up endorsing Vallas. Going into the race, Vallas had about $4.5 million in financial support. Blagojevich and his father-in-law began to raise a great deal of money. Of course, they had most of the ward committeemen behind them. Very easily, they raised about $8 million for Blagojevich's campaign.

There I was with my measly little $1 million pot. I ended up getting another half million from my businessman friend, so I ran my race with about $2.2 million, which means I had only $700,000 from contributors other than my businessman friend.

Vallas and I split the suburban and the Chicago vote. Blagojevich came in third in the suburbs and Chicago, but he won big downstate. He had put big money into those downstate Democratic operations, and those county chairmen delivered for him. That's how it went down in the

Primary, not more than 40,000 or 50,000 votes separating all three of us;, but Blagojevich, the big moneymaker, came out as the nominee. In the General Election, Blagojevich went up against two-term Attorney General, Jim Ryan. Ryan lost that contest, making Blagojevich Illinois' 40th governor.

Republican, former state's Attorney General, Jim Ryan, and I are very good friends. I try my best never to make enemies in the political arena. People can ascertain the truth of that statement by counting how many friends I have across party lines. I'll give you respect as a person, whether you are a democrat, a republican or an independent, but I'll not hesitate to fight you politically and challenge your issues politically. One thing I very seldom have ever done, or will do, was campaign negatively against another democrat.

On numerous occasions, I have been hurt by negative campaigning, but I try not to engage in it myself. Of course, there's been a time or two that I've had to do negative campaigning against a republican, but even then I did so only *after* my opponent had first campaigned negatively against me. I hate it nonetheless. My philosophy has always been to tell the people what I'm going to do for them; and that's it. I'm not going to start off tearing down the other person in order to build myself up. I want people to select me over the other candidate because of what I'm promising to do for them, not because of how bad I made that other person appear.

Staying away from all that negative stuff was why some T.V. consultants became bitter towards me. When I ran for attorney general in '90, I had hired one political consultant group but I would not allow that group to create negative commercials against Jim Ryan for my campaign. Might I remind you, I still beat Ryan without the negative ads. Due to those consultants' continued bitterness, when I ran for governor in 1994, for the Primary, my former consultant group went to work for my opponent, Dawn Clark Netsch. In the campaign world, switching sides in that way as unheard of. A political consultant just did not become a consultant against a former client.

I suppose my problem in politics was that I was too Pollyannaish. I believed that if you did a good job and brought a clear message to the people, those people would vote for you and keep you in office. Well, in American politics, that is not always the case. Some people actually look forward to all of the negative attacks in a campaign. Unfortunately, as voters, they fall for those messages and rely on that information in their decision-making processes. I would not succumb to the mud-slinging involved in negative campaigning, but I've had more than my share of negativity thrown my way; even in the years which followed my last gubernatorial campaign. For instance, Mark Kirk (in his 2010 run for senate) used my picture in his commercials about corruption. Kirk didn't have a bit of evidence to show where I had ever been corrupt. In fact, no type of corruption has ever been associated with me in campaigning or while in office, during my entire political life.

In 2002, I suffered my third strike at the governorship. As the rule goes, after being allowed three strikes, with my third loss for the governor's chair, I was out. Without the necessary funds available for campaigning, I felt once again, that this was certainly the end of politics for me; or so I thought. Partnering with my campaign manager and friend, Fred LeBed, I set up a consulting business. Our company was named Burris Lebed, and we became rather successful in our field. By this time, my son had become a lawyer as well and opened up his law firm, to which I became counsel. Besides working at my firm and my son's firm, I enjoyed just being at home with family.

Announcements, Inaugurations and In-Office Photographs

1976: Governor Dan Walker and Roland Burris, Walker's Cabinet level appointee, Director of General Services

Lobbying on behalf of the National Association of State Comptrollers and Treasurers, Illinois Comptroller Roland Burris meets with Senator John Glenn (D-OH), Chairperson, Senate Operations Committee

Illinois State Comptroller Roland W. Burris expresses his appreciation to Senator Ted Kennedy (D-MA) who was keynote speaker at Burris' 1982 fundraiser for re-election as State Comptroller

Roland Burris, Senatorial candidate Carol Moseley Braun, and U. S. Senator Paul Simon

Chicago Black elected officials: Roland Burris, center; from left: Timothy Evans, Clifford Kelly, Wilson Frost, Eugene Sawyer, Benny Stewart, and Cecil Partee, unknown official; from right: Tom Fuller, Bill Henry, Howard Brookins, and Ethel Alexander

Congressman Dan Rostenkowski, (D-IL); Mayor Richard Daley; Roland W. Burris; and George Dunne, Cook County Democratic Party Chairperson

Roland W. Burris and former President William Jefferson Clinton

Senator Roland W. Burris and Secretary of State Hillary Rodham Clinton

Illinois Comptroller Roland W. Burris and First Lady, Rosalyn Carter on reviewing stand for Columbus Day Parade in Chicago

Chicago Mayor, Richard J. Daley and Attorney General, Roland W. Burris

Roland W. Burris and Congressman Robert Kennedy II (D-MA)

U. S. Attorney General Janet Reno and Illinois Attorney General Roland W. Burris

From left: Alderman Eugene Sawyer; Cook County Board President, John Stroger; Eleanor Sawyer; Alderman Wilson Frost; Roland Burris; Dr. Berlean Burris; State Senate President Cecil Partee; and Georgia State Representative Ben Brown

Hon. Roland W. Burris and Dr. Berlean Burris chat with Vice President Walter Mondale

Hon. Roland W. Burris and Dr. Berlean Burris share a moment with Senator Charles Percy (R-IL)

Chicago Mayor Harold Washington and Roland W. Burris

Dr. Berlean Burris, Roland W. Burris, daughter, Rolanda Burris; and U. S. Senator Charles Robb of Virginia

At the podium, President Jimmy Carter has a word with Illinois Comptroller Roland W. Burris

Roland Burris speaks from the stage at Council of State Governments meeting

Roland Burris and Andrew Young, former Mayor of Atlanta and Congressman from Georgia's 1st Congressional District

Burris and Governor Doug Wilder of Virginia

From left: Vel Phillips, Secretary of State, Wisconsin; Carol Moseley Braun, Illinois State Rep.; Henry Parker, Treasurer, Connecticut; Congresswoman Cardiss Collins (D-IL); Roland W. Burris, Comptroller, Illinois; Lenora Cartwright, Chicago Commissioner of Health and Human Services; Barbara Flynn Curie, Illinois State Rep.; and Richard Austin, Secretary of State, Michigan

Chapter Fifteen

Sights on the Senate

Paving a Better Way

After becoming the first black statewide elected official for Illinois in 1978, it felt at times that my life existed under a microscope. I watched my every move, careful not to do anything that would reflect negatively on me, my family or my entire race for that matter, since the media was always there waiting for my shoelaces to be untied or something; anything for a headline. As a trailblazer, I did not view my passion for governmental service as a burden; instead, I viewed it as a privilege accompanied by a serious obligation. That obligation is not unique to me, but belongs to all black leaders of the past, present and future that were, are, and will be determined to pave a better way for the generations of black people yet to pass this way.

Since my teen years, I have felt the obligation to carry that banner and let it be known to the world that black people are just as humanly capable as anyone to run successfully for political office and, more importantly, to represent in a successful and appropriate manner all races and ethnic groups while in that office. For this reason, I do not believe that any of my campaigns, including the failed ones, were in vain. After all, look at Illinois' record. There are only a few states in the U.S. that have elected as many, or more, black statewide elected officials as we have in Illinois. Even so, that number is still only a handful: Carol Moseley-Braun, Barack Obama, Jesse White and Roland Burris. Illinois has also been able to bridge any type of racial divide in terms of its elected officials. Proof of that claim is that no other state has sent more black U.S. senators to the United States Senate than Illinois.

In fact, during the Reconstruction era--that brief period beginning in 1863 after the Emancipation Proclamation and culminating in 1877 when the last of the federal troops protecting the interests of African-Americans were removed from the South, two African-Americans from Mississippi, Hiram R. Revels and Blanche K. Bruce, were elected to the U.S. Senate by the Mississippi State Legislature.

While I served as a member of the U. S. Senate, I could count only four additional black U. S. senators since the Reconstruction era.[cxxviii] Those four were Republican Edward Brooke from Massachusetts; and Carol Moseley Braun, Barack Obama and Roland W. Burris--all from the State of Illinois. Since leaving the Senate, however, I note the recent appointments of Senator Tim Scott (R-SC) and Senator Mo Cowan (D-MA), although as of this writing, Senator Cowan has been replaced. In addition, I am also happy to note the election of Senator Cory Booker (D-NJ), which brings the total number of black U.S. senators in our national history to an unimpressive total of nine.

When I make the claim that Illinois has been able to bridge any type of racial divide in terms of its elected officials, I am referring to that great divide in our state that separates the downstate voter from the Chicago voter. I come from downstate, being born and raised in Centralia, Illinois. My elementary and high school years, and even my college years, were spent downstate. I have family members who still live downstate. I know the mentality of the downstate voters. All you have to do to win their approval is to be straight up with the people, which is how I've always been. Of course, there's still racism in downstate Illinois, as there is everywhere. There are some people who just don't like you because of the color of your skin. You probably won't ever be able to change the opinions or the biases of those people. The majority of the people are not that way. For the majority, no matter what color you are, if you have their back, they'll have yours. In fact, for a good many of these good people, the fact that you are from Chicago might raise more of an objection than your racial identity. One thing about the people of downstate Illinois, though, is if they sense you don't have their back, they will drop you like a hot potato. Fellow trailblazer, Carol Moseley-Braun, comes to my mind, as I make that statement.

The relationship between Carol and I goes all the way back to the late 1970's when she was an Illinois state representative. My first impression of Carol, who is ten years my junior, was that she was a very bright, politically astute young lady with an insatiable amount of political ambition. In 1988, after ten years in the house, she was ready to get out of Springfield. I can't remember any specifics surrounding her decision, but basically she's no different than a lot of legislators who simply want out after so many years. It's a really tough business. Even though serving as a state representative is considered a part-time job, it is definitely a job which *fully* consumes your life, your family's life and which influences almost every personal decision you make. The public loves you one day, hates you the next, and the media can be your worst enemy any day. All of that, with little pay, can take its toll on even the most passionate public servant.

Carol Mosley-Braun made her way back to her hometown of Chicago. In 1988, as the newly-elected Cook County Recorder of Deeds, she was esteemed as the first African-American *and* the first woman to hold an executive office in Cook County government. On the flip side of her history-making accomplishment was the fact that of the seven elective Cook County offices, Recorder of Deeds was the lowest paid, not even matching the salaries of the county clerks, commissioners, or the treasurer. Needless to say, by 1990, she was aspiring for more and, accordingly, set her sights on the United States Senate.

I had just become Illinois' attorney general when Mosley-Braun started talking about running. She called me one day to share the news of her decision and, naturally, I offered my opinion, *"You're running for senate against Alan Dixon? That's definitely not a wise decision. You know, as County Recorder of Deeds, you can become president of the county board or you can run state-wide. Since you're a lawyer, you can become Attorney General, for that matter. Just be patient; you have a bright future!"*

"I know, Roland," she shot back, *"but this is the lowest county office; it's just the pits! It certainly doesn't pay any money. Actually, I'd rather be in private practice than doing this. I've gotta do this."*

I conceded, *"Well, okay, but, rest assured that if you're the nominee, I'll be with you. However, in the primary I can't pull back my commitment to Alan."*

Of course, Carol Mosley-Braun understood that Alan Dixon was a good friend of mine. In 1978, Alan had been elected secretary of state as I had been elected to my first term as comptroller. In 1981, he became a U.S. senator from Illinois. In 1991, his senate vote was one of the fifty-two that confirmed Clarence Thomas to the Supreme Court, in the midst of the highly publicized Anita Hill sex accusations towards Thomas. That move on Alan's part was just the fuel that Mosley-Braun needed to heat things up in her favor on the campaign trail!

In the 1992 Illinois senate primary race, to the shock of many, Carol Mosley-Braun beat Alan Dixon, the incumbent. A win over an incumbent U.S. senator had not occurred in over ten years; and it had never been accomplished by a woman! Just as I had promised her, and just as I had done with Paul Simon when he beat me in the primary for United States Senate, I put all my efforts behind her campaign. I spoke everywhere on her behalf, traveling state-wide supporting her election. I especially traveled downstate into those southeastern Illinois communities like Fairfield, Lawrenceville, Carmi and Ridgeway. Lo and behold, lightning struck twice, and in November of 1992, Carol Moseley Braun beat Richard S. Williamson to become the first African-American woman to be elected to the U.S. Senate. I was truly proud of her!

Later, in 1998, as I conducted my second run for Governor, Carol Mosley-Braun ran for re-election as senator. I headed back down to those same southern Illinois counties, only that time I sought out support for my own campaign. I was totally caught off guard by the angry conversations some of the locals darted at me. *"Hey Roland, you came here campaigning for Carol Mosley-Braun. It's been six years and we haven't seen her yet!"*

Because of their disappointment with Carol Mosley-Braun, and because I was going up against Glenn Poshard, who was a heavy favorite in those parts, I didn't fare well at all in those downstate counties. As I mentioned before, there is a great divide in Illinois; an imaginary east-west line, if you will, stretching across the state beginning near the city of Champagne, which is one hundred thirty-five miles south of Chicago. South of that imaginary line, people are pretty loyal to their downstate officials and are very sensitive to the way they are served. So, even though I was a downstate native who was known to the people and who had received their support in the past, I sensed that it just wasn't going to fly that time. Without the downstate vote, I lost that race. Carol Mosley-Braun was also unsuccessful in her re-election bid.

The State Senate Race

In 1992, during the early years of my term as Illinois' attorney general, I began to catch the buzz about a rising young, black, community crowd-pleaser. He was thirty-something years old, a lawyer and an organizer enthusiast. With a team of volunteers, his voter registration drives registered hundreds of thousands of unregistered black citizens throughout Chicago and its suburbs. Folk would tell others about him. *"Some guy named Oba…"* they would hesitate before completing his name, never quite sure if they were pronouncing it correctly.

In 1995, Illinois Representative, Mel Reynolds, lost his U.S. House seat due to an indictment, which paved the way for his successor, Jesse L. Jackson, Jr. to win that seat in the 2nd Congressional District in a special election. Also, during that time, there was confusion involving then-Illinois state senator, Alice Palmer, who had decided she was not going to run for re-election in 1996, as she had set her sights on running for Congress. After entering that 2nd Congressional District race, she dropped out and tried to re-enter the state senate race for a chance at winning back her old seat. By that time, Barack Obama had made his first foray into the political arena, casting his lot for that vacated seat. As it turned out, Palmer did not qualify for a place on the ballot, and Obama went on to win that 1996 election.

That win launched Obama's career as a public servant and transformed him from community organizer to politician. Even though I had only met him briefly during his race, once he became State Senator Barack Obama, he supported me in my gubernatorial efforts in 1998 and 2002, both of which I lost in the primaries. My first and ongoing impression of my new supporter was that he was a very strong-willed, yet pleasant, young man. So strong was Obama in his conviction that in 2000, and certainly contrary to all conventional wisdom, he made what many of us felt would be a politically disastrous decision of challenging

Illinois' U.S. Representative, Bobby Rush, for his seat in Congress.

I ran into Obama at a meeting one day after he had made his bid, and I pointedly asked him, *"Senator, what are you doing? Bobby is the incumbent. He's got seniority* (four-term seniority at that)*! You're trying to take him out? I don't see how I can support your efforts in that."*

Senator Obama replied, *"Well, look; you've got to do what you've got to do. For family reasons, I have made this decision."*

"You've got a bright future, man," I came at him with more sincerity because I really liked him. *"You can be attorney general, governor, and we can prepare to run you state-wide. Don't mess up by taking on Bobby Rush."*

Realizing that my concern fell on deaf ears, I left the topic alone. I didn't know what he meant when he said "for family reasons," but he so firmly defended his position that I didn't question him further about it. I just respected his decision to run against Bobby, as he respected my decision to not support him in his effort to unseat Bobby Rush. When State Senator Donne Trotter (my Senator) also entered that race against Bobby Rush, I could not support him either. Perhaps Bobby was off his game a little during that time, giving those guys reason to believe he was vulnerable. In the end, it became apparent that Bobby was *not* vulnerable, and as I had predicted, the community rallied behind him leading him to victory. Of all the opponents, Obama came in a fairly close second place in that 2000 race. I came to know Obama pretty well after that and respected him even more.

Self Incrimination at its Best

When 2004 rolled around, the events following the retirement of Republican United States Senator, Peter Fitzgerald led to a chapter of my own political life that played out with more intensity than I could have ever imagined. For starters, early media polls showed investment entrepreneur Blair Hull, enjoying a substantial lead in the March 2004 Primary Election to fill the vacancy created by Fitzgerald's retirement. New to the political scene, there was no doubt that Hull's positioning resulted from his own personal wealth and on the fact that in the end he spent over $33 million on his campaign.

Prior to Hull's announcement of his candidacy, Fred Lebed, my partner in our consulting business, had signed on as his consultant. Therefore, I scheduled a lunch meeting with Hull to feel him out about his upcoming campaign. Soon after we were seated, I got right to the point, *"Well, how much money do you plan to spend on the senate race?"*

Hull looked at me nonchalantly and stated, *"Twenty million dollars."*

"Whoa. What?"

"Twenty million." He coolly repeated.

"Are you going to raise that?" I asked with avid curiosity.

"Not necessarily," He replied.

What I did not know at that time was Hull's net worth topped out at about $500 million. More than anything I was just enthralled by his confidence. It was because of that confidence that, when I got back to the office later that day, I gave Fred thumbs up regarding Hull, *"Okay, friend, you've got yourself a good client there."*

I began working with Fred, counseling him with Hull. However, I felt more compelled to offer my assistance to Obama rather than to Hull. The only problem was that I could not really get to Obama's people. Then there came an occasion when I was able to give Obama some pointers.

Eventually, I backed off from Hull and started solely talking up Obama. Hull remained the leader in that primary which consisted of six or seven candidates. Obama was polling third.

Things were looking great for Hull when, lo and behold, Fred approached me one day about this "situation" Hull had. He said, *"You know, Blair has a sealed divorce. What do you think about someone with a sealed divorce?"* I only had to think for a minute before giving him my most honest, straightforward reply, *"Well, Fred, if you can get Blair to get that divorce unsealed and let it get early exposure before Election Day, that's your best shot."*

Fred took that suggestion to Hull. Fred also got on the phone with all those big time Washington, D.C. consultants to whom Hull paid gobs of money and they all said emphatically, *"No, no, no! The courts aren't going to unseal the divorce. If they do unseal it, we will be well able to handle it."*

Fred argued with Hull, who stood firmly opposed to revealing the details of his divorce. Fred backed off and decided not to take it further.

As it goes in the world of politics, word leaked out about the divorce anyway. Around late December of 2003 or early January of 2004, the matter went into litigation, and Hull's decree was ordered unsealed just three or four weeks before the March Primary Election. Up until that time, he had comfortably held the lead with around 33% of the vote. However, as soon as the divorce papers disclosed that he had allegedly threatened to kill his wife, his percentage dropped like a rock.

Naturally, Obama benefited from the allegations about Hull's incriminating threats to his former wife, immediately rising in the polls and eventually clenching the primary nomination. During this time, on the other side of the playing field, Jack Ryan was running in the Republican Primary and was favored to spar with Democrat Barack Obama. By that time, I was working for Obama and I found out that, like Hull, Ryan had a sealed divorce too. *What in the world is going on?"* I asked myself.

On the night of that Primary Election, I offered political commentary on WGN-TV. Ryan's divorce was a hot topic. *"Go back and look through the records,"* I proposed, *"If you all think that that divorce is not going to be unsealed and that Jack Ryan will not find himself in trouble, then you've got another thought coming."* His divorce from actress wife, Jeri Ryan, had occurred in California, so loads of red tape slowed the process.

At the end of March, a California judge ruled that only a few of the Ryans' divorce records would be opened to the public, but the rest would remain sealed. Finally, however, near the end of June 2004, Ryan's remaining files were ordered unsealed. None of that would have occurred had it not been for the tenacity of *The Chicago Tribune* newspaper and Chicago's ABC affiliate, WLS-TV, in initiating the litigation. Allegedly, and I must say allegedly because I didn't read those files, Ryan attempted to get his wife to join him at sex clubs and swap clubs to do couple swapping.

Whether or not those allegations were true, that whole ordeal led Jack Ryan to withdraw his candidacy from the U.S. Senate race in Illinois. With just a short time to go before the General Election, the Republican Party then pulled Alan Keyes out of their magician's hat. Keyes previously had made fruitless attempts at winning a senate seat in Maryland, and, as it turned out, his Illinois effort would fare no better.

Although a well-educated, perhaps even brilliant, Harvard educated political scientist, Keyes somehow seemed flawed. I quickly formed one personal opinion of Keyes based on his behavior: *"He appears to be an educated fool."*

In that senate race, Keyes' whole platform was abortion and gays; he was against both. Okay, that's all fine and good. However, what *wasn't* fine was that no matter what issue was brought up by his opponent in the campaign, he took everything back to that same abortion and gay debate. He appeared on Channel 7 talking about abortion and the gay debate; he hit the streets making speeches about abortion and the gay debate; you knew without question that Alan Keyes was against abortion and that he did not support the rights of the lesbian, gay, bisexual and transgender (LGBT) community.

The clincher? It turned out that Alan Keyes' own daughter is a lesbian! It had been reported that he knew her sexual preference during the time he was campaigning. Can you believe that? Did he think that no one would ever find out? Not to mention, because of Keyes' rigid insistence on focusing on abortion and the gay debate, he literally forced his family to re-live the trauma of their daughter's "coming out," only this time, through the eyes of the public. For me, these actions confirmed my initial impression of him as an educated fool.

Barack Obama trounced Alan Keyes in the 2004 U.S. Senate General Election with 70% of the vote. In fact, Obama's plurality of 2.2 million votes over Keyes still stands today as the highest in Illinois' history. If anyone was a non-believer in divine intervention, that senate victory should have made a believer out of them. Once Obama secured his spot in that General Election, all he had to do was stand by and watch his opponents defeat themselves: two of them due to exposed sealed divorces and the one due to his foolish insensitivities. For Obama, all of these occurrences had to be more than lucky breaks. For him to have had the opportunity to make the Keynote Address at the 2004 Democratic Convention in Boston as if signaling his arrival on the national scene like he did...well, again, that *had* to be more than luck. Some people would rather refer to it as the stars being lined up for Obama. No matter what reasoning one applies, things don't just happen the way they did without divine direction. To those of us who anchor our faith in Christianity, God had Obama in the right place, at the right time.

Not for the Faint of Heart

Anyone who knows anything about being a politician knows that, divine direction or not, politics is not for the faint of heart. From the old school machine-style patronage politics; through all the negative, mug-slinging campaigns; to the modern day, up-to-the-second, in-person impact polling that social media advocates, I can tell you without a doubt, that you have to really love serving, in order to withstand what comes your way. Sometimes a health matter is something to withstand.

For instance, since 1988, I've dealt with a health condition that I never let slow me down from my political duties. During a regular check-up when I was fifty-years-old, my doctor discovered blocked arteries in my heart, a condition which he further diagnosed as heredi-tary. Because I had a negative reaction to the prescribed medication, I could only fight this disease with proper diet and exercise, which I did successfully for sixteen years. After that, a more aggressive plan of treatment was deemed necessary. In 2004, my condition required quin-tuple bypass surgery to open up five clogged arteries in my heart. Of course, there's never a *good* time to have surgery, but the timing of that surgery was especially bad. My surgery was on March 3, 2004. I came out of the hospital on March 8, 2004 with the U.S. Senate Primary Election just eight days away. I felt well enough, so I was certainly not going to miss participating in that race. March 16, 2004, after the polls closed, I appeared on WGN-TV doing political commentary.

My niece, Carol Nadine Giboney Young, who lives in California, happened to catch me on WGN- TV and thought, *"I'm sure that is a re-run since he's still recuperating from his heart surgery."* Realizing it was real-time dialogue, she immediately called Chicago.

"Yeah, Carol, that's your uncle on T.V. live," confirmed my wife.

Berlean knew that she could not have talked me into staying at home that day during those primaries, whether I was fully recovered from my heart surgery or not. Serving is what God put me here to do. Therefore, I've always had the heart for politics. In 2004, I literally gained an even stronger heart! Just in time, too, as three short years later my sights would be fixed on my own journey to the chambers of the United States Senate.

Chapter Sixteen

My Appointment

Obama Decides to Run

"They ain't gonna elect no black man president of this country!"

Boy, if I had a dollar for every time I heard that statement in 2007! U.S. Senator Obama had only been in the senate for two years when he decided to run for the presidency of the United States. To be truthful, I feared that he would be assassinated if elected, and I certainly was not the only one in his camp who shared that trepidation. A good friend of mine was Dr. Eric Whitaker who, traveled with Obama on the campaign trail. Whitaker and I were chatting one day when he confided in me how concerned he was for Obama's safety, as well.

Soon after that, I ran into Michelle Obama at an event, where the room was all abuzz with talk of the presidential race. I approached her both curiously and respectfully, seeking her perspective on the whole matter. *"Michelle, I have to bring this up to you. Have you thought about what could happen if he does this? I mean, Barack could be assassinated!"* She politely responded, *"Roland, I appreciate your asking that, because we have talked about it. The whole family has sat down and said that is a real possibility. Then we came to the conclusion that if that's the price we have to pay to try to move in this direction, then that's the price we're willing to pay."* *"You're kidding me, Michelle."* I was struck by her frankness.

She said, *"No."*

Even more inspired than before, I immediately replied, *"Then count me in, Michelle. I'm on board!"*

I knew that if the Obama's were willing to pay that ultimate price to move our race forward in accomplishing great things, like electing an African-American as president of our nation, then *I* had to be willing, as well. I began talking up Obama everywhere I went, to which came the response, *"They ain't gonna elect no black man president of this country!"*

Before the January 2008 Iowa caucuses, Oprah Winfrey had Senator Obama on her show. Oprah then joined him in Iowa and on some of his campaign events. With Iowa being the traditional and formal start of things for the delegate selection process, Obama got a stellar start. As many young predominately white college kids in Iowa got excited about Obama for president and became involved in the ground roots political process which led Obama to a resounding victory, they shattered the old belief that an African-American could not be elected as president of the United States. Encouraged by the results of the Iowa primary, students on both white and black campuses across America jumped on board as well. Soon, that belief factor spread like wildfire among young and old alike. For instance, Senator Tom Harkin's annual Iowa fish fry typically draws 2,000 to 3,000 people, which was considered a rather successful headcount. However, when Obama appeared at this fish fry in 2007, the event attracted more than 10,000 people.

Lobbying for that Vacant Seat

After those 2008 caucuses, blacks in America took notice of Obama's victory in ninety-six-percent-white-populated Iowa, and suddenly Obama had gained a tremendous amount of support. Next, came Super Tuesday in February which saw Obama capture thirteen states and a total of 847 delegates, as it became quite apparent that he could win the Democratic nomination. By that time, it was also pretty clear that Obama's Republican opponent would be Arizona Senator, John McCain, against whom a victory was certainly plausible. At that point, I started painting a scenario in the minds of my friends about an empty senate seat to which someone would have to be appointed by Governor Blagojevich if Obama became president. During the months to follow, especially after that big day in June when Obama won all those primaries, I kept rehearsing that scenario. In June, Blagojevich held a fund-raiser in Chicago that I attended and to which I made my standard contribution of a $1,000 check. While there, I continued to plant seeds by suggesting my appointment to members of Blagojevich's staff: guys like Doug Scoffield and John Wyma. I stated repeatedly, *"If Obama wins, Blagojevich will make the replacement appointment. Keep me in mind."*

None of them said anything of significance in response, which was okay. My goal was just to keep planting the seeds. And that is exactly what I did, especially as July rolled around, and I began to sense that we were going to the Democratic National Convention (DNC) for sure. I attempted to get a few moments with Michael Madigan, Speaker of the Illinois House of Representatives. I also attempted to get a few moments with Dick Durbin, Senior U.S. Senator from Illinois.

In July, I attended a state convention in Springfield, where Durbin and I engaged in a conversation about the upcoming elections. Naturally, I eased our conversation towards the senate seat, *"You know, Dick, since you're close to Blagojevich..."*

"No, no, I'm not that close." He interrupted.

I continued with my plea, as though not hearing him *"Look, if Obama wins this thing, I'm interested in his senate seat."*

That conversation I had with Durbin, as did those I had with most other people, went nowhere. But whether they even believed the seat would become vacant or not, I continued to share with anybody and everybody who would listen, my interest in being appointed to the vacant senate seat that would be available in the event of an Obama win. Throughout the summer months and leading into November, I expended a great deal of energy towards achieving that goal.

In July, I invited Alonzo "Lon" Monk, the governor's *former* chief of staff, over to my consulting firm for a discussion about his clients. Lon, a consultant himself, would experience a conflict of interest if he took on certain clients, due to the "revolving door" statute. The "revolving door" statute defines how long persons who go into private employment after having left government service must wait before engaging in certain types of representational activity on behalf of their private employers.[129] I proposed to Lon that he refer those particular clients to the consulting firm that Fred and I operated, since we were not affected by those restrictions.

At the conclusion of our meeting, I looked him square in the eye and stated, *"Lon, if Obama wins the presidency, I want you to let the governor know that I'm interested in getting appointed to that seat. After all, I'm black and from Illinois. We have a black Illinois senator. I have a huge state-wide base, being elected all these times state-wide."* He replied, *"Well, I know your credentials. You're a good case for it. I'll certainly let the governor know."*

I don't know whether or not Lon ever said anything to the governor on my behalf, but there I was lobbying to yet another person for that appointment. Of course, all that seed planting is what would ultimately bring about many of the false allegations made against me in the press.

The Democratic National Conventions

As I carried out my duties in that 2008 campaign, calling the black Democratic National Committee members to see where they stood on Obama as delegates, I also knew that I desired to be one of the at-large delegates at the convention. The only problem was that I could not be appointed as a convention delegate because I was not in office at that time. That's when I decided to run for that position, even though Obama's people felt that I probably shouldn't run because of the need to balance the male and female delegates.

I, on the other hand, felt that the delegate slot was mine; I was sure that no one could beat me in that district. Besides, the best way I could explain my intention was to tell them, *"You're likely to get a real big turnout if I'm on the ticket."* Sure enough, I ran for delegate in my congressional district and won with 123,000 votes, almost as many as Congressman Bobby Rush received when he ran for re-election. Naturally, from there, I got elected to the 2008 Democratic National Convention as an Obama delegate.

While relishing my victory and preparing to take on my responsibilities as a convention delegate, my mind took me back fifty-six years, when I first yearned for that electrifying convention experience. I was a sophomore in high school in 1952 when the Republican convention, which was held in Chicago, resulted in the nomination of Eisenhower. I was a republican in those days, as were my parents. I listened intently as Donny King declared over the radio, *"Mr. Chairman, the state of Illinois cast blah, blah votes for the next president of the United States..."* I couldn't wait to get to my civics class the next day and share what I had heard with Miss Boody, my teacher. She heard it all too. *"I'd love to do that!"* I declared to her, as I made up my mind right then and there that I wanted to go into politics.

Fast forward twenty-eight years to 1980. The location was Madison Square Garden, New York City. The event was the Democratic National Convention where Jimmy Carter and Ted Kennedy vied for the democratic presidential slot. I was forty-three-years-old and co-chair of the Illinois delegation when I actually lived the moment I dreamed of since my high school days, by rising on the convention floor and declaring: *"Madame*

Chairman, the great state of Illinois casts 139 delegates for the next president of the United States, Jimmy Carter, and 15 for Senator Kennedy!" Standing before the convention and uttering those same words that I had heard others before me declare was electrifying! In fact, in many ways, it was literally a dream come true!

For me, the 2008 Democratic National Convention, which was held in Denver, was even more exhilarating as the 1980 convention which fulfilled my early dreams. It was exciting being in the midst of all the people, attending all the receptions and parties, and watching all the convention goers converging from everywhere. Even with my previous convention experience, I must admit I had never quite seen anything like it! Although Denver is a great city, it sometimes seemed there were just too many people invading the available space all at one time to expect everything to run smoothly.

Since I had been a vice president of the DNC, I knew quite a few of the key democratic figures from across the country that were in attendance. In one way or another, I had worked with the majority of them, including guys like Jim Lewis from New Mexico and many others from Ohio, Minnesota, and many other places.

I had established a good networking base dating all the way back to Clinton's conventions in New York in 1992 and Chicago in 1996. As a result of these experiences, by 2008 I was considered such an old war horse that they kept me right up front in our Illinois delegation. In fact, the entire Illinois delegation was up front, too, both in the convention hall and in the football stadium, since we were Obama's state. With a cascade of mountains as the backdrop, it was truly magical to listen to all the eloquent speeches, especially Obama's acceptance speech, reverberate throughout the vast openness in the south end section of Denver's Invesco Mile High stadium.

The Governor's Brother Keeps Calling

With Election Day soon approaching, I received a phone call one October day from Robert "Rob" Blagojevich, the governor's brother and fund-raiser. Rob initiated the conversation by apologizing for an incident during my 2002 gubernatorial race when he had mistakenly called me Jesse White, who is the Illinois secretary of state. I had forgotten all about it, but we joked about that incident for a few moments until he segued into the real purpose of his call. *"I'm now the governor's fund-raiser,"* he began, *"and we're trying to raise funds for the governor's re-election.* " I replied, *"Well, Rob, you've got to call me back later; sometime after November. We have this election coming up soon that I'm focused on, and you're talking about a race that's not until 2010. We have candidates hitting us up for money for this election. Call me back after the election next month."*

Later, I told my consulting partner, Fred, that the governor's brother had called me, trying to raise funds for Blagojevich. I told him what my response was to Rob. Fred looked at me and said, *"Well, I think Blagojevich is in trouble. Some of these guys had been sentenced. I wouldn't give him any money."*

"Oh!" was my only response. Although I respected Fred's opinion not to donate, I decided to pose that same question to my law partner, Tim Wright, in order to elicit his opinion as well. *"Do you think we should donate anything, Tim?"*

"No. The governor's in trouble," Tim echoed Fred.

Back in 2006, we had given Blagojevich $5,000 towards his campaign. I personally gave $1,000; the partnership gave $1,500; and the law firm gave $2,500. For 2010, both my partners were of the opinion that we should not give him anything.

On November 4, 2008, General Election Day finally arrived. As we expected, U.S. Senator Barack Obama won, becoming our nation's 44th president and the 1st African-American president in the nation's history. In Chicago's Grant Park that night, tears were flowing from almost everyone's eyes, including mine. Watching all the celebrations of that historical event on television proved so contagious that I decided at the last minute to go downtown to join in the celebration of Obama's election. When the electoral vote count reached 281 votes, or something like that, I jumped out of my seat and said, *"I'm going down to the park!"*

I was about ten blocks from the park, so it didn't take me very long to get there. Since some of the cops who were standing watch knew me, they helped out quite a bit by ushering me towards the front of that mass of people who were gathering there. Once I got closer to the front, I saw that some of the state police who had provided me with security at some point in my twenty years in state government were also there, and they assisted me further by opening a path, which allowed me to get even closer to the front while telling people, *"He's the former Attorney General."* One of the officers even helped me climb over an unanticipated fence! Finally, I stood in awe among thousands of others listening to our new president deliver his history-making acceptance speech.

Even before leaving the park that night, I slipped back to lobbying mode. I ran into Rick Garcia, a major leader in the gay and lesbian community. While chit-chatting about what had just transpired, I posed this question, *"Rick, what do you think about who will take Obama's place?"*

"I don't know," he replied.

"What about me?" I asked.

Rick gave a slight nod as if to imply, *"Why not?"* Unfortunately, that one minute dialogue ended up as an article with twisted facts thanks to the pen of an unscrupulous columnist inaccurately implying that there was something wrong or illegal about "Burris trying to get the appointment." I was simply lobbying every angle I could, which never went one step further than letting people know that I have a legitimate interest in the position.

On November 8th, four days after the election, the governor's brother called me back as I had suggested in our previous conversation where I told him to contact me after the election. As soon as he announced himself, I started right in, *"Well, Rob, I don't know how to get any money for you and the governor, but I've got some more people to talk to. Let me talk to them and call me back in about a week. I'll let you know."*

On one hand, I found myself telling Rob I would help his fundraising efforts; while on the other hand, I knew I had no resources from which to pull any money. I mainly wanted to placate the governor's brother to put him off for the time being. With an interest in the senate seat, I knew I could not raise money for the governor; yet, at the same time, I wanted to remain on the good side of the governor and his brother.

Around November 13th, Rob called again. I can see why the governor selected his brother as fundraiser, as he was certainly relentless in his approach. Upon answering the phone I asked, *"Are you calling me to let me know that I'm being appointed to the senate seat?"*

"Huh?" he responded, tipping me off right away to the fact that he was calling once again for a donation for the governor.

I don't know why, but during that phone conversation I ran my mouth. Giving no specifics, I told the governor's brother that our law firm *might* be contributing to the governor's campaign when, in fact, I already knew that Tim would not be sending a dime. I also told Rob that I was experiencing a business "problem" at that time. In other words, I couldn't give money because our consulting business was unstable and on the verge of splitting up because clients weren't renewing their contracts. Yet, in the midst of all these excuses, I said to Rob, *"I'll send you a check."*

Part of the reason I said this was that for me making such a donation was normal practice. I had always made some sort of donation to the governor's campaign, and I had also always written the governor's campaign a check for $1,000. My promised check that time would be for that same amount: $1,000. However, before ending our conversation and hanging up the phone, I made sure that Rob knew that I was well aware of the rules. I said, *"Now, Rob, I can't raise any money for you, because it would look like I'm trying to buy the seat."*

After I hung up the phone, I chastised myself, *"Roland, you can't give a $1,000! You can't do that! Why did you say you would?"*

I had conjured up all those excuses; all just to cover myself and stay in good with Rob. I didn't know it at that time was that during that entire phone conversation, I was being taped.

Blagojevich is Arrested

I continued lobbying for the seat, this time by calling my classmates in my hometown of Centralia and asking them to write to the governor's office requesting my appointment. One of my friends, Richard Barber, of Somerset, New Jersey, wrote a five-page letter to the governor's office entitled: Why Burris should be appointed to the senate. In that vein, I continued with my aggressive strategy of lobbying everyone to contact the governor's office. In mid-November, a minister friend of mine with contacts in the governor's office informed me that I was on the short list for the appointment to the senate seat. Yet, in the media, other people, such as Valerie Jarrett and Jesse Jackson, Jr., were being talked about as viable appointees, without my name ever being mentioned. That started to concern me as I lamented to my wife, *"Honey, they aren't even mentioning my name. What is going on? I thought I was on the short list? Who can I call?"* I voiced my concern to Fred, *"Fred, they aren't even mentioning my name. I need to call the governor's chief of staff and try to find out what's going on up there."*

Sometime right after Thanksgiving, I called Springfield to follow up on the status of a job for which my nephew had submitted an application. Even though he was well-qualified for the position, he was told it had to be signed off by John Harris, the Chief of Staff. I called Harris to get an update and he said assuredly, *"Your nephew has good credentials. We're looking at his application."* I thanked him then took a quick opportunity to ask about the senate seat. *"Have you heard anything on the appointment for the Senate seat?"* Harris replied abruptly, *"No!"* Before I could say another thing, he hung up! I wasn't quite sure how to interpret that very unfriendly response. At around 7:30 in the morning on December 9th, I received a phone call from Fred. He said, *"General, the governor has been arrested!"*

"What?" I just knew I heard incorrectly.

"The governor's been arrested for trying to sell the senate seat." Fred repeated slowly.

All I could say was, *"Oh my God."*

As I rushed to the T.V. to turn on the news, I tried to wrap my brain around the stunning information that Fred had just given me, both about the governor's arrest and about the charges being made against him. I thought to myself, *"Who in the world would be trying to buy the senate seat? What was that all about?"*

For most of the day I remained glued to the story as more and more reports revealed the allegations of wrong doings. Governor Rod Blagojevich had been arrested. His chief of staff, John Harris, had been arrested. His deputy governor, Bob Greenlee, had resigned. That afternoon in a press conference, the U.S. Attorney made an announcement about the criminal enterprise in which the governor was alleged to have been involved.

One week prior to all that, as I was telling Fred about the unpleasant phone incident with Harris, I decided that despite the abrupt manner that he had hung up on me, I would just call him back and inquire as to what was transpiring with the appointment. As I stared at the news programming on T.V., I was so glad that I never got around to making that call.

Should I Take It?

That night, at a meeting with my group, Coalition of African-American Leaders (COAL), several of us sat around after the meeting talking about the governor's arrest. I had previously informed them that I was on the short list, so they all wanted to know the status of the appointment. Some of the guys spoke up in support of my appointment, indicating that they felt I was clearly the best person for the senate seat. I expressed my appreciation for their vote of confidence and assured them that, *"I've been trying to get my name out there."*

"Well, you've got to come up with a strategy," they suggested.

There were a lot of my middle-class black friends in that group. They agreed to stand behind me on whatever strategy I devised. I rushed home that night with plans forming in my head. The next day, I shared everything with Fred, *"Fred, I've got a group that would back me for the senate seat. We have to get some kind of press exposure, maybe get a press conference called, so we can get out a message. Let's get a group of supporters of Roland Burris and say, 'the best person to take over this seat is [Attorney] General Burris'."*

While the media continued to buzz with stories about the selling of the seat, Fred and I worked out a plan for me and notified all my supporters from my COAL group. We also hired a black public relations firm that agreed to work with us to bring my name before the public as the best person for the senate seat. We planned the press conference in which my friends would put my name out there. At the same time, there was a debate as to whether or not my term would be for two years only, just until the term expired for that vacated seat. About thirty of my friends showed up for the press conference on December 13th. Some of those who spoke on my behalf included Sheila Smith, a major supporter of mine and previous candidate for lieutenant governor who ran on the ticket with me in '94; Bill Cousins, a former appellate court judge; and Eddie Read, a community leader.

After my supporters spoke, I came forward from the back of the room and joined those who had spoken out in support of my appointment to the vacant senate seat. First, I thanked them for their support in putting my name forward. I then answered questions from the press, such as how long I would serve. Initially, I didn't want to get myself locked into that particular issue, but I thought about my answer one last time and then briefly replied, *"Well, I'll take it for the two years."*

Attorney General Madigan had already filed a suit against Blagojevich regarding his competency not only to make the senate appointment, but also to perform any gubernatorial functions. She had been quoted as saying that whether or not they could find a statute to sue the governor for his actions and whether or not the competency statute would apply, he really was *not* incompetent. The next question posed to me by the press was, *"You're a former attorney general. What do you think about Lisa Madigan's suit?"*

Even though I wanted to stay on the good side of Blagojevich for purposes of the assignment, I had no choice but to answer honestly and forthrightly, *"Well, if I were General Madigan, I'd have to pursue every legal angle. It's your sworn duty as a constitutional officer to take that action. If I were the attorney general right now, I would be doing the same thing to see if that statute would apply to the situation. If the governor would appoint me, more than likely I will accept the appointment."*

Christmas day came, and we celebrated it in our usual way as a family; yet my thoughts were anything but normal during that time. Blagojevich was determined to appoint someone, saying that he had no alternative but to carry out his constitutional duty to make an appointment in the wake of no legislation being passed to hold a special election for that seat. His lawyers, father and son team, Sam Adams, Sr. and Sam Adams, Jr. had viewed my press conference and advised the governor that if he was going to appoint someone to the seat that I would be the best person for him to appoint.

The day after Christmas, just as my wife and I had done for years, we prepared to attend a black-tie dinner affair at the downtown Hyatt Hotel, hosted by "The Assembly," a group of one hundred or so black males. The guest list for this annual event has always included anywhere between 1,500 to 2,000 people. Around three o'clock that afternoon, I received a call from a woman stating that one of the governor's counselors was trying to reach me. Just then, my other phone rang. As soon as I answered it, Sam Adams Jr.'s voice came across the receiver saying, *"I've got to talk to you."*

"About what?" I inquired.

He repeated, *"I've got to talk to you, but I can't do it on the phone. Are you home?"*

"Yes," I replied." *Come on over."*

Within twenty minutes, Adams was ringing my doorbell. As soon as he sat down on the sofa, he started right in, *"This is what I want you to know. My father and I have been talking to the governor, and the governor is going to make an appointment to the senate seat. We're advising him that the best person he can appoint is you."*

"What? You did?"

"That's right," he confirmed, *"What do you think about it?"*

I said, *"Well, that's great, but yeah, uh, I've got to think about it."*

I was taken aback even though it was the very thing for which I had been lobbying my can off.

I immediately requested more time to think about my response: *"I need some time. I need at least a week."*

"No, no, you don't have a week. The governor's going to make an appointment in the next few days. This is now the 26th of December. He's going to appoint somebody in the next few days."

"How much time, then? I need to talk to my wife."

Berlean was at the beauty parlor getting ready for the black-tie dinner. I asked for more information but Adams would not comply with that request either. He continued to press upon me the urgency of the matter at hand, *"My father and I have convinced the governor that the best person he can appoint is you. You've got the credentials and the credibility. If you'll accept this appointment, the governor will appoint you."*

"Okay, how much time do I have?"

Adams finally let me off the hook from having to give an immediate answer, *"How about Sunday afternoon?"* I took a deep breath and answered, *"Okay, I'll let you know by Sunday at four o'clock."*

My heart started racing at the possibility that the appointment that I had been seeking might actually coming into fruition, and in such an entirely unanticipated way. I ushered Sam Adams, Jr. to the door and once he had left, attempted to collect my racing thought. Within the hour, Berlean came home, and I couldn't wait to tell her everything that transpired.

"Are you kidding? She started, looking confused. *"And you don't want to take it?"* She was surprised that I had not told Adams 'yes,' right on the spot. I got our son and daughter on the phone and queried them. My son was all for me taking the appointment; my daughter was on the fence regarding the whole matter. I wanted to see what the public had to say about it, so I decided to ask the opinions of as many of my friends as I could at that dinner we were attending that evening. That's exactly what I did.

My conversation was something like: *"If the governor were to appoint me to the senate seat, should I take it?"* I went from person to person all night long until I had talked to about two hundred friends. Every person that I approached and queried that evening felt strongly that I should take the appointment. The one person who spoke against my taking the appointment said, *"No, you should not take it because the governor is tainted. But when you do take it, I need a job!"* Needless to say, that decision-making process dominated our household conversation for the duration of the weekend. We talked about it all the way home from the dinner. I stayed on the phone all day and all evening on Saturday, polling my friends across the state with the same question I had asked the dinner guests. All of them basically said, *"You're the best person for it. Illinois needs someone like you in the United States Senate. Go for it. If the governor appoints you, take it!"*

Adams called around two o'clock Sunday afternoon. I told him my family would be eating dinner at three o'clock and that he could come over at four o'clock. Promptly at four on the nose, Adams and his assistant showed up at my door. I had my lawyers and Fred there, as well as some of the other people with whom I had talked back and forth. My wife and I had agreed that I would take the appointment, so I was relieved and quite ready to give my unwavering answer.

"Now, Roland, I want to know your answer," Adams cut right to the chase. *"If the governor calls you and offers you to the appointment to the United States Senate, would you accept it?"*

I said, *"If the governor calls me, I'd tell him, 'Yes, I'll accept the appointment.'"*

He replied, *"Okay, let me get him on the phone."* Adams went outside and called Blagojevich on his cell phone. He and—presumably--Blagojevich talked for a few minutes before Adams concluded his telephone conversation and came back inside where the rest of us were waiting. He said to me, *"The governor's going to call you in three minutes."*

A few minutes later, just as Adams had predicted, my phone rang. It was Governor Blagojevich on the line, telling me, *"General, you deserve it. You're the best qualified person for it. We couldn't have anyone better in the United States Senate. It's my pleasure to appoint you to the United States Senate for the great State of Illinois. Will you accept my appointment?"*

I firmly stated, *"Governor, I accept."*

Blagojevich's final words to me were, *"The staff will work out the other details. Thank you. Good-bye."*

285

Chapter Seventeen

To Be Seated or Not to Be Seated

I Accept the Seat!

I t was Sunday evening, December 28, 2008 when that brief phone dialogue I shared with Governor Blagojevich changed my life forever. After the fateful telephone call one of the governor's lawyers, Sam Adams. Jr., and I agreed there would be a press conference, but not until Tuesday. That essentially meant sitting on my acceptance until the press conference. On the other hand, my own lawyers, as well as close friends of mine, were advising me to make phone calls and to start letting everyone know I was going to accept the appointment. *"You've got to call Durbin,"* they instructed. *"You've got to call this person and that person."* On and on it went.

Going against all these suggestions, I did not make any calls at all on Monday. Nevertheless, news of the appointment had leaked out to the press by Monday evening, which forced me to start calling key officials on Tuesday morning. One of the calls I personally made was to Illinois Senior Senator Dick Durbin. When I told him my intentions, right away he said with much fervor, *"Don't accept an appointment from the governor! Don't accept it!"*

"Why not, Dick?" I inquired.

He gave no explanation for his position, but just kept telling me in a variety of ways not to accept the governor's appointment: *"You can't be a seat warmer."* *"You won't be able to run."* *"You have to have $20* *million." "We want somebody in there who can hold onto that seat."*

At the time of that conversation, little did I know that Durbin had already obtained the signatures of fifty-two of the Democratic senators on a letter stating that they planned to object to the seating of *any* individual appointed by the governor, regardless of the identity of the appointee? In our phone conversation, Durbin never once mentioned that letter to me.

In response to all the reasons that Durbin kept spewing out about why I should not accept the appointment, I simply said, *"I'm sorry, Dick. I appreciate all that, but I have already accepted the appointment."*

Next, I called Secretary of State Jesse White to let him know about the governor's appointment and my decision to accept the offer. Initially, he congratulated me, but then called me back about two hours later singing an entirely different tune. *"Well, I'm not going to sign the governor's appointment document if he appoints you."*

I couldn't believe my ears. How could the secretary of state hope to veto a legitimate appointment by the governor? Jesse's only explanation for throwing the legal monkey wrench he had just thrown at me was that he had stated publicly he would not sign any appointment made by the governor. So, it was what it was. As I prepared for the press conference, I tried to push that conversation out of my head. Although, I knew there would be a lot of "stuff" to deal with once the announcement was made that afternoon; never could I have predicted just how much "stuff" that would turn out to be.

At the press conference, after informing the public of my appointment, I read my statement of acceptance. Instantly, the undercurrent of tension that already filled the room became so tangible I could almost hear the criticism and see the strategic wheels of opposition turning in the heads of my detractors. What I was witnessing in that room, was the "coalitioning" of the brain power that was already busy at work devising reasons to block my appointment. *"It's not going to happen. It's not going to happen."* I could imagine them muttering amongst themselves, as reporters fired off questions and even hurled accusations at me.

All of this happened in spite of the fact that in naming me as his appointee to the senate, Governor Blagojevich had made an earnest appeal to the media and others. *"Please don't allow the allegations against me to taint this good and honest man,"* he said when he announced my appointment to fill the senate seat vacated by Obama.

Before opening my mouth to speak any further, I mentally fought off the allegations I knew would soon surface, with two fundamental points of rationalization: First of all, there was the fact that ultimately, Illinois had to get *someone* in that seat; secondly, there was the fact Blagojevich was still governor and had the legal authority to make the senate appointment. Period. Those two points of common sense and legitimacy were all that mattered to me.

Just then, I spotted Congressman Bobby Rush in the back of the room, and invited him up to the microphone. Bobby used that opportunity to chastise the members of the press for their attacks on me. He specifically admonished them on the race issue and rejected outright the suggestion Blagojevich selected me solely because of race. In that particular press conference, Bobby provided a good buffer for me; however, I knew very well no buffer could shield me from what lay in store for me in the weeks ahead.

The Senate Rejects My Seating

After being officially appointed on December 30, 2008, the next thing I should have been doing, along with the other new senators, was preparing for the swearing-in ceremony, which was to take place on January 6, 2009. Instead, I was working with a team of lawyers straight through the holiday to prepare a legal action to take before the Illinois Supreme Court to force our secretary of state to sign the governor's appointment documentation.

On New Year's Day, the lawyers continued working on the *Writ of Mandamus,*[cxxx] which in essence was a legal document to force the secretary of state to perform his duty. After the holiday, when the courthouse was open again, we filed the necessary legal documents. Over the next couple of days, I prepared to travel to Washington, D.C., anxious to bring the entire appointment situation to a successful conclusion.

Sunday, January 4, 2009, in celebration of my appointment, there was a major rally held for me at the New Covenant Missionary Baptist Church, where Rev. Stephen Thurston is pastor. Berlean and I stood gratefully before a church sanctuary filled with people who included

288

supportive members of the congregation of New Covenant, family, friends and people from all sectors of the community. Through their congratulations and prayers for my success, they evidenced their strong support for my appointment, as I completed preparations for my Monday morning departure to D.C.

As I left my house that next morning heading to the airport, one of the first things that became apparent to me was the majority of the people in the crowd that had gathered outside my home certainly did not share the warm sentiments that had been expressed by the people of New Covenant Missionary Baptist Church on Sunday. Instead, the reporters and cameramen who headed the crowd outside my home advanced towards me like vultures circling their prey. They wanted any comments I would give them. Those reporters, along with their news truck crews, had stationed themselves outside my house for days; in fact, they had been camped out ever since my press conference. I didn't know what to make of all the fuss! Apparently, it was all because I had been appointed to the seat by the governor, and, even worse, I had the audacity to accept the governor's appointment and the nerve to be headed to Washington to be seated in the U.S. Senate.

We still had not obtained the signature of the secretary of state or the official seal at the bottom of the appointment document we had already sent in to the U.S. Senate. Therefore, the big question still looming as I arrived in D.C. was whether or not I would be sworn in along with the other new senators.

To help ensure I would be sworn in, I had brought a team with me to Washington, having personally paid for seven airline tickets for my team members out of my own pocket. That team included Fred LeBed, my partner; Jason Erkes, a young man who handled my media matters; Tim Wright, head of my legal team; Eddie Read, a community activist; and Kenny Sawyer and Chris Russo, a couple of my close friends and longtime supporters.

The swearing-in ceremony was scheduled to take place at noon on the day after I arrived in the capital with my team. The members of my team and I strategized all day and all night regarding how I would get seated. Some of the lawyers on my team had remained in Illinois to go before the Illinois Supreme Court and appeal for the court's issuance of a *Writ of Mandamus* against the secretary of state. Tim, the head of my legal team, also had a team of lawyers in D.C. tirelessly researching and writing up a brief based on the legal premise that pursuant to the governor's legitimate appointment; it would have been unconstitutional *not* to seat me.

To assist the team in that critical task, Tim also recruited some of the best and brightest legal talent available, including a Howard University Law School research team headed by Kurt Schmoke, Dean of the Howard Law School and former Mayor of Baltimore; Charles J. Ogletree, a Harvard Law School professor; and William Jeffers, one of the most well-respected and high-powered lawyers in D.C.

Activity and conversation amongst us flourished nonstop. Who was going to do what? When were we going to arrive at the senate? Would we try to go to the senate floor? Would I perform a sit-in at the senate chamber doors? Yes, things had begun to get a little crazy and rather intense, and especially so by the time talk of the sit-in came up as a potential strategy. Finally, I laid down the law when the strategizing suggestions reached the point of name calling and threats of leaving.

"Look," I told the members of my team, *"we can't do any of that. We've already talked to the sergeant at arms, who said we will not be able to enter the chamber."*

Fortunately, though, I knew the sergeant at arms, Terry Gainer, from his days as Illinois State Police Director and from my days as Illinois Attorney General. I talked my guys out of using any of their scene-causing strategies and instead, made arrangements with Terry for us to get into the Senate building in the morning, prior to the noontime ceremony, so as not to disrupt the swearing in of the other new senators. My lawyers had informed me in order to file a case based on my not being seated; I first had to be rejected officially by the senate.

On the morning of January 6, in the pouring rain, my team and I began our five-block trek from the hotel to the senate on Constitution Avenue. Just seconds after we emerged from the hotel, several reporters fell in step with us, poking microphones in my face, as my team and I attempted to make our way to the senate office building, through the very rainy Washington D.C. streets. As if the raindrops pelting our faces weren't bad enough, the media presence grew stronger by the minute, with the growing numbers of press people soon forming a tighter bubble around me every one hundred yards or so.

I could not see anything to my left, to my right, or in front of me except microphones, cameras and tape recorders, all attached to outstretched arms. I couldn't even tell exactly where we were, so I had no way of knowing how close we were to reaching our destination. As we reached the Capitol grounds, the Capitol Police officers did their best to control the media; but, somehow, in the process, a female police officer was inadvertently knocked to the ground.

Finally, we made it to the senate building and through security, where the sergeant of arms met us. At that point, there were about twelve of us in my party. We were escorted to the third floor, where we met in the office of Senate Secretary Nancy Erickson. She, along with the senate parliamentarian and a group of lawyers, were there waiting for us.

As soon as we sat down, the lawyers from both sides began talking back and forth about my appointment documents. *"The appointment papers are not properly executed according to the Senate Rule 2. They must be signed and sealed, yet these papers have not been signed and sealed by the Illinois Secretary of State."*

Once my lawyers heard that statement, they declared, *"Okay, we've been rejected from being seated; that's what we needed to hear."* That statement by the lawyers for the senate constituted the senate's formal refusal to seat me on that date. That formal rejection by the senate parliamentarians and lawyers meant my lawyers could proceed with the preparation to file a federal suit. At the conclusion of our meeting, my party and I left the office of the senate secretary at around eleven o'clock in the morning. It goes unsaid that my party and I departed in a very professional manner, being especially careful to cause any disturbance to the new senators or those gathering to see them sworn in.

By the time my party and I finally exited the building, it was literally raining cats and dogs. In spite of that, I held a brief press conference, with team member, Howard University Dean Schmoke, holding an umbrella over my head. To open that press conference I stated, *"I am the junior senator from Illinois. This morning, I presented my credentials to be seated and was refused seating in the United States Senate."*

D.C. Meeting

Back in the hotel room, I watched the swearing-in of my colleagues on T.V. Several of my friends, including Mark Begich (D-AK), and the Udall cousins, Tom (D-NM) and Mark (D-CO), and about four others I knew very well, were sworn in. I got goose bumps and teary-eyed watching the ceremony, especially since I knew I should have been there among the newly sworn in senators.

Nevertheless, I had to focus on the meeting I had with senate leaders Durbin and Reid the next day to discuss what needed to happen to remove the legal obstacles to my own swearing in as a senator. I had never met Senator Reid before, so prior to my meeting with him, I called my friend Frankie Sue Del Pappa, a former attorney general for Nevada, and asked her to put in a good word about me. *"Call Senator Reid and tell him that I'm not a bad guy."* I knew former Senator Richard Byran of Nevada also, so I called him as well with the same request. Both of them called Reid and put in a good word on my behalf. Of course, I already knew my own Senator Durbin. By that time, I also had heard about an effort afoot in the U.S. Senate to reject anyone appointed to that body by the governor; however, I still did not know it was Senator Durbin, himself, who was the chief architect of that letter-writing campaign. I should have realized since he was definitely not a Blagojevich fan, he would pretty much regard me in a similarly negative manner.

There had been many rumors swarming around about my upcoming meeting with Reid and Durbin and the demands they would be making on me. Then, as though all of that wasn't enough, on that same day I was scheduled to go before the Illinois Impeachment Committee back in Springfield to answer some questions. Their subpoena for my appearance on January 7th had stated the hearing would be, *"in reference to your appointment by the governor to a United States Senate seat."* My lawyers and I knew we could not make it to that hearing in Springfield, IL on the 7th, so we sent an affidavit explaining how the appointment came about and informing the members of the committee that I could appear before the committee on January 8th.

Understandably, in anticipation for what the next day held, I got very little sleep that night. What helped to calm my anxiety were the many people who let me know they were pulling for me to make it through all the legal and political red tape and emerge as a senator. I remained encouraged by all the bipartisan support and good wishes I received throughout the day from people I saw in the hotel and from people all over the country, some whom I didn't even know personally.

For example, I received a phone call in my hotel room from former President Jimmy Carter encouraging me to stick with my effort to be seated. Michael Steele, who had lost the race for senate from Maryland and who was later elected president of the Republican National Committee, stopped by my hotel room to wish me well.

Senator James Inhofe (R-OK) introduced himself to me at the restaurant where I had dinner that evening and said to me, *"You deserve to be seated. You're a good young man."*

"Thank you, Senator," I replied, chuckling inside at the implications of his description of me as a "young man," since I was seventy-one-years-old at the time. Inhofe, one of the most conservative guys in the entire senate, and I soon thereafter became good acquaintances. We have even discussed the possibility of taking a trip to Africa together.

The next morning, while my entourage waited for me in Reid's office reception area, the two senators and I finally sat down for our meeting. First, I told them a little bit about myself. Reid confirmed with me that both Frankie Sue and Governor Bryan had put in a good word for me. He then said, *"There was another lawyer who lives in Las Vegas who wrote an article; he's a former Chicago lawyer. He wrote this very favorable article on you."* Reid had taken the time to retrieve the article, cut it out and bring it with him.

"Yeah, his name is Earl Malkin," I said. It pleased me to know that Earl, who said he was going to put something in the Nevada newspapers supporting me, was a man of his word. So, my conversation with Reid was very warm and very friendly. In contrast, my interaction with Durbin remained cold for the duration of the meeting. In wrapping up the meeting, both men advised me to go to the Impeachment Committee hearing, give my testimony and see what would come out of it. Next, I was advised to get my papers in order by obtaining the necessary signature in order to meet Rule 2 of the senate. After that, they indicated they would consider the next step, which would possibly be sending my request to the Senate Committee on Rules and Administration (Rules Committee).

Springfield Meeting

We darted out of D.C., that same evening, the evening of January 7th.

There were about nine of us flying back to Chicago, then driving to Springfield on the morning of January 8th, so I could go before the Impeachment Committee, as I had promised in the first affidavit. Actually, it was that first document that created a great deal of the problems for me. The last item of that affidavit said, *"Prior to December 26, 2008, no one in the governor's office or a governor's representative or my representative had said anything to Roland Burris with reference to appointing him to a senate seat,"* That was the one sentence in the affidavit of that the members of the press clearly had no understanding; otherwise, they would not have been creating senseless mass frenzy, saying I had lied in order to get seated.

During that impeachment hearing in Springfield, I had all kinds of "off track" questions thrown my way. One Republican kept zeroing in on what happened way back during my 2002 gubernatorial race when my friend (he didn't use the term "friend") with the broadcasting station loaned my campaign $1.5 million and on the fact I still owed that individual $1.2 million. From my perspective, that had nothing at all to do with my senate appointment; yet, some of the other legislators raised similarly irrelevant questions as well, over and over. It began to be very confusing.

Then, that same Republican who raised the question about the loan, rattled off a list of names, including the name of the governor's brother, Rob Blagojevich. He looked up from his list and asked me, *"Well, did you talk to and have contact with all these people?"*

"Yes, I've talked to those people." I answered with an edge to my voice by this time, *"They're not the only people I talked to, though. I talked to a lot of my friends."*

Then someone on the committee made reference to Lon Monk. There had been a meeting between Lon and I, so I told them about it in order to clarify the actual content of that meeting.. *"The only person I really sat down and talked to about wanting to get appointed was Governor Blagojevich's former chief of staff, Lon Monk. That took place in my office at the end of July. That's the only person with whom I had a conversation."* So we focused on Lon Monk for a little while.

Other legislators were asking questions. At one point, a female legislator, who asked a question earlier, came back with another inquiry, *"Now is there anybody else that you talked to?"*

To that question, I answered, *"No, I don't recall anybody else. I talked about the appointment with all my friends, and I can give you all kinds of names of people I talked to about my interest in getting an appointment."*

They later tried to get me on the basis of perjury, because I had not given the governor's brother's name when that woman legislator asked if I recalled speaking to anyone else about the appointment. The reason I did not give his name in response to her question was I was a little confused by the redundancy of her question, especially since I had already gone on record admitting I had spoken to the governor's brother when I admitted having talked to the people whose names appeared on the list produced by the first legislator. When I admitted to having talked to the governor's brother and the other people on the list, I also pointed out I had spoken to many other people in my lobbying for the senate seat. Once it had been established I had spoken to the governor's brother, I provided the additional information that the brief discussions between the governor's brother and I had been exclusively about fund-raising, although no one on the Impeachment Committee ever asked me anything about fund-raising. It was this testimony, which was freely given by me in response to the questions asked of me, that led to most of the controversy concerning my acceptance of the appointment from Blagojevich and to the unsubstantiated allegation I had lied to the Impeachment Committee in order to be seated.

Seated!

After I completed my testimony before the committee, having answered all their questions, we all shook hands and my group and I prepared to leave. It seemed to me that everything was okay and final. On the other hand, my lawyer, Tim Wright, thought otherwise, and informed the members of the committee that, *"We are going to review this transcript, and if anything is missing, we'll clear up the senator's answers afterwards. We'll submit information after we read the transcript."* Even that statement given by my lawyer was left in the testimony. On that note, the meeting was adjourned, and we headed back to Chicago to continue our battle over whether or not the Illinois Secretary of State could legally refuse to certify my appointment, in the Illinois Supreme Court.

By Thursday, January 9th, the Supreme Court still had not issued a ruling on the matter regarding the secretary of state! Finally, on Thursday evening, the court ruled the secretary of state could not veto an act by the governor; therefore, his refusal to sign my appointment had no effect. The secretary of state was ordered to issue a certified copy of the appointment with his signature and seal on it. On Friday, January 10, 2009, we received the certified copy of the appointment we had been asking for since December 30, 2008. When all was said and done, that ten dollar certified copy came by way of a motion; a reply to the motion; and a reply to the reply, all to the tune of about $150,000 in legal fees. Next, the big question was whether or not the senate would accept the documentation with the governor's signature on one page and the secretary of state's signature and seal on the attached page. We didn't know if that would be sufficient, but that following Sunday afternoon, Tim headed back to D.C. to meet with the governor's chief of staff.

The next morning, the two of them met and presented the newly signed document to the parliamentarian and the secretary of the senate. After the senate received the appointment documents, the word on the Hill was it might be sent to the Rules Committee to stall my appointment, although the official reason was there were some concerns as to whether or not Rule 2 was being violated, because the governor's and secretary of state's signatures and seal appeared on separate pages.

In the meantime, through the force of public opinion, the pressure continued to build around the entire situation. Were they going to seat Burris, or were they not going to seat Burris? Heated and sharply divided discussions sprung up about my situation throughout Illinois and across the nation. Chicagoans were up in arms. Citizens from places all around the country were calling their senators saying, *"We know Roland Burris. He's qualified and deserving of the seat." "Seat Roland Burris!"* Unfortunately, the continual news-streaming surrounding the senate's non-decision soon threatened to overshadow both the national excitement and the historic significance of the upcoming Obama inauguration.

In light of that fast approaching inauguration, something had to be done quickly. To assist in expediting matters, the Chicago City Council, along with the Black Caucus and my alderman, Fredrenna Lyle, joined together to hold a special council meeting. With Mayor Richard M.

Daley presiding, the council passed a resolution calling for me to be seated. I was humbled by the wonderful comments made about me by those in attendance, particularly Ms. Lyle, as they extolled my spotless public record. In the midst of all the negative opposition I had been facing, the opportunity to sit in that room and to hear all those nice things being said about me, went a long way towards recharging my spirit and energizing me for the work that remained to be done.

On Monday, January 11th, my lawyers prepared briefs and were ready to file suit the next day in the D.C. District Court to challenge the failure of the senate to seat me. They were ready to go into court to start the litigation, because if the senate had been allowed to send my certified appointment paperwork to the Rules Committee for thirty or sixty days, it is likely I would never have been seated.

It became that tight of a battle. Every minute of every day was so crucial. Though my stomach and nerves were in knots, I had to maintain my composure, especially every time a microphone or camera was shoved in front of me.

Finally, my prayers were answered. I was told Senator Dianne Feinstein (D-CA), exiting Rules Committee Chairwoman, stated adamantly, *"You all are not sending that to the Rules Committee! That man ought to be seated!"* Next, Senator Russell Feingold (D-WI) spoke up and said, *"Burris should be seated."* Then Senator Charles Schumer (D-NY), newly selected Chairman of the Rules Committee, said, *"We don't need it in the Rules Committee."* That was when the word became official on Tuesday, January 12, 2009 that I, Roland W. Burris was to be seated in the United States Senate as the new Illinois junior senator!

The next big decision that had to be made quickly was who was going to conduct my swearing in ceremony? Would it be Vice President Dick Cheney or Vice President-Elect Joe Biden? We were told due to Cheney's schedule, he would not be available January 13th through 15th, so we contacted Biden's office, and it was confirmed Biden would officiate at my swearing in ceremony. Shortly thereafter, however, we received a call back from Cheney's office informing us the vice president *would* be available on the 15th after all. My swearing in ceremony was finally scheduled for 1:00pm on January 15, 2009.

We were still in Chicago, so you can imagine what a zoo our household instantly became, as my wife and I hastily packed and then round-ed up my daughter, my son, my daughter-in-law, two grandsons and a nephew. Also joining us were Fred LeBed, my business partner; Jason Erkes, my media person; Tim Wright, my law partner; and Eddie Read, Kenny Sawyer, and Chris Russo, my colleagues and friends. I purchased roundtrip plane tickets for the entire entourage, and not at the discounted rate either! Once our party arrived in D.C., there would be hotel and eating expenses to consider. Thank goodness Fred agreed to put about $15,000 worth of expenses on his credit card. When all was said and done, I absorbed the remaining amount of our grand total of approximately $50,000!

Sworn In!

Early Thursday morning, on January 15, 2009, we all boarded our flight for D.C. What a great day that turned out to be! I refused to allow my concern about the expenses incurred on that trip to enter my mind at a time of such great vindication, not wanting anything to spoil my "seventh-heaven" feeling. Once we landed, my cloud-nine high was again challenged; this time by a flood of angst over the confusion of where to go, what to do and who would take us there. Unfortunately, that confusion would continue for the first couple of weeks in the senate, as I fumbled my way through operations and procedures of the senate and through the corridors and passageways of all those buildings without much assistance. Thank goodness on that first day, though, we were picked up from the airport by the Capitol police and chauffeured to the Dirksen building where we were directed to my temporary office on the fifth floor.

After examining my office, which consisted of four sections, my entourage changed clothes and then began our witch hunt for the senate dining room, where my family and I ate lunch before my swearing in ceremony. Throughout my long career, I have had ample opportunity to experience both defeat and victory, but it is truly difficult to describe the feeling of tremendous accomplishment, happiness, and family support I felt on this special day when I became a member of the United States Senate. As I looked around, I could see that the entire family was there, including my wife, Berlean; my daughter, Rolanda; my son, Roland; his wife, Marty; their two sons Roland Theodore and Ian Alexander, and my wife's nephew, Ron Miller. Together, we enjoyed an elegant, personally meaningful, and historic luncheon in the Senate Dining Room, the most exclusive dining chamber in the nation's capital and, perhaps, in the world.

Lo and behold, when I sat down in the dining room, who should be seated with his family at the very next table, but Vice President-elect Joe Biden. I have known Biden since the 1970's and have always appreciated his genuine friendliness. Before Obama got into the presidential race, I was a Biden supporter. In fact, before Obama announced his candidacy, I had already given his campaign a $1,000 check. I became torn at that point, but eventually pulled back from supporting Biden and threw my support behind Obama instead. Doing so created such an awkward situation for me that I had never confronted Biden personally or his staff about my change of heart. Fred had smoothed it over for me with Biden's staff. I figured seeing Biden in that dining room that day was an opportunity to explain my change of allegiance personally, so I approached him. After we exchanged pleasantries, I confessed, *"I want you to know, I couldn't continue to support you, Mr. Vice President-elect, when my friend was running for President."*

"Roland, I understand that," he said with a big smile.

"But," I assured him, *"I did support you for Vice President."*

We shared a few more minutes of good conversation, which gave me some relief over that whole circumstance. Talking with Biden also helped to settle the butterflies in my stomach in anticipation of soon becoming a United States Senator. After everything I had been through to get seated, those butterflies were rather justified, if I do say so myself. I knew I was starting out on an uphill climb with concerns by some of the senators about my appointment. I tried not to let that overwhelm me unduly, since I already had some experience in facing a similar situation many years ago when I had started out at the bank. Just as I had known I would have to work hard and do well to win the confidence and respect of those at the bank, I knew and accepted the fact that I would have to do the same things in order to earn the confidence and respect of my fellow senators.

Finally, the moment for which I had waited for so long, had arrived. Believe me, it was a moment worth waiting for, because it made up for all the hours and days of ridicule, slander, travesty, and hatred, which had been so unjustly directed at me. Around one o'clock that afternoon,

I presented myself at the senate door that opened to the center aisle of the chamber.

Senator Dick Durbin met me there at the entrance, while my family and guests were directed up into the seating reserved for them in the gallery. Those guests included classmates from Howard University Law School, as well as classmates from Southern Illinois University. As they watched from the gallery, they would never know how much gratitude I felt, knowing they were in attendance to lend me their much appreciated support.

Durbin and I proceeded down the aisle to the spot where Vice President Cheney stood waiting to administer the oath. During those moments, my heart was beating so fast and so loudly it seemed almost to drown out Cheney's words, as I became a United States Senator. Standing nearby was Secretary of the Senate, Nancy Erickson. With a smile on her face so large it caused me to smile proudly as well, she handed me the pen to sign the senate book. I signed my name and made it all official.

So many thoughts of trials and triumphs flooded my mind at that moment. One thought in particular was that of a young, anxious public servant ready to blaze much needed trails in my home state of Illinois. When I left law school in Washington, D.C. in 1963, I told myself I would only come back to D.C. as the Vice President of the United States or as a United States Senator. I never imagined my goal would take forty-six long years to come to fruition, but praise God, it did. As I repeated that oath, I shed tears of joy.

When the administration of the oath was completed, senators from all over the chamber came forward and congratulated me. One of them asked me if my family was there.

I turned around, pointed up to the gallery and noted, *"Yes, they are. There's my wife right there."*

Just then, another senator tapped me on the shoulder and instructed, *"Senator Burris, you just violated one of the rules of the Senate."*

"What's that?"

"You're not supposed to refer to anybody in the gallery, or look up and point to the gallery."

I gasped. That rattled me, as I thought, *"Oh, my God, I haven't been here five minutes and already I've violated the rules!"*

Perhaps making me look up into the gallery was a little initiation gag they pulled on newcomers. Whether it was or not, it didn't make me feel any better knowing I had violated a rule.

There was no time to dwell on rules at that moment, though, as we all swiftly headed over to the old senate chamber to re-enact the entire ceremony for the sake of a photo shoot. I wish I could have stayed in the chamber to hear the speech Durbin gave, in which he mentioned me, my background and made other remarks about my being sworn in; however, between the re-enactment of the oath, and all the congratulatory activity and picture taking on my behalf in the hallway, I missed his speech entirely. I was under continuous bombardment there in the hallway with a lot of hugging, laughing, and picture-taking going on. Members of the media with their cameras were everywhere; some Black Caucus members had gathered there in the hallway as well. In all the joyous confusion, I couldn't even see where my family had gone!

From this flurry of activity outside the chamber, we were ushered into a lavish reception held in my honor. My family and friends attended, along with lots of other people, most of them senators. Many of those senators approached me, offering their congratulations and shaking my hand. Senator Charles Schumer (D-NY) was one of them. I made a point of thanking him, as well as Senator Diane Feinstein (D-CA), because I had previously learned both of them had been instrumental in ensuring my appointment had not been consigned to the Rules Committee like some senators had suggested. Senator Daniel Inouye (D-Hawaii) was another one who shook my hand; he was followed by Senator John Kerry (D-Mass). Being personally congratulated by so many officials, many of whom I had never met in person, but only seen on T.V., was truly an added benefit of this event.

First Order of Business

From the moment I arrived in D.C. that morning, to the reception given in my honor after the ceremony, I floated on cloud nine. However, my "cloud" riding encountered an abrupt interruption several hours after my ceremony when duty called for a vote on the TARP 2, a revised plan to spend the remaining $350 billion of an ineffective Bush Administration TARP financial stability initiative. Some of my family members were just heading to the airport to return home, when I had to rush back to the senate chamber for my first order of business. Having not quite figured out everything, I went up to the table when it was time for me to cast my vote and lingered between the Democratic and the Republican tables realizing no one had informed me which table was which.

Suddenly, Hillary Clinton came up behind me offering a warm greeting, *"Roland, how are you doing?"*

"Secretary of State-designee, it's so good to see you." I replied, as we exchanged smiles and a few congratulatory words.

"Madame Secretary, I'm casting my first vote!" I very proudly stated.

In equal exhilaration, she added, *"Well, guess what, Roland? I'm casting my last vote in the United States Senate!"*

Just then, someone tapped me on the shoulder, and I turned around to greet none other than Joe Biden. *"Hello, Mr. Vice President-elect!"* I respectfully greeted him with his new title for the second time that day, as we hugged.

"Roland, I'm getting ready to cast my last vote in the senate," he added to the conversation Hillary and I were having when he approached us.

The senate operates by seniority, so it meant a lot to me when members of Capitol Hill like Joe and Hillary and several other senior senators embraced me and encouraged me by letting me know they had my back, and that they were there for me. As I became the 100th senator, I knew I had to work really hard to gain the respect of the other senators, since most of them had been opposed to my appointment. Before too long, though, I moved up in rank, which not only allowed them the opportunity to get to know me better, but helped to boost my confidence as well. I became the 97th ranking senator when three more senators were appointed: Ted Kaufman taking Joe Biden's seat, Kirsten Gillibrand taking Hillary Clinton's seat, and Michael Bennet taking Ken Salazar's seat when Salazar became Secretary of the Interior. The very last senator to come in was Al Franken from Minnesota, who didn't arrive until July of 2009, when his litigation matter ended. He then took the 100th spot, pushing me to number 96 in the U.S. Senate.

There have been less than 2,000 people who have been United States Senators in all the history of this country. At age seventy-one, I wasn't even the oldest one to become a member; as senate history reports there was an eighty-five-year-old man sworn in. Even though I couldn't reach a senate milestone, such as thirty-six years of service like Patrick Leahy, I like to think t my twenty-three months of decision-making and the actions I voted on concerning all parts of the world were ones that will help to create a positive environment for many American citizens and others around the world.

Political Photographs

Roland W. Burris makes Acceptance Speech after his first election as State Comptroller

Inauguration as Illinois State Comptroller: Illinois Appellate Court Justice Kenneth Wilson administers the Oath of Office to Roland W. Burris as Dr. Berlean Burris holds Bible

After the inauguration, Roland W. Burris and his family pose for picture in Illinois Comptroller's Springfield office

Illinois State Comptroller Roland W. Burris delivers 1979 Inaugural Address in Springfield

Illinois State Constitutional Officers and their wives (1979)
Lt. Governor and Mrs., Dave O'Neal; Attorney General and Mrs. William Scott; Secretary of State and
Mrs. Alan Dixon; Comptroller and Mrs. Roland W. Burris; and Treasurer and Mrs. Jerry Cosentino

1983 Inauguration as Illinois State Comptroller: Roland W. Burris is administered the Oath of Office by Illinois Appellate Court Justice Glen Johnson as daughter, Rolanda Burris (partly obscured); wife, Dr. Berlean Burris; and son, Roland Burris II look on

Flanked by wife, Dr. Berlean Burris ,son, Roland Burris II, and Chicago Bears tackle Jim Osborne, Roland W. Burris announces his 1984 candidacy for US Senate

Comptroller Roland W. Burris and Dr. Burris arriving at 1987 Inauguration in Springfield

1987 Swearing In Ceremony with Rolanda Burris, Comptroller Roland W. Burris, Dr. Berlean Burris, Roland Burris II, and Illinois Appellate Court Justice Glen Johnson

Illinois Constitutional Officers and their wives at 1987 Inauguration: Secretary of State and Mrs. Jim Edgar; Attorney General and Mrs. Neil Hartigan; Lt. Governor and Mrs. George Ryan; Governor and Mrs. James Thompson; Comptroller and Mrs. Roland W. Burris; and Treasurer and Mrs. Jerry Cosentino

National Association of State Comptrollers
Seated, from left: Robert L. Buckham, Director of the Division of Accounts, Tennessee; Roland W. Burris,, Immediate Past President, National Association of State Comptrollers, Illinois; and Earl B. Morris, Comptroller-General, South Carolina; Standing, from left: Louis L. Goldstein, Comptroller, Maryland; Edward J. Mazur, Comptroller, Virginia; Edgar Ross, Director of Accounts, Kentucky

Comptroller Roland W. Burris at Check Awarding Ceremony for $40 million for Illinois Lottery winners in the first Multimillion dollar Lottery in Illinois history

Illinois Comptroller Roland Burris and Presidential candidate, Massachusetts Governor Michael Dukakis meet on the 1988 campaign trail

Comptroller Roland Burris speaking at Democratic National Convention in Atlanta, 1988

Comptroller Roland Burris greets students and teachers as he arrives at Chicago elementary school to address students in school assembly

Illinois Comptroller Roland W. Burris holds Chicago Press Conference to announce his 1990 candidacy for Illinois Attorney General

Vince de Musizo, Illinois Democratic State Party Chairman; Neil Hartigan, candidate for Governor, Jerry Cosentino, candidate for Secretary of State; Roland Burris, candidate for Attorney General, and Paul Simon, candidate for the U. S. Senate (1990)

1990 Illinois State Wide Office Democratic Ticket: Dawn Clark Netsch, Comptroller; Jerry Cosentino, Secretary of State; Peggy Breslin, Treasurer; Jim Byrnes, Lt. Governor; Neil Hartigan, Governor; Paul Simon, United States Senate; and Roland W. Burris, Attorney General

1990 Inauguration: Roland W. Burris, the first Illinois Black Attorney General being sworn in by Charles Freeman, the first Black Illinois Supreme Court Justice, as Roland Burris II, Rolanda Burris proudly look on, and Dr. Berlean Burris holds the Bible

*Illinois Attorney General Roland W. Burris hosts
the National Association of Attorneys
General annual meeting in Chicago*

*Illinois Attorney General Roland W. Burris
(First row, third from right) and visiting Attorneys
General pose after a friendly East v. West ball
game at White Sox Park*

*Attorney General Roland Burris is flanked by
law enforcement officers as he holds a Press
Conference on Indictment of Drug Dealers*

*Illinois Attorney General Roland Burris
and Hubert Humphrey III,
Minnesota Attorney General*

Attorney General Roland Burris is greeted by a staff member on a visit to the Illinois Attorney General's Regional Office in Peoria, Illinois

Attorney General Roland Burris with Attorney General Pam Carter of Indiana (left) and Attorney General Rosalie Simmons Ballentine of the Virgin Islands (right)

Roland W. Burris is applauded by supporters as he declares his 1995 candidacy for Mayor of Chicago

Roland W. Burris announces his candidacy for Governor with wife, Dr. Berlean Burris; nephew, Steve Burris; Representative Danny K. Davis; daughter, Rolanda Burris; son, Roland Burris II; and other supporters

Roland W. Burris holds Centralia Press Conference to announce his candidacy for Governor of Illinois

Roland Burris II, Marty Burris; Illinois State Senator Obama, candidate for a U.S. Senate; Dr. Berlean Burris, Rolanda Burris, and Roland W. Burris

Sign carrying Burris advocate in 2002 Illinois Governor's contest is surrounded by other Burris supporters (from left) Illinois *Congressmen* Danny Davis and Bobby Rush; Joe W. Freelon, *Mayor* of Maywood; and *Alderman* Anthony Beal

Chapter Eighteen
Adjusting to the Senate

President Obama's 2009 Inauguration

As though becoming a U.S. senator wasn't enough of a thrill in my lifetime, the thought of attending Barack Obama's history-making presidential inauguration spurred a level of excitement and pride inside that I cannot adequately put into words. I had attended other inaugurations in years past, but there was little doubt in my mind that somehow President Obama's historic inauguration would be different. Back in 1960, since I was already there in D.C attending law school, I had made it to the mall area for President Kennedy's inauguration. My second inaugural experience was on the occasion of President Jimmy Carter's swearing in on January 20, 1977.

That one was extra special because my son, Roland II, who was turning ten-years-old around that time, had been personally invited to the inauguration by the newly elected president. Roland II had written President Carter a letter, and the president had graciously sent him a personal response, along with an invitation to sit in a special section at the Inauguration and in the grandstand at the Inaugural parade. Roland II and I traveled to D.C., bundled up and prepared to brace ourselves against the Capitol's bitterly cold weather. The fact I had with me a young boy who had an invitation, allowed us an advantage in terms of our Inaugural viewing, as people with big hearts made way for us to move closer to the front.

After the ceremony, we made our way to the grandstand where we waited and waited in anticipation of catching a glimpse of President Carter and First Lady Rosalyn walking right in front of us down Pennsylvania Avenue. In doing so, my son and I nearly froze! His coat, hat, gloves and boots, which we had thought would be sufficiently warm, were hardly enough to protect him against the intense cold of that January day. Therefore, before getting to view the First Couple up close, we hustled out of there in search of a warm building. Little did I know it at the time, but since all the shops and buildings along Pennsylvania Avenue were closed for the Inauguration; there was not one open building to be found anywhere nearby. In our attempt at making a quick getaway, I made the mistake of exiting underneath the grandstand. Guess what was happening down there? So many people were so jammed underneath there, huddled as close together as possible for warmth, like us, trying to escape the cold, that no one could go anywhere. To add insult to injury, I noticed some young thugs picking the pockets of some of the unsuspecting people in the crowd! When several victims finally realized what was happening, a lot of shoving started within a whole line of people. Instructing my son to hold onto my coattail, I began pushing a pathway out of there. It was very hectic and scary, but we finally found an opening, emerged onto the street and attempted to hail a cab, which turned out to be an impossible task, as no cabs were in sight.

As a result, we walked all the way up 14th Street NW to Lafayette Square, which is right across from the White House, where we finally found an open building that happened to be the exclusive Hay-Adams Hotel.

Once inside and sipping hot chocolate in the lounge, we viewed the parade on T.V. As the president and first lady appeared on the screen walking past the grandstand, I shook my head and laughed. *"Well, son, that is where we would have been."*

In 2009, I was not sure I knew what differences to expect between attending the Inauguration as a senator and attending as a private citizen. What I had already discovered as a new senator was you must be fast on your feet in learning the senatorial rules, including those that applied to attending the Inaugural ceremony. I received word the senators were all supposed to gather in the chamber that morning and march down together to the section designated for us, which was located behind the president's podium.

Only those senators in some leadership role had specially assigned seats in that section. Because I was new and did not know the protocol, I kept stepping back when we lined up, allowing others to go in front of me thinking we would *all* settle in our assigned seats. I had to laugh at myself when I found out otherwise and ended up seated further back than I would have been had I better understood the protocol.

Nevertheless, I enjoyed a good view of the president, along with a spectacular view across the mall where people thronged for as far as the eye could see. Being on that platform, as a part of that history-making ceremony, was surreal. There I sat, watching someone whom I personally knew being sworn in as *the* President of the United States. Wow! That moment had me pinching myself and asking, *"Is this real? Is this really happening in these United States of America?"*

As monumental as it all was, it was problematic as well. The biggest of all the problems was getting tickets to the Inauguration. The question of whether or not I would "inherit" the three hundred and thirty Inaugural tickets that came compliments of Obama's senate seat was still up in the air. Fortunately, however, it was eventually decided I would receive those tickets. Unfortunately, the media got wind of that decision and plastered it all over the news. As a result, people came out of the woodwork requesting tickets! Suddenly, so many people became my "best friends."

Between my home phone, my law office phone, my senate office phone and my cell phone, I received thousands of phone calls for tickets. Family members were the worst! I could not believe the audacity of one family member who called me and demanded fifteen tickets. *"Who the heck are you talking to?* I asked him following that impetuous request. *You'll be lucky if you get one ticket."*

"Well, I need fifteen," he insisted.

"Wait a minute; my statement meant no!"

I couldn't believe it, but all I could do was take it all in stride, as the decisions I was forced to make about those tickets caused me to lose some friends and to anger some family members. Several days after I was sworn in, while my staff and I worked tirelessly through lists of names trying to decide which ones should receive invitations to the Inauguration, I was made aware of a group of thirty or so Chicago eighth-graders who had been promised a visit to their classroom by then Senator Obama, as well as tickets to the Inauguration for them and their teachers. I headed back to Chicago to fulfill both parts of that promise. Fortunately, the tickets were delivered to me the night before my visit to the school. During the classroom visit, I enjoyed a great question and answer session with those students. At the end of our time together, I said, *"Oh, and by the way, you each get to attend the Inauguration."* That caused such a joyful pandemonium in that place! I felt so privileged to be a part of that.

Aside from ticket mayhem, the day of the Inauguration lent itself to a level of chaos most of us had never seen before. I kept hearing horror stories about people not being able to get into the viewing area after having walked for miles in the cold. Hotel rates were exorbitant. People found out hotel rooms they had reserved weeks, or even months, earlier had been sold out from under them, leaving them scrambling at the last minute for new accommodations. Everywhere you turned, there were frustrated people forced to work through very trying situations. In spite of all that, though, the record-breaking crowds persisted, and on January 20, 2009, they received the thrill they sought.

After the Inauguration, we ended up back at my office for awhile and then were off to the hotel, where I was still living, so I could get dressed for a full night of glitz and glamour. All over town, there were balls to attend. The only problem was that the excessive gridlock kept anyone from getting anywhere fast. The same chauffeur who had driven for me since my arrival in D.C. drove four of us around, but even with his experience and knowledge of the city, it required over an hour for us to travel just ten blocks from the hotel to the convention center. We considered getting out and walking, but were told that, while the special senate license plates we displayed in the window of the car would get us through security, we did not have credentials to get through security on foot. Therefore, we had no choice but to remain in the car with our very knowledgeable driver and to pack on a lot of patience. Besides, the night was young.

One thing I wasn't quite prepared for that night was all the "pleasant" attention I received from the media. My face had become very recognizable because of all the controversial T.V. coverage surrounding my appointment, so people everywhere pointed, waved and spoke to me. All night long, I heard, *"That's Senator Burris! Hey Senator Burris!"* People opened doors for me, shook my hand, and requested autographs, pictures and interviews: the whole nine yards! I was even directed to walk down a red carpet at one of the events.

That night, I was "the guy who took Obama's seat," a fact which drew all kinds of positive energy my way. I was very accommodating to everyone, mainly because that is just my nature, but also because I knew to take all of that attention with a grain of salt and not get too caught up in the moment. It would only last for a little while, just long enough for those who now sang my praise to conjure up some other reason to hang me out to dry.

We attended event after event until well into the wee hours of the morning, but we never did have any personal contact with either the president or the first lady. They were at the Illinois ball at the same time we were there, but because of the massive crowds, we never connected. It was funny to me how people I talked with that night would ask if I could get them into the White House celebration planned for later that evening. They assumed because I was a senator, I had easy access to the president and I would be at the White House for some of the private gatherings that were going to be held there. I informed them to the contrary: that, like everyone else, I, too, had limited access to the president.

Setting Up Shop

The president's Inaugural activities were a welcomed break from the full schedule I had been keeping since the moment I had been sworn in as a U.S. Senator. From the time we arrived, getting a full staff was the first order of business, so Fred LeBed, my business partner; and Jason Erkes, my media person immediately began the task of trying to hire people for my office staff. Their quest for eligible and competent staff led them to John Sassaman, Ethics Committee chief counsel and staff director. When they asked him about the appropriate procedures they should use to bring individuals onto the senate payroll, he responded with a cold look accompanied by a stern inquiry, *"Who are you, and what authority do you have to hire people?"*

"We're representing Senator Burris," Fred respectfully replied.
"Are you federal employees?"
"No, we're just volunteers."
"Well, you can't negotiate anything. You can't talk about senate employees or volunteers if you're not an employee. You have to be on the payroll."

Neither Fred nor Jason wanted to go on my payroll, since they were just there temporarily to help me get settled. However, Sassaman allowed them no leeway whatsoever. Our only recourse was to place Chris Russo and Kenny Sawyer on the payroll as assistants with each of them earning around $28,000 a year. Only then could we continue to put together a staff for my office.

For starters, we were given several volunteers. These volunteers handled logistics, helped with the staff hiring, or did whatever was needed to get the office up and running. The office scene in those early days was characterized by lots of people running around trying their best to do many things, but with no real direction. I also remember the phones in my office were not hooked up right away either. And even when they had been installed, my volunteers did not know how to manage the voicemail system properly. That issue turned into a huge public relations headache, as we later learned calls had been flooding in like crazy, so much so, in fact, that the phone system overloaded and crashed for a day or two!

Many of the calls that did not come through during that chaotic time were from members of the press, many of whom were attempting to interview me. As it happened, however, the senate was in the midst of a major piece of legislation that week, so even if my phones had been working properly, I would not have been available to conduct those interviews. As a result of that whole fiasco, some Illinois reporter wrote a slanderous article about me entitled, *"The Senator you can't find."* The article criticized my work ethic with phrases like: *"Where's Burris?"* *"He doesn't answer the phone."* *"We couldn't get in touch with him."* Of course, after those members of the press who had printed negative things about not being able to reach me, found out about the phone system problem, which had prevented me from even knowing anyone was trying to reach me, they never bothered to print an apology or retraction of their offensive statements. This, unfortunately, was simply par for the course.

In addition to receiving a massive number of phone calls, in those first few days, resumes poured in via email at an overwhelming rate. My staff reviewed resumes from people as far away as California and New York, but found none of the applicants had the Senate experience we desperately needed. A young woman, Vera Baker, who had some background experience in the House of Representatives, had worked on my 2002 gubernatorial race as a fundraiser. She showed up on day one as a volunteer. She was eventually made deputy chief of staff.

A real jewel named Carolyn Mosely soon joined our staff. When we received word from someone that the lady who ran the Obama senate office was available for hire, my immediate words to my staff were, *"Find her!"* A couple of hours later, she was in my office for an interview. When Obama resigned from the senate on November 16, 2008, Carolyn's work there ended, and she had been given sixty days to get hired somewhere else on the grounds or face the prospect of being removed from the federal payroll. I interviewed her on her 60th day at around two o'clock in the afternoon. At the conclusion of the interview, I told my staff to do whatever it would take to hire her right away. We made it happen, and she started working for me the very next day. Finally, we had someone who knew how both the phones and the senate operated. *"Oh, thank you Jesus!"*

Carolyn came to our rescue that day and remained so loyal to me and so dedicated to getting my office up and running, that even though she anticipated going to work for President Obama's administration, she turned down the initial job offer the new administration made. When the administration made her a second job offer, she turned it down again, all the while continuing to get my staff and office squared away. A couple of months later in April, after we moved into our permanent office in the Russell Building, Carolyn figured she probably should not turn down the third offer from the White House. We agreed with her, and, with very grateful hearts, bid her farewell. As of this writing, Carolyn works in the Department of Labor.

From the beginning, I knew that I needed a chief of staff. Fortunately, I had met Senate Majority Leader Reid's top advisor, Darrell Thompson, who became my acting chief of staff. Darrell was literally an answer to prayer, bringing with him the experience necessary to help me grasp

312

the operations of the senate. Acquiring him wasn't an easy feat, though, considering the fact Reid didn't want to give him up, and the fact Darrell was hesitant about coming over. However, being the pretty good persuader I am, by the first week in February, I did get him to come aboard, at least temporarily, as my acting chief of staff.

Darrell was a true life saver in helping to assemble the remainder of my staff. Among other positions, we hired a communications director, Jim O'Connor from Illinois, who had worked on Blair Hull's campaign for the United States Senate. We also hired a legislative director, Brady King. We filled those positions in a very short period of time in order to get on to the larger order of business: building legislative strategies in order to shorten my learning curve for senate operations, rules and voting.

Rules of Order

A shorter learning curve was an essential element of my being able to function effectively in the senate in the shortest possible amount of time, especially since the complex and unfamiliar senate rule book tugged at my attention. There was still staff hiring to manage, the media to deal with, votes that needed researching, and also, there was the matter of Blagojevich's impending impeachment. No doubt, Blagojevich's situation had influenced some of my colleagues to act coldly towards me and to keep their distance, as though I was connected to Blagojevich and his troubles. In spite of it all, I dove into that rule book, literally devouring it every night. I easily got wrapped up in all those secondary amendments and side-by-side amendments. Up until then, I thought I was a pretty good parliamentarian, having studied parliamentary procedures as practiced under *Robert's Rules of Order.* I prided myself in knowing how to run a meeting and how to keep a debate moving. In fact, members of some of the organizations I belonged to over the years called me "Little Caesar," because of how tenaciously I followed the rules during a meeting. They referred to those impositions that I always insisted upon as *"Burris' Rules of Order."*

However, the Senate rules were quite different from the rules I had learned and practiced under *Roberts Rules of Order*; they were much more confusing. The situation in which I found myself reminded me of my first day in my contracts class at Howard Law School, when the professor walked into the classroom, introduced himself, and asked *"How many of you all had business law in undergraduate school?* A few confident students shot their arms up in the air and smiled at the prospect of having an advantage over the rest of us. Instantly, that professor burst their bubbles when he said, *"Take your hands down. Whatever you learned in business law, forget it. Don't bring it into this contracts class."* In much that same way, the underlying attitude in this case was that I should not bring anything t I knew to be true in *Robert's Rules of Order*, into the senate, because that was not the way the senate operated.

Because I had missed the presiding orientation with the other freshmen senators, it was decided I would have a special orientation and that I would be assigned some time as the acting President Pro Tem of the senate. I was instructed on what to do when sitting in the chair. It was explained to me about the "people down in front of me." I learned that even though I was in charge, I had to get my instruction from the parliamentarian, who would then give me my procedural moves. As acting President Pro Tem of the senate, it was my job to keep the rules and regulations in force.

I loved all that! I loved presiding over the senate sessions, because it really gave me a chance to learn. Soon, rather than regarding the senators merely as legislative figures whom I had seen on T.V., I actually knew who they were. I remember my first couple of days of presiding in the chamber and listening very intently as the various senators talked from the floor. Others, when they presided, often would be reading and looking like they were only halfway paying attention to the senator speaking, but I listened. One day, I recognized Orrin Hatch (R-UT) to speak from the floor. I heard quite a lot about him and as he spoke, I found myself agreeing with some of what he said. The next day, I complimented him on his speech.

"Yeah, I noticed that you were listening rather attentively," he said, *"which was very nice of you. Most of the time the presider's don't even pay us any attention."*

From then on, Hatch and I took a liking to each other and became close acquaintances. He would always tell me, *"I wish you weren't so darned liberal."*

I'd respond with, *"Oh, Orrin, you're just too conservative. We've got to meet on middle ground. So let's both..."*

314

He would interrupt, *"No, I'm not moving to the middle!"*

We would both get a kick out of joking like that. In fact, in the midst of all the seriousness that took place in the senate, I must say I had some laughable moments. One such moment that comes to mind was on my very first roll-call vote. The A's were being called; then the B's. As soon as I heard the clerk say, *"Burr,"* I quickly stated my vote. Those around me shook their heads right away and corrected me, *"No, no, no, you don't vote now."*

"I don't?" I asked.

"No, that's for Burr. You're Burris, not Burr. Senator Richard Burr is a conservative Republican from North Carolina."

I promptly responded, *"Oh, his family didn't know how to spell their last name. They left off the last two letters."*

Laughter broke out across the room, as I waited for the next name to be called: *"Burris."* I hesitated to make sure it was truly my name and then raised my hand and replied, *"Aye"* on that vote. That was only my second vote, but there would be many more over the course of my twenty-three months in the senate.

Me? Resign?

After being in the senate for about a month, I made up my mind that I wanted to remain past the completion of that appointed term, so I prepared to campaign for a full term. At the same time, though, I needed to make lots of fund-raising phone calls to help pay off all those legal fees I had racked up in the process of getting to the senate chamber: a whopping $400,000 worth of fees, or so I thought. Little did I know that by the time all the legal fees came in, they totaled over $800,000!

Most of the crazy and frenzied activity by the media who hounded me day and night from the time of my appointment through my swearing in ceremony had slowed down slightly, allowing me to catch my breath. That all changed on February 13, 2009, as I sat making calls in the Democratic Senatorial Campaign Committee (DSCC) headquarters across the street from my senate office. The frenzy, which appeared to have died down, now threatened to reach new and higher levels and to ignite new flames. It all started when Darrell, my chief of staff, received a call from my office saying a *Chicago Sun-Times* reporter wanted to talk to me.

"About what?" I inquired.

Darrell responded, *"They understand that you talked to the governor's brother."*

"Well, yeah, I talked to the governor's brother; so, what's the problem?" I asked, very agitated that some reporter was inquiring about something that had already been addressed during the governor's impeachment hearing.

"Well, they have you on tape talking to the governor's brother. But they said you didn't put that in your testimony when you testified before the Impeachment Committee." Darrell continued.

I didn't know what tape the guy was talking about, but I snapped back a response that sounded like I knew about it. *"We supplied an affidavit to the committee covering all that information!"*

"What affidavit?" Darrell repeated their question to me. I quickly realized that the whole affidavit ordeal was like a hand grenade from which the press had pulled the safety pin.

The *Sun-Times* requested a copy of that second affidavit. I had my lawyers in Chicago immediately fax them exactly what they wanted. Whether or not that reporter ever read the first affidavit in conjunction with the second affidavit and the impeachment transcript, I'll never know. One thing was certain: if he did read it, he completely ignored the truth it revealed and chose, instead, to detonate that bomb by fabricating his story, beginning with a false headline: *"Burris changed his story to get seated."* In other words, according to *his* interpretation of everything, and totally contrary to the findings of the Illinois Impeachment Committee, I lied to get seated.

On that next day, Saturday, I headed home for our week-long President's Day holiday break. I arrived in Chicago just as all havoc was breaking loose over the media's handling of the affidavit issue.

The root of the problem was the tremendous amount of misinformation which was created and disseminated by the media. As a means of helping to quell the frenzy, I felt it was paramount I quickly clarify things for the public, so I held a press conference that Sunday afternoon. I stated in that press conference that yes, I had spoken to the Robert (Rob) Blagojevich, the governor's brother, and that his name was on a list of names of people I had already admitted talking to when I had been questioned by the republican legislator in Springfield. The press acted as if the revelation that Robert Blagojevich and I had talked was a major revelation. In fact, it had never been a secret there had been communication between the governor's brother and me.

I also pointed out I had never been questioned on the details of that conversation during the hearing. It was only after listening to that transcript later that my lawyers advised me to recount in an affidavit to the impeachment committee the details of the conversations I had with each of the individuals on that list. Even in doing as my lawyers had requested, I had absolutely never changed my story as a means of getting seated.

Apparently, many of those in the media chose not to accept any of what I had just explained to them, because that Monday morning, as I emerged from my home, I was greeted by the loud humming noises of the media's big generator trucks parked in front of my house and stretching all the way down the block. Immediately, reporters scrambled out of their trucks and ran up to me with microphones shoved in my face to ask more questions about my conversation with the governor's brother. *"Is there no end to all this?"* I wondered, as I brushed past them. I am sure that my neighbors were not too pleased by all that noise, or the prospect of having this media circus go on for weeks to come.

That morning, I held a meeting on the West Side of Chicago in order to give West Side elected officials an opportunity to meet their senator and to discuss issues important in their districts. I left that meeting to attend a major gathering of black religious community leaders, which was being held at Friendship Missionary Baptist Church. These leaders wanted to re-affirm their support of me in light of all the media attacks and false reporting. Upon leaving that meeting, eighty-year-old Rev. Willie Barrow happened to be walking along beside me. As we conversed, she grabbed my elbow for support, and we locked arms and proceeded to our cars. Would you believe the press even twisted *that* around? Someone wrote an article stating I was hiding behind an eighty-year-old woman to shield myself from the press!

Following that meeting at the church, I immediately headed downstate to begin a three-day fact-finding tour in Bloomington, Peoria and other central Illinois communities. Everywhere I went, from my house, to the West Side, and then on to Central Illinois, the media appeared, bringing along with them the persistent murmur: *"Burris talked to the governor's brother."*

While in Peoria, I attended a luncheon with labor leaders, met with the mayor and his staff, met with the President of Bradley University, and took a tour the campus; later that evening, I spoke at the Peoria Democratic Annual Dinner. At that event, I was presented an achievement award by the Peoria Democratic Party. At each of those events, the press hounded me about the governor's brother.

Hoping to bring clarification and closure to the matter, I held a major press conference after the dinner to try once again to explain to the press what actually happened. Afterwards, in evaluating my efforts, Darrell and others thought I had done an excellent job explaining step by step exactly when I had spoken with Rob Blagojevich and exactly what had been discussed in our conversation. However, despite our confidence that the controversy had been put to rest, in a spectacular demonstration of ignoring, rather than reporting, the facts, the next morning the *Chicago Tribune* headlines read, *"Burris admits that he tried to raise funds for the Governor."*

Once again, members of the media had proven beyond a shadow of any doubt they had only one agenda: their clear priority was to ramp up their attacks against me, not to report the truth. To achieve their goal, they grew more vicious than ever in their slanderous headlines. Their focus became the second affidavit, its inconsistency with the first affidavit, and whether or not I lied to get seated by not testifying I had talked to the governor's brother.

Soon thereafter, on February 17, 2009, an investigation into the issue of perjury was initiated against me when Illinois House Speaker, Michael Madigan, forwarded a letter to Sangamon County State's Attorney, John Schmidt, in Springfield, Illinois.[cxxxi] With that letter, he also submitted the transcript of my testimony before the Illinois Impeachment Committee and my two affidavits. His purpose was to determine whether or not I perjured myself in the Impeachment Committee hearing.

Even Senator Dick Durbin got wind of what was happening with my situation all the way overseas in Greece, where he was traveling for the week. When we returned to Congress after the Presidents' Day recess, he and I met. Right off the bat, he wanted to know what I was going to do. *"What do you mean, what am I going to do?"* I sharply responded. *"I'm not going anywhere, Senator. I haven't done anything wrong."*

"Well, you took the appointment from the governor. I told you not to take the appointment. The man was toxic." Durbin was not letting me off the hook one bit.

"So what does that have to do with me? I wanted to be a senator, and the governor had the authority. He appointed me; I took the appointment; and that's the extent of it. So, yes, all I did was take the appointment. I did not pay to play." I was sick of having to defend that one point.

"Yeah, but he also was tainted, and it's rubbing off on you. See what all those people in the media are saying about you? See what they're doing to you?"

"Well, tainted or not, he did not try to sell me the seat, and I did not try to buy it!" I continued, refusing to back down from Durbin's accusations. *"As a matter of fact, I'm planning to run for the seat."*

That got Durbin off my back for a while, but not until he first held a press conference about me. He told the media that he advised me to consider resigning. In a separate interview, the White House's press secretary Robert Gibbs chimed in with a statement saying I have the weekend to decide. *"Decide what?"* I thought to myself.

I wasn't going anywhere, because I had done nothing wrong! How could I get to Gibbs, though, and tell him that? Not only could I not reach him and tell my side of things, but I was also hampered by not knowing of anyone who could reach him and tell him the truth on my behalf.

In fact, many democratic officials in Illinois quickly started singing a common tune: *"Burris should resign. Burris should resign."* Later, those same people had to apologize when they learned the real truth. Illinois Governor Quinn, who took over after Blagojevich's impeachment, was one of them, as was Illinois Treasurer Alexi Giannoulias. Alexi learned the hard way the ramifications of being one of the first ones to call for my resignation.

After announcing his candidacy in the summer of 2009 for the 2010 U.S. Senate race, he ran into problems getting people to back him. I still have a good base of constituents in Illinois, so he really got ahead of himself jumping out there condemning me like he did. Despite his condemnation, however, I remained a good sport about it and even endorsed him for the senate seat. Apparently, there simply was not enough overcoming for him, as he went on to lose that senate race to Illinois Republican Mark Kirk.

Two of the few people who did *not* put my head on the chopping block or call for my resignation, were Chicago Mayor Daley and Majority Leader Reid. People could learn a lot from the way those two men carried themselves throughout the entire controversy: remaining poised on the sidelines with a *"Let's wait and see what happens?"* attitude. I truly respect and appreciate them for that. Eventually, prominent leaders of the community told all my Democratic accusers to back off, stating, *"If you want to continue to have this base out there in the community, you'll have to back off Burris."* Most obliged; some never did.

Quid Pro Quo (Pay to Play)…Not!

Reflecting back over the time period following my appointment, I am now convinced my team of lawyers and I should not have volunteered to send those affidavits to the Illinois General Assembly Impeachment Committee. Clearly, had I *not* submitted that second affidavit, there would not have been such a media frenzy and so much controversy once that second affidavit was juxtaposed against the first one and the impeachment transcript.

The first affidavit was sent to the committee to inform them I could not appear before the committee on the seventh of January, as requested, but I could be there on the eighth instead. Paragraph eleven of that first affidavit stated I had not engaged in a conversation with anyone about my appointment to the senate seat prior to meeting with the governor's lawyer, Sam Adams, Jr., on December 26, 2008. During the hearing, a republican legislator gave a list of names of people, which included the name of the governor's brother, Rob, and asked if I had spoken to them. I confirmed I had.

As we wrapped up that hearing, my lawyers said they wanted to review the transcript from the hearing and would present the committee with any necessary clarifications to the testimony I had given. My lawyers received their copy of the transcript the last week in January and, in reading through it, realized I had not sufficiently clarified my conversations with all those names on the list that had been presented to me by the republican legislator. At the time, various legislators had zeroed in on one name, the former chief of staff to the governor, Lon Monk, the only person I ever sat down and talked with about the appointment. Monk had recently become a lobbyist, and I met with him to inquire about any possible conflicts he might be experiencing with prospective clients, since his new position held him subject to the Illinois *"revolving door law."* That law required that for a one year period following his separation from the governor's administration, he was prohibited from conducting business with certain clients. I told him I would appreciate it if he would refer to me those clients he was legally prohibited from serving. That was the main topic we spoke about during our meeting.

However, at the very end of our conversation, I mentioned to Lon my interest in the senate appointment. He said he felt t I was very well qualified and would make a good senator. He also said he would let the governor know of my interest. That was all that was said between us, and that was exactly what I testified to at the governor's impeachment hearing. After my lawyers read the transcript, they approached me with their recommendation: *"Senator, we think that you ought to let the Impeachment Committee know what you said to each one of the people on that list. Therefore, you ought to do a second affidavit."*

The people they referred to were men such as the governor's brother, Rob, and some of the governor advisors, including Doug Scofield, John Harris and John Wyma.

"Okay, let's do an affidavit," I agreed. I sat down with my lawyers, and, almost word for word, to the best of my recollection, I told them everything I had said to everyone on that list. In that affidavit, which then became the second affidavit, was a paragraph explaining how the governor's brother had called me on three different occasions about fund-raising for the governor's 2010 re-election. It was made very clear his conversations with me concerning the gubernatorial race had included no mention of the senate appointment.

The first time Rob called me for a donation for his brother was in October of 2008. At that time, I told him the governor's 2010 election was too far off for me to think about, because our firm had people coming to us for donations for the upcoming November elections. That first phone conversation pretty much ended on that note. However, Rob did not waste any time, and called back on November 8th, immediately after that election, which was when we had our second conversation about the governor's 2010 fund-raising.

At that time, I suggested Rob call me back a week later, because I had not yet found anyone who would agree to raise funds for the governor. Fred and others had been telling me they would not give money to or raise money for Governor Blagojevich's campaign at all, based on rumors the governor was "in trouble." Nevertheless, in an attempt to remain on Rob's good side, I once again put him off and told him to call me back in a week, rather than telling him "no" to a campaign donation.

On November 13, 2008, Rob called again. By that time, I was very curious about where the senate appointment was headed, so I queried him about it right after I said hello. He wouldn't even entertain my question. During that phone call with him, I promised to send a check, the same personal campaign contribution I normally gave; but in my next breath, I also told him I could not raise funds for the governor at the same time I was trying to be appointed by him to the senate seat.

Everything I recounted in my second affidavit can be confirmed on the recorded tape of that November 13th conversation between Rob and me, which I didn't even learn about until February 13, 2009. On that tape, I can be heard rambling on about how the business Fred and I owned was not doing so well at that time and how I could not contribute to the governor's campaign. What I said about the business was not totally true, but it came out that way in my weak effort to bow out gracefully from raising funds.

A federal judge authorized the release of the tapes of my recorded conversation with Rob Blagojevich to the public in April of 2009, a couple of months into the investigation being conducted by State's Attorney, John Schmidt. Even before U.S. Attorney Fitzgerald, released the tapes, my enemies in the press, via leaked information, implied the tapes proved I had bargained for the seat in quid pro quo: a pay to play scheme. I kept hearing from various sources that, *"Burris is on tape talking to the governor's brother." "Burris was talking to the governor's brother about fund-raising."*

While I spoke about the appointment briefly on the phone to Rob, he did not talk about the appointment at all, except to say that I and a thousand other people were interested in the seat. The press tried to relate that brief "appointment" statement of mine to the "act of appointing" by Governor Blagojevich. I wanted so badly for the public to understand that there was a difference between the two statements.

I needed the public to know that nothing occurred between Rob and me about quid pro quo, or anything like what the press was stating. On the tape, it was clear what the governor's brother was NOT saying to me was, *"I will do this if you do that."* No, no, no, he was only talking about me helping to raise funds for his brother's gubernatorial race. *I,* on the other hand, *did* talk about the appointment on that phone conversation, but only to the extent of trying to find out what was happening with the appointment.

I could not help raise funds for the governor *and* get appointed by him, which is why I'm heard on the tape saying, *"That would look like I'm trying to buy the seat. I can't be raising money for the governor."* That would have an implication of impropriety.

I remember thinking during that phone call that I didn't know what influence Rob had on his brother in terms of his brother making the appointment. So, since I already knew without any doubt I could not raise any funds for the governor, I was just really placating him. My business partner, Fred, had already said, *"We can't raise any funds for that campaign."* My law partner, Tim, said he wasn't going to raise any funds, because the governor was in trouble. I also remember practically kicking myself as soon as I hung up the phone thinking, *"Now, why did I say I was going to send a check?"* After Schmidt's four-month long thorough investigation that involved talking to lots of people, including Senator Durbin and Fred, I was totally exonerated of any wrongdoing. According to Schmidt, there was insufficient evidence to indicate I had not told the truth or to charge me with perjury.

In Schmidt's June 19, 2009 letter back to Madigan, he noted it was clear the purpose of my taped conversation, which was initiated by the governor's brother *"was to raise money for Governor Blagojevich and not to discuss the vacant Senate seat."* He further commented the various conversations I had with people about the appointment were merely legitimate ways to let the governor know I was interested in being appointed, not a discussion about *how* to get the appointment. Finally, he concluded the second affidavit was the proper thing to do to supplement my committee testimony, that it was consistent; that it had been filed long before I knew my phone conversation with Rob had been taped; and that it was submitted prior to the completion of the work of the Impeachment Committee.

In spite of all that, some members of the press continued to be relentless in slinging their ridiculous accusations at me. Their justification in doing so was that even though the state's attorney had found nothing criminal in my acts, the Senate Select Ethics Committee's investigation of me was still under way. Slanderous attacks came from all directions. I felt very strongly the unsupported allegations that were being reported about me were more than any innocent person should have had to bear. When one reporter got in my face in front of my house asking me about the affidavits, I fired back at him, *"What about the affidavits?"*

He replied, *"Well, you didn't tell the truth in the second affidavit."*

"Listen here," I went at him, nose to nose, *"have you read the affidavit? Did you read the transcript? Have you read the second affidavit?"*

I became so furious, because even though the reporter had done no due diligence or read anything, there he was telling me that *I* wasn't telling the truth. I continued staring him square in the face and said, *"I'll talk to you when you've read the affidavits. If you read them, you will see that there is no conflict."*

Of course, this encounter was reported on the T.V. news as *"Burris is angry."* First, I was guilty; next, I was lying; and then, I was angry, but none of it was their fault. The sad thing about the media is the public is constantly being deceived into believing all the negative things they hear reported to them, even when these things are being reported through the media without due diligence. Then, when the person who is targeted gets angry about the injustice, the offenders in the media twist that around as well.

The media attacks had grown so incredibly fierce towards me that Darrell, my acting chief of staff, found himself constantly quarterbacking verbal responses, while accompanying me on that February downstate Illinois tour. It all became too intense for him, especially as he contemplated his own future career in the senate. As a result, Darrell made the decision to leave me and return to Reid's office. I then promoted my legislative director, Brady King, to interim Chief of Staff.

By the time July rolled around, I decided not to run for the senate. Four months later, on November 20, 2009, that six-person Ethics Committee reached *its* conclusion about whether or not I perjured myself. Based on State Attorney Schmidt's ruling, as well as its own findings, the Ethics Committee claimed in a Public Letter of Qualified Admonishment that I did not break any laws.[cxxxii]

They did say, however, the admonishment letter was issued as a result of my actions and statements in connection with my appointment, which, the Committee felt reflected unfavorably upon the senate. The letter stated *"While the Committee did not find that the evidence before it supported any actionable violations of law, senators must meet a much higher standard of conduct."*

I certainly feel that senators, as well as *all* elected officials, should be held to a higher standard of conduct than the general public. However, I find the statement targeted at me by the Ethics Committee quite interesting, given the fact that everything concerning my conversations with Lon Monk, Rob Blagojevich and others occurred while I was a private citizen, not while I was a senator!

In spite of how everything went down and what everyone thinks, one thing I still do believe about the Blagojevich appointment is that had the governor *not* been arrested, I never would have been appointed, because I was not on any list of his, either long or short. I did not appear on the governor's radar until he was advised by his lawyers, Sam Adams, Sr. and Sam Adams, Jr., to find someone who had a clean political record. After those lawyers witnessed a press conference held on December 13, 2008 by my friends, and once it was known that the legislature was not going to hold a special election to fill that seat, the lawyers strongly suggested to the governor that it would be in his best interest to appoint Burris to the senate seat.

Along with being an individual who was known from not backing down from a challenge, I have to believe that my stature, credibility, extensive political experience and ever-increasing commitment played a big part in my being appointed. After all, just because I was not on the governor's original list of candidates does not mean I was some nobody plucked up out of nowhere and brought in to represent the people of Illinois, which is precisely what the media would have loved for people to believe about me. Whatever their reasons, there were definitely those in the media who had no intention of focusing on my thirty plus years of impeccable political service and on my many corporate and political "firsts." No, none of the good and innocent stuff seemed to matter when those who controlled the press wanted a juicy story. But, I was the man who stood up to be seated in the United States Senate. It didn't matter to me what Blagojevich's intention was with anyone else, because I knew he never offered the senate seat for sale to *me*, so I certainly wasn't going to resign from that seat under pressure just because of what others thought. Had any of those newspaper reporters done their homework, instead of just feeding off one another's limited information, things would never have gotten to the point where I was being pressured to resign or being investigated for perjury!

No Justice from the Media

All I wanted during that time, and now, was for the public to under-stand what truly happens in this media-frenzy, wolf-pack mentality world of ours where supposedly, newsworthy information is publicized instantly across the airwaves without proper research and without a total understanding of the issues being posted out there for public scrutiny. From there, misinformation gets repeated and twisted, and usually ends up snowballing out of control.

Not only did this type of unethical practice cause unnecessary dis-tress and suffering for me personally, but it also had negative effects on my career. The newspapers' erroneous reporting caused a huge and negative effect on potential fund-raising to support any future aspirations I might have had in the senate. The extreme viciousness and unfairness of the media was also terribly upsetting to my entire family.

In fact, living through the experience prompted my wife to write a book entitled, *"Just Stand: God's Faithfulness Never Fails."* In the book, she highlights the journey to the senate from the perspective of a politician's wife. The underlying theme shows how faith and prayer got us all through that whole traumatic ordeal. My entire family had to remain very strong in order to survive all the harassment caused by the false reporting of the media. I must admit, however, there were times when it did not seem faith was going to be enough to get me through the ordeal. Gradually, the constant negative activity from the press began to wear on me, especially after that February 13th date when the media attacks truly went into second gear. As I mentioned, those news trucks stayed parked outside our house and around the block for hours each day, starting very early in the morning. Sometimes they stayed well into the night. There were also huge spotlights on our home so they could see what was going on in our home when they were reporting the nine or ten o'clock nightly news. One time, a friend of ours who was watching the news told me the reporter outside my house said, *"The light just went out in the kitchen."* That was just how intrusive things got.

If the incessant hounding by the press wasn't bad enough, I also had to deal with death threats. I was forced to fire a Springfield employee for making threats; I had a disgruntled veteran walk into our office making verbal threats; and I lost count of the number of anonymous, nasty, and lewd phone calls made to my office and home. We had to turn all those calls over to the police department for investigation by the Capitol police. An interrogator was involved in the entire process as well.

Eventually, we had to get security cameras installed outside our home. For a couple of weeks during that February time period, we had Chicago police officers stationed outside of our home 24/7, because the alleged threats were at a high alert level. People did not hesitate to get right in my face and call me a liar, a crook, a thief and ask me how much I paid for the senate seat. With that kind of boldness on the part of strangers, it was hard to predict just how far someone would go in their anger and disdain. That caused us to become overly cautious, at the advice of the police authorities.

One day, a large anonymous package addressed to me was mailed to my Chicago home, while I was in D.C. It arrived on a Wednesday, but I was not due home until Thursday night. Berlean opened the package and found a smaller box inside. She opened that one and found an even smaller box inside. She called me about it, and I told her to get it out of the house, and put it in the garage. We called our friend and Senate Sergeant at Arms Terry Gainer's office, and the people there called the Chicago police, who had the bomb squad at our house within thirty minutes. They cordoned off the neighborhood, while the bomb squad took the box to the back yard and opened it. It turned out that some anonymous individual had sent us a cookbook. That incident really shook us up a little bit.

Because so many in the media believe in subjecting the public to the "guilty until proven innocent" mentality, I adamantly blame them for some of the injustices citizens are up against in this society. The totally irresponsible approach of some individuals in the media puts an innocent person in more danger than the average person could ever begin to imagine; unless, heaven forbid, it happens to them one day, and *they* and their families are placed in that same predicament. Unfortunately, such irresponsibility is allowed within the media industry today. Erroneous reporting goes unchecked by anyone.

I will argue this point with anyone: the media is the only professional entity not policed by outside or internal forces. If you are a doctor, you are governed by medical boards, and you have the threat of malpractice looming over your head, as a means of keeping you in line. If you are a lawyer, there is a disciplinary committee you have to answer to in the event of any wrong doing. Judges on a bench can be questioned by their peers; insurance and real estate professionals can have licenses revoked; the financial industry has the SEC, FDIC and other governing bodies.

Irresponsible or biased members of media, on the other hand, are free to run amok, ruin a person's reputation; and, in some cases, even destroy his or her legitimate means of financial livelihood, and no one can hold them accountable! In fact, reporters, columnists, journalists, paparazzi, and the like are given the confidence to do so, all under the aegis of the First Amendment, that good ole' freedom of the press. Well, freedom of the press should never mean the press has freedom to lie or to withhold the truth!

There was a policy luncheon in the senate one day, where we had the *New York Times* and other top national newspaper publishers as our guests. I raised the question to one of their big media moguls about who polices them. The man said, *"Well, we police ourselves or we police each other."*

"Ah hah! That's the problem!" I replied. No outside accountability to induce a writer or an editorial person to do the right thing. A perfect example was a *Chicago Tribune* editorial on June 6, 2010 about the Illinois senate race between Kirk and Giannoulias. The columnist wrote, *"Burris has told five different lies and three of them were under oath."* Now, how could he say that in an editorial and get away with it without being under any obligation at all to prove his statements? The statement of the reporter is not only an affront to me and to my reputation, but it is also an insult to the competence of the Illinois Impeachment Committee

and the Senate Ethics Committee, two totally unconnected bodies, that thoroughly investigated my case and found no evidence of dissemination on my part.

If I lied under oath, as this reporter alleged, I would have been convicted of perjury, which I wasn't, because I didn't. Plus, it was old stuff he was drumming up long after the state's attorney and the ethics committee cleared me of any wrong-doing. Unfortunately, I was not surprised that I could not find a single attorney who was willing to take on the *Tribune* newspaper and go after them in a libel suit, which is a fact that many less scrupulous journalists count on.

Many journalists are arrogant in their injustice, simply because they know they can be frequently arrogant and sometimes inaccurate, and get away with it. One such arrogant and inaccurate journalist who comes to mind is *Sun-Times* columnist, Mark Brown. In February 2009, he wrote a column stating *"Burris, the sneaky little liar." "Lied three times—he's a sneaky little liar."* What? As I understand it, Mr. Brown was able to reach these conclusions from reading the only information he was given, which consisted of some quotes from the transcript of the impeachment testimony.

Mind you, Mr. Brown never bothered to read the entire transcript, a precaution you would think even a cub reporter would take before attempting to write any story for publication. One has the strong feeling Mr. Brown's statement that *"Burris...lied three times—he's a sneaky little liar,"* is, for him, a foregone conclusion, which is not fair, not impartial, and has no connection to the facts of the situation.

This media issue is obviously a sore spot with me both because I strongly oppose the tendency of some who are in the media to hide behind the first amendment freedom of speech, while committing slander and libel with impunity, and because of the unwarranted stress an unethical media brought upon me and my loved ones.

Over the years, as a public official, from time to time, I have had occasion to differ with what the media has reported. That was my right, just as it was their right to report the story and their duty to do so as honestly as possible. I can truly say, however, I have never felt as unfairly victimized by the press as I have over the months prior to my confirmation as Senator from the State of Illinois in the Senate of the United States.

When the headlines screamed, "*Burris discussed buying the senate seat with the governor's brother,*" I was not troubled, because as the secretly recorded tapes show, this conversation did occur. What the media consistently overlooks, however, is the fact the tapes also show neither the governor's brother or I ever made any mention at all to buying or selling a seat in the U.S. Senate. "*Burris is a liar,*" other headlines proclaimed as *fact,* as the media bombarded the unsuspecting public with unverified, unsupported, and even uninvestigated sensationalist journalism is, on the other hand, of the lowest quality.

Although I am troubled about some of the untrue things the media said about me, I am even more disturbed by what they neglected or refused to say. When the media learned the conversation I had with the governor's brother was perfectly innocent, did they take back any of the statements they made which assassinated my character, or attempt to undo the harm they had done to my entire career of public service or attempt to wipe away the unwarranted grief they brought to my family and friends? The answer to all those questions is a resounding "No!"After using all that ink to smear my name based on lies and unsupported assumptions, the media demonstrated no remorse and took absolutely no responsibility for the harm they had done.

When I was cleared of *all* wrong doing by the U.S. Senate Ethics Committee, the media wrote as little as possible on the committee's finding, apparently because they felt my proven innocence did not make for as sensational a story as my presumed guilt. Although the media duly reported the fact the governor's brother was cleared of all charges of illegal activity pertaining to selling the senate seat, including the conversation he had with me, they refused to print a single word of retraction to correct the many untruths they printed earlier about me attempting to buy the seat. The deliberate silence of the media, and their refusal to tell the news objectively is every bit as tyrannical as filling the minds of their readers with falsehoods and misinformation. Neither approach is in the service of truth.

The experience I had with the media stands as a clear warning to all of us that the media *must* be held to a high standard of responsible and honest reporting. This is especially important nowadays with a 24/7 news cycle, courtesy of the Internet, YouTube and the social media gamut; the race to get a story picked up is very tight. I've lived long enough to see how investigative reporting has unfortunately become a part of that vicious cycle.

As we go to press with this book, the Chicago Tribune continues to demonstrate its totally biased position on anything related to my name. When Illinois Comptroller Judy Topinka recently died, the Tribune went out of its way to snub me deliberately by not including my name anywhere among the names of the former state officials asked to pay tribute to Topinka, although I had served as Illinois Comptroller for twelve years.

A few days later, however, when the Tribune's attention had wandered to the question of whether or not lame-duck Governor Pat Quinn would be making an appointment to Topinka's vacant office, since a new governor will take office in a few weeks, the Tribune did not hesitate to use my name in a cartoon in which a befuddled looking Governor Quinn appears to be thinking about whether or not to make a last minute appointment, and is being told by an aide that "Roland Burris is available."

When a Letter to the Editor supporting me was sent to the Tribune, it was duly printed, but only after the Tribune had gutted more than 90% of the letter, leaving nothing more than a string of phrases, completely robbed of all sense and meaning.

I cannot say how this kind of "one way" journalism might look to others, but from my vantage point, the Tribune's continued failure to abide by the rules we have a right to expect from ethical journalists makes it abundantly clear that the Tribune is unwilling to pay the basic fairness and objectivity which must always underwrite the privilege of freedom of the press. The real question is, *How long will this be tolerated by the public? How many more people's lives will be destroyed before there is mandated accountability?*"

I can only pray this problem is corrected in my lifetime.

Chapter Nineteen

Life in the Senate

Committees, Congressional Delegations and Confirmations

I n addition to serving on a number of committees, senators are also very much a part of a number of confirmatory processes, including ratification of members of the president's cabinet and members of the US Supreme Court. Along with voting on the floor, senators also vote in committees to which they are appointed. I had hoped to serve on the Banking and Finance Committee and perhaps the Budget Committee as well, given my extensive financial background. However, those options were not mine to choose. On my second day as a senator, Majority Leader Harry Reid handed me a list of three committees he had selected for me: Veterans Affairs committee, Armed Services committee, and the Homeland Security and Government Operations committee (HS and GO). I graciously accepted them, realizing I had fared pretty well based upon the ratings that senate committees are given. The Armed Services and HS and GO committees are "A" rated and the Veterans Affairs is a "B." I also sat on six sub-committees: three with the Armed Services and three with Homeland Security.

With the Homeland Security committee, I traveled to San Diego to observe our border patrol operations and to gain additional insight on immigration issues. On this trip, during a demonstration by the patrol officers showing us how they catch smugglers and uncover the genius decoys, a real incident occurred, as an automobile tried to smuggle drugs into the U.S. That turned out to be one of the biggest drug busts in a long time! Serving on this committee, also allowed me to deal with all types of issues regarding the District of Columbia and the United States Postal System. I was especially interested in the effort to find solutions to the Postal Service's $7 billion shortfall.

I considered my assignment to the Armed Services a very big deal and a particularly honorable assignment as well. That group focuses on dour military operations and on the wars in which our country is involved. I visited our military installations around the country to gain firsthand knowledge of those operations. With the Armed Services committee, I traveled to Iraq and to many other foreign countries, including some in Eastern Africa. However, due to our senate calendar, I never made it to Afghanistan.

My Eastern Africa trip was to gain knowledge and information about AFRICOM,[cxxxiii] a new command established by the U.S. in 2007 to work directly with the fifty-three countries on the continent of Africa. I was there to learn from the military leaders; to listen to the concerns of the troops; and basically to see how General William E. Ward felt about his command. Since AFRICOM was a new command, the U.S. had not yet had the opportunity to provide the training or sufficiently laid the necessary groundwork to allow the African countries to fully understand the U.S. reason for creating the command. That confusion brought about a lot of friction for the commanding officer, General Ward.

Fortunately, I had hired a retired Brigadier General on my staff, General Roosevelt Barfield, who was very familiar with the operations of AFRICOM. He accompanied me to Stuttgart, Germany, AFRICOM's headquarters, where we met with our military leaders and received a briefing. From there, we traveled to Djibouti where we visited Fort Le Monier, our only base on the African continent. I learned what our troops were doing, particularly around the Horn of Africa dealing with Yemen and Somalia and addressing some of the other events which were transpiring in the area.

We also traveled to Addis Ababa, Ethiopia, where we met with Donald Booth, the newly confirmed Ambassador to Ethiopia, who briefed us on the relations between the U.S. and Ethiopia, and on the relations between Ethiopia and Eritrea. I also met Ambassador Michael Battle, our representative to the African Union. The African Union is the centralized, primarily military, organization for all of the African states on the continent of Africa, with the exception of Morocco. Coincidentally, Ambassador Battle was also a former professor at Chicago State University and taught there at the same time my wife served there as a dean. That common bond created quite a homecoming meeting with him. From there, we traveled to Nairobi, Kenya where the Ambassador to Kenya and other U.S. officials gave me briefings about what was happening along the eastern African coast with Somalia and about the issues of piracy and military action.

In carrying out our duties as congressional members, we also traveled throughout the world on official visits known as Congressional Delegations (CODELS). I went on two such parliamentary exchanges, one to China and the other one to London. Senator Patty Murray (D-WA), Senator Christopher Bond (R-MO), and I went on that China trip together, with Senator Murray as our senior representative. On the London trip, Senator Patrick Leahy (D-VT) was the senior representative for a CODEL, which was comprised of Bernie Sanders (I-VT), Thad Cochran (R-MS), Judd Gregg (R-NH) and, me, Roland Burris (D-IL). We met with the members of the Parliament in both the House of Commons and the House of Lords to discuss the various relations between Great Britain and the United States.

One of my biggest thrills in life was engaging in the advice and consent of our nation's Supreme Court Justices. I had the opportunity to have personal meetings and extended discussions with appointees Justice Sonia Sotomayor and Justice Elena Kagan. I can readily affirm how exquisitely knowledgeable these women are in the finer points of our legal system as well as how fortunate we are to have them on our highest court. Confirming two appointees during one Senate term was a rare occurrence, so I felt doubly privileged. As a lawyer and a former attorney general I can appreciate, perhaps more so than the average person, the magnitude of the decision-making process those justices will encounter over the years they serve on our highest court. As I contemplated the role I played in their assignments and the vastness of these responsibilities for many years to come, my heart overflowed with pride and gratitude at being a member of the U.S. Senate. The experience was absolutely more than I could have ever dreamed it would be.

Keeping Family a Priority

I was pretty shocked when I first learned that senators don't receive a housing allowance for the temporary living quarters they must maintain in D.C. in addition to their permanent residences in their respective home states. After arriving in D.C. for my swearing in, my wife spent a few days shopping around for my housing. She reluctantly settled for a rather expensive, furnished apartment about six blocks from Capitol Hill. Because I would be spending four or five days a week there, I also had to budget for groceries, laundry and a whole lot of other normal living expenses. My schedule had me leaving Chicago Sunday evenings or Monday mornings, working on Capitol Hill through Thursday and then returning home Thursday evenings or Friday mornings. It is amazing to think about how members of Congress keep up those types of dual schedules and living expenses for years on end.

During the Christmas senate session in 2009, that four or five-day work week turned into about fifteen days straight as the members of Congress locked horns over healthcare reform legislation. As a matter of fact, when I realized the extended session was about to interfere with my wedding anniversary, I approached Senate Majority leader, Harry Reid with what I thought was a fair demand. *"I'm going home. It's my 48th anniversary."*

He quickly abolished my request, citing as his reason the fact that if I went home, I would run the risk of not making it back to D.C. in time for the critical Healthcare Reform vote. He was probably right, as we were in the middle of one of the worst snowstorms in D.C.'s history. *"You can't go,"* he firmly replied, *"We need your vote on the healthcare bill."*

"Well, it's my anniversary," I spoke sincerely, hoping for a little sympathy from the leader. If I did not make it back to Chicago for our anniversary, it would mark the first time in our forty-eight years of marriage that Berlean and I would be apart on our special day. Well, no sympathy came from Harry. He did, however, ask me for my wife's first name and our home address.

On December 23, 2009, much to my wife's surprise, a bouquet of flowers arrived at our home. The card read, *"Happy Anniversary. Sorry we've got Roland, but he'll be home soon. Harry Reid"* Berlean loved that gesture and has kept that card to this day. I'll always be grateful to Harry for turning that dilemma into a positive and memorable outcome.

He is great at handling situations of all degrees in such a diplomatic manner.

Aside from missing important occasions like that, I had grown accustomed to being away from my family quite a bit due to my many years spent maintaining dual residency between Springfield and Chicago. There were some difficulties with that type of schedule, since our children were young and needed so much attention, but I give Berlean all the credit she deserves for standing in the gap and raising our children to become the fine adults they are today. One tradition we incorporated back then that helped us through those times was "the family Sunday dinner." I made it a point to be at home on most Sundays, and all of us sat at the table together for dinner promptly at three o'clock in the afternoon.

My children are now grown and living on their own; yet, three o'clock Sunday dinners are still a priority among all of us. It's funny, but our empty nest is anything but empty, especially with the presence of our two grandchildren, Roland and Ian who are ages nine and six, respectively, as of this writing, for whom Berlean frequently baby sits. Now that I am semi-retired, I get to enjoy them as much as she does, instead of just over the weekend, as I did when I was restricted by my senate schedule.

Sacrificing time spent with family was just one of the negative necessities that came along with the duties of a public servant. The plane rides to and from D.C. were another. When I worked for the state government, commuting wasn't a problem, as we had our own state planes and flew in and out of Chicago's downtown airport, Meigs Field. From my office in Chicago, I could get to Meigs Field and then to Springfield, all in just forty-five minutes.

Commuting as a senator to and from our nation's capital certainly did not provide me with the same convenience and luxury, as commuting to and from Springfield had. There were no private planes and no Meigs Field to save me from Chicago's eternally congested O'Hare Airport or from the huge inconvenience of getting there every week. My weekly travels to D.C. began with a forty-five to sixty-minute trip just to get from my house to O'Hare Airport. Once at O'Hare, there were the frequent weather and maintenance delays that are synonymous with commercial airline travel.

Keeping a Healthy Perspective

Being the only black person in the U.S. Senate presented its own set of unique obstacles. Even after I had gotten my staff up and running, my office could barely handle all the demands, questions, and requests for assistance, interviews, and meetings that came from all across the nation, from California to Connecticut and from Texas to Minnesota. Keeping all those plates spinning and balls juggling sometimes seemed overwhelming, to say the least!

My office started off with three or four people who did nothing but answer the telephones. That number soon grew to six. One day, I spent a great amount of time receiving the phone calls coming into the office. Much to the callers' surprise, a senator was answering their calls. I was equally surprised at some of the things they were requesting and the far-fetched reasons for some of the calls. It was just plain hectic; the telephones never stopped ringing!

A large number of minorities who lived in the jurisdiction of other senators would call my office looking for *me* to help them with various issues. My staff would usually try to refer them back to their own senators, often against their will, especially if there were two Republican senators representing their state. I remember sending some issues from North Carolina over to Senator Kay Hagan (D-NC) saying, *"Alright Kay, this is something one of your constituents called me about. You'll want to take a look at it."* Often, I also received calls from South Carolina, where there were no Democratic senators, so I had to refer those callers to House Representative James Clyburn (D-SC).

Traveling with other senators, both democratic and republican, proved very beneficial in that I really got to know them better and began to get a feel for their personal sides. To my surprise, that personal side was sometimes a lot better than the side displayed in the senate chamber! It was my hope that during those days and weeks of travel, the other senators would also get to know the real me, as well. I wanted them to see I was a solid, committed person of integrity. I wasn't that big old egotistical, arrogant person with horns the media led people to believe. In fact, I believe I entered into that honorable legislative body in the most humbling fashion possible. As the newest kid on the block, why would I enter any other way? Having come into situations like that before, as I did when I was appointed a member of Governor Walker's cabinet, I knew I had to learn the law of the land before I could be effective. As a newcomer, there was no way I could hope to know as much as people with twenty years seniority, especially if I came in with the attitude I had it all figured out.

When I became state comptroller and attorney general, I had to take over those operations from the top, so that required a more authoritative approach. Going into the senate, the approach that worked best was similar to the approach that worked for me when I worked in the banking business: being willing to work hard, to listen intently, and to learn the ropes, as expediently as possible. That was how I worked my way up through the ranks to become the first black bank officer of Illinois' largest bank, Continental Illinois National Bank.

With the senate, I knew once I really got exposed to the environment and learned the ground rules; I could then be effective and begin to have an impact on the issues which were the daily business of the senate. I also relied on my past Washington experience and background to shorten my learning curve in the senate. In the summer of 1962, I had worked as a summer intern in the Kennedy White House. That, along with the knowledge and experience gained through my tenures as Vice-Chairman of the Democratic National Committee; President of the National Association of State Auditors, Comptrollers and Treasurers; and President of the National Comptrollers Association, where I spent years lobbying Congress, all counted for something.

I had extensive background experience and knowledge to bring to the Senate office. I anticipated having the opportunity to put much of it to use in serving the people of Illinois and of America. Unfortunately, the twenty-three months spent on Capitol Hill was much shorter than I would have liked them to be. I can't be ashamed of that time, though, and I am very proud of every vote I cast. With those votes, I sponsored more than sixty bills and co-sponsored over three hundred bills for the benefit of my fellow Illinois citizens and the good of the country.

Senate Photographs

Vice President Dick Cheney administers the Oath of Office to Illinois Senator Roland W. Burris as wife, Dr. Berlean Burris, holds the Bible

Senator Daniel K. Inouye (D-HI), President Pro Tempore of the U.S. Senate, greets Senator Roland W. Burris

Senator Burris shares a moment with Senator Patrick Leahy (D-VT), President Pro Tempore of the U.S. Senate

Senator Roland Burris and Dr. Berlean Burris chat with Senator John Kerry (D-MA)

Senator Burris shares a light moment with Senator Lamar Alexander (R-TN)

Flanked by Rep. John Lewis (D-GA) and Rep. Ed Markey (D-MA), Senator Burris greets Edward Brooke, first Black popularly elected to the U.S. Senate and first black Attorney General in the US

Senator Burris greets Senator Robert Byrd (D-WV), President Pro Tempore of the Senate

Senator Roland W. Burris and family pose with Vice President Dick Cheney after Swearing-In Ceremony

Burris Family relaxes at the Senate Reception after the Swearing-In Ceremony
From left: nephew Ron Miller; daughter-in-law and grandson Marty Burris and Roland Theodore Burris; son and grandson Roland Burris II and Ian Alexander Burris; daughter Rolanda Burris; and wife Dr. Berlean Burris

Congressional Black Caucus Dinner: First Lady Michelle Obama, Senator Roland W. Burris, President Barack Obama

Senator Burris signs Registry after delivery of
George Washington Farewell Address to the U. S. Senate

enator Burris has a word with Representative Donald M. Payne (D-NJ)

enator Burris poses on Capital Steps with some of the members of his Washington, DC Senate staff

On fact seeking tour of modern Iraq, Senator Burris poses with members of U. S. military at Ziggurat Tomb (circa 2113 BC) excavated on the site of ancient city of Ur

Senator Roland W. Burris poses with the Golden Gavel Award, one of two he received for serving as presiding officer of the U. S. Senate for 100 hours

Senator Burris sits beneath the Presidential Seal as he waits to meet with the president in the Executive Office Building

Senator Burris focuses on testimony being presented to Senate Armed Services Committee

Senator Burris examines signed copy of historic Affordable Health Care Act

...nator Burris speaks at Southern Illinois University reception honoring his donation of political papers to the \ ...niversity's Special Collections Research Center of Morris Library

Dr. Berlean Burris, Senator Roland W. Burris, and grandson, Roland Theodore Burris, chat with Southern Illinois University Dean of the Library in front of the display honoring Burris in the SIU Morris Library

Senator Burris does a little "catching up" with Bill Norwood, former member of the SIU Board of Trustees and main speaker at the 2011 ceremony commemorating the donation of Senator Burris' papers to the Southern Illinois University's Morris Library

Chapter Twenty
Farewell to the Senate

What a Great Ride It Was

As the adage goes, "All good things must come to an end." And so it was in November of 2010 with my time in the senate and with my political career as well. Both my career and my time in the senate were truly memorable times, even though my time in the senate was short-lived. I will especially cherish the time I spent presiding over the senate, an activity which I thoroughly enjoyed. In fact, I currently hold the record for being the only freshman senator with two Golden Gavels. In order to earn a gavel, you have to preside in the chair for one hundred hours. I became only the fourth freshman senator to acquire one hundred hours and the first freshman senator in the 111th Congress to log in a second one hundred hours.

While presiding, I listened intently to what the senators were saying and would often take notes. Sometimes, I agreed with the various speakers; sometimes, I disagreed with them. Either way, they appreciated my attentiveness. Democratic colleagues would come to me expressing their appreciation when I was in the chair, since they were accustomed to most of the presider's doing their own work, writing or reading: anything but listening. I listened to Byron Dorgan (D-ND), who shared so much great history. Sheldon Whitehouse (D-RI) really impressed me as quite the orator. I remember Sherrod Brown (D-OH) getting very wound up over certain issues.

There were also some senators we didn't hear much from at all, such as Evan Bayh (D-IN) and Herb Kohl (D-WI), and every now and then, we would hear something from Daniel Akaka (D-HI). However, the standard ones, so to speak, senators like Amy Klobuchar (D-MN) and Debbie Stabenow (D-MI), spoke often. Debbie was very good at keeping a record of the filibusters. Just before we adjourned from our first session in 2009, she brought to the attention of our caucus that there had been approximately one hundred and three filibusters, the most ever in the history of the senate. We went back into the second session of the Congress and by March or April, experienced an additional forty or fifty filibusters! The number of stops was awful; even on advice and consent, and on appointments. Without the required sixty votes, we couldn't even get the nominations of some of the judges to the floor. We had to get closure on everything, which wrecked the heck out of our schedule, making it impossible to address some of the other pressure-point issues that confronted us. I must say, though, in spite of it all, we tackled many issues and passed a lot of meaningful legislation. Although introducing and debating legislation are certainly important, I liked it best when we were passing legislation, because I like action. Action means progress is taking place. To get progress we had to vote. I don't think I missed more than three votes during my entire term in the senate, meaning I was present and voted on 99.8 percent of the bills presented. That wasn't a bad voting record, considering all the traveling time factored into the dual residency I maintained throughout my term in office.

Healthcare Reform

The most interesting and difficult piece of legislation I voted on during my time in the senate was, without a doubt, the Healthcare Bill. President Obama proclaimed it his "front line" fight to do something to change health care delivery in this country. He said ten presidents before him had tried to pass legislation to improve our health care system and he did not intend for a twelfth president to work on it. He wanted comprehensive healthcare reform to pass on his watch. Boy was it an all out battle to defend and pass such a major bill that would reform healthcare for the future!

In early February of 2009, at the time the legislation came out of committee on a partisan vote, we did not have the necessary sixty votes required to pass it. Unfortunately, Senator Kennedy (D-MA), who led this healthcare fight for many years, had become seriously ill at the inauguration luncheon due to brain cancer and was not able to attend subsequent senate sessions. In addition, Al Franken (D-MN) had not yet resolved his battle for the Minnesota senate seat. That left us with only fifty-seven Democratic Senators and a whole lot of doubt. Senator Chris Dodd (D-CT) took up Kennedy's mantle at the direction of Senate Majority Leader Reid and had the bill called. On February 10th, Kennedy then came to the senate, with the aid of a cane and wheelchair, to give us vote number fifty-eight, but we still needed two more votes.

The republicans had been lobbying hard and heavy to put votes on the bill. After hours of debate and defeat of many republican amendments, the motion to proceed was voted on. In order to beat the filibuster, we needed two republican votes; however, the republicans who decided to support the motion did not want to be the 60th vote. Therefore, we needed three republicans' votes. Senators Olympia Snowe (R-ME) and Susan Collins (R-ME), as well as Senator Arlen Specter (R-PA), seemed to be the ones most likely to vote for the bill, as they were known for their past willingness to facilitate bipartisan compromise. Their votes on February 10th brought the vote to 61-37, which got that bill onto the floor for debate.

I had taken a very strong position on the element of the healthcare legislation calling for a public option, which would allow people who could not get insurance the option to go to the government for an insurance program, creating competition for the insurance companies. I worked hard to amend the bill for the public option, while other senators were staking out their positions. Senator Lieberman (I-CT) was against the public option and against reducing the Medicare age to fifty-five. The floor debate went back and forth on the numerous positions with Senator Mary Landrieu (D-LA) backing her own position, along with fellow Democrats Senator Blanche Lincoln (D-AR) and Senator Ben Nelson (D-NE). That meant we really didn't have all fifty-seven democrats on board with the bill. After numerous debates, defeated amendments and many Democratic Caucus meetings, the time had come to cut through the debate and just vote—again, though, we needed sixty votes in order to do that.

I held back on my vote, since there was no public option put forward for the bill. Lieberman had knocked out the option to lower the age for Medicare age lowering, so the opportunity for a public option was still out there. I figured it would take direct talks with President Obama by me to deal with Lieberman not backing the public option. In my meeting with the president, he expressed his total commitment to passing health care legislation and informed me if I held to the public option as stated, the legislation would die in the senate. As a matter of fact, *any* of us democrats could have killed the bill, since we didn't have the votes to pass it. I complied with the president and in order to keep the bill alive, I worked out a compromise that the bill should contain three major elements: accountability, cost savings and competition. Those elements ended up in the final bill.

When we finally moved to cut off the debate, it appeared the sixty votes were not there. We only had fifty-seven votes. Again, it took some heavy lobbying of the three republicans to stick with us to cut off the debate. Senator Kennedy could not come back to the senate. In fact, Mrs. Kennedy even called the three senators to explain how grave her husband's condition was and how it would certainly not be in his best interest health-wise to come in to vote. They were convinced and those three republicans added to our fifty-seven votes to give us the sixty votes needed, but we were missing one democrat senator, Sherrod Brown of Ohio, who was home attending his mother's funeral. Because a commercial flight could not get him back in time for the midnight vote deadline, he was flown back to D.C. in a government airplane. Brown cast the sixtieth vote close to 11:00pm on February 13, 2009 to end the debate.

Months later, the Democratic House, under the leadership of Nancy Pelosi (D-CA), passed a strong health care bill containing the public option and sent it to the senate. Meetings and more meetings were held trying to work out a compromise among the democratic amendments. We all wanted something different. The republicans just didn't want the bill at all.

Senator Franken of Minnesota had finally resolved his legal issues and had been seated in July of 2009; Senator Kennedy died on August 25, 2009; and Senator Paul Kirk had been appointed to finish out Kennedy's term. That gave us fifty-nine senators, which meant we were still in need of one more vote. Because of the Republican Caucus' determined anti-Obama stance, Senator Specter would no longer accept their position and he quit the republicans to join us democrats. That gave us our sixty votes for the first time.

In December of 2009, just before Christmas, we finally achieved closure on the bill after a very, very late night session. I had already missed my 48th wedding anniversary on December 23rd because, due to a horrible snow storm, it would have been impossible for me to make it home and back in time to vote. It was one of the biggest storms in the history of D.C. As stormy as the weather was outside, the atmosphere inside the senate chamber proved even stormier. Things were so contentious during this time that on December 22nd, I tried to lighten up matters by creating and then reciting from the senate floor my own rendition of "The Night before Christmas."[cxxxiv] Those who were in the chamber at the time liked the poem so much that word about it spread to others who were elsewhere in senate meetings and even to some people in Chicago and throughout the country.

Around 2:00am on Christmas Eve morning, with all senators, now totally fatigued, but poised and in their seats, a roll call vote was held, and we passed the Health Care bill with sixty votes. Senators could finally go home to their families to celebrate the holidays. Even with that huge victory, we knew the health care legislation battle was far from over. In fact, it seemed to be just beginning. The Senate and House bills had differences, so in order to reconcile the two bills, a conference committee was set up and began when Congress resumed following the holidays.

However, by the time the 2nd session of the 111th Congress got underway in January of 2010, Senator Kennedy's seat had been won by a Republican Senator named Scott Brown. That left us once again with only fifty-nine votes, and we could not pass anything agreed to in the conference committee without our sixty votes.

In February of 2010, a year after the passing of the Healthcare Bill in the senate, the democratic leadership of the Senate and House came together on a plan to reconcile the two bills. The House, through its reconciliation procedure, accepted the senate bill. That House action was taken, because the conference committee bill would not have been accepted, since the democrats did not have sixty votes. Finally, on March 23, 2010, President Obama signed that bill at a White House ceremony marking a historical accomplishment that was ninety-seven years in the making: a major healthcare legislation that would benefit millions of Americans.

My Farewell Speech

On Thursday, November 18, 2010, I stood in the senate chamber one last time and delivered my farewell speech. So many thoughts had run through my mind, as I had prepared that speech, thoughts about the rough journey I had been forced to take in order to reach the senate and about the high points I witnessed and experienced while serving there. There were also thoughts of milestones like being only one of six Black-Americans to ever hold a seat in the senate in two hundred and twenty years.

There were thoughts of the surreal moments like being in the presence of two of our greatest members, Senator Ted Kennedy and Senator Robert C. Byrd, who both passed away while I was a member of the Senate, as well as voting on the confirmation of two Supreme Court Justices, Sonia Sotomayor and Elena Kegan. I approached my time in the Senate with much resolve and fortitude, so as I gathered all those thoughts, I hoped and prayed my speech would reflect even a glimmer of what I felt. Here is the result…

Mr. BURRIS. *"Madam President, as you know, one of the first duties delegated to freshman Senators is the high honor of presiding over the Senate. I remember the very first time I sat where you are sitting now, Madam President. Throughout my time as a Member of this august body, I have had the opportunity to spend more than two hundred hours in the Presiding Officer's chair and have earned two Golden Gavels. I also had the honor of delivering our first President's—President George Washington's—Farewell Address on his birthday this year to this august body. From the chair, I have had the opportunity to listen to the words of my colleagues and reflect upon the great debate that unfolds each and every day, as it has always done throughout our Nation's history, in this, the greatest deliberative body in the world.*

We come to this Chamber from every State in the Union: Democrats, Republicans, and Independents alike. Each of us carries the solemn

346

responsibility of giving voice to the concerns of those we represent. Although we do not always agree, as the debate on this floor will often show, I am always struck by the passion that drives the Senators to stand in this singular place in the world and to speak their minds. It is this passion that will always define this Chamber for me. For all the weight of history, for all the great and eloquent sentiments that have been expressed by our forefathers, on a fundamental level, this remains a very human place.

We stand today, as the Members of this body have done frequently throughout our great Republic's history, at a critical moment. Partisanship and obstructionism threaten somewhat to paralyze this great institution. But it is a testament to the inherent wisdom and durability of the Senate, of the rules and the tradition that govern this institution, that even in the face of great discord, we have had the high privilege of serving in the most productive Congress in generations.

Despite our many differences, I believe the men and women who make up this Senate remain its greatest strength. It has been the honor of my lifetime to once again represent the people of Illinois and to do so in the Senate. First, as a cabinet member for our Governor, as the Illinois State Comptroller, and as Illinois Attorney General, the people of my State placed in me a sacred trust and one that throughout my thirty years in public service I made into my life's work: to serve the people of my State to the very best of my ability.

In my younger years, shortly after graduating from law school at Howard University, not far from where we stand today, I was turned off by a city with far too much government. I headed to Chicago, convinced that I would not return to this city unless I could be an effective and meaningful part of the solution to the many challenges we face and dreaming of a time I might come back to Washington as a Senator or as Vice President of the United States.

That dream took longer to achieve than I could have imagined that day, but in a towering testament to the vibrancy of the American dream, that day came. After decades of experience in the executive branch of Illinois government, I was sworn in as a Senator of Illinois, and this was my introduction to serving as a legislator. It was the steepest of learning curves, but with the warm assistance of my Senate colleagues, the steady support of my loving family, and the dedication of my tireless staff, I could not be more proud of what we have been able to accomplish together.

To my family, my friends, and my staff I owe the deepest thanks. My wife, Berlean, has always been by my side, and I will always be grateful beyond words for her constant support. My son, Roland II, and his wife, Marty, and my daughter, Rolanda, are the pride and joy of my life. Of course, they were just here yesterday, but it is my two grandchildren, Roland Theodore and Ian Alexander, to whom I dedicate my service and for whom I have the greatest hopes and even greater expectations.

To my friends and supporters from Chicago to Centralia, I will never forget your smiles and your kind words during even the most difficult of times. To my staff, in D.C., and those in Springfield, Moline, and Car-bondale, you have been some of the most dedicated, talented, and professional individuals with whom I ever had the privilege to serve. From the front office staff assistants and interns answering the endlessly ringing telephones, to my circle of senior advisers who gave me wise and thoughtful counsel throughout, my team has been indispensable to me, and they have all served the people of Illinois with distinction. I am deeply grateful for their service.

Madam President, I ask unanimous consent that the complete list of my staff be printed in the Record following my remarks."

The PRESIDING OFFICER (Mrs. Hagan). *"Without objection, it is so ordered."*

(See exhibit 1, p. xiv)

Mr. BURRIS. *"Thank you, Madam President.*

I wish to extend a special word of gratitude to my old friend who is sitting right there, the Sergeant at Arms, Terry Gainer; the Secretary of the Senate, Nancy Erickson; the Secretary for the Majority, Lula Davis; for their many kindnesses, and a thank you to the Senate Chaplain, Dr. Barry Black, for his counsel and prayers during my time here.

I also wish to acknowledge my fellow freshman Senators: Senators Begich, Bennet, Franken, Gillibrand; the Presiding Officer, the North Carolinian, Senator Hagan; as well as Senators Merkley, Shaheen, Mark Udall, Tom Udall, Mark Warner, and our just departed Senator Kaufman from Delaware. They are tremendous individuals possessing incredible talents and have been a very supportive group for me. Thank you, my freshman colleagues.

In a broader sense, I wish also to thank all of those who serve under this hallowed dome with quiet and often unheralded dignity and duty. The Senate floor staff, you all do a heck of a job: the maintenance crews, the elevator operators, the Capitol Police, the Senate train drivers, the dining room servers, and the scores of others whose hard and important work ensures the smooth and constant operations of the business that takes place within our Capitol.

As I stand to address this Chamber for the last time, I cannot help but reflect on the unlikely path that led me to this point and upon the challenges we continue to face. When I first came to the Senate nearly two years ago, our Nation was only days away from inaugurating an African-American man from Chicago as the 44th President of the United States of America. It was a national milestone I never thought I would ever live to see, an incredible moment that speaks volumes about the progress our country has made even in my lifetime.

As a child, I knew the injustice of segregation. When I was only about fifteen years old, I helped integrate the swimming pool in my hometown of Centralia, IL. Although that incident drove me to pursue a life of public service, dedicating myself to the goals of becoming both a lawyer and a statewide elected official, there was never any guarantee that such a path would be open to me. There were no people of color in elected office in those days, especially not in Illinois and not in Centralia, and there was no path to follow. So I knew from the start that I would have to blaze a trail.

Despite the lack of established role models, my parents provided nothing but support and encouragement. They nurtured my dreams and helped me develop the skills to achieve them. In the end, they and my older brother Earl, who is now deceased, and my sister, Doris, God bless her, who is still living, were the only role models I needed.

The values they instilled in me, of hard work, determination, and unwavering dedication to principle, have guided me throughout my life, and the same values have driven me to take an interest in the next generation.

It is that focus on the future that constantly drives all of our legislative energy, to improve the quality of life for the generations to come.

Not too many generations ago, my family roots told a different story. I stand in this Chamber as the great-grandson of a man who was born into slavery, in an era when this Senate debated whether he and others like him were worthy of freedom and equal treatment under the law. Yet today, I stand among my colleagues on the Senate floor, a Member of the highest body of lawmakers in this land. In some ways, this is a remarkable testament to our Nation's ability to correct the wrongs of generations past, to move always toward that "more perfect Union."

However, in other ways, it is a solemn reminder of how far we still have yet to go. In a country as progressive and diverse as any on this planet, I am today the only Black-American Member of this Senate. Aside from myself, I can count the number of Blacks who have served in this body on the fingers of a single hand: Blanche K. Bruce, Hiram Revels, Edward Brooke, the last two from Illinois Carol Moseley-Braun, and our President, Barack Obama.

Throughout two hundred and twenty years of Senate history and 111th Congresses, only six Black-Americans have been able to serve. This is troubling in its own right. But when the 112th Congress is sworn in this coming January, there will not be a single Black-American taking the oath of office in this Chamber.

This is simply unacceptable. We can and we will and we must do better. In this regard, and in others, our political process has proven less successful and less representative than it ought to be. Although I have never allowed my race to define me, in a sense it has meant that my constituency as a Senator has stretched far beyond the boundaries of Illinois.

Letters, emails, and telephone calls have poured in to my office from Black-Americans from all across the country, and at times, as I have tried to bring their voices to this Chamber, I have acutely felt the absence of any other Black person to represent them.

Our government hardly resembles the diverse country it was elected to represent. Partisan bickering has driven moderates out of both parties and made principled compromise more difficult for those who remain. Too often, our politics seem to have become a zero-sum game. It is easy for people to believe that the best argument or the plainest truth would not necessarily win the day anymore.

In such a destructive political environment, people are often left wondering who will speak up for them. The media certainly isn't blameless. News outlets which could play a critical role in educating the

American public with facts too often bow to ratings or quick sales and, in the process, end up choosing to pursue the entertainment value of conflict over thoughtful analysis. This is the harsh reality we face.

America just cannot afford this any longer. We should check these notions at the Cloakroom door. This is a critical moment.

So I believe it is the responsibility of everyone in this Chamber to take ownership of this process once again, to demonstrate leadership, and pledge a return to more responsible rhetoric, and more responsive government.

What we face is a test, not only of our willingness to meet the challenges we face, but of the democratic institutions designed to cope with these challenges.

Here in the U.S. Senate, this question is paramount.

Have our destructive politics left this great body locked in a stalemate, unable to move forward, because of the petty obstructionism that has taken root?

Or can this Chamber be made to address these problems once again? Can it be redeemed by the good people who serve here?

I have confidence that it can.

It will require the concerted effort of all one hundred Senators to overcome the partisanship that has paralyzed this Chamber, and the obstructionist tactics that have become the rule rather than the exception.

Colleagues, this is the moment to summon the strength of our convictions, and fight for the principles in which we all believe.

This is the hour for principled leadership, originating right here in the U.S. Senate. But even as we look to the future and debate the agenda for the upcoming years, I must note with regret that my time here is nearly at an end.

Serving as a Member of this body, alongside so many fine colleagues who have become good friends, has been the honor of a lifetime.

Together we have achieved passage of the most ambitious legislative agenda since the Great Depression. And a great deal of the credit for our success is owed to Leader Harry Reid.

I am proud of every vote I cast in the name of the people of Illinois, and proud of the more than sixty bills I sponsored and over three hundred I have co-sponsored.

In the twenty-two months I have been a Member of the Senate, I have advocated for comprehensive health care reform designed to meet the goals of a public option, and fought to address health care disparities that separate minority communities from the population as a whole; I have pushed for redirection of subsidized funds that made $68 billion available for new Pell grants and extended new opportunities for minority students to attend historically Black colleges and universities, as well as predominantly Black institutions; I have stood up for minority-owned businesses, and made sure they will have equal opportunity to share in America's renewed prosperity as our economy continues to recover; I have worked hard to extend unemployment insurance, improve access to COBRA benefits, and create jobs for the people of Illinois and across the country; I have voted for the sweeping stimulus package that brought this country back from the brink of economic disaster and started us on the road to recovery; I have introduced legislation that would improve transparency and accountability as stimulus dollars are spent, so the American people can keep their elected officials honest; I have co-sponsored legislation to repeal the military's discriminatory "don't ask, don't tell" policy, so all of our soldiers, sailors, airmen, and marines can serve openly, and had a press conference on that.

I say to my colleagues, don't filibuster that issue. We need all of our individuals to have an opportunity to serve in the military service, regardless of their sexual orientation. Don't be surprised if I come back for that vote. I am from Chicago, and I will vote twice. I supported major credit card reforms, to prevent credit card companies from abusing their customers; I fought for equal pay and benefits for women, to cut down on workplace discrimination; I fought for additional impact aid funding, to shore up Federal support for school districts that serve military communities and other Federal activities; I have honored the accomplishments of pioneers like Vice Admiral Samuel Gravely, the first African-American to serve as a flag officer in the Navy, and the Montford Marines[cxxxv], the first African-American Marine division; I have supported the Matthew Shepard Act, which will help make sure those who target people based on sexual orientation, race, or other factors are brought to justice; I have raised my voice on behalf of Main Street, and all those who have been left behind in our continuing eco-

nomic recovery, so that everyone can share in the benefits; I have introduced legislation calling for the Department of the Interior to study a historic site called New Philadelphia[cxxxvi], IL, the first settlement founded by a freed African-American slave, for its preservation as part of the National Park System.

I hope, as a legacy to ROLAND BURRIS, that someday that legislation will pass. I raised awareness of youth violence, which threatens our children and tears our inner cities apart and which must be stopped; I have fought for veterans' benefits, including the implementation of the new GI bill, so we can honor the service of those who defend our freedom. And now, as we are ready to close the books on the 111th Congress and the long and significant chapter of legislative accomplishment, it is time for a new class of Senators to join this fight.

I am deeply grateful to my friends on both sides of the aisle for the passion they bring to their work every day. I have witnessed it from the Presiding Officer's chair, and have had the privilege not only to watch the debate but to take part. But now it is time for me to find new ways to serve.

This is the arena where great ideas are put to the test on a national stage. This is where our identity is forged anew, every day, and where our principles are challenged. It is the heart of our democratic process. Although there will be few easy solutions for the problems we face, I will never forget the courage and patriotism that I have seen from countless citizens of Illinois and America over the course of my time here.

This is a trying time for our Nation. But as long as the American people have the wisdom to elect leaders like the ones I have come to know in this Chamber, and as long as this Senate remains true to the people we serve, I will never lose faith in our ability to overcome these challenges together.

These are my parting remarks from this body. I treat this as an opportunity of a lifetime, and I treat this with great respect and dignity for all of those I have worked with and have come to know in this body. With that, I thank the Chair, I thank all my colleagues, and I yield the floor for the final time. God bless you all. Thank you."

The Four P's

It is not by accident that I achieved what I did in life. Even though I am a very fortunate man, setting goals and a lot of hard work, integrity and trust in God have been the components of the winning combination for me. Throughout the years, I've operated by a simple rule of The Four P's: Preparation, Patience, Perseverance and Prayer. It is my hope that having read my life's account, including my trail-blazing journey to public office, the reader of these memoirs can detect the presence of those principles, as I stayed true to my family, my loved ones and the ones to whom I was called to serve. It is also my hope that these same four P's will be incorporated by future leaders throughout our country to ensure our legislative energy contains the moral values necessary to constantly improve the quality of life for Americans here and abroad for generations to come.

Epilogue

Afterwards

As I look back over my career in public service, which spans more than three decades, first, as a statewide elected official in Illinois, and, most recently, as a member of the United States Senate, I feel very proud and very humbled to have had the unique opportunity to serve the people of Illinois and the people of this country. Not many people are fortunate enough to set career and life goals early in life as I did and then go on to achieve those goals in a straightforward manner with little deviation from the original plan. The path I travelled was certainly not one which was strewn with roses; in fact, my path was sometimes made nearly impassable by obstacles of every imaginable kind: resources were often scarce or non-existent; hard work was a given; and personal sacrifice became second nature to me. Over all these years of sacrifice, overcoming, and achievement, I have become much less impressed by transitory things and more and more appreciative of things which have enduring value.

For me, one of these things is a stronger sense of the meaning and the richness of the past. Embracing my own past awakened in me a profound awareness of the importance of our history. I quickly understood that unless we learn from our history, we will almost certainly be condemned to repeat the mistakes of the past.

This sense of history enveloped me when I had the honor of becoming only the sixth African-American in U.S. history to serve in the U.S. Senate. It also informs me that far too few minorities have served in that national legislative chamber and in other high offices throughout the land; and it cautions me that we must not continue to squander the dedication, the patriotism, and the incredible talent of the men and women of color who, if given the opportunity, would serve their country capably and well.

Another enduring quality I have come to appreciate is the priceless value of all the opportunities I have had throughout my career to make a difference in the world: by strengthening families, by rebuilding communities, and by striving to make ours a more equitable and just society for all people. I am proud to say that over the years, I have been very opportunistic in taking advantage of every chance which presented itself to bring about positive change.

Finally, I have also learned to appreciate less obvious, but tremendously important things, such as the unflinching optimism it takes to be steadfast in our belief in the future. This is most crucial when it comes to interacting with our young people in our roles as parents, teachers, mentors and members of the generation from whom, one day, they must accept the torch that will light the way to the future.

As I revisited my life's events in the making of *The Man Who Stood Up To Be Seated*, young people who will hopefully read and learn from my story, were never far from my thoughts. In this book, I wanted to reach out to them and encourage them to dream. I hope that my experience will show young people all over the world that, if you have the determination and enthusiasm to overcome obstacles, dreams do come true.

Throughout my career, I have always insisted on setting aside time to interact with our country's future leaders. I would speak to them in the schools and bring them in to my office as interns. Even today, I remain a strong advocate for education and other programs that provide opportunities for the safe and positive development of our youth.

One of my first actions as a member of the United States Senate was to return to Chicago, so I could personally deliver tickets to the Inauguration of the first African-American president in our nation's history to a class of inner-city students who were thrilled to have the opportunity to be participants in such a singular moment.

In terms of our future generations, I am extremely excited, grateful and humbled by the fact that my *alma mater,* Southern Illinois University in Carbondale, has requested and received all of my political papers, dating all the way back from my election as the first black comptroller in the history of the State of Illinois to my historic appointment to the U.S.

Senate. These papers will be stored in the Special Collections section of the university's Morris Library. I am so pleased that these papers will be available to future historians and political scientists who may be able to use these documents as a means of gaining a fuller understanding and a more complete knowledge of the history of our state and our nation.

As my tenure in the U.S. Senate came to an end, I had many mixed emotions. Although I have never been one to say never, I was more than content to direct my attention away from politics and onto other matters which, besides writing and editing this memoir, included spending more time with Berlean, our children, and our grandchildren. I also began serving alongside my son, Roland Burris II, as legal counsel for a Chicago law firm.

As I look back over the pathway I blazed from Centralia to Springfield and on to the nation's capital, one thing has become clear to me. No matter how satisfying it feels to have achieved so many of my life goals, it has never really been about the success alone.

More importantly, it's about the joy of helping to better our society. It's about the sense of fulfillment knowing our young people and future leaders have a positive influence to follow. Most of all, it's about me being thankful to God for a very splendid journey.

Roland W. Burris, *Chicago, 2014*

Appendix

1. Biography of Roland W. Burris

2. Family Tree (Partial) for Roland W. Burris

3. Letter from John Schmidt to Michael J. Madigan, June 19, 2009, regarding Senator Roland W. Burris' testimony before the Special Investigative Committee of the Illinois House of Representatives.

4. Public Letter of Qualified Admonition from the Senate Ethics Committee to Senator Burris, November 20, 2009

5. Senator Burris' "The Night before Christmas" presentation to the Senate, December 22, 2009 (on the eve of the passage of the Affordable Health Care Act)

6. A List of Firsts for Senator Roland W. Burris

Appendix 1
Biography

Roland Wallace Burris, the youngest of three children of Earl and Emma Burris, was born on August 3, 1937 in Centralia, a small southern Illinois community where he was raised and received his early education. The Burris family tree traces the family's roots as far back as the slavery era, with origins mostly in the southern states of Georgia, South Carolina and Tennessee.

In 1955, Burris graduated from Centralia High School and enrolled at Southern Illinois University (SIU) in Carbondale where, in 1959, he received a Bachelor of Arts degree in political science. After graduation from SIU, Burris received a fellowship to become an exchange student at the University of Hamburg in Germany where he studied international law. Upon his return to the USA in 1960, he enrolled at the Howard University Law School where, in 1963, he earned the *Juris Doctor* degree.

After graduation from law school, Burris accepted a position as a national bank examiner for the Office of the Comptroller of the Currency of the U.S. Treasury Department. From 1964 to 1973, he worked at Continental Illinois National Bank and Trust Company (now Bank of America), serving as tax accountant, tax consultant, commercial banking officer, and vice-president. While at Continental, Burris also headed a commercial group that covered government guaranteed loans and minority business banking.

In 1973, he was appointed by Illinois Governor Daniel Walker as Director of the Department of Central Management Services, a position in which he served until 1977 when he became National Executive Director and Chief Operating Officer for Operation PUSH (now Rainbow PUSH Coalition).

In 1978, Burris became the first African-American to win election to statewide office in Illinois, when he was elected Illinois Comptroller, a position which he had sought unsuccessfully in 1976. In 1984, in the second of his three successful terms as Illinois Comptroller, Burris also ran an unsuccessful campaign for the U. S. Senate.

In 1990, Burris was elected Illinois Attorney General, the first African-American to be elected to this position in Illinois. After his tenure as Illinois Attorney General, Burris served as managing partner for the law firm of Jones, Ware, and Grenard. He also served as counsel to the law firm of Gonzalez, Saggio and Harlan, L.L.C., where his areas of legal concentration were business transactions, estate planning, wills, trusts, probate, and consumer affairs. Burris was also a partner in the political consulting firm, Burris and LeBed.

In 1994, 1998, and again in 2002, Burris was an unsuccessful candidate for the Democratic nomination for Governor of Illinois. In 1995, he ran as an independent for Mayor of Chicago, losing to incumbent Richard M. Daley.

In 2008, Burris was appointed by Illinois Governor Rod Blagojevich to replace President-Elect Barack Obama as the junior Senator from Illinois. After a protracted battle defending the legality of his nomination by the governor and the ethics of his acceptance of the position, Burris and his legal team prevailed and he was seated as a senator from the State of Illinois on January 15, 2009.

Burris has served in many state, regional, and national positions, such as Vice-Chairman of the Democratic National Committee, and Chairman of the Illinois Commission of African-American Males, the National Association of Attorneys General Civil Rights Commission, and the Illinois State Justice Commission.

Burris was Vice-Chairman of the Committee on Illinois Government, President of the National Association of State Auditors, Comptrollers and Treasurers, President of the Association of State Comptrollers, and a Trustee for both the Financial Accounting Foundation and the Government Finance Officers Association of U.S. and Canada.

He was a member of the Board of Directors of the Better Business Bureau, the Roosevelt University Auditorium Theater of Chicago, and the National Center for Responsible Gaming.

In addition, Burris was on the Board of Directors of the Inland Real Estate Corporation as an Independent Director and was Chairman of its Governance and Nominating Committee. He has also served as an Adjunct Professor in the Master of Public Administration program at Southern Illinois University, Carbondale.

Burris is a rank-and-file member of the Howard University Law School Alumni Association, the Southern Illinois University Foundation, the Mental Health Association of Greater Chicago, the U.S. Jaycees, the Chicago Area Council of the Boy Scouts of America, the National Association for the Advancement of Colored People, the Southern Illinois Alumni Association, Alpha Phi Alpha fraternity, the Western Consistory of Ancient and Accepted Scottish Rite Free Masons, and Sigma Pi Phi Fraternity, Beta Boule.

Burris is married to Berlean Miller Burris, *Ph.D.* They are the parents of two adult children, Rolanda S. Burris, *Ed.D.* and Roland W. Burris II, *Esq*. The Burris' also have two grandsons, Roland Theodore Burris, and Ian Alexander Burris.

Appendix 2: Burris Family Tree (Partial)

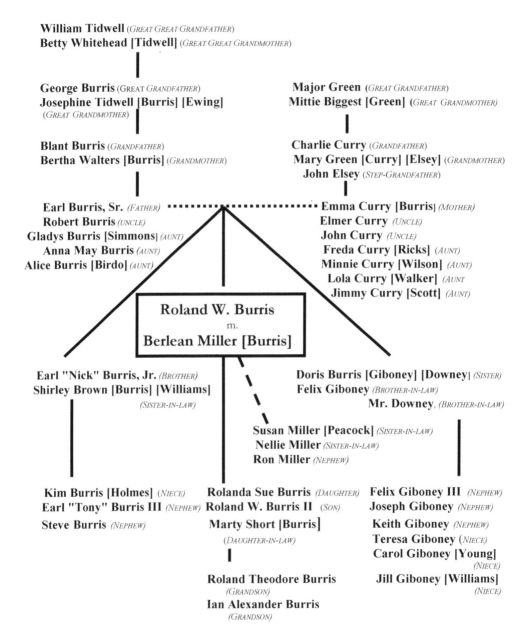

William Tidwell *(GREAT GREAT GRANDFATHER)*
Betty Whitehead [Tidwell] *(GREAT GREAT GRANDMOTHER)*

George Burris *(GREAT GRANDFATHER)*
Josephine Tidwell [Burris] [Ewing]
(GREAT GRANDMOTHER)

Major Green *(GREAT GRANDFATHER)*
Mittie Biggest [Green] [Green] *(GREAT GRANDMOTHER)*

Blant Burris *(GRANDFATHER)*
Bertha Walters [Burris] *(GRANDMOTHER)*

Charlie Curry *(GRANDFATHER)*
Mary Green [Curry] [Elsey] *(GRANDMOTHER)*
John Elsey *(STEP-GRANDFATHER)*

Earl Burris, Sr. *(FATHER)*
Robert Burris *(UNCLE)*
Gladys Burris [Simmons] *(AUNT)*
Anna May Burris *(AUNT)*
Alice Burris [Birdo] *(AUNT)*

Emma Curry [Burris] *(MOTHER)*
Elmer Curry *(UNCLE)*
John Curry *(UNCLE)*
Freda Curry [Ricks] *(AUNT)*
Minnie Curry [Wilson] *(AUNT)*
Lola Curry [Walker] *(AUNT*
Jimmy Curry [Scott] *(AUNT)*

Roland W. Burris
m.
Berlean Miller [Burris]

Earl "Nick" Burris, Jr. *(BROTHER)*
Shirley Brown [Burris] [Williams]
(SISTER-IN-LAW)

Doris Burris [Giboney] [Downey] *(SISTER)*
Felix Giboney *(BROTHER-IN-LAW)*
Mr. Downey, *(BROTHER-IN-LAW)*

Susan Miller [Peacock] *(SISTER-IN-LAW)*
Nellie Miller *(SISTER-IN-LAW)*
Ron Miller *(NEPHEW)*

Kim Burris [Holmes] *(NIECE)*
Earl "Tony" Burris III *(NEPHEW)*
Steve Burris *(NEPHEW)*

Rolanda Sue Burris *(DAUGHTER)*
Roland W. Burris II *(SON)*
Marty Short [Burris]
(DAUGHTER-IN-LAW)

Felix Giboney III *(NEPHEW)*
Joseph Giboney *(NEPHEW)*
Keith Giboney *(NEPHEW)*
Teresa Giboney *(NIECE)*
Carol Giboney [Young]
(NIECE)
Jill Giboney [Williams]
(NIECE)

Roland Theodore Burris
(GRANDSON)
Ian Alexander Burris
(GRANDSON)

Appendix 3: Illinois House of Representatives Impeachment Committee:

Letter from John Schmidt to Michael J. Madigan, June 19, 2009, regarding Senator Roland W. Burris' testimony before the Special Investigative Committee of the Illinois House of Representatives

June 19, 2009

Honorable Michael J. Madigan
Speaker House of Representatives, Room 300
State House
Springfield, IL 62706

Re: *Senator Roland Burris*

Dear Speaker Madigan:

Pursuant to our telephone conversation and your letter dated February 17, 2009 this office has concluded the review of Senator Burris' testimony before the House Special Investigative Committee. Our office interviewed numerous individuals and reviewed transcripts and affidavits. For the reasons set forth below there is insufficient evidence to charge Senator Burris with the offense of perjury.

Before a prosecutor charges an individual with a criminal offense, he must review all known evidence both inculpatory and exculpatory and determine whether or not based upon the known admissible evidence there is a reasonable likelihood of a success at trial. Thus, any decision to charge must be based solely on the evidence.

In Illinois, the offense of Perjury (720 ILCS S/32-2) is committed when an individual under oath makes a false statement and at the time of the statement he believes it into to be true. *Illinois Pattern Jury Instruction 22.01.* Moreover, an individual does not commit perjury if he corrects the known falsity before the adjournment of the tribunal. This provision accomplishes the legislative intent of the law of perjury which is to get complete and truthful information before the tribunal.

Beginning with the 2008 Democratic National Convention and through the election of President Barack Obama, Roland Burris told anyone he thought had the attention of Governor Rod Blagojevich that he was interested in being appointed to President Obama's vacant senate seat. These conversations occurred at fundraisers where Senator Burris would see individuals he thought were speaking to the governor, and in telephone conversations. The one-on-one conversations were brief and were characterized by the individuals he spoke to as not memorable, and "in passing." In the November 13, 2008 phone conversation with Robert Blagojevich, Mr. Blagojevich called Senator Burris and asked him if he would raise money for Governor Rod Blagojevich. During the call Burris asked how the appointment process was going and asked Robert Blagojevich to remind his brother he (Burris) was interested in the senate appointment. It is clear from the conversation that Robert Blagojevich's call was to raise money for Governor Blagojevich and not to discuss the vacant senate seat.

In a telephone conversation in late November 20-08 with John Harris Chief of Staff to Governor Rod Blagojevich, Senator Burris inquired about a job for a family member. He then asked Harris to tell the Governor he was interested in being appointed to the Senate seat.

These conversations were not substantive discussions concerning how to get the appointment, but rather Burris imploring the listener to tell Governor Blagojevich he was interested in the appointment.

When Representative Durkin asked Senator Burris if he spoke to member of the Governor's staff or family members regarding his interest in the Senate seat, Burris responded, "I talked to some friends about my desire to be appointed, yes." *Transcript House Impeachment Committee January 8, 2009 page 941 lines 9-20.* This is a truthful answer. While Senator Burris failed to mention the phone conversations with Rob Blagojevich or John Harris, he did say he spoke to friends about his interest. The Illinois Supreme Court has consistently held the burden is on the questioner to pin the witness down as to the specific object of the questioner's inquiry, *People v. Robert Willis, 71 Ill 2nd 138 (1978).* Next, Senator Burris was asked:

REPRESENTATIVE DURKIN: I guess the point I was trying to ask, did you speak to anybody who wan on the Governor's staff prior to the Governor's arrest or anybody, any of those individuals or anybody who is closely related to the Governor.

MR. BURRIS: I recall having a conversation meeting with Lon Monk about my Partner and I trying to get continued business. ...*Transcript January 8, 2009, Page 941-942*

Senator Burris answered the question by recalling a conversation with Lon Monk. The fact he did not mention others does not make the statement perjerous. It makes it incomplete. Again, the burden is on the questioner to ask specific questions. Senator Burris truthfully stated he had a conversation with Lon Monk.

The same analysis applies to Senator Burris's responses to Representative Tracy. Senator Burris is asked to whom he expressed senate seat interest and the time frame September of 2008 or as early as July of 2008. *Transcript 998 Lines 13-17.* Burris responded that one person he spoke with was his law partner. Chairwoman Currie stated, "Is that when you talked to Lon Monk?" Then Representative Tracy asked, "Was it Lon Monk was that the extent of it Lon Monk." *Transcript pages 998-999.* Senator Burris reiterated his conversation where Lon Monk told him he was qualified to be in the U.S. Senate.

Transcript page 999. Senator Burris was asked, "So you don't recall that there was anybody else besides Lon Monk that you expressed an interest to at that point?" He responded, "No, I can't recall because people were coming to me saying Roland you should pursue the appointment. . ." *Id.* Moreover, Senator Burris volunteered to give names of individuals the committee could contact regarding his interest in the senate seat. See *Transcript page 1000, Line 17-21.*

Burris' responses cannot support a perjury charge. He said he could not recall anyone specific because there were many individuals urging him to run. The answer was incomplete, but that is not perjury, given the form of the questions.

This is not a criticism of the questioners. The committee was finding facts concerning the possible impeachment of Governor Blagojevich. Asking broad questions allowed a great deal of information to be discussed without the need to constantly ask follow-up questions. However, such questioning makes difficult the prosecution the crime of perjury which is a knowingly untruthful answer to a precise question. Case law clearly mandates very specific questions be asked and knowing false answers be given to support perjury. Answers subject to different interpretations or incomplete are insufficient to support perjury.

The two affidavits signed by Senator Burris dates January 5, 2009 and February 4, 2009 are not inconsistent, thus do not support a perjury charge. The January 5, 2009 affidavit only describes the actual appointment process of Governor Blagojevich appointing Roland Burris to the vacant senate seat. It is insufficient to support perjury charges based upon Burris's testimony before the House Impeachment Committee.

The February 4, 2009 affidavit was requested by the Committee and filed to supplement Burris' testimony. This affidavit does not support perjury charges based upon Senator Burris' answers to the House Committee. This affidavit supplements and expands answers while the tribunal was still convened. It should be noted the affidavit was filed with the Special Committee long before Senator Burris knew his conversation with Robert Blagojevich was captured on tape. This fact supports

Senator Burris' claim the affidavit was meant to supplement the record while the tribunal was in session.

In sum, based upon our review of the fact and the applicable law, there is insufficient evidence to charge Senator Roland Burris with perjury.

Sincerely,

JOHN SCHMIDT

cc: Honorable Tom Cross
        Minority Leader Illinois House of Representatives

Appendix 4:
Senate Ethics Committee

Public Letter of Qualified Admonition from the Senate Ethics Committee to Senator Burris, Nov. 20, 2009

United States Senate
Select Committee on Ethics
Hart Senate Office Building, Room 220
Second and Constitution Avenue, NE
Washington, DC 20510-6425

November 20, 2009

The Honorable Roland W. Burris
United States Senate
Washington, DC 20510

Public Letter of Qualified Admonition

Dear Senator Burris:

After an extensive investigation, the Select Committee on Ethics is issuing you this Public Letter of Qualified Admonition for actions and statements reflecting unfavorably upon the Senate in connection with your appointment to and seating in the Senate.

The Committee found that you should have known that you were providing incorrect, inconsistent, misleading, or incomplete information to the public, the Senate, and those conducting legitimate inquiries into your appointment to the Senate. The Committee also found that your

November 13, 2008 phone call with Robert Blagojevich was inappropriate. Although some of these events happened before you were sworn in as a U.S. Senator, they were inextricably linked to your appointment and therefore fall within the jurisdiction of the Committee.

While the Committee did not find that the evidence before if supported any actionable violations of law, Senators must meet a much higher standard of conduct. Senate Resolution 338 gives the Committee the authority and responsibility to investigate Members who may engage in "improper conduct which may reflect upon the Senate."

To make its determination, the Committee conducted interviews with multiple witnesses; requested and reviewed a tape of the November 13, 2008 phone conversation between you and Robert Blagojevich; and looked carefully at tour numerous sworn and unsworn statements to the Illinois House of Representatives Special Investigative Committee on Impeachment, to the press, and to the Senate, including your responses to this Committee. Based on all the evidence before it, the Committee reached the following conclusions:

<u>Your sworn affidavit and sworn testimony before the Illinois House of Representatives were inconsistent, incomplete and misleading.</u>

In your January 5, 2009 affidavit, you state that you did not have any contact with Governor Blagojevich or any of his representatives about your appointment to the Senate before December 26, 2008. In your January 8, 2009 testimony before the Impeachment Committee, despite repeated and specific questioning, you did not disclose having any conversations about your desire to seek the U.S. Senate appointment or about fundraising with anyone associated with the Governor, except Lon Monk. It was not until your second affidavit and subsequent press statements that you disclosed additional contacts with associates of the Governor.

These omissions in your sworn statements are particularly noteworthy given their context. The Governor had recently been arrested and charged with corruptly using his authority to make a Senate appointment in exchange for campaign contributions and other benefits, and these charges were the subject of the impeachment hearings conducted by the Illinois House of Representatives, as well as intense media scrutiny. Therefore, you should have known that any conversations you had about your desire to seek the Senate seat and about any possible fundraising for the Governor were critical to these inquiries. In addition, your testimony on January 8, 2009 was one of the factors the Senate leadership said they would consider in your seating, and its truthfulness was important and relevant to your seating.

Your shifting explanations about your sworn statements appear less than candid.

You gave multiple and at times contradictory explanations for failing to disclose all your contacts with the Governor's associates, which individually and collectively gave the appearance that you were being less than candid. For example, you said you believed that affidavit referred only to your appointment after it was made and not to conversations about seeking it. You then said certain questioners during the hearing did not give you enough time to give full answers about those contacts, despite the fact that you were asked the question multiple times and the pauses before and after your answers gave ample time for elaboration. Later, you said that when you answered that you had talked to friends it was your intention to include many of the people specifically mentioned in the question. Most recently, however, you told this Committee that at the time of the hearing, you did not recall speaking to anyone besides Lon Monk.

Your November 13, 2008 phone call with Robert Blagojevich, while not rising to the level of an explicit *quid pro quo*, was inappropriate.

When Robert Blagojevich called you on November 13, 2008, he was explicit about the purpose of his call: to raise campaign funds for his brother. Yet during this conversation in which you appeared to agree to write a check and even potentially raise money for Governor Blagojevich, you repeatedly brought up your desire to seek the Senate set. You also implied that the people you might raise money from would be unhappy if you did not receive the appointment. The Committee finds that this conversation was inappropriate in its content and implications.

In determining the proper conclusion to this matter, the Committee took into consideration many factors, including the fact that the Sangamon County State's Attorney found that your sworn statements and affidavits were not actionable violations of law. We were also aware that these issues surrounding your appointment to and seating in the Senate have been subject to intense public criticism.

Again, the Committee has found that your actions and statements reflected unfavorably on the Senate and issues this Public letter of Qualified Admonition.

Sincerely,

Barbara Boxer, *Chairman*   Johnny Isakson, *Vice Chairman*

Mark Pryor, *Member*   Pat Roberts, Member

Sherrod Brown, *Member*   James E. Risch, *Member*

Appendix 5:
The Night before Christmas

From The Congressional Record - Senate, December 22, 2009, S13721

The PRESIDING OFFICER. The Senator from Illinois.

Mr. BURRIS. Mr. President, as this debate draws to a close and my colleagues and I prepare to vote on a health care reform bill, I recognize that long hours and tense negotiations have left some nerves and tempers frayed. This is why I come to the floor.

Although our work keeps us away from our family and friends for much of this holiday season, I see no reason why we cannot share good cheer with one another right here in Washington.

So in the spirit of the season, I would like to share my own version of a classic holiday story with my good friends on both sides of the aisle.

It goes something like this:

'T'was the night before Christmas and all through the Senate
The Right held up our health bill, no matter what was in it.
The people they voted -- they mandated reform --
But Republicans blew off the gathering storm.
"We'll clog up the Senate!" they cried with a grin,
"And in midterm elections, we'll get voted right in!"
They knew regular folks need help right this second --
But fundraisers, lobbyists and politics beckoned,
So, try as they might, Democrats could not win
Because their majority was simply too thin.
Then, across every State there arose such a clatter
The whole Senate rushed out to see what was the matter!

All sprang up from their desks and ran from the floor
Straight through the cloakroom, and right out the door.
And what in the world could be quite this raucous?
But a mandate for change! From the Democratic caucus!
The President, the Speaker, and of course Leader Reid
Had answered the call in our hour of need.
More rapid than eagles the provisions they came,
And they whistled, and shouted, and called them by name:
"Better coverage! Cost savings! A strong public plan!
Accountable options? We said, 'yes we can!"
"No exclusions or changes for pre-existing conditions!
Let's pass a bill that restores competition!"
The Democrats all came together to fight for the American people,

That Christmas Eve night.
And then, in a twinkle, I heard under the dome –
The roll call was closed! It was time to go home.
Despite the obstructionist tactics of some,
The filibuster had broken -- the people had won!
A good bill was ready for President Obama,
Ready to sign, and end health care drama.
And Democrats explained, as they drove out of sight:
"Better coverage for all, even our friends on the right!"

And I say to all my colleagues: In this season, Merry Christmas and a
happy, happy New Year.

Mr. President, I yield the floor.

Appendix 6: A List of Firsts

Accomplished through the years by Senator Roland W. Burris (D-IL)

- First African-American youth, along with brother, Nick, to deliver *Centralia Sentinel*
- First African-American to swim in the municipal pool at Centralia, Illinois
- First African-American resident of Centralia, Illinois to become a lawyer
- First Southern Illinois University, African-American recipient of exchange student scholarship to the University of Hamburg, Germany
- First African-American bank examiner in the U.S. for the U. S. Treasury Office of the Comptroller of the Currency
- First African-American officer and Vice-President for Continental National Bank and Trust, the largest bank in Illinois and the 7th largest in the U.S.
- First African-American to head the Department of Central Management Services for the State of Illinois
- First African-American Regional Director and National Director for the Illinois Jaycees
- First African-American to be elected to statewide Comptroller office in Illinois
- First African-American to be elected as Attorney General in Illinois, the second African-American to be elected as Attorney General in the U.S.
- First African-American president of the National Association of State Auditors, Comptrollers, and Treasurers
- First African-American President of the National Association of State Comptrollers
- First African-American, non-lawyer to serve on the Board of Trustees of the Illinois CPA Society

374

- First African-American to run in three consecutive races for the office of Illinois Governor
- First African-American in the U.S. appointed to the U.S. Senate, the sixth African-American to serve in the Senate

Guide to Photographs

Section I: Family Photographs, between Chapters 3 and 4	
Panel	**Photograph Description**
Family-1	**P-1** Josephine Ewing, *great grandmother* **P-2** Mittie Biggest, *great grandmother*
Family-2	**P-3** Bertha Hinds, *great aunt* **P-4** Ada Bell Scott, *great aunt* **P-5** Ada Bell Scott, Bertha McGinnis, Bertha Hinds, *great aunts* **P-6** John Henry Curry, *uncle* **P-7** Elmer Curry, *uncle*
Family-3	**P-8** George Burris Jr., Acy Burris, Joe Burris, Russell Burris, Sam Burris *great uncles*, and Blant "Papa" Burris *grandfather* **P-9** Kim Burris Holmes, *niece*; Steve Burris, *nephew*; Rolanda Burris, *daughter*; Jill Giboney Williams, *niece*; Roland W. Burris, Teresa Giboney, *niece*; Felix Giboney, *nephew*; Doris Downey, *sister*; Earl Burris III, *nephew*; Dr. Berlean Burris, *wife*, and Roland Burris II, *son*
Family-4	**P-10** Emma Burris, *mother*; Earl Burris, Sr., *father*
Family-5	**P-11** Freda Ricks, Lola Walker, Minnie Wilson, *aunts* **P-12** Earl Burris, *brother*

Family-6	**P-13** Roland Burris and *son*, Roland II, at son's Morgan Park graduation
	P-14 Roland Burris II receives diploma at St. Ignatius College Prep
	P-15 Dr. Berlean Burris, Roland Burris, Roland Burris II, and Rolanda Burris confer in family backyard
	P-16 Roland Burris, Rolanda Burris, and Dr. Berlean Burris pose prior to Rolanda's Debutante Ball
	P-17 Roland Burris, Rolanda Burris, and Dr. Berlean Burris at Rolanda's graduation from Harvard-St. George High School
Family-7	**P-18** Rolanda Burris receives her doctoral hood at her Ed.D. graduation from Northern Illinois University
	P-19 Second row: Roland Burris, *father*; Dr. Berlean Burris, *mother*; Roland Burris II, *brother*; First row: Elder Cleotis Peacock, *uncle*; Susie Peacock, *aunt*; and Nellie Miller, *aunt* at Rolanda's NIU graduation
Family-8	**P-20** Family Photograph: Roland Burris II, Dr. Berlean Burris, Roland Burris, Rolanda Burris
Family-9	**P-21** Dr. Berlean Burris receives Ph.D. from Northwestern University with family: Cleotis (Cleo) Peacock, *brother-in-law*; Susie Peacock, *sister*; Mattie Townsend, *aunt;* Nellie Miller, *sister*; Rolanda Burris, *daughter*; Roland W. Burris, Dr. Berlean Burris; Roland Burris II, *son*; Mamie Lewis, *sister*; Johnny Miller, *brother*; Hallie Miller, *sister-in-law*; and Henry Miller, *brother*
	P-22 Roland W. Burris and Dr. Berlean Burris pose at her Ph.D. commencement at Northwestern University
	P-23 Roland W. Burris and Dr. Berlean Burris display Dr. Burris' newly awarded Master's degree from Moody Bible Institute
Family-10	**P-24** Roland W. Burris and Dr. Berlean Burris with *son*, Roland II at his graduation from Northwestern University Law School
	P-25 Roland Burris II receives congratulations from Dean at his graduation from Northwestern University Law School
Family-11	**P-26** Roland W. Burris, Roland Burris II, *son*; Roland Theodore Burris, *grandson*; and Ian Alexander Burris, *grandson*

Family-12	**P-27** Dr. Berlean Burris with *grandsons*, Roland Theodore Burris and Ian Alexander Burris **P-28** *Son*, Roland Burris II; *daughter-in-law*, Marty Burris; and *grandsons* Roland Theodore Burris and Ian Alexander Burris

Section II: Education Photographs, between Chapters 5 and 6

Panel	Photograph Description
Education-1	**P-29** Roland W. Burris [first row, third from left] and first grade class at Lincoln Elementary School, Centralia, Il **P-30** Roland W. Burris [first row, center] and eighth grade class at Lincoln Elementary School, Centralia, Il
Education-2	**P-31** Roland W. Burris, second grade photograph, Lincoln Elementary School, Centralia, Il **P-32** Mr. William Walker, *principal*, Lincoln Elementary School, Centralia, Il
Education-3	**P-33** School photograph of Roland W. Burris, Upper grade, Lincoln Elementary School, Centralia, Il **P-34** School photograph of Roland W. Burris, Freshman, Centralia High School **P-35** School photograph of Roland W. Burris, Sophomore, Centralia High School **P-36** School photograph of Roland W. Burris, Junior, Centralia High School **P-37** School photograph of Roland W. Burris, Senior, Centralia High School **P-38** School photograph of Roland W. Burris, uniform number 12, Centralia High School Football Team
Education-4	**P-39** Roland W. Burris [top row, second from left] Centralia High School Freshman Football "B" Team **P-40** Roland W. Burris [second row, second from left] Centralia High School Sophomore Football "B" Team
Education-5	**P-41** Sophomore, Roland W. Burris [fourth row, far right] Centralia High School Track Team **P-42** Centralia High School Varsity Football Team, Roland W. Burris [first row, third from right]
Panel	Photograph Description
Education-	**P-43** Centralia High School Track Team, Roland W. Burris [third

6	row, far right] **P-44** Centralia High School Varsity Football Team Roland W. Burris [first row, third from right]
Education-7	**P-45** Southern Illinois University chapter of Alpha Phi Alpha fraternity, Roland W. Burris [row one, fifth from left] and Southern Illinois University members of Alpha Phi Alpha fraternity **P-46** Southern Illinois University Inter-Fraternity Council, Roland W. Burris [row three, far right] **P-47** Southern Illinois University Young Republicans, Roland W. Burris[row two, far right]
Education-8	**P-48** Southern Illinois University Freshman Football Team: Roland W. Burris [far right] **P-49** Roland W. Burris, Senior Class Photograph, Southern Illinois University
Education-9	**P-50** Roland W. Burris and members of the Southern Illinois University chapter of Alpha Phi Alpha fraternity at celebration of the Senator's donation of his papers to SIU library **P-51** Senator Roland W. Burris donates his papers to Southern Illinois University library: Former SIU trustee William "Bill" Norwood, *Key note speaker*; David Carlson, *Director of Library Affairs*, Morris Library; former SIU *Vice Chancellor* Harvey Welch; Senator Roland W. Burris; Chris Shelton, *president* of the Beta Eta Chapter of Alpha Phi Alpha fraternity; SIU *Chancellor* Rita Cheng; and SIU *President* Glenn Poshard
Education-10	**P-52** Exchange student, Roland W. Burris [far left] and students at the University of Hamburg, Germany **P-53** Howard University Law School Senior Class president, Roland W. Burris [third from left] and other class officers **P-54** Howard University Law School Senior Class, Roland Burris [first row, far right]
Education-11	**P-55** Howard University Law School Moot Court, Roland W. Burris [far right] **P-56** Howard University Law School chapter of Delta Sigma Tau law fraternity, Roland W. Burris [far left]
Education-12	**P-57** Howard University Law School chapter of Delta Sigma Tau law fraternity, Roland W. Burris [far right] **P-58** Roland W. Burris Senior Class photograph, Howard University Law School **P-59** Roland W. Burris poses in his graduation gown prior to his graduation from Howard University Law School in 1963 **P-60** Roland W. Burris returns to Howard University Law School graduation as Commencement Speaker

Section III: Celebrities Photographs, between Chapters 7 and 8

Panel	Photograph Description
Celebrities-1	**P-61** Michael Jordon, Chicago Bulls superstar, poses with Roland W. Burris
Celebrities-2	**P-62** Chicago Bull, Bill Cartwright and Roland W. Burris **P-63** Chicago Bull, John Paxton and Roland W. Burris **P-64** NBA star Isaiah Thomas and NFL star Ahmad Rashad and Roland W. Burris
Celebrities-3	**P-65** Don McHenry, US Ambassador to the United Nations and Roland W. Burris **P-66** Chicago columnist, Irv Kupcinet, Mayor Eugene Sawyer, and Roland W. Burris
Celebrities-4	**P-67** Publisher John Johnson, Dr. Berlean Burris, and Roland W. Burris **P-68** Chicago Bears star Richard Dent and Roland W. Burris
Celebrities-5	**P-69** Israeli Prime Minister and future Israeli president, Shimon Peres, and Roland W. Burris **P-70** Radio and television host, Larry King and Roland W. Burris
Celebrities-6	**P-71** World Heavyweight boxing champion, Mohammed Ali, and Roland W. Burris
Celebrities-7	**P-72** Chicago Bears Walter Payton and Vince Evans and Roland W. Burris **P-73** Historian John Hope Franklin, singer Etta Moten Barnett, and Roland W. Burris
Celebrities-8	**P-74** Polish Prime Minister Tadeusz Mazowiecki and Roland W. Burris **P-75** Boxer, Tommy Hearns and Roland W. Burris
Celebrities-9	**P-76** Composer Eubie Black and Roland W. Burris **P-77** Entertainer, Hostess, Entrepreneur Oprah Winfrey and Roland W. Burris
Celebrities-10	**P-78** Entertainer Liza Minnelli and Roland W. Burris
Celebrities-11	**P-79** Entertainer Sammy Davis Jr. and Roland W. Burris
Celebrities-12	**P-80** South African Revolutionary and President, Nelson Mandela, Dr. Berlean Burris, and Roland W. Burris

Section IV: Celebrations Photographs, between Chapters 10 and 11

Panel	Photograph Description
Celebrations-1	**P-81** Banker Roland W. Burris meets with members of Group 4-B, a small business loan section which he headed **P-82** Banker Roland Burris and members of Continental Bank Alumni Association
Celebrations-2	**P-83** Banker Roland W. Burris and Continental Bank Vice President, Fred Shewell **P-84** Roland W. Burris speaks at Ten Year Tribute for Outstanding Service as Illinois Comptroller
Celebrations-3	**P-85** Secretary of the Navy and former Mississippi governor, Ray Mabus and Roland W. Burris
Celebrations-4	**P-86** Goodwill Industries presents Roland W. Burris with Man of the Year Award **P-87** Former HUD Secretary Patricia Roberts Harris and Roland W. Burris
Celebrations-5	**P-88** Roland W. Burris [second from right] and other recipients of the Black Book Award **P-89** Actress, Ruby Dee speaks with Roland W. Burris as Ill. Rep. Benny Stewart and businessman Ted Jones look on
Celebrations-6	**P-90** Dr. Benjamin Alexander, president of Chicago State University presents Roland W. Burris with Presidential Citation for "exemplary service and outstanding contributions to the university." **P-91** Dr. Berlean Burris and Roland W. Burris with Centralia friend Bill Norwood, and his wife, Molly Norwood
Celebrations-7	**P-92** The Burris family celebrates Burris' 50th birthday at Chicago residence **P-93** Former Attorney General Neil Hartigan joins Attorney General and Dr. Burris and family for 50th birthday celebration
Celebrations-8	**P-94, P-95** Members of Comptroller Roland Burris' staff celebrate his 50th birthday in Springfield
Celebrations-9	**P-96** Burris speaks with Centralia residents Dorothy Brady and his great aunt, Bertha Hines [far right) **P-97** The Burris family, along with sister, Doris, celebrate Burris' 50th birthday

Celebrations-10	**P-98** The Burris family with friend Betsy Kourdouvelis at Burris' 50th birthday celebration in Centralia **P-99** The Burris family celebrates the couple's 20th wedding anniversary
Celebrations-11	**P-100** Roland and Berlean Burris repeat their wedding vows on 25th wedding anniversary **P-101** Dr. Berlean Burris and Comptroller Roland W. Burris with friends, Dr. and Mrs. Conrad May
Celebrations-12	**P-102** Dr. Berlean Burris and Comptroller Roland W. Burris at 25th wedding anniversary reception

Section V: Announcements, Inaugurations, In-Office Photographs, between Chapters 14 and 15

Panel	Photograph Description
Announcements-1	**P-103** Illinois Governor Daniel Walker and Roland W. Burris, Director of General Services
Announcements-2	**P-104** Senator John Glenn and Illinois Comptroller Roland W. Burris **P-105** Senator Ted Kennedy and Illinois Comptroller Roland W. Burris
Announcements-3	**P-106** Senatorial candidate, Carol Mosley Braun; Senator Paul Simon, and Illinois Comptroller Roland W. Burris **P-107** Roland W. Burris and other Chicago Black elected officials
Announcements-4	**P-108** Congressman Dan Rostenkowski, Mayor Richard Daley, Comptroller Roland Burris, and Cook County Democratic Chairman George Dunne **P-109** Former President William Clinton and Roland W. Burris
Announcements-5	**P-110** Secretary of State Hillary Clinton and Roland W. Burris **P-111** First Lady Rosalyn Carter and Illinois Comptroller Roland W. Burris
Announcements-6	**P-112** Chicago Mayor Richard J. Daley and Roland W. Burris **P-113** Congressman Robert Kennedy II and Roland W. Burris
Announcements-7	**P-114** US Attorney General Janet Reno and Roland W. Burris **P-115** Alderman Eugene Sawyer, Cook County Board President John Stroger, Mrs. Sawyer, Alderman Wilson Frost, Roland W. Burris, Dr. Berlean Burris, State Senate President Cecil Partee, and Georgia Representative Ben Brown

Announcements-8	**P-116** Vice President Walter Mondale, Dr. Berlean Burris, and Roland W. Burris **P-117** Senator Charles Percy, Dr. Berlean Burris, and Roland W. Burris
Announcements-9	**P-118** Chicago Mayor Harold Washington and Illinois Comptroller Roland W. Burris **P-119** Senator Charles Robb, Dr. Berlean Burris, Roland W. Burris, and Rolanda Burris
Announcements-10	**P-120** President Jimmy Carter and Roland W. Burris **P-121** Roland Burris speaking at National Council of State Governments
Announcements-11	**P-122** Former Atlanta Mayor, And Congressman, Andrew Young and Roland W. Burris **P-123** Virginia Governor Doug Wilder and Roland W. Burris
Announcements-12	**P-124** Illinois Comptroller, Roland W. Burris, center, poses with black Illinois lawmakers and 3 of the 5 black elected state officials in the USA: Vel Phillips, Secretary of State, Wisconsin; Henry Parker, Treasurer, Connecticut; and Richard Austin, Secretary of State, Michigan

Section VI: Politics Photographs, between Chapters 17 and 18

Panel	Photograph Description
Politics-1	**p-125** Roland W. Burris makes acceptance speech after winning the 1978 race for State Comptroller **P-126** Roland W. Burris takes the oath of office as Illinois State Comptroller as administered by Illinois Appellate Court Justice Kenneth Wilson and as Dr. Berlean Burris holds the Bible **P-127** Roland W. Burris and his family pose at the State Comptroller's office in Springfield
Politics-2	**P-128** Illinois Comptroller Roland W. Burris speaks at 1979 Inauguration in Springfield **P-129** Illinois State Constitutional Officers and their wives
Politics-3	**P-130** Comptroller Roland W. Burris takes oath of office from Appellate Court Justice Glen Johnson as Roland Burris and Roland Burris II look on and as Dr. Berlean Burris holds the Bible. **P-131** Flanked by Dr. Berlean Burris, Roland Burris II, and Chicago Bears tackle Jim Osborne, Roland W. Burris announces his 1984 candidacy for Senator **Photograph Description**

Politics-4	**P-132** Comptroller Roland W. Burris and Dr. Berlean Burris arrive at the 1987 Inauguration in Springfield **P-133** Comptroller Roland W. Burris takes the oath of office as administered by Appellate Court Justice Glen Johnson while Dr. Berlean Burris holds the Bible and Rolanda Burris and Roland Burris II look on
Politics-5	**P-134** Dr. Berlean Burris (seated, second from right) and Comptroller Roland W. Burris (standing, second from right) and other Illinois constitutional officers at 1987 inauguration **P-135** Roland W. Burris, past president of the National Association of State Comptrollers and other national officers
Politics-6	**P-136** Illinois Comptroller Roland W. Burris presents $40 million check to lottery winners **P-137** Illinois Comptroller Roland W. Burris and presidential candidate Michael Dukakis **P-138** Roland W. Burris speaks at Democratic National Convention in Atlanta **P-139** Comptroller Roland W. Burris arrives to speak to Chicago elementary school assembly program
Politics-7	**P-140** Illinois Comptroller Roland W. Burris announces his candidacy for Attorney General **P-141** Vince de Musizo, Democratic Party Chairman and democratic candidates; Neil Hartigan (*governor*), Jerry Cosentino (*secretary of state*), Roland W. Burris (*attorney general*), and Paul Simon (*senator*)
Politics-8	**P-142** Roland W. Burris [far right] and other members of the 1990 Democratic Statewide Ticket **P-143** As Roland Burris II and Rolanda Burris look on and Dr. Berlean Burris holds the Bible, Roland W. Burris takes the oath of office for Illinois Attorney General as administered by Illinois Supreme Court Justice Charles Freeman
Politics-9	**P-144** Roland W. Burris speaking at convention of National Association of Attorneys General in Chicago **P-145** Attorney General Roland W. Burris [first row, third from left] and other attorneys general at Chicago's White Sox Park **P-146** Illinois Attorney General Roland W. Burris is flanked by drug enforcement agents at press conference on indictment of drug dealers **P-147** Illinois Attorney General Roland W. Burris and Minnesota Attorney General Hubert Humphrey III
Politics-10	**P-148** Illinois Attorney General Roland W. Burris pays a visit to his regional office in Peoria, Il **P-149** Illinois Attorney General Roland W. Burris, with Indiana Attorney General Pam Carter [left] and Virgin Islands Attorney

	General Rosalie Simmons Ballentine [right]
Politics-11	**P-150** Roland W. Burris is applauded by supporters as he announces his candidacy for Mayor of Chicago **P-151** Dr. Berlean Burris, Rep. Danny Davis, Rolanda Burris, and Roland Burris II watch as Roland W. Burris announces his candidacy for Governor of Illinois **P-152** Surrounded by family and friends, Roland Burris announces his candidacy for Governor of Illinois in Centralia
Politics-12	**P-153** U.S. Senate candidate Barack Obama [third from left] and Roland Burris II, Marty Burris, Dr. Berlean Burris, Rolanda Burris, and Roland W. Burris **P-154** Burris for Governor supporters include Rep. Danny Davis, Rep. Bobby Rush, Mayor Joe Freelon of Maywood, and Alderman Anthony Beal.

Section VII: Senate Photographs, between Chapters 19 and 20

Panel	Photograph Description
The Senate-1	**P-155** Senator Roland W. Burris is administered the oath of office by Vice President Dick Cheney while Dr. Berlean Burris holds the Bible
The Senate-2	**P-156** Senator Roland W. Burris and Senator Daniel K. Inouye, *President Pro Tempore* of the Senate **P-157** Senator Roland W. Burris and Senator Patrick Leahy, *President Pro Tempore* of the Senate
The Senate-3	**P-158** Dr. Berlean Burris, Senator Roland W. Burris and Senator John Kerry **P-159** Senator Burris and Senator Lamar Alexander
The Senate-4	**P-160** Flanked by Rep. John Lewis and Rep. Ed Markey, Senator Burris greets Edward Brooke, the first black popularly elected to the US Senate **P-161** Senator Roland W. Burris greets Senator Robert Byrd, *President Pro Tempore* of the Senate
The Senate-4	**P-162** After swearing in, Senator Burris and his family pose with Vice President Dick Cheney **P-163** Members of the Burris family relax before reception in honor of Senator Burris' swearing in as a member of the US Senate. From left, *nephew* Ron Miller, *daughter-in-law* Marty and *grandson* Roland

	Theodore, *son* Roland II and *grandson* Ian Alexander; *daughter* Rolanda Burris, and *wife* Dr. Berlean Burris
The Senate-6	**P-164** President and Mrs. Obama pose with Senator Roland W. Burris at Congressional Black Caucus dinner **P-165** Senator Burris signs Registry after delivering the George Washington Farewell Address to the Senate
The Senate-7	**P-166** Senator Roland W. Burris and Representative Donald M. Payne **P-167** Senator Roland W. Burris poses with some members of his Washington, DC staff on the steps of the capitol
The Senate-8	**P-168** On fact-finding trip to Iraq, Senator Burris poses with US servicemen at Ziggurat Tomb at the site of the ancient city of Ur (circa 2113 BC) **P-169** Senator Roland W. Burris poses with one of the two Golden Gavels he was awarded for presiding over the US Senate
The Senate-9	**P-170, P-171** Apparently unaware of the presidential seal above his head, Senator Roland W. Burris awaits a meeting with President Obama
The Senate-10	**P-172** Senator Roland W. Burris listens intently to testimony during a hearing of the Senate Armed Services Committee **P-173** Senator Roland W. Burris examines a signed copy of the historic Affordable Health Care Act
The Senate-11	**P-174** Senator Roland W. Burris speaks at the program celebrating the donation of his political papers to the Southern Illinois University Morris Library
The Senate-12	**P-175** Senator Burris, Dr. Berlean Burris, grandson, Roland Theodore Burris, and Director of Library Affairs, David Carlson, look at the display honoring the Senator in the Southern Illinois University Morris Library **P-176** Senator Burris and Keynote speaker, Bill Norwood, chat at program featuring the donation of the Senator's political papers to the Southern Illinois University library

Index

End Notes and Explanatory Notes

[i] My great, great-grandmother, Lola Tidwell, a Blackfoot Indian, was a descendent of the "original people" who were often referred to as the Niitsítapi Confederacy which consisted of three First Nations Indian bands [the Blackfoot, Bloods, and Piegans] in Canada and the United States. See http://www.jstor.org/stable/658663

[ii] As a child I learned that among African-Americans "passing for white" indicated the intentional and undetected assimilation of a fair skinned black person of mixed ancestry into the white race, usually to avoid the racial discrimination and economic disadvantages faced by most African Americans. When a person "passed for white," he or she usually had to cut all ties with black family members and friends. In telling his life story, Oscar DePriest, a very fair-skinned Chicago African American politician often recalled the fact that when he first arrived in Chicago from the South, he frequently had to "pass for white" in order to get jobs that were not open to African Americans.

[iii] The Illinois Central Railroad (IC), *the Main Line of Middle America*, provided employment for my father and many others in Centralia, and was one of a very few US railroads to serve markets along a north-south route from Chicago to New Orleans and the Gulf Coast. See http://www.american-rails.com/illinois-central.html

[iv] The story of the blizzard conditions in which our son, Roland II was born are detailed in the Chicago Tribune. Chicago Blizzard. Chicago Tribune online.
See: http://www.chicagotribune.com/news/politics/chi-chicagodays-1967blizzard-story,0,1032940.story.

[v] William H. Upton, *Negro Masonry: Being a Critical Examination of Objections to the Legitimacy of the Masons Existing Among the Negroes of America,* (New York: AMS Press, 1975). The African-American Masonic organization to which my father belonged is a branch of organized North American Freemasonry founded by Prince Hall in the 18th century because African Americans were not generally welcome in the white Masonic lodges. One of the reasons I was so impressed by my father's Masonic regalia is the high sense of mystery which was associated with those objects and the great secrecy associated with the Masonic rules, regulations, and rites.

[vi] The Order of the Eastern Star, to which my mother belonged, is the largest Masonic-related fraternal organization in the world. The organization is based on a belief in a supreme being and is based on practical ideas such as a desire to acquire additional

knowledge and a desire for self-improvement. The first lodge for black women was established in 1874 in Washington, D.C. See http://dwperkins29.org/about_oes

[vii] The *Pittsburgh Courier* which my brother, Nick and I distributed on Saturdays, was once the country's most widely circulated black newspaper with a national circulation of almost 200,000, a readership which was almost as large as the readership of The *Chicago Defender* and The *Afro-American*.
See http://www.pbs.org/blackpress/news_bios/courier.html.

[viii] The status of my Lincoln Elementary School principal, Mr. Walker, as a former Tuskegee Airman was a definite plus, even in those days before the airmen had attained the fame they enjoy today. To us, the exclusion of African-Americans from flying or from any full participation in the U.S. military was a personal affront. We supported the civil rights organizations and the black press which exerted pressure and helped to bring about the creation of the Tuskegee Airmen program in 1941. Of course, for the children at Lincoln Elementary School where Mr. Walker was principal, and for many of the adults in Centralia's African American community, Mr. Walker was an instant hero. See http://tuskegeeairmen.org/explore-tai/a-brief-history/.

[ix] The television program that my friends and I always watched on Saturday evenings at the home of Conrad Mays, *Your Show of Shows,* was a live, original, 90 minute, comedy starring comedians Sid Caesar and Imogene Coca. The show was broadcast weekly throughout the US on NBC between 1950 and 1954. During the preparation of the manuscript, we learned of the passing of Sid Caesar on February 12, 2014 at the age of 91. See http://www.imdb.com/title/tt0042173/

[x] The Negro leagues were professional baseball leagues which consisted of teams made up of African American and other minority players, primarily Latin Americans, who, because of their race, were excluded from the fame and the financial advantages afforded by major league baseball. Melvin Duncan, my cousin's uncle, was a right hander who pitched for the Kansas City Monarchs and the Detroit Stars in the early 1950s, although, ironically, even then, the Negro Baseball leagues were in decline, due to the integration of baseball by Jackie Robinson in 1947 and the subsequent acceptance of minority players in the previously all-white major baseball leagues. See http://www.negroleaguebaseball.com/

[xi] The National Council of African-American Men, Inc. which honored me in 2010 as the *Illinois African American Man of the Year*, is a not-for-profit organization located in Champaign, Illinois which has the mission of addressing critical issues, such as community improvement, capacity building, and community development, which affect the African American community.

See http://www.nonprofitfacts.com/IL/National-Council-Of-African-American-Men-Inc-Ncaam-Ncaam-Inc.html#ixzz2rRZoLSKU.

[xii] During my term in the Senate, I was a member of the Congressional Black Caucus, an organization composed of the black members of Congress. In addition to their mission to represent their constituencies, the member of the caucus also work to ensure fairness for African-Americans and others and to promote equity for all, both at home and abroad. See http://cbc.fudge.house.gov/.

[xiii] My friend Bill Norwood was the first black pilot for United Airlines, and the first black to be promoted to captain for United as well. His achievement was memorialized by his induction into the Illinois Aviation Hall of Fame. Retrieved:
See http://www.ilavhalloffame.org/members_07.html

[xiv] Bobby Jo Mason, who excelled in several sports at Centralia High School, went on to become a member of the world-renowned Harlem Globetrotters for fourteen years! See http://www.harlemglobetrotters.com/harlem-globetrotter-legend/bobby-joe-mason

[xv] Dr. Delyte Morris, President of SIU who believed that "higher education should be available to all who seek it regardless of race, nationality, gender, economic circumstance or physical limitations" demonstrated this belief by integrating student housing for females at SIU during my freshman year.
See www2.wsiu.org/outreach/070122excellence/profiles.shtml.

[xvi] Because few public or private medical facilities were open to African Americans, Dr. Daniel Hale Williams. An African-American surgeon, established Provident Hospital, the first Black-owned and operated hospital in the U.S., in Chicago in 1891. See http://www.providentfoundation.org/history/.

[xvii] My college fraternity, Alpha Phi Alpha (AΦA), which was founded on December 4, 1906 at Cornell University in Ithaca, New York, is the oldest of all black Greek fraternities. Its motto is *First of All, Servants of All, We Shall Transcend All.* See http://www.alpha-phi-alpha.com/index.php.

[xviii] To me and my fellow Alphas, our chief competitor fraternity at SIU was the Kappas [Kappa Alpha Psi (KAΨ). This predominately African American fraternity which was founded at Indiana University in Bloomington, Indiana on January 5, 1911, has more than 150,000 members in the United States and abroad.
See http://www.kappaalphapsi1911.com/.

[xix] Because I personally witnessed firsthand the suffering of students who did not have adequate financial support when I was an undergraduate at SIU, I established the

Roland W. Burris Scholarship at SIU to provide emergency assistance to students who needed such assistance in order to remain enrolled in school.. See http://siualumni.com/s/664/2012/1col.aspx?pgid=350.

[xx] Although he was a few years ahead of me, Dick Gregory was one of my classmates at Southern Illinois University. See http://news.siu.edu/2009/10/100209cjm9250.html.

[xxi] Prior to my arrival at SIU, Dick Gregory was a student there and had led a protest which resulted in the opening of the previously segregated Varsity Restaurant to all regardless of race. In fact, when I arrived at SIU as a candidate for the football team, I was told by the coaching staff that the Varsity was one of the four places in Carbondale that African-Americans could eat. Despite the integration of The Varsity and a few other places, however, no further action was taken regarding the segregation of the majority of the hotels and restaurants in Carbondale, until my senior year when I worked with other students and SIU President Morris to eliminate those barriers throughout the city of Carbondale.

[xxii] I have known Tom Burrell since we were both college students dreaming about the future. I met him during the summers that I used to spend working in Chicago. See www.thehistorymakers.com/biography/thomas-j-burrell-40.

[xxiii] Burrell Communications Group L.L.C. is a full-service communications company and one of the largest minority marketing firms in the world. It was founded by Chairman Emeritus Thomas (Tom) J. Burrell, and is headquartered in Chicago, IL. See http://burrell.com/company/our-approach.

[xxiv] The Young Executives in Politics (YEP) was a group I created for individuals between the ages of 36-55 who worked in major corporations. The purpose of the group was to teach participants how to maximize their participation in politics. In many ways this groups was a continuation of the Young Professionals.

[xxv] One of my friends at SIU was Donald F. McHenry, future U.S. Ambassador to the United Nations. See http://www.eurasia.org/people/donald-f-mchenry.

[xxvi] US Ambassador to the UN, Andrew Young, was asked to resign by President Jimmy Carter after it was discovered that he had held a secret and unauthorized meeting with Zehdi Terzi, the UN representative of the Palestinian Liberation Organization. See http://www.biography.com/people/andrew-young-jr-9539326.

[xxvii] As my own experience clearly indicates, Dr. Delyte Morris was actively involved with students. He regularly had students over for dinners and made an honest effort to be involved with multiple aspects of student life. When presented with a list of

businesses which prohibited African-American clientele, he went before the Carbondale Chamber of Commerce and successfully persuaded them to discontinue segregation in Carbondale businesses.
See http://www2.wsiu.org/outreach/070122excellence/profiles.shtml.

[xxviii] Although today, the Fulbright Scholar program is a racially diverse program, I do not believe that in the earliest years of the organization's history, it was always able or willing to rise above the racial norms which were dominant in 1946 when the program was created. Although my research has been limited, the earliest African American Fulbright scholars that I could find were John Hope Franklin, the noted historian and Gladys Kidd Jennings, nutritionist who both were awarded Fulbright awards in 1954. I could not find any minority recipients between 1946 when the program was instituted by Congress and 1954.

[xxix] The Suez War occurred when Egypt took control of the Suez Canal in July 1956. To retake the canal by force, Israeli forces attacked Egypt troops in Sinai and British and French aircraft bombed Egyptian naval bases. Under international pressure, the attacks were called off and Israeli forces eventually left the Sinai.
See http://ehistory.osu.edu/middleeast/WarView.cfm?WID=33.

[xxx] The Hungarian Revolution of 1956 was the first major threat to Soviet control of Eastern Europe since World War II. The spontaneous nationwide revolution against the government of the People's Republic of Hungary and its Soviet-imposed policies took place between October and November of 1956.
See http://www.historylearningsite.co.uk/hungarian_uprising_1956.htm.

[xxxi]. Brown v. Board of Education, 347 U.S. 483 (1954), was a landmark United States Supreme Court case in which the Court struck down and declared unconstitutional state laws establishing separate public schools for black and white students, thereby overturning the Plessy v. Ferguson decision of 1896, which allowed state-sponsored segregation in public education under a 'separate but equal 'clause. According to the unanimous (9–0) decision of the Warren Court: "separate educational facilities are inherently unequal" and de jure racial segregation was ruled a violation of the Equal Protection Clause of the Fourteenth Amendment of the United States Constitution. This ruling was a major civil rights victory of the era.
See http://www.nationalcenter.org/brown.html

[xxxii] Freedom Riders were civil rights activists who rode interstate buses usually from Northern cities into the segregated southern United States in 1961 and following years to challenge the non-enforcement of the United States Supreme Court decisions Irene Morgan v. Commonwealth of Virginia (1946) and Boynton v. Virginia (1960), which ruled that segregated public buses were unconstitutional.

See http://www.history.com/topics/black-history/freedom-rides.

xxxiii The Voice of America (VOA) station on which I depended so heavily when I was homesick during my year as an exchange student at the University of Hamburg, is the official external broadcast "voice" of the United States which promotes freedom and democracy through the transmission of programming about America and the world to a vast audience overseas. See http://www.voanews.com/.

xxxiv To illustrate to my German hosts some of the social, economic, and political problems which arise when a majority population feels threatened by minorities, I used the example of the Notting Hill Race Riots which erupted in 1958 and the escalating hostility between white British working class families and the more than 100,000 new Caribbean immigrants who [the whites felt] were taking jobs from them. See http://www.itzcaribbean.com/nottinghillraceriots.php

xxxv BBC News: The 'forgotten' race riot, British Broadcasting Corporation, 21 May 2007. Just prior to the Notting Hill riots, there was racial unrest in Nottingham, which began on Saturday, 23 August and went on intermittently for two weeks.

xxxvi The Berlin Wall was a barrier which was originally constructed by the German Democratic Republic in 1961 to divide communist East Berlin and democratic West Berlin and to isolate West Berlin completely from surrounding East Germany. As the Cold War waned, there was significant improvement in relationships between the US and the Soviet Union and their allies, the physical Wall itself was primarily destroyed by 1989, paving the way for German reunification, which was formally concluded in 1990. See http://history1900s.about.com/od/coldwa1/a/berlinwall.htm.

xxxvii Historically black colleges and universities (HBCUs), like Howard University where I attended law school, are now officially defined as institutions of higher education in the United States that were established before 1964 with the intention of serving the African-American students. There are 106 historically black colleges and universities (HBCUs) in the United States, with most of them located in the former slave states and territories of the U.S. See http://hbcuconnect.com/history.shtml

xxxviii According to the Howard University official history, Howard came into being in November of 1866, shortly after the end of the Civil War, when members of the First Congregational Society of Washington met to consider establishing a theological seminary for the education of African-American clergymen. Howard University, the institution which emerged as a result of this planning session was named for General Oliver O. Howard, a Civil War hero who was both a founder of the University and, a Commissioner of the Freedman's Bureau. See www.howard.eduhistory of Howard University.

405

^{xxxix} Although I was never a staff member for the *Howard Law Journal,* since some of my friends were on the staff, I occasionally hung around the *Law Journal* office where I did a little "gofer" work from time to time, including running the messy mimeograph machine which was the copier of that era. ... As the principal scholarly publication of the Howard University School of Law, the *Journal* is dedicated to promoting the civil and human rights of all people, in particular those groups who have been the target of subordination and discrimination. See www.howard.eduHoward University School of Law.

^{xl} Thurgood Marshall (July 2, 1908 – January 24, 1993) was an Associate Justice of the United States Supreme Court, serving from 1967 until his retirement in 1991. Marshall was the Court's 96th justice and its first African American member. See http://www.thurgoodmarshall.com/.

^{xli} Constance Baker Motley (September 14, 1921 – September 28, 2005) was an African-American civil rights activist, lawyer, judge, state senator, and Borough President in Manhattan, New York City. In 1966, she became the first black woman to be appointed to a federal judgeship. See http://www.biography.com/people/constance-baker-motley-9416520.

^{xlii} Jack Greenberg (born December 22, 1924, in Brooklyn, New York) is an American attorney and legal scholar. He succeeded Thurgood Marshall as Director-Counsel of the NAACP Legal Defense Fund (LDF) from 1961 to 1984. See http://www.naacpldf.org/jack-greenberg-biography.

^{xliii} Another civil rights attorney, Oliver White Hill, Sr. (May 1, 1907 – August 5, 2007), was a classmate and close friend (and friendly rival) of Thurgood Marshall in law school. They worked together on numerous cases for the NAACP and LDF, most famously the *Brown* cases at the Supreme Court. Among his numerous awards is the Presidential Medal of Freedom, awarded by President Bill Clinton in 1999. See http://brownat50.org/BrownBios/BioOliverHill.html.

^{xliv} The NAACP Legal Defense and Educational Fund, Inc., an offshoot of the Legal Department of the National Association for the Advancement of Colored People (NAACP), is a leading United States civil rights organization and law firm based in New York City. The Defense Fund was originally created by Charles Hamilton Houston in the 1930s, but spun off from the NAACP in 1939. However, it was not until 1957, that Thurgood Marshall established the Legal Defense Fund as a new organization, totally independent of the NAACP. See http://www.naacpldf.org/.

^{xlv} Spottswood William Robinson III (July 26, 1916 – October 11, 1998) was Dean of the Law School during my years in law school. After he left Howard, Spottswood

became a Judge who, in 1966, was appointed by President Lyndon Johnson as the first African-American member of the United States Court of Appeals for the District of Columbia Circuit. He later became the first African-American to become Chief Judge of the District of Columbia Circuit Court. See http://www.blackpast.org/aah/robinson-spottswood-william-1916-1998.

[xlvi] Charles Hamilton Houston (September 3, 1895 – April 22, 1950) was a prominent African-American lawyer, Dean of Howard University Law School, and NAACP Litigation Director whose role in dismantling racially discriminatory laws earned him the title "The Man Who Killed Jim Crow". He is also well known for having trained future Supreme Court Justice Thurgood Marshall and for defining what he called "the social engineering responsibility of the [African-American] attorney." See http://www.charleshamiltonhouston.org/.

[xlvii] McNeil, *Groundwork* at 71 (1983), *quoting* Charles Hamilton Houston, "Personal Observations on the Summary of Studies in Legal Education as Applied to the Howard University School of Law," (May 28, 1929). *"[The] Negro lawyer must be trained as a social engineer and group interpreter. Due to the Negro's social and political condition . . . the Negro lawyer must be prepared to anticipate, guide and interpret his group advancement. . . . [Moreover, he must act as] business advisor . . . for the protection of the scattered resources possessed or controlled by the group. . . . He must provide more ways and means for holding within the group the income now flowing through it."*

[xlviii] http://www.naacp.org/pages/naacp-history-charles-hamilton-houston.

[xlix] http://www.nytimes.com/1998/09/02/us/james-a-washington-jr-83-judge-and-dean-of-law-school.html. New York Times Obituary: James A. Washington.

[l] http://www.nytimes.com/1991/06/16/obituaries/herbert-o-reid-sr-75-lawyer-who-taught-many-black-leaders.html. New York Times Obituary: Herbert O. Reid, Sr.

[li] http://www.highbeam.com/doc/1P2-797312.html. Washington Post Obituary (July 24, 1996): Dorsey E. Lane Dies; Lawyer Battled Bias.

[lii] http://www.washingtonpost.com/wpdyn/content/article/2006/11/18/AR2006111180093 3.html. Washington Post Obituary: Newton Pacht, 82; Howard Law Professor, classical Musician. Retrieved.

[liii] Freedmen's Hospital, the forerunner of Howard University Hospital, was established in the District of Columbia in 1862 to meet the medical needs of the thousands of African-Americans who came to Washington, DC, during and after the Civil War, seeking freedom and social, economic, and political opportunity. The first hospital of

its kind to provide medical treatment for former slaves, Freedman's Hospital later became the major hospital for the area's African-American community. See http://www.nlm.nih.gov/hmd/medtour/howard.html.

[liv] The Cuban missile crisis was a 13-day confrontation in October 1962 between the combined forces of the Soviet Union and Cuba and the United States over the Soviet Union decision to place missiles in Cuba, within striking distance of the United States – in violation of the Monroe Doctrine (1823) which stated that all efforts by European nations to colonize land or interfere with states in North or South America would be viewed as acts of aggression which would require U.S. intervention. The confrontation ended on October 28, 1962, when Kennedy and United Nations Secretary-General U Thant reached an agreement with Khrushchev, who agreed not to place missiles in Cuba on the condition that the U.S. would not take military action against Cuba and remove its missiles from Turkey. See http://www.history.com/topics/cold-war/cuban-missile-crisis.

[lv] During my internship at the White House, I worked with the National Defense Executive Reserve Files (NDER) program which is a recruitment and training program for experienced business executives and other civilian personnel to serve in key government positions during periods of national emergency. Reservists augment the staffs of federal departments and agencies when organizations must rapidly mobilize to respond to national security emergencies. See http://www.archives.gov/records-mgmt/rcs/schedules/general-records-schedules/n1-grs-87-010_sf115.pdf.

[lvi] When I heard the strains of "Pomp and Circumstance," the march played at my Howard Law School graduation, which was composed by Sir Edward Elgar and which has been a favorite for US graduation ceremonies for more than 100 years, neither the loftiness of the music nor the happiness of the occasion could erase from my mind the individuals who had started out with us in law school, but who never made it to graduation.

[lvii] Will Cooley, "Moving On Out: Black Pioneering in Chicago, 1915-1950," Journal of Urban History 36:4 (July 2010), 485-506.

[lviii] Panic Peddling. Encyclopedia of Chicago History. See http://www.encyclopedia.chicagohistory.org/pages/147.html

[lix] Kramer, Barbara (2003). *Mahalia Jackson: The Voice of Gospel and Civil Rights.* Berkeley Heights, New Jersey: Enslow Publishers. ISBN 0766021157. Because I now live in the former home of gospel singer Mahalia Jackson, I am very familiar with some of the things she experienced in the house. For example, although internationally known, Miss Jackson still encountered racial prejudice. When she bought the house

where I now live, someone fired a shot through her large living-room windows and she had to contact the police for protection.

lx Office of the Comptroller of the Currency. See http://www.occ.treas.gov.

lxi http://www.occ.gov/about/what-we-do/history/An-OCC-Pioneer-First-African-American-Bank-Examiner.pdf.

lxii United States General Accounting Office.
See http://www.gao.g+ov/archive/1997/gg97096.pdf.

lxiii Abraham M. Saperstein (July 4, 1902 – March 15, 1966) was an owner and coach of the Savoy Big Five, which later became the Harlem Globetrotters. He was born in London, England to a Jewish family. See http://en.wikipedia.org/wiki/Abe_Saperstein.

lxiv Since its founding in 1920, the United States Junior Chamber of Commerce, or Jaycees, has been a leadership training and civic involvement organization whose members include both men and women between the ages of 18 and 40. The not-for-profit organization focuses on business development, management skills, individual training, community service, and international connections.
See http://usjayceefoundation.org/.

lxv For more than 100 years, Mental Health America of Illinois has been the leading non-profit, non-governmental, statewide organization in Illinois concerned with the entire spectrum of mental and emotional disorders. MHAI is dedicated to promoting mental health, working for the prevention of mental illness and improving care and treatment for persons suffering from mental and emotional disorders.
See http://www.mhai.org/.

lxvi http://encyclopedia.chicagohistory.org/pages/774.html. The Daley Machine.

lxvii http://en.wikipedia.org/wiki/Cook_County_Democratic_Organization.
The Machine in Kennedy's 1962 Election.

lxviii William Levi Dawson (April 26, 1886 – November 9, 1970) was a state central committeeman for the First Congressional District of Illinois 1930-1932; alderman for the second ward of Chicago 1933-1939 and Democratic committeeman since 1939. He was elected as a Democrat to the Seventy-eighth and to the thirteen succeeding Congresses and served from January 3, 1943, until his death November 9, 1970. See http://bioguide.congress.gov/scripts/biodisplay.pl?index=d000158.

lxix Oscar Stanton De Priest (March 9, 1871 – May 12, 1951) was a member of the Cook County Board of Commissioners (1904). He was also elected to the Chicago city council where he served for one term before being indicted for protecting South Side gamblers. After winning acquitted in 1917, he later became a national symbol of racial pride as the first African American congressman elected to the House of Representatives from a northern state. He served in the House until 1934 when he was defeated. After leaving the House of Representatives, De Priest served one term on the Chicago City Council and devoted his time to his real-estate business. See http://www.encyclopedia.chicagohistory.org/pages/2402.html

[lxx] Richard J. Daley (May 15, 1902 – December 20, 1976) An Irish Catholic native of Chicago's Bridgeport neighborhood, Richard J. Daley won a number of elective offices between 1936 and 1955 when he ousted incumbent mayor Martin Kennelly in a bitterly contested Democratic primary, then beat Republican Robert Merriam in the general election. He secured reelection five times, the last in 1975. His earlier elective position included state representative, state senator and senate minority leader, state director of revenue, Cook County clerk, and chairman of the Cook County Democratic Party. See http://www.encyclopedia.chicagohistory.org/pages/1722.html.

[lxxi] The Committee on Illinois Government was formed by young independent democrats like Adlai Stevenson, Dan Walker, Dawn Netsch, and Victor de Grazia to oppose the regular Chicago Democratic machine.

[lxxii] Adlai Ewing Stevenson III, is the great-grandson of Vice President Adlai Ewing Stevenson and a former US Senator. He was a member of the Illinois house of representatives from 1965-1967, treasurer for the State of Illinois from 1967-1970, and elected to the US Senate by special election on the death of Everett Dirksen in 1970. Stevenson was re-elected to the Senate in 1974, served in the U. S. Senate from November 17, 1970, to January 3, 1981. He ran unsuccessful gubernatorial campaigns in 1982 and 1986 and is currently a resident of Hanover, Illinois. See http://bioguide.congress.gov/scripts/biodisplay.pl?index=s000890.

[lxxiii] http://baic.house.gov/member-profiles/profile.html?intID=56. Black Americans in Congress.

[lxxiv] The 29th District Voter Education Conference was a group organized by Gus Savage and Bill Cousins to involve and inform voters about critical issues in electing a senator for the newly created 29th Senatorial District.

[lxxv] http://articles.chicagotribune.com/1986-07-04/news/8602170728_1_chew-rolls-royce-seat-belt-law Chicago Tribune online.

[lxxvi] Leon M. Despres. *Challenging the Daley Machine: A Chicago Alderman's Memoir.* (Evanston, Ill.: Northwestern University Press, 2005) pg 90.

lxxvii The Chicago Maroon, The University of Chicago. Retrieved 2012: See http://chicagomaroon.com/2009/5/12/leon-despres-chicago-alderman-and-civil-rights-activist-with-university-ties-dead-at-101/.

lxxviii The Independent Political Organization was an organization I founded with the idea of providing voters with alternatives to the Regular Democratic Party. I was the first president of the organization.

lxxix Timuel D. Black, *Bridges of Memory: Chicago's First Wave of Black Migration* (Evanston, Ill.: Northwestern University Press, 2003); and *Bridges of Memory: Chicago's Second Generation of Black Migration* (Evanston, Ill.: Northwestern University Press, 2007).

lxxx Dan Walker Memoir–Illinois Digital Archives. Retrieved from www.idaillinois.org/utils/getfile/collection/uis/id/4479/filename/4480.pdf.

lxxxi http://www.worldjewishcongress.org/en/biography/54.

lxxxii Cumulative voting. . . is a multiple-winner voting system intended to promote more proportional representation than winner-take-all elections. See http://en.wikipedia.org/wiki/Cumulative_voting.

lxxxiii http://news.google.com/newspapers?nid=1499&dat=19851017&id=72waAAAAIB AJ&sjid=UyoEAAAAIBAJ&pg=7169,7960051Nixon Lauded as Creator of Black Capitalism..

lxxxiv http://articles.chicagotribune.com/1996-05-03/news/9605030367_. Chicago Tribune Obituary: David Kennedy.

lxxxv http://news.google.com/newspapers?nid=1243&dat=19681211&id=t_5XAAAAIB AJ&sjid=AvcDAAAAIBAJ&pg=3272,1374818.

lxxxvi The Small Business Administration (SBA) is a United States government agency that provides support to entrepreneurs and small businesses by providing support designed "to maintain and strengthen the nation's economy by enabling the establishment and viability of small businesses and by assisting in the economic recovery of communities after disasters". The agency's activities are summarized as the "3 Cs" of capital, contracts and counseling. See http://www.sba.gov/.

lxxxvii The Small Minority Business Capital Corporation, which I worked with extensively while at Continental Bank, is an organization created by the Small Business Administration to identify and access additional equity funding for minority businesses.

411

[lxxxviii] John Harold Johnson (January 19, 1918 – August 8, 2005) was an American businessman and publisher. He was the founder of the Johnson Publishing Company. In 1982, he became the first African-American to appear on the Forbes 400. In 1996, he was awarded the Presidential Medal of Freedom. See http://www.thefamouspeople.com/profiles/john-h-johnson-149.php.

[lxxxix] Johnson Publishing Company, Inc. is an American publishing company founded in November 1942 by John H. Johnson. Johnson Publishing is the preeminent publisher of EBONY and JET magazines and owner of Fashion Fair Cosmetics. The company's products reach over 72% of African-Americans over 18 years old. See http://www.johnsonpublishing.com/

[xc] John Herman Henry Sengstacke (November 25, 1912 – May 28, 1997) was an African-American newspaper publisher of *The Chicago Defender*. He worked with President Franklin D. Roosevelt to have African-American reporters in the White House and to create jobs in the United States Postal Service for African-Americans. . .President Harry Truman named Sengstacke to the commission he formed to integrate the military. Sengstacke established the National Newspaper Publishers Association, which was an endeavor to unify and strengthen African-American owned papers. See http://www.topfamousbiography.com/biography/29961/john_herman_henry_sengstacke_biography.html

[xci] *The Chicago Defender* is a Chicago-based weekly newspaper founded in 1905 by an African American for primarily African-American readers. In 1919–1922 the *Defender* attracted the writing talents of writers like Langston Hughes, Gwendolyn Brooks and Willard Motley. It was published as *The Chicago Daily Defender,* a daily newspaper, from 1956 to 2003, when it returned to a weekly format. See http://en.wikipedia.org/wiki/The_Chicago_Defender.

[xcii] Judge Henry Parker was a migrant from the farms of rural Montgomery County in Tennessee who started his sausage business using home recipes he learned from his mother. In 1921, Mr. Parker acquired enough money to purchase a plant and several refrigerated delivery vehicles, providing the first opportunity for black route salesmen to drive commercial delivery trucks which enabled him to break the racial barrier for meat distributors and to become not only the first African American to own and operate a meat processing plant in the Midwest, but also the first to control his own distribution of his product. Parker House Sausage Company was incorporated in. See http://parkerhousesausage.com/The_Beginning.html.

[xciii] http://articles.chicagotribune.com/1994-03-13/news/9403130235_1_mr-troy-illinois-racing-board-optometrist. Chicago Tribune Obituary: Cecil Troy.

^{xciv} George Ellis Johnson, Sr. (born June 12, 1927) is an American entrepreneur and the founder of Johnson Products Company, an international cosmetics empire, and Independence Bank, both headquartered in Chicago, Illinois. Johnson is perhaps best known for being the first African American to have his company listed on the American Stock Exchange. See http://www.blackpast.org/aah/johnson-george-ellis-sr-1927#sthash.yjCW3y3F.dpuf.

^{xcv} http://www.idvl.org/thehistorymakers/Bio3.html. The History Makers: Ed Gardner.

^{xcvi} http://www.idvl.org/thehistorymakers/Bio27.html. The History Makers: Demsey Travis.

^{xcvii} http://www.newspapers.com/newspage/6327327/. The Danville Register.

^{xcviii} The Reverend Jesse Louis Jackson, Sr., founder and president of the Rainbow PUSH Coalition, is one of America's foremost civil rights, religious and political figures. Over the past forty years, he has played a pivotal role in virtually every movement for minority empowerment, civil rights, gender equality, and economic and social justice. On August 9, 2000, Presidents Bill Clinton awarded Reverend Jackson the Presidential Medal of Freedom, the nation's highest civilian honor. See http://rainbowpush.org/pages/jackson_bio.

^{xcix} http://articles.chicagotribune.com/2002-05-02/news/0205020166. The Chicago Tribune.

^chttp://childcarecenter.us/provider_detail/les_finch_learning_tree_day_nurs_school_chicago_il#.Us2MmRDvPw. Finches Childcare Center.

^{ci} http://www.seawaybank.us/a_history.html. Seaway Bank and Trust Company website.

^{cii} http://www.CCPTV.com. Central City Productions.

^{ciii} http://www.nytimes.com/1988/05/11/obituaries/richard-b-ogilvie-is-dead-at-65-illinois-governor-from-68-to-72.html. New York Times Obituary: Richard Buell Ogilvie

^{civ} http://articles.chicagotribune.com/2005-04-09/news/0504090270_1_mayor-richard-j-daley-democratic-quintessential-politician. Chicago Tribune Obituary: Victor R. De Grazia.

^{cv} Leslie Waller, *The Banker* (Garden City, N.Y., Doubleday, 1963).

[cvi] http://myloc.gov/Exhibitions/gettysburgaddress/Pages/default.aspx. Library of Congress website.

[cvii] http://en.wikipedia.org/wiki/Edwin_M._Stanton.

[cviii] http://www.ioc.state.il.us/index.cfm/about-our-office/history/. State of Illinois Comptroller website.

[cix] *"It's Your Money"* is a monthly publication I made available to Illinois citizens to provide them with a precise and accurate financial statement and accounting of their tax dollars.

[cx] Harold Washington (April 15, 1922 – November 25, 1987) was a member of the Illinois house of representatives from 1965-1976, a member of the Illinois senate from 1977-1980, and a member of the US House of Representativesfrom1981-1983. In 1983, Washington was elected mayor of Chicago. He was reelected in 1987 and served until his death in Chicago on November 25, 1987.
See http://bioguide.congress.gov/scripts/biodisplay.pl?index=W000180.

[cxi] In 2004, all three of our rankings went down a notch when then-Illinois State Senator Barack Obama beat Alan Keyes for the U.S. Senate seat. Obama's whopping win, by 2.2 million votes, stands today as the highest plurality in Illinois election history

[cxii] Washington, Pittman & McKeever, LLC (WPM) is a certified public accounting and management consulting firm which was founded in 1939 by Mary T. Washington, the first African-American female CPA in the United States. WPM provides businesses and individuals with audit, accounting, tax and advisory service and is one of Chicago's most established accounting/consulting firms.
See http://www.linkedin.com/company/washington-pittman-%26-mckeever-llc.

[cxiii] http://www.thehistorymakers.com/biography/lester-mckeever-39. The History Makers: Lester McKeever.

[cxiv] Remembering Ms. Washington: Mary T. Washington Wylie, the nation's first African-American female CPA, blazed a trail for other black accountants. See http://www.icpas.org/hc-insight.aspx?id=1732.

[cxv] Founded in 1987, The Bronner Group is a unique professional services firm focused on services for both government and the public sector. Consultants and subject matter experts selected to join Bronner come from a range of backgrounds, including high-ranking positions within government, professional services firms, not-for-profit organizations and private industry. See http://www.bronnergroup.com/about_us/.

[cxvi] Gila J. Bronner, CPA is President and CEO of Bronner Group, LLC, a woman-owned, multi-disciplined professional services company that delivers comprehensive strategy, transformation and accountability consulting services to state and local governments and federal agencies.
See http://www.bronnergroup.com/about_us/gila_j_bronner/.

[cxvii] Lyndon Hermyle LaRouche, Jr. (born September 8, 1922) is a controversial American dissident, political activist and founder of the LaRouche movement. LaRouche was a presidential candidate eight times between 1976 and 2004, running once for his own U.S. Labor Party and campaigning seven times for the Democratic Party nomination. See http://en.wikipedia.org/wiki/Lyndon_LaRouche.

[cxviii] The LaRouche movement is a political and cultural network promoting Lyndon LaRouche and his ideas. It has included many organizations and companies around the world, which promote a revival of classical art and a greater commitment to science; advocates the development of major economic infrastructure projects on a global scale; and calls for a reform of the world financial system to encourage investment in the physical economy and suppress financial speculation.
See http://en.wikipedia.org/wiki/LaRouche_movement.

[cxix] The Solidarity Party was an American political party founded by Senator Adlai Stevenson III in the state of Illinois. It was named after Lech Wałęsa's Solidarity movement in Poland, which was widely-admired in Illinois at the time (Illinois has a very large Polish American population, especially around Chicago). The party was founded in 1986 in reaction to the Democratic Party's nomination of two followers of Lyndon LaRouche in the race for high state offices.
See http://en.wikipedia.org/wiki/Solidarity_Party.

[cxx]http://uselectionatlas.org/RESULTS/state.php?fips=17&year=1986&f=0&off=5&elect=0. Illinois election results.

[cxxi] In 1962, Edward Brooke became the first African-American to be elected as any states Attorney General when he was elected for Massachusetts and he would soon go down a road to become the first African-American to join the senate in 1966. See http://mvafricanamericanheritagetrail.org/edward-brooke.html.

[cxxii] It took the Supreme Court to sort out this centuries-old fishing dispute. See http://www.ledgersentinel.com/article.asp?a=9743. Ledger Sentinel online newspaper.

[cxxiii] The Young Professionals was a group that I created for young college graduates between the ages of 25-35. The purpose of the group was to acquaint these young people with ways to maximize their political effectiveness and to enhance their upward mobility.

[cxxiv] The National Assembly of Black Elected Officials is an organization that I created with other black state officials including Representative Ben Brown of Georgia, to provide a forum for blacks elected to statewide positions in the US. Four of the five black elected officials at the time participated in the organization included Vel Phillips, *Secretary of State*, Wisconsin; Henry Parker, *Treasurer*, Connecticut; Richard Austin, *Secretary of State*, Michigan; and Roland W. Burris, *Comptroller*, Illinois.

[cxxv] Inspired by an extended stay on the continent as a young legislator, Texas Representative George Thomas "Mickey" Leland (November 27, 1944 – August 7, 1989) poured his energy into focusing attention on a disastrous East African famine and raising funds for relief efforts. Leland worked tirelessly as chairman of the House Select Committee on Hunger, which he had lobbied Congress to create. Leland was also chair of the Congressional Black Caucus. He became a martyr for the cause of eradicating world hunger, perishing in a plane crash on a humanitarian mission to transport supplies to an Ethiopian refugee camp.
See http://history.house.gov/People/Detail/16887.

[cxxvi] Among her many accomplishments and accolades, Dr. C. Delores Tucker marched with Dr. Martin Luther King, Jr. in Selma, Alabama. She was the first black Secretary of State (PA). In 1984, she was the founding chair of the National Political Congress of Black Women and in 1992 succeeded the late Hon. Shirley Chisholm as national chair of the organization now called the National Congress of Black Women. See http://www.visionaryproject.org/tuckercdelores/.

[cxxvii] Richard M. Daley went on to become the longest serving mayor in Chicago history with 22 years in office, only surpassing the tenure of his father, Richard J. Daley.

[cxxviii] As of this writing, there have been only nine blacks who have been seated as U.S. Senators in our history. In addition to the four mentioned in this book (Edward Brooke, Carol Mosely Braun, Barak Obama and myself), the other two were from the Reconstruction Era (1865-1877). Hiram Revels, a Republican from Mississippi, served in 1870 and 1871 and another Mississippi Republican, Blanche Bruce, served from 1875 until 1881. Both of these men were appointed by the state legislature. More recently, there were two Senate appointments of African-Americans, Tim Scott, a Republican from South Carolina and Mo Cowan, a Democrat from New Jersey. Although Cowan did not run when his appointment expired, Senator Scott was subsequently elected to complete the term of former South Carolina Senator Jim DeMint. In 2013 Cory Booker was elected to the US Senate from New Jersey. Another African American Senator, who is not included in the total of nine, was P. B. S. Pinchback of Louisiana who was denied a Senate seat in 1875 on the basis of a contested election.

[129] Congressional Research Service. *Post-Employment, "Revolving Door," Laws for Federal Personnel.* CRS Report for Congress authored by Jack Maskell, Legislative Attorney. Retrieved May 12, 2010. See http://www.fas.org/sgp/crs/misc/97-875.pdf.

[cxxx] *Writ of Mandamus.* In Illinois, one may petition the circuit courts for a writ of mandamus "to command a public official to perform some ministerial nondiscretionary duty in which the party seeking such relief has established a clear right to have it performed and a corresponding duty on the part of the official to act." The authority of the respondent to comply with the writ must also be clear. Finally, the petitioner must show that a demand was made on the official concerned but that he refused to comply. This is to make sure that the officer in question has the option of performance before the court exacts compliance.
See http://www.dcbabrief.org/vol121099art6.html.

[cxxxi] See Appendix, Section 3: Letter from John Schmidt to Michael J. Madigan, June 19, 2009, regarding Senator Roland W. Burris' testimony before the Special Investigative Committee of the Illinois House of Representatives.

[cxxxii] See Appendix, Section 4: Public Letter of Qualified Admonition from the Senate Ethics Committee to Senator Burris, November 20, 2009.

[cxxxiii] The United States Africa Command (USAFRICOM or AFRICOM)is one of six of the U.S. Defense Department's geographic combatant commands and is responsible to the Secretary of Defense for military relations with African nations, the African Union, and African regional security organizations. See http://www.africom.mil/about-the-command.

[cxxxiv] See Appendix, Section 6: Senator Burris' "Night Before Christmas" presentation to the Senate, December 22, 2009 (on the eve of the passage of the Affordable Health Act)

[cxxxv] In 1942, President Roosevelt established a presidential directive giving African-Americans an opportunity to be recruited into the Marine Corps. These African-Americans, from all states, were not sent to the traditional boot camps of Parris Island, South Carolina and San Diego, California. Instead, African American Marines were segregated - experiencing basic training at Montford Point - a facility at Camp Lejeune, North Carolina. Approximately twenty thousand (20,000) African-American Marines received basic training at Montford Point between 1942 and 1949. Twenty years after World War II, in the summer of 1965, over four hundred former and active duty Marines, representing seventeen States attended the Montford Point Marines reunion in Philadelphia which led to the establishment of the Montford Point Marine Association,

417

a non-profit veteran organization chartered in Philadelphia. Today the Association proudly boasts 33 active chapters throughout the United States. See http://www.montfordpointmarines.com/.

cxxxvi The founder of New Philadelphia, Illinois was Thomas McWorter. Born a slave in South Carolina in 1777, Frank McWorter moved to Kentucky with his owner in 1795. He married Lucy, a slave from a nearby farm, in 1799. Later allowed to hire out his own time, McWorter was able to buy his freedom in 1819 after first purchasing the freedom of his wife in 1817. In 1830, Frank and Lucy McWorter and four of their children left Kentucky for Illinois where they bought a farm in Pike County's Hadley Township and platted the town of New Philadelphia in 1836. McWorter promoted New Philadelphia strenuously, and engaged in other enterprises, managing to buy the freedom of at least sixteen family members. The town itself became a racially integrated community long before the Civil War. According to the 1850 and subsequent U.S. Census, New Philadelphia was the home of both black and white families. Frank McWorter died at New Philadelphia in 1854. A son, Solomon, assumed family leadership. Bypassed by the railroad in 1869, the townspeople slowly dispersed from the scene from the late 1880s. Today, the town site is an open field. See http://www.newphiladelphiail.org/.